Food Lit

"Perhaps one can say that the subject of cookery has never received so much and so intelligent attention as at the present time."

—from *The Compendium of Cookery and Reliable Recipes*, 1890

"Tell me what you eat, and I will tell you what you are."

—Jean Anthelme Brillat-Savarin in *Physiologie du goût* (*The Physiology of Taste*), 1825

Food Lit

A Reader's Guide to Epicurean Nonfiction

Melissa Brackney Stoeger

Real Stories
Sarah Statz Cords, Series Editor

LIBRARIES UNLIMITED

AN IMPRINT OF ABC-CLIO, LLC
Santa Barbara, California • Denver, Colorado • Oxford, England

Library of Congress Cataloging-in-Publication Data

Stoeger, Melissa Brackney.
  Food lit : a reader's guide to epicurean nonfiction / Melissa Stoeger Brackney.
    pages cm. — (Real stories)
  Includes bibliographical references and indexes.
  ISBN 978-1-59884-706-2 (hardback) — ISBN 978-1-61069-376-9 (ebook)
1. Food—Bibliography.   I. Title.
  Z5776.F7S86—2013
  [TX353]
  016.6415—dc23   2012038052

ISBN: 978-1-59884-706-2
EISBN: 978-1-61069-376-9

17   16   15   14   13   1   2   3   4   5

This book is also available on the World Wide Web as an eBook.
Visit www.abc-clio.com for details.

Libraries Unlimited
An Imprint of ABC-CLIO, LLC

ABC-CLIO, LLC
130 Cremona Drive, P.O. Box 1911
Santa Barbara, California 93116-1911

This book is printed on acid-free paper (∞)
Manufactured in the United States of America

Contents

Series Foreword

For years I have been involved in a serious love affair—with nonfiction books.

What a pleasure it continues to be, therefore, to keep meeting other readers who prefer history, biographies, memoirs, travel narratives, current affairs books, or true crime titles (to name but a few nonfiction genres) to the latest novels. I still read fiction—many nonfiction readers do—but more often than not when I am looking for "a good book" what I am really looking for is a "good nonfiction book."

The continuing mission of the reading guides in the *Real Stories* series is to help library staff and all those who work with readers (not to mention readers themselves) learn more about various nonfiction genres and types, as well as to identify specific titles and authors which may be of interest to them. For too many years the tools available to readers' advisors focused exclusively on fiction, but in the recent past the explosion of literary blogs, other online literary commentary, and the inclusion of non-fiction titles in book recommendation databases has helped to augment such classic guides to fiction as Diana Tixier Herald's *Genreflecting* titles and Joyce Saricks's *Readers' Advisory Guide to Genre Fiction*. It is our hope that the specific titles in the *Real Stories* series, which now includes guides to Biographies, Food Writing, Investigative Writing, Life Stories, Travel Narratives, and Women's Nonfiction, will be of particular use to those still looking for cohesive nonfiction genre and subgenre groupings, booklists, and other nonfiction resources.

My best piece of advice for reading this volume, Melissa Stoeger's delectable exploration of Food Writing, echoes that given to grocery shoppers: don't read it when you're hungry. Not only has Melissa identified and annotated hundreds of nonfiction titles on food, food preparation, and those who love and work with food (this is no small task—very few resources exist to help readers and readers' advisors identify these titles, and subject headings on cookery are as likely as not to lead you to cookbooks when you might be looking for something with more narrative), she has written about them in such a way that you not only want to read all of them, immediately, but you also find yourself with your stomach growling and your mouth watering. She has also described read-alikes for these highly evocative books in the most evocative ways, which is only fitting.

Melissa has also been good enough to provide extensive supporting materials on the titles that have been written by famous chefs, fiction titles that revolve around food, food magazines and blogs, food documentaries and TV shows, and award-winning food books. What gold mines for professionals seeking that sometimes-elusive goal of providing whole library readers' advisory! It's the rare reader's guide that can take you all over the library—through the Dewey stacks, into fiction, and continuing on into magazines and DVDs—and this one does so, all on the trail of that perfect meal, the best restaurant, the most demanding chefs, the most satisfy-ing and sustaining foods.

I hope you enjoy this book. And I invite you to not only use this guide (and others in the *Real Stories* series) when helping patrons or when performing readers' advisory, but also when you personally need a "good nonfiction book."

Acknowledgments

Writing this book has been such a challenging and rewarding experience. I am so grateful to Sarah Statz Cords and Barbara Ittner of Libraries Unlimited/ABC-CLIO for this opportunity. I hope you are as proud of it as I am. Thank you, thank you, thank you, Sarah, for your encouragement, advice, and support. Without you, this book never would have made it to publication. Thanks to Rick Roche for your advice and expertise with regards to indexing.

The most enjoyable part of this project has been reading all these great food books. But there is a downside. I can't tell you how hard it is to spend hours reading about cake or French bread or looking at gorgeous blog photos of food and not immediately run to the kitchen to try to recreate it. Thank you to my trainer, Melissa Bentsen, who kept me from indulging in every recipe I came upon and gaining five hundred pounds. I think *not* putting on weight during this project is a huge accomplishment.

Thank you to my family and friends, who have listened to me talk about food books for the past two years. Unfortunately, I can't promise that I won't be talking about them anymore. To my friend Jody Wilson, thank you for your never-ending encouragement, enthusiasm, and chicken articles.

And last, but never least, thank you to my husband Kent, for your support and your patience. This book took longer than I anticipated and you've been a really good sport about picking up the slack while I've been engrossed in food books. Thank you for indulging me as I talked about bees, meat, farming, or whatever else I was reading about at the time. Thank you for taking me to secret suppers on rooftops and to see Anthony Bourdain. Thank you for gamely trying the recipes I made, both good and bad. And thank you a million times for building me a beautiful kitchen!

Introduction

Have you ever heard someone say "I don't like food?" I would bet that you haven't. You may have heard someone say that they don't like a *particular* food, or that they don't like *cooking* food, but you would be hard pressed to find someone who dislikes food altogether. It is not difficult, however, to find plenty of people who willingly admit to loving food.

Food is a very powerful thing. Every living being needs it to survive. It nourishes us and sustains us. It comforts us. It can trigger memories, reminding us of our childhood or of a particular person. It entertains us. It can even define us. Jean-Anthelme Brillat-Savarin claimed in his famous work *The Physiology of Taste*: "Tell me what you eat, and I will tell you what you are" (Brillat-Savarin 1971, 15). Food is also one of the few things that all human beings have in common. Although we may eat different foods, everyone must eat. Food can bridge cultures and bring people together.

It seems only natural that our need for and enjoyment of food would lead to books about food. People have been writing about food for thousands of years. Initially these were records of food production and allocation. Soon collections of recipes began appearing. In 1825 Brillat-Savarin's *The Physiology of Taste* was the first to define gastronomy and became the first gastronomic essay. Since then, food writing has become a popular topic. *The Compendium of Cookery and Reliable Recipes*, published in 1890, mentions that cookery had never received more attention than it was receiving at that time (Blakeslee 1890). One could say that today.

Definition of Food Lit

When I told people I was writing a book about food books, the first response was always: "Oh, like cookbooks?" When I replied that the book would not contain cookbooks (or very few cookbooks), I got a few quizzical looks. Cookbooks are certainly books about food and there is an abundance of them, but the purpose of this book is to encompass Food Lit, which is more than just a collection of recipes.

So what is Food Lit? Journalist Molly Seltzer states that "the category of food books is hard to define. It might include recipe books, celebrity chef biographies and memoirs, gastronomy, environmentally sensitive cuisine, wine, food travel books, or food histories" (Seltzer 2008). NoveList uses the term "Food Writing" and defines it as including biography, memoir, history, reporting, and narrative cookbooks, with the focus on either "the importance, preparation, consumption, or meaning of food." Darryl Campbell states that food writing also "has the unique capacity to tell us something about our social norms and attitudes" (Campbell 2011). Similarly, in *American Food Writing: An Anthology with Classic Recipes*, editor Molly O'Neill explains that food writing serves as a window into our wider culture, providing a glimpse of our values and ideals (O'Neill 2007).

In the case of this book, Food Lit encompasses nonfiction titles. There are fiction titles that include food as a plot element and even include recipes; however, the food is not usually the focus of the story. In Food Lit, food is the primary focus, and as journalist Kathryn Hughes points out, is about more than just recipes (Hughes 2010b). Food is a universal part of culture, history, and memory and can be found in memoir, biography, science, history, and travel writing. Food Lit can describe the role of food in an individual's life or its role in a society or company's history. It can also describe the physical aspects of food, such as the growing, preparation, obtaining, or consumption of it.

Why a Reader's Guide to Food Lit Is Needed

Food is a hot topic right now and interest in it shows no sign of letting up. Not relegated to only cookbooks anymore, the topic of food is creating a number of best-selling books, magazines, movies, and television shows—there are even television channels devoted to food.

In 2007, there were over 13.9 billion cooking and entertaining books sold nationwide, which was a 12 percent increase since 2004. In 2007, 3,004 new cooking titles were released, which was a 53 percent increase from 2002 (Seltzer 2008). Nielsen's website has a large graphic across the top reading: "In a falling economy, cookbook sales rose 5%" (Nielsen February 27, 2011). But cookbooks aren't the only food books that are exploding in popularity. Kathryn Hughes says that ever "since Anthony Bourdain's *Kitchen Confidential* rocked into town and gave food writing such a hard slap that it has never quite known which end to stand on ever since" (Hughes 2010b). Bookstores are now creating special sections for food writing. Laura Shapiro says that when it comes to autobiographies and memoirs, sex and substance abuse are still best sellers, but food is catching up (Shapiro 1998). More and more writers are recounting meals from their past. Aside from showing up on best-seller lists, food books are often included in notable lists, such as the *New York Times'* Notable Books and the American Library Association's Notable Books lists. Michael Pollan's books *The Omnivore's Dilemma: A Natural History of Four Meals* and *In Defense of Food: An Eater's Manifesto*, Barbara Kingsolver's *Animal, Vegetable, Miracle: A Year of Food Life*, Peter Pringle's *Food, Inc.: Mendel to Monsanto—The Promises and Perils of the Biotech Harvest*, Eric Schlosser's *Fast Food Nation: The Dark Side of the All-American Meal* have all been included on notable lists. And it's not just food politic topics that are making the lists. Memoirs such as Frank Bruni's *Born Round: The Secret History of a Full-Time Eater*, Phoebe Damrosch's *Service Included: Four Star Secrets of an Eavesdropping Waiter*, and Bill Buford's *Heat: An Amateur's Adventures as Kitchen Slave, Line Cook, Pasta Maker, and Apprentice to a Dante-Quoting Butcher in Tuscany* have also made these lists.

Food magazines are also gaining in popularity. In 2002, the magazine industry as a whole saw a decline in business, except for epicurean magazines. The epicurean genre had the highest growth, with a 12 percent jump in readership. The Publishers

Information Bureau reported that 12 new magazines in the epicurean category were launched in 2006 (Seltzer 2008). Although the landmark culinary magazine *Gourmet* was discontinued at the end of 2009, Holly Hughes, editor of the *Best Food Writing* series, says that food writing is more popular than ever. Food writing is no longer limited to food magazines and the food sections of newspapers. Food writing, especially provocative food journalism is popping up in general interest magazines, such as *The New Yorker*, *The Oxford American*, *The New York Times*, *GQ*, and the *Atlantic Monthly* (Hughes 2010a). Food writing is also appearing all over the Internet. In fact, Hughes believes that much of today's best food writing is being published online. There are a number of professional food web sites, not to mention the thousands of individual blogs that are focused on food.

The Food Network premiered in 1997 and has brought fame to cooks and chefs such as Rachel Ray, Emeril Lagasse, Paula Deen, and Mario Batali. The Food Network launched a second channel in 2010, the Cooking Channel. Cooking and food shows are popping up on other networks as well, such as the Travel Channel and TLC (The Learning Channel). Shows such as *Top Chef*, *Iron Chef*, *Hell's Kitchen*, *Ace of Cakes*, *Kitchen Nightmares*, *Man vs. Food*, and *No Reservations* all have large followings.

In 2009 the movie *Julie & Julia*, an adaptation of Julie Powell's memoir *Julie and Julia: 365 Days, 524 Recipes, 1 Tiny Apartment Kitchen* and Julia Child's memoir *My Life in France*, was a box office success; and earned Meryl Streep several award nominations and a Golden Globe award for her portrayal of Julia Child. The 2008 documentary *Food, Inc.* also received an Academy Award nomination.

The increased popularity of food may be due to social trends. Up until the second half of the 20th century, cooking in the home was primarily seen as the woman's responsibility. But changes in women's roles in the home and more equality in the division of labor have brought more men into home kitchens. Men now comprise 35 percent of the Food Network's audience and 40 percent of the Cooking Channel's audience (Levine 2011). Restaurant cooks were often seen as servants and cooking was considered a blue-collar career. But memoirs such as Anthony Bourdain's *Kitchen Confidential: Adventures in the Culinary Underbelly* have changed the image of restaurant cook from blue-collar worker to sex-filled, rock-star lifestyle, which makes for a more appealing image. Today chefs are celebrities and people send their children to cooking camps.

The increased desire for healthy living may also be a driving force in the increased interest in food. With over 60 percent of adults in the United States tipping the scales as either overweight or obese and increases in diseases such as diabetes and high blood pressure, Americans are starting to examine their food and dietary habits. Consumers are constantly inundated with messages to eat locally and seasonally, and to question the ingredients found in their food. In addition to desiring healthy living, there has also been an increased awareness of the environmental and global effects of the American diet. Americans are starting to consider where food comes from and how the production of that food may affect the environment and the local population. Some also believe that the events of September 11, 2001, as well as the troubled economy, have encouraged more people to do their entertaining at home, creating more interest in food and cooking (Granatstein 2002).

For a vast array of reasons, the interest in food does not seem to be a short-lived fad. Luckily, there is no shortage of Food Lit titles that will satisfy a variety of interests. The difficulty comes in connecting the reader with these titles. When I got puzzled looks from people who didn't understand what kind of books I would be including in this compendium, my standard examples were Michael Pollan's *The Omnivore's Dilemma*, Anthony Bourdain's *Kitchen Confidential*, or Julie Powell's *Julie and Julia*. Even if most had never read them, they had heard of them and were familiar with the topics. These titles are great recommendations to give readers looking for Food Lit, but there are so many more titles that rarely get off the library shelves simply because they don't get the publicity that Pollan's or Bourdain's books receive. For example, Marco Pierre White's *The Devil in the Kitchen: Sex, Pain, Madness, and the Making of a Great Chef* is an excellent choice for fans of Anthony Bourdain, but unless the reader is British or reads a lot of Food Lit, she has likely never heard of White.

For a reader who is simply browsing, finding Food Lit titles will be difficult. Much of it will be found in the 641s, but there are so many cookbooks in this section, it's difficult to pick out the Food Lit unless you know what you are looking for. There are also many Food Lit titles scattered throughout the Dewey numbers that will be missed. For example, Sue Fishkoff's *Kosher Nation* is located in 296. Unless a reader is specifically looking for this topic, a casual Food Lit reader would not usually think to look in this section. Gabriel Thompson's *Working in the Shadows: A Year of Doing the Jobs (Most) Americans Won't Do* is located in 331 and the subject headings ("immigrants," "foreign workers," and "minimum wage") do not indicate a relation to food, yet this book would certainly be an enjoyable read for readers interested in the issue of where their food comes from.

In libraries, Readers' Advisory has long been considered a service for fiction titles, whereas Reference has been assigned to nonfiction titles. But this is no longer the case. As Sarah Statz Cords mentions in *The Real Story: A Guide to Nonfiction Reading Interests*, sales for nonfiction titles have increased and more and more readers are turning to nonfiction for leisure reading (Cords 2006). More and more nonfiction is being written with a narrative style that has many of the same appeal elements as fiction, which is more appealing to readers than the traditional dense, scholarly-like titles readers used to associate with nonfiction. Readers' Advisory is a service that is now performed across both fiction and nonfiction. NoveList, formerly a database for fiction titles, has incorporated nonfiction titles into its database. While nonfiction readers' advisory guides do address food literature, such as Cords's *The Real Story* and Neal Wyatt's *Readers' Advisory Guide to Nonfiction*, it is given a brief overview and only the most popular titles, or benchmark, "sure bet" titles are included. This guide seeks to define the various topics within Food Lit, and provide a wide variety of Food Lit titles as well as other titles that may be of interest.

Appeal of Food Lit

Food Lit is appealing for many reasons. The Reader's Advisory database NoveList broadly states that food writing is fun to read (Wyatt 2007a). This is certainly true for some of the titles, but there are quite a few, particularly in the Investigative Food Writing chapter, that I would not call *fun*. Interesting, inspiring, educational, and even shocking, but not always fun. Author and *Library Journal* columnist Neal Wyatt says that the chief reason readers enjoy food books is the element of learning, or for the vicarious experience (Wyatt 2007b). Readers can experience the life of a chef or experience the flavors of a five star restaurant. They can also learn how food is produced and where it comes from. Details and language are also strong appeal elements. Lynn Z. Bloom states that food writing is evocative and full of emotion, energy, sensory details, and sensuality (Bloom 2008). Descriptive details of elaborate meals or exotic foods are highly appealing to readers. Character is another appeal element, particularly with memoirs. A wide variety of characters from chefs to home cooks to farmers bring their strong personalities to the page and create connections with the reader. As mentioned before, food often has the ability to spark a memory, reminding us of the family meals of our childhood, holiday gatherings with friends and family, social gatherings, or learning to cook from one's parent or grandparent. Barbara Frey Waxman suggests that Food Literature will appeal even to reluctant readers. Everyone eats, therefore food provides an unthreatening context that is familiar to everyone (Waxman 2008). Molly O'Neill believes that we enjoy reading about food "because reading about food reminds us that we are human and alive and a tangle of contradictions, some of which can be eased by a meal and some of which can be resolved by remembering and imagining what it feels like . . ." (O'Neill 2007).

The Selection Process

Although not a comprehensive list, this guide attempts to broadly cover the most popular and most current Food Lit titles. Most of the titles included were published between 1995 and 2011, although some classic or benchmark titles, published prior to 1995, are also included. I began by collecting titles from my own collection of favorite Food Lit titles. Then I consulted well-known Readers' Advisory guides, such as Nancy Pearl's *Book Lust* and *More Book Lust*, Neal Wyatt's *Readers' Advisory Guide to Nonfiction*, Sarah Statz Cords's *The Real Story*, and the Novelist and Readers' Advisory Online databases. These were helpful in identifying benchmark titles and authors.

I then culled titles from award winners and notable book lists. The most prestigious food writing awards are the James Beard Foundation Awards and the International Association of Culinary Professionals Awards. Many of these winners are cookbooks, but there are a number of Food Lit titles that have received awards. Food Lit titles that won either of these awards between 2000 and 2010 were included. Yearly lists of notable books, such as the American Library Association's Notable Books, the *New York Times* Notable Books, the Indies' Choice Book Awards (formerly the American Booksellers Association's Book Sense Book of the Year Awards), and Amazon's Editor's Picks were also considered for inclusion.

In addition, *Publisher's Weekly*, *Library Journal*, and *Booklist* were consulted for Food Lit titles that were given starred reviews. Finally, I found many titles simply by browsing the nonfiction stacks in a large public library with a very impressive collection of food titles (Shout out to Skokie Public Library!) as well as those in bookstores.

What Is Not Included

There are so many Food Lit titles that it would be impossible to include them all; and the intention of this guide is to provide a broad but selective, rather than a comprehensive, list. Certainly, there are titles that were published outside of the scope of publication dates covered that have been missed. Titles that are scholarly or academic were passed by as well, as this book is meant to provide suggestions for leisure readers. And with few exceptions, cookbooks are not covered. As previously mentioned, cookbooks do not fit into Food Lit as defined here, and there are such a vast number of cookbooks in print that it would be impossible to cover them. However, it is worth noting that readers who enjoy Food Lit also like to read cookbooks, whether or not they intend to use the recipes. Therefore, there is a chapter of narrative cookbooks, as well as an appendix of well-known food figures and their cookbooks. Some cookbooks are also mentioned in the "Now Try . . ." section of the annotations.

How to Use this Book

Organization of the Chapters

This book is divided into four sections:

- Life Stories

- Nonfiction Genres

- Nonfiction Subject Interests

- Stylistic Genres

Life Stories include memoirs and biographies. Nonfiction Genres include travel and adventure. Nonfiction Subject Interests include history and science. Stylistic Genres include investigative writing, narrative cookbooks, and essays. In addition, the appendices include lists of popular cooks and their cookbooks, fiction titles with food, food writing awards, and suggestions for other formats that may be of interest to readers of Food Lit, such as blogs and documentaries.

Format, Annotations, and "Now Try" Recommendations

For each title annotated here you will find a brief summary of the title, as well as the appeal factors. The publication information is provided, along with page numbers and ISBNs. Each annotation also includes subject headings based on Dewey Decimal classification, as well as popular appeals, such as "Quick Reads." Following each annotation, additional titles that may be of interest to the reader are suggested in "Now Try." These titles include fiction and nonfiction selections, as well as other formats that may be of interest.

"Consider Starting With . . ."

Each chapter concludes with a list of titles that are recommended as a good place to start for librarians and readers who are not familiar with that particular genre. These titles are considered benchmarks of that particular genre and are often sure bets.

Conclusion

Journalist Kathryn Hughes suggests that we are currently experiencing a renaissance in food writing (Hughes 2010b). This is an exciting time for Food Lit. There is an abundance of titles that cover a variety of topics, from history to travel and everything in between. Librarian S. R. Ranganathan famously proposed: "every book its reader," meaning that every book has a reader who will enjoy it (Ranganathan 1931). This is certainly the case for Food Lit. Any reader interested in Food Lit should be able to find a title that suits her taste. The trick is connecting the reader with this book. Since this "renaissance" of Food Lit is relatively recent, there are not a lot of resources dedicated to this task. My hope is that this book will help readers and librarians connect with a variety of Food Lit titles that they will enjoy.

References

Blakeslee, E. C. 1890. *The Compendium of Cookery and Reliable Recipes*. Chicago: D. R. Ingersoll & Co.

Bloom, Lynn Z. 2008. "Consuming Prose: The Delectable Rhetoric of Food Writing." *College English* 70 (4): 346.

Brillat-Savarin, Jean-Anthelme. 1971. *The Physiology of Taste: Or Mediations on Transcendental Gastronomy*, translated by M.F.K. Fisher. New York: Knopf.

Campbell, Darryl. 2011. "Our Meals, Ourselves: A Short History of Food Writing." *The Millions*. Available at www.themillions.com (accessed February 25, 2011).

Cords, Sarah Statz. 2006. *The Real Story: A Guide to Nonfiction Reading Interests*. Westport, CT: Libraries Unlimited.

Granatstein, Lisa. 2002. "Comfort Food: Epicurean Titles Are Adding Readers as More Americans Do Their Entertaining at Home." *Mediaweek* 12 (21): 32.

Hendrick, Bill. 2011. "Percentage of Overweight, Obese Americans Swells, Americans Are Eating Poorly, Exercising Less, and Getting Bigger, Survey Finds." *WebMD Health News*. Available at www.webmd.org (accessed February 25, 2011).

Hughes, Holly. 2010a. *Best Food Writing 2010*. Cambridge, MA: Da Capo.

Hughes, Kathryn. 2010b. "A Taste for Words: In the 10 Years Since Anthony Bourdain Revealed the Shocking Secrets of Life as a Chef and Celebrity Cooks Dominated the Best-seller Lists, Food Writing Has Moved Out of the Kitchen and On to the Bookshelves." *The Guardian* (June 19).

Levine, D. M. 2011. "Getting Food Right: Brooke Johnson, President of the Food Network and Cooking Channel, on the Shift from Cooking to Watching." *Adweek*. (September 21). Available at http://www.adweek.com/news/television/getting-food-right-134922 (accessed February 2, 2012).

The Nielson Company. 2011. www.nielson.com (accessed February 27, 2011).

O'Neill, Molly. 2007. *American Food Writing: An Anthology With Classic Recipes*. New York: Library of America.

Ranganathan, S. R. 1931. *The Five Laws of Library Science*. Madras, India: Madras Library Association.

Seltzer, Molly. 2008. "Chicagoans Hungry for Books About Food, Publishers Happy to Serve up More." *Medill Reports*. Chicago: Northwestern University.

Shapiro, Laura. 1998. "Memories of Meals Past: Sex Still Sells Biographies, But Cookery is Catching Up." *Newsweek* 13 (15): 68.

Waxman, Barbara Frey. 2008. "Food Memoirs: What They Are, Why They Are Popular, and Why They Belong in the Literature Classroom." *College English* 70 (4): 363.

Wyatt, Neal. 2007a. "Getting up to Speed in . . . Food Writing." NoveList. Available at www.ebscohost.com/novelist (paid subscription, check your local library).

Wyatt, Neal. 2007b. *The Readers Advisory Guide to Nonfiction*. Chicago: American Library Association.

Part I

Life Stories

Chapter 1

Food Memoirs and Autobiographies

Definition of Food Memoirs and Autobiographies

Memoirs are nearly as old as writing itself, as Ben Yagoda points out in his book *Memoir: A History* (Yagoda 2009). People have been writing about their lives since at least the 5th century. At that time most memoirs were confessions of sin, but by the first half of the 19th century, a quarter of all memoirs were written by criminals. Today the topics range anywhere in between and are more popular than ever. In 2007, memoirs accounted for 12.5 percent of nonfiction deals and were outpacing debut novels (Minzesheimer 2008). Yagoda cites less concern for privacy and our therapeutic culture as reasons for the increase in popularity of memoirs.

Readers often use the terms memoir and autobiography interchangeably. Although memoirs are a form of autobiography, there is a difference between the two. While both are histories of a writer's life, memoirs are a slice of life (Wyatt 2007), recounting an experience usually focused on a specific period of time in the writer's life. An autobiography is typically a lengthier work and tends to detail the writer's entire life. In her guide on life stories, Rosalind Reisner says that autobiographies are usually written by someone who is famous in their own right, whereas writers of memoirs often become famous for having written their memoir (Reisner 2009). In his memoir *Palimpsest*, Gore Vidal gave this definition: "a memoir is how one remembers one's own life, while an autobiography is history, requiring research, dates, facts double-checked" (Vidal 1995).

Despite the immense popularity of the memoir, Vidal's criteria for memoir are exactly why so many memoirs have come under intense scrutiny. A person's memory can be sketchy, so it stands to reason that memoirs may be lacking in certain details, or events, dates, and conversations may not be entirely accurate. How one person remembers an event differs from another's memory of the same event. One of the most publicized falsified memoirs was James Frey's *A Million Little Pieces*, which was chosen as an Oprah book-club selection. When it was revealed that Frey took liberties with his memoir, Oprah berated Frey on television for his lies. But such scandals are not new. Yagoda points out that falsified slave memoirs were sparking controversy before the Civil War (Yagoda 2009). As a result, it is common now for authors to include a statement at the beginning of his or her memoir, acknowledging that the events are true to the best of his or her knowledge and memory. In addition, to protect the privacy of others as well as condense stories, many writers acknowledge that multiple characters have been condensed into one, and events, dates, and times have also been condensed. Rosalind Reisner states that "life stories are literature and that may be the only truth" (Reisner 2009). Regardless of the creative license writers often take with their memoirs, they remain one of the most popular forms of nonfiction writing. Sarah Statz Cords suggests that the success of the memoir genre indicates that most readers aren't particularly concerned with the absolute truth (Cords 2006).

Food is quickly becoming a popular topic for memoirs. Food writer Laura Shapiro pointed out that "sex and substance abuse are still the big issues in autobiography, but food is catching up fast" (Shapiro 1998). Since cookbooks and memoirs continue to be popular sellers, Food Memoirs are a natural union. Dubbing them "foodoirs," former food editor of the *New York Times Magazine*, Christine Muhlke said that these memoirs have "captured the money-making imagination of the publishing industry" (Muhlke 2009). Food Memoirs are frequently found on the *New York Times* best-seller list. Anthony Bourdain's *Kitchen Confidential: Adventures in the Culinary Underbelly*, which was released in 2000, continues to pop up on the *New York Times* best seller for trade nonfiction and Elizabeth Gilbert's *Eat, Pray, Love* spent over 200 weeks on the list. Steve Dublanica's *Waiter Rant*, Frank Bruni's *Born Round*, Julie Powell's *Julia and Julia*, and Gabrielle Hamilton's *Blood, Bones & Butter* are just a few other Food Memoirs to reach the best-seller lists.

Barbara Frey Waxman states that Food Memoirs chronicle the growth of the writer through the lens of food memories (Waxman 2008). Food Memoirs and Autobiographies incorporate food as a major element of the writer's experiences. The writer is typically either employed in a profession related to food, such as a chef, or has a passion for food that plays a big role in his or her life, such as a home cook or a food blogger. A large portion of these memoirs are focused on food, either in the preparing of it or in the eating of it, and many often include recipes as well.

Appeal of Food Memoirs and Autobiographies

A strong appeal factor of Food Memoirs is the focus on character. Memoirs give readers the opportunity to escape into someone else's life and share a journey with the writer. Unlike biographies, which are also character-focused, memoirs frequently have the added appeal of voice. Memoirs provide a more personal connection because they create a direct connection between the reader and the subject. There is an intimacy achieved through memoir found in no other form, because it is the author speaking directly to the reader. Because they share the writer's thoughts and feelings, readers often feel that they can identify with the writer. Memoirs can also impart a "gossipy connection" (Wyatt 2007), enhancing the personal connection between reader and writer.

Food Memoirs allow a reader to live vicariously through the writer. Readers can experience something they might not get to experience in their own day-to-day lives. Perhaps they will never be a professional chef, but they can experience the frenzy, chaos, and heat of the kitchen through memoirs like Jason Sheehan's *Cooking Dirty: A Story of Life, Sex, Love and Death in the Kitchen*. Readers may not want to grow their own food, but they can "feel vicariously virtuous" (Yabroff 2007) reading about Barbara Kingsolver's sacrifices in *Animal, Vegetable, Miracle: A Year of Food Life*. Memoirs can also be inspiring or cathartic experiences for the reader. Often stories of challenges faced by the author, such as difficult childhoods or illnesses, and the ability of the author to overcome obstacles can be very inspiring to the reader. Or a reader may have experienced similar obstacles and reading about another's struggles can be a source of commiseration and comfort. Several writers have described their struggles with illness, tragedy, and even addiction and their use of cooking to overcome their problems.

Food Memoirs are popular for their elements of detail, settings, and tone. Wyatt writes that "writers of culinary memoirs have often spent their lives writing about food and honed their descriptive skills crafting restaurant reviews and essays" (Wyatt 2007). Therefore, these memoirs often include lush descriptions of food, detailed descriptions of restaurants and kitchens, and humorous stories of coworkers, employers, and restaurant patrons.

Rosalind Reisner also points out that memoirs are popular because they are literary. They are shaped like a novel, with a beginning that focuses on character development, a middle that often includes climactic events, and an end, which usually offers a resolution (Reisner 2009). Readers enjoy memoirs for the same reasons they enjoy fiction: memorable characters, unique literary styles, absorbing stories, and detailed settings.

Readers who enjoy Food Memoirs for their character appeal may also enjoy Food Biographies for the in-depth details of the figure's life. The Immersion Journalism stories in the Investigative Food Writing chapter may also be appealing for the accounts of the author's personal experiences. Many of the Food Travel titles have many similar appeal elements as well, including personal experiences, details, and strong settings.

Organization of the Chapter

One of the most popular subgenres of Food Memoirs is the **Working Life** theme. Anthony Bourdain's hugely successful *Kitchen Confidential: Adventures in the Culinary Underbelly* paved the way for other Food Memoirs from those working in the food industry, whether it be as a chef, waiter, bartender, or even cheesemonger. Closely related to this theme is that of the **Personal Endeavor** memoir. Today it seems that anyone who undertakes a new hobby or project inevitably will write about it. Many of these personal stories are related to food in some way, whether it's someone's attempt to raise their own food or learn to cook. **Foodie Memoirs** encompass works by famous food critics, food writers, as well as home cooks, bloggers, and those for whom food has played an important role in his or her life. **Comfort Food** is another popular subgenre of Food Memoirs. These writers have turned to food or cooking to help them through difficult times such as illness, tragedy, failed relationships, or addiction.

Working Life Memoirs

In public appearances, Anthony Bourdain has been known to say that when he wrote *Kitchen Confidential: Adventures in the Culinary Underbelly*, he only intended for it to be read by some of his friends and colleagues. He never thought it would even be read by anyone outside of New York. But his story quickly hit the *New York Times* best-seller list, making Bourdain a celebrity and creating a market for other gritty, entertaining inside tales of the restaurant business. Since then, several other chefs have hopped on board, penning their own memoirs. Although not as prolific (yet), waiters and bartenders have started writing their own memoirs, balancing the mix with stories about the front of the house. Other careers in food also provide interesting fodder for memoirs, such as restaurateurs, restaurant critics, and even cheesemongers.

The Working Life memoirs of chefs, waiters, and bartenders are tremendously appealing for several reasons. Many of us have a romantic view of the chef's job. We see him or her dressed in chef's whites creating artful dishes. But so many writers have dispelled this view by giving us an inside, personal look at what really goes on in the back of the house (and the rich, often complex and/or conflicted characters who work there). Readers can also experience the life of a chef without subjecting themselves to the harsh environment of a restaurant kitchen. The detailed descriptions of the working conditions, pace, and heat make the reader feel like they are right there in the kitchen. Some writers also impart a gossipy feel to their writing, telling stories about customers and owners. The pace of Working Life memoirs is often quick. The tone tends to be grittier, since many stories focus on the darker side of the food business. Some memoirs have an element of humor, whether it's from stories of pranks in the kitchen or commentary on demanding customers.

> Working Life Food Memoirs are memoirs written by a variety of individuals who work in the food industry, describing their careers and work environments. They tend to be quickly paced, extremely evocative of food and the surroundings in which it is made, and often adopt a gossipy or even somewhat gritty tone.

Readers who enjoy the Working Life Memoirs may also enjoy memoirs that illuminate other careers. From flight attendants to retail associates, nannies, and nurses, there is a memoir for just about any career one could think of. Readers may be interested in Investigative Food Writing, as there are a number of titles that go behind the scenes in restaurants and culinary schools. Although usually lighter in tone, fiction titles that feature chefs, bakers, and caterers as the main character may also be enjoyed.

Achatz, Grant, and Kokonas, Nick

Life on the Line: A Chef's Story of Chasing Greatness, Facing Death and Redefining the Way We Eat. New York: Gotham Books, 2011. 390pp. ISBN 9781592406012.

> Achatz is the chef and co-owner of the Chicago restaurant, Alinea, one of the top restaurants in the country. Achatz begins by recalling his childhood in Michigan, where he was around kitchens from an early age. After attending the Culinary Institute of America, he went on to work for Thomas Keller and Charlie Trotter. In 2005, Achatz partnered with Kokonas to open Alinea, where he created his unique menu and earned a reputation as a leader in molecular gastronomy. In 2007, Achatz was diagnosed with stage IV tongue cancer. The recommended course of action was to remove his entire tongue; however, hoping to save his career, Achatz chose to undergo an aggressive alternative treatment, which had horrible side effects. Despite the pain, he continued to work, and within five months was cancer-free and earned the James Beard Foundation award for Outstanding Chef in America.
>
> **Subjects:** Cancer, Chefs, Health Issues, Men's Lives, Midwest, Restaurants
>
> **Now Try:** Readers may enjoy Achatz's beautifully photographed pictorial of his famous restaurant, *Alinea.* What is molecular gastronomy? Try *Molecular Gastronomy: Exploring the Science of Flavor* by Hervé This. *Blood, Bones, & Butter: The Inadvertent Education of a Reluctant Chef* by Gabrielle Hamilton is a memoir by another chef who faced personal struggles throughout her career. *Ferran: The Inside Story of El Bulli and the Man Who Reinvented Food* by Colman Andrews is the biography of another leading chef known for his creative culinary talents. Readers may also enjoy other memoirs about battling illness, such as *It's Not About the Bike: My Journey Back To Life* by Lance Armstrong or tennis champion Arthur Ashe's memoir *Days of Grace*, in which he recounts his struggles against racism and AIDS.

Boulud, Daniel

Letters to a Young Chef. New York: Basic Books, 2003. 165pp. ISBN 9780465007356.

> French chef and restaurateur, Boulud has been named Chef of the Year by *Gourmet* magazine and won the James Beard Award for Outstanding Chef of the Year in 1994 and Outstanding Restaurateur in 2006. His most famous restaurant, Daniel, in New York City, was awarded four stars by

the *New York Times* and three stars from Michelin. In this short book, Boulud speaks to those who are considering entering his profession. Part memoir and part advice, Boulud explains what it takes to be a successful chef and restaurant owner. He also describes his career path and what it's like to work in a restaurant and offers honest advice for young chefs on what to expect. Although written for chefs, readers will appreciate the inside look at the restaurant business and thoughts from this successful chef. Boulud's advice will ring true for any ambitious person: work hard and pay your dues.

Subjects: Business, Chefs, Quick Reads, Restaurants

Now Try: Leslie Brenner provides a look at what it's like to work for Daniel Boulud in *The Fourth Star: Dispatches from Inside Daniel Boulud's Celebrated New York Restaurant*. Readers may want to peruse Boulud's *Café Boulud Cookbook*. Anthony Bourdain dispenses advice to those considering a career as a chef in the chapter "So You Wanna Be a Chef" in *Medium Raw*. Eric Ripert, chef of the famed Le Bernardin restaurant, describes the workings of his restaurant in *On the Line*. Readers may enjoy the personal stories from famous chefs in *How I Learned to Cook: Culinary Educations from the World's Greatest Chefs* by Kimberly Witherspoon and Peter Meehan and *Chef's Story: 27 Chefs Talk About What Got Them into the Kitchen* by Dorothy Hamilton and Patric Kuh. Michael Ruhlman's books also provide a good perspective on becoming a chef; they include *The Making of a Chef* and *The Soul of a Chef*.

Bourdain, Anthony

Kitchen Confidential: Adventures in the Culinary Underbelly. New York: Bloomsbury, 2000. 307pp. ISBN 9781582340821.

Before he was a television celebrity, Anthony Bourdain was a New York chef. In this entertaining memoir, Bourdain introduces readers to the underbelly of the restaurant business. While visiting France as a child, he discovered a passion for food that led to his first job (of many) working in a restaurant, schooling at the Culinary Institute of America, and finally, achieving a position as head chef. Bourdain chronicles the fast paced, chaotic, and demanding life of a chef, as well as the darker side of working in restaurants: late nights, partying, sex, drugs, and pranks on coworkers. Readers who have ever romanticized the life of a chef will find this an eye-opening read.

Subjects: Bourdain, Anthony, Chefs, Culinary School, Humor, Men's Lives, New York City, Profanity, Restaurants

Now Try: Readers who enjoy the fast-paced and behind-the-scenes aspect of *Kitchen Confidential* should try Jason Sheehan's *Cooking Dirty: A Story of Life, Sex, Love, and Death in the Kitchen* and Bill Buford's *Heat: An Amateur's Adventures as Kitchen Slave, Line Cook, Pasta-Maker, and Apprentice to a Dante-Quoting Butcher in Tuscany*. Joe Bastianich's *Restaurant Man* is another entertaining account of running a restaurant. Other inside looks at different aspects of the restaurant industry may also be appealing, such as Phoebe Damrosch's *Service Included: Four Star Secrets of an Eavesdropping Waiter* or Steve Dublanica's *Waiter Rant: Thanks for the Tip—Confessions of a Cynical Waiter*. Bourdain cites Nicolas Freeling's 1970 title, *The Kitchen: A Delicious Account of the Author's Years* *as a Grand Hotel Cook* as one of his favorite books and the one that inspired him to write *Kitchen Confidential*. Fans of Bourdain's writing style should try some of his other books, such as *The Nasty Bits* or *Medium Raw* or even his fiction novels, *Gone Bamboo* or *Bone in the Throat*. Readers may also be interested in other Working Life memoirs, such Claire Lewis's *Exposed: Confessions of a Wedding Photographer* or Jeff Martin's *The Customer Is Always Wrong: The Retail Chronicles*.

Cecchini, Toby

Cosmopolitan: A Bartender's Life. New York: Broadway Books, 2003. 238pp. ISBN 9780767912099.

Cecchini introduces readers to the life of a New York City bar owner. He illustrates the hectic pace of a popular bar on a Saturday night, describes some of his regular customers and some of the more demanding customers who have frequented his bar with their strange behaviors and requests, and discusses why he hates making margaritas and refuses to make mojitos. But Cecchini also explores the idea of the neighborhood bar: what a bar can be to people, how it can create community bonds, and become a comfortable, familiar place where people can connect, and why it's important to have a place where everybody knows your name.

> **Subjects:** Bars, Bartenders, Cocktails, Community Life, New York City

> **Now Try:** Readers may also enjoy Ty Wenzel's memoir *Behind Bars: The Straight-Up Tales of a Big City Bartender*. Debra Ginsberg's *Waiting: The True Confessions of a Waitress* includes stories of restaurant life and the customers. Readers who enjoy the idea of the neighborhood bar as a place for community may also enjoy *The Tender Bar: A Memoir* by J. R. Moehringer or *Little Chapel on the River: A Pub, a Town and the Search for What Matters Most* by Wendy Bounds. Christine Sismondo traces the history of the bar as part of American life in *America Walks into a Bar: A Spirited History of Taverns and Saloons, Speakeasies and Grog Shops*. *Later, at the Bar: A Novel in Stories* by Rebecca Barry is a fiction novel about the regulars that frequent the local bar. Drink Dogma (www.drinkdogma.com) is a blog written by the owners of a Houston bar, who share opinions on cocktails and stories from the world of bartending.

Damrosch, Phoebe

Service Included: Four Star Secrets of an Eavesdropping Waiter. New York: William Morrow, 2007. 228pp. ISBN 9780061228148.

After graduating from Barnard College, Damrosch was trying to figure out what to do with her life. Deciding that she would get a job waiting tables, she decided to set her sights on the best job she could find. When Thomas Keller opened his restaurant Per Se in New York City, Damrosch was hired as one of its first servers. Keller is known for demanding perfection and precision, so this is not just any story of waiting tables at a mid-level restaurant. Damrosch describes the in-depth training she received on service etiquette, the exacting standards she was expected to meet, and the anxiety over a review from the *New York Times*. While she provides a behind-the-scenes look at working in a restaurant, it is a much tamer view than those taken by many chefs, but readers will enjoy the unique look at this famous restaurant.

> **Subjects:** Bruni, Frank, Keller, Thomas, Per Se, Restaurants, Waiters, Women's Nonfiction
>
> **Awards:** *New York Times* Notable Book
>
> **Now Try:** Readers may also enjoy Debra Ginsberg's memoir *Waiting: The True Confessions of a Waitress* and Steve Dublanica's *Waiter Rant: Thanks for the Tip—Confessions of a Cynical Waiter*. Readers who are captivated by the exacting standards of Thomas Keller and the attention to every detail from the food down to the forks may want to try *The Fourth Star: Dispatches from Inside Daniel Boulud's Celebrated New York Restaurant* by Leslie Brenner or *Knives at Dawn: America's Quest for Culinary Glory at the Bocuse d'Or, the World's Most Prestigious Cooking Competition* by Andrew Friedman, which capture the exacting standards of haute cuisine. Danny Meyer's *Setting the Table: The Transforming Power of Hospitality in Business* is an interesting treatise on restaurant hospitality. One of Thomas Keller's cookbooks may also be appealing. Try one that showcases his restaurants, such as *The French Laundry Cookbook* or *Bouchon*.

DeLucie, John

The Hunger: A Story of Food, Desire, and Ambition. New York: Ecco, 2009. 233pp. ISBN 9780061579240.

John DeLucie began his working career in financial services. After several unhappy years, he quit his job to take a 12-week cooking course. After completing the course, he went on to find a job working at the upscale market Dean & Deluca's. Although he quickly bored of his position, he realized that his happiness lay in a career in cooking. DeLucie goes on to recount his experiences working in various restaurants: the hectic and chaotic pace of the kitchen, the initiations and pranks from fellow coworkers and the after-hour partying. Eventually DeLucie partners with Graydon Carter, editor of *Vanity Fair*, to purchase the popular Waverly Inn in Greenwich Village, which comes with its own set of difficulties.

> **Subjects:** Career Change, Chefs, Men's Lives, New York City, Restaurants
>
> **Now Try:** A number of Food Lit memoirs feature authors who left unfulfilling careers. Kathleen Flinn recalls her unhappiness in a corporate career and her decision to become a chef in *The Sharper Your Knife, the Less You Cry: Love, Laughter, and Tears in Paris at the World's Most Famous Cooking School*. Doug Psaltis recounts his road to becoming a chef and finally opening his own restaurant in *The Seasoning of a Chef: My Journey From Diner to Ducasse and Beyond*. Gesine Bullock-Prado left her Hollywood career to open her own bakery in *My Life From Scratch*. Steven Jenkins shares his love of food and his career working in the famous New York City grocery story, Fairway Market, in *The Food Life: Inside the World of Food with the Grocer Extraordinaire*

at Fairway. Other memoirs by people who left unfulfilling careers to follow their passion may also be appealing, such as John Wood's *Leaving Microsoft to Change the World.*

Dublanica, Steve

Waiter Rant: Thanks for the Tip—Confessions of a Cynical Waiter. New York: Ecco, 2008. 302pp. ISBN 9780061256684.

When Dublanica took a job as a waiter, he intended it to be a temporary gig. But after several years, he found himself still waiting tables, blogging about the life of a waiter. In this book, he shares insight into the workings of an upscale New York City restaurant, but he also has a lot to say about one topic we don't hear much about in chef memoirs: the customers. Dublanica says that restaurants bring out the worst in people, and after spending years working as a waiter in upscale restaurants in New York, he has plenty of stories of rude, obnoxious, selfish, and just plain mean, customers. Although not as humorous as some of the other titles in this subgenre, this book feels like a gossip-y tell-all.

Subjects: Blogs, Humor, New York City, Profanity, Quick Reads, Restaurants, Waiters

Now Try: Dublanica seems to be trying for a voice similar to Anthony Bourdain, so a good choice would be Bourdain's *Kitchen Confidential: Adventures in the Culinary Underbelly.* Readers that enjoyed the gossip of Dublanica's tale may also enjoy *Service Included: Four Star Secrets of an Eavesdropping Waiter* by Phoebe Damrosch. Other gossip-y customer-service stories that may appeal to readers are A. J. Adams's entertaining collection of customer horror stories, *The Customer Is Not Always Right: Hilarious and Horrific Tales of Customers Gone Wrong,* Freeman Hall's *Retail Hell: How I Sold My Soul to the Store,* or Michael Fazio's *Concierge Confidential: The Gloves Come Off—and the Secrets Come Out! Tales from the Man Who Serves Millionaires, Moguls, and Madmen.* Readers may also want to consider Dublanica's exploration of tipping: *Keep the Change: A Clueless Tipper's Quest to Become the Guru of the Gratuity.*

Edgar, Gordon

Cheesemonger: A Life on the Wedge. White River Junction: Chelsea Green Publishing, 2010. 236pp. ISBN 9781603582377.

A cheesemonger, as Edgar points out, is one who buys and sells cheese. Not to be confused (necessarily) with a lover of cheese. Although an Antique Gruyere turned Edgar into a lover of cheese, Edgar became a cheesemonger before he developed his love of cheese. In this passionate account, Edgar recounts his path to cheesemonger of a San Francisco grocery co-op, and what his job entails. Tales of mistakes made along the way, rodent issues, difficult distributors, and interesting customers make this an entertaining story. Edgar also covers the intricacies of cheese production, industry issues, and elaborate profiles of cheeses.

Subjects: Cheese, Food Industry, Grocery Trade, Retail

Now Try: Eric LeMay shares his love of cheese and his quest to learn more about it in *Immortal Milk: Adventures in Cheese*. Liz Thorpe shares an inside look at the cheese industry in *The Cheese Chronicles: A Journey Through the Making and Selling of Cheese in America, From Field to Farm to Table*. Readers may also enjoy the brief, but interesting history *Cheese: A Global History* by Andrew Dalby. Steve Jenkins, a cheese expert, shares his experiences selling various products, particularly cheese, in *The Food Life: Inside the World of Food with the Grocer Extraordinaire at Fairway*. Readers may also want to check out blogs such as Curd Nerds (curdnerds.com) or It's Not You, It's Brie (itsnotyouitsbrie.com). For fun, readers may want to try Avery Aames's Cheese Shop mystery series. Start with *The Long Quiche Goodbye*.

Febbroriello, Courtney

Wife of the Chef. New York: Clarkson Potter, 2003. 281pp. ISBN 9780609611067.
This entertaining, behind-the-scenes memoir proves that having a chef for a husband isn't all that it's cracked up to be. Febbroriello and her husband own a small restaurant in Connecticut. As chef, her husband gets all the glory. As wife of the chef, Febbroriello manages all of the day-to-day operations and gets no recognition. Frank yet humorous, she describes what her typical hectic day running a restaurant includes: labor and immigration issues, condescending salesmen, cranky customers, and unreliable suppliers. She is on the run from the early morning until she collapses into bed. Although stressful, she and her husband seem to thrive under the pressure and are proud of the business they have created together.

Subjects: Chefs, Marriage, Restaurants

Now Try: Kenny Shopsin's book *Eat Me: The Food and Philosophy of Kenny Shopsin* is an entertaining account of running a family restaurant. Pino Luongo's *Dirty Dishes: A Restaurateur's Story of Passion, Pain, and Pasta* also depicts the challenges of running a restaurant. Alyssa Shelasky shares what it's like to be in a relationship with a busy chef in *Apron Anxiety: My Messy Affairs In and Out of the Kitchen*. Melinda Blanchard recounts how she and her husband left their life in Vermont to open a restaurant on the island of Anguilla in *A Trip to the Beach: Living on Island Time in the Caribbean*. In *Julie and Julia: 365 Days, 524 Recipes, 1 Tiny Apartment Kitchen*, Julie Powell relates her quest to cook from Julia Child's cookbook with her husband's support.

Flinn, Kathleen

The Sharper Your Knife, the Less You Cry: Love, Laughter, and Tears in Paris at the World's Most Famous Cooking School. New York: Viking, 2007. 285pp. ISBN 9780670018239.

At 36, Flinn found herself miserable and unhappy with her career as an executive at a major software company. When her job was eliminated, she took a chance on a lifelong dream and moved to Paris to study at the famous Le Cordon Bleu culinary school. Readers will enjoy her descriptions of daily life in Paris, and the difficulties of her classes (especially because she speaks little French). Flinn finds fulfillment in her successes, the friendships she makes, and her developing romance.

Subjects: Career Change, Culinary School, France, Le Cordon Bleu, Relationships, Women's Nonfiction

Now Try: *Under the Table: Saucy Tales From Culinary School* by Katherine Darling is another account of an unhappy career left for culinary school. Other books about women and self-discovery may be suggested, such as *Julie and Julia: 365 Days, 524 Recipes, 1 Tiny Apartment Kitchen* by Julie Powell, *Animal, Vegetable, Miracle: A Year of Food Life* by Barbara Kingsolver, *Educating Alice: Adventures of a Curious Woman* by Alice Steinbach, or *Eat, Pray, Love* by Elizabeth Gilbert. Readers who enjoyed the Paris setting may also enjoy David Lebovitz's *The Sweet Life in Paris: Delicious Adventures in the World's Most Glorious and Perplexing City* or Amy Thomas's *Paris, My Sweet*. Jenny Nelson's novel *Georgia's Kitchen* is the story of a chef who leaves her problems in New York to work in a trattoria in Italy.

Ginsberg, Debra

Waiting: The True Confessions of a Waitress. New York: Harper Collins, 2000. 286pp. ISBN 9780060194796.

Debra Ginsberg began waiting tables as a teenager, and continued in the profession for over 20 years. She recounts her experiences working in various restaurants and provides juicy, gossipy stories about various customers, from the overly demanding to the bad tippers. She shares her perspective on the back-of-the-house employees, like the chefs and dishwashers, and how the front and back of the house interacts. A single mother, Ginsberg also describes what it's like to be a waitress while pregnant, raise a child on a waitress's wages, and how she dealt with other's perceptions of her choice to work in this field.

Subjects: Restaurants, Waiters, Women's Nonfiction

Now Try: Phoebe Damrosch's *Service Included: Four-Star Secrets of an Eavesdropping Waiter* is another enlightening account of waiting tables. After his experiences waiting tables and earning poor tips, Steve Dublanica examines the concept of gratuity in *Keep the Change: A Clueless Tipper's Quest to Become the Guru of Gratuity*. Candacy Taylor interviews career waitresses in *Counter Culture: The American Coffee Shop Waitress*. Readers may enjoy the behind-the-scenes gossip of retail sales in Freeman Hall's *Retail Hell: How I Sold My Soul to the Store Confessions of a Tortured Sales Associate*. A. J. Adams collects shocking and humorous stories of customer horror stories in *The Customer Is Not Always Right: Hilarious and Horrific Tales of Customers Gone Wrong*. Other

People's Dirt: A Housecleaner's Curious Adventures by Louise Rifkin is an intimate look at the lives of a housecleaner's clients. Readers may also want to consider Ginsberg's memoir of raising her son, *Raising Blaze: Bringing Up an Extraordinary Son in an Ordinary World*, or her novels, which include *Blind Submission* and *The Grift*.

Hamilton, Gabrielle

Blood, Bones, and Butter: The Inadvertent Education of a Reluctant Chef. New York: Random House, 2011. 291pp. ISBN 9781400068722.

Gabrielle Hamilton, chef and owner of the New York restaurant Prune, is an unlikely success story. Hamilton had an idyllic childhood until her parents' marriage ended in divorce when Gabrielle was 13. With her mother gone and her father inattentive, Gabrielle's childhood was shattered and she was left to take care of herself; as a rebellious teenager, she began lying and stealing. At the age of 16, she moved to New York City, where she worked as a waitress until she was arrested for stealing. Her French mother had instilled a love of good food in Hamilton, and she began catering and cooking for a children's summer camp. With her life finally on track, Hamilton went back to school for a writing degree, then decided to go into the restaurant business. Marriage, motherhood, a successful career, and a close relationship with her sister seem to have brought Hamilton peace. Hamilton's evocative and emotional writing make this different from the typical fast-paced chef memoir.

> **Subjects:** Chefs, Family Relationships, Marriage, New York City, Restaurants, Women's Nonfiction

> **Now Try:** *Spiced: A Pastry Chef's True Stories of Trials by Fire, After-Hour Exploits, and What Really Goes on in the Kitchen* by Dalia Jurgensen is another chef memoir from the woman's perspective. In *Cakewalk: A Memoir*, Kate Moses describes her family's complex, and often painful, history and her ability to find comfort in food and cooking. Readers may also enjoy the fiction novel *Girl Cook* by Hannah McCouch. Mary Karr's *Liars' Club: A Memoir* is another raw, frank account of growing up in a dysfunctional family. Another possible suggestion is Piper Kerman's *Orange is the New Black: My Year in a Woman's Prison*, about another rebellious woman who spent time in jail for her youthful transgressions but went on to turn her life around.

Henderson, Jeff

Cooked: From the Streets to the Stove, From Cocaine to Foie Gras. New York: William Morrow, 2007. 275pp. ISBN 9780061153907.

Jeff Henderson grew up in the inner city and began stealing at an early age. He soon turned to dealing drugs and became a very successful and wealthy criminal. It wasn't long before he was caught and sent to prison. While in prison, Henderson discovered an interest in cooking and soon channeled his passion into a new career. After his release Henderson went on to work for some well-known chefs and restaurants and is now the executive chef of Café Bellagio in Las Vegas. The first half of the book is focused on Henderson's early life of crime and violence, as well as life in prison. Henderson also recounts the difficulties he faced after his release finding a position and convincing employers to take a chance on him. His determination to overcome his obstacles and his rise to success creates a unique and inspiring story.

Subjects: Chefs, Crime, Inspirational Stories, Men's Lives, Prison

Now Try: Although Gabrielle Hamilton did not spend time in prison, for a time her life was headed in that direction. Hamilton's memoir *Blood, Bones, and Butter: The Inadvertent Education of a Reluctant Chef* details her journey to turn her life around and create a successful career. Anthony Bourdain describes his use of drugs while he was struggling as a chef in *Kitchen Confidential: Adventures in the Culinary Underbelly*. Readers may also enjoy Geoffrey Canada's inspirational *Fist Stick Knife Gun*. Canada, a Harlem school administrator, grew up on the streets, resorting to violence to get by, but now tries to provide a school environment where youngsters don't have to resort to violence and crime. Nathan McCall's gritty memoir, *Makes Me Wanna Holler: A Young Black Man in America* describes his violent youth and prison sentence, his rehabilitation, and his subsequent decision to do something more affirming with his life.

Jenkins, Steven

The Food Life: Inside the World of Food with the Grocer Extraordinaire at Fairway. New York: Harper Collins, 2008. 256pp. 9780061231681.

Fairway Market is a New York grocery chain that opened its first storefront shop on the Upper West Side of Manhattan in the 1970s. The store is known for offering a vast selection of fresh fruits and vegetables, as well as unique, high-end, specialty items at low prices. Jenkins, a cheesemonger and VP at Fairway, recounts his 30-some years in the business. He begins with a history of the company, from its early inception in the 1920s to its current upscale operation and the experience of shopping at Fairway. He recalls the various employees who have come and gone, those who have made a lasting impression on him and those whose names he can't remember. Covering each department, from the butcher to the fishmonger, Jenkins is most passionate about his specialty: cheese. Waxing poetic about cheese, he denounces factory-made, mass-produced cheeses and recalls the cheeses he has introduced over the years. Jenkins conversational tone, humor and passion for his profession and the foods he sells comes through in this quick read.

Subjects: Business, Cheese, Grocery Trade, Recipes, Quick Reads

Now Try: Jenkins's *Cheese Primer* won a James Beard Award. Gordon Edgar recounts his career as a cheesemonger in *Cheesemonger: A Life on the Wedge*. Kenny Shopsin, owner of Shopsin's in New York City, first a grocery store and later a restaurant, delivers a humorous and entertaining narrative cookbook, *Eat Me: The Food and Philosophy of Kenny Shopsin*. Readers may want to consider histories of some of America's biggest grocery store chains, such as

The Great A&P and the Struggle for Small Business in America by Marc Levinson and *The Trader Joe's Adventure: Turning a Unique Approach to Business into a Retail and Cultural Phenomenon* by Len Lewis.

Jurgensen, Dalia

Spiced: A Pastry Chef's True Stories of Trials By Fire, After-Hour Exploits, and What Really Goes on in the Kitchen. New York: J. P. Putnam's Sons, 2009. 274pp. ISBN 9780399155611.

The majority of chef memoirs are written by men, so this woman's perspective is a fresh take on a chef's life. Jurgensen is a pastry chef, who has worked in several upscale New York restaurants, as well as for Martha Stewart's TV show. Although she does have a few raunchy stories, unlike her male counterparts' tales, she focuses more on the food. She intricately describes the dishes she creates and their preparation and the technical aspects of the job. Like all chefs, she experiences the long hours, fast pace, and demand for perfection that come with the job, but the tone is a little calmer and less frantic than some of her colleagues' accounts.

Subjects: Baking, Chefs, Restaurants, Stewart, Martha, Women's Nonfiction

Now Try: *Blood, Bones, and Butter: The Inadvertent Education of a Reluctant Chef* by Gabrielle Hamilton is another memoir by a female chef. Melanie Rehak recalls her time working in a small restaurant kitchen in *Eating for Beginners: An Education in the Pleasures of Food from Chefs, Farmers, and One Picky Kid*. Like Jurgensen, she experiences long hours and fast pace, but the tone is calmer than other chef memoirs. Gesine Bullock-Prado describes her decision to leave her job in Hollywood to open her own bakery, a demanding yet rewarding career, in *My Life From Scratch: A Sweet Journey of Starting Over, One Cake at a Time*. Michael Krondl profiles sweet-makers from the past and present from around the world in *Sweet Invention*. Readers may enjoy other memoirs by women in typically male-dominated careers, such as *Tough As Nails: One Woman's Journey Through West Point* by Gail O'Sullivan Dwyer or *The Hungry Ocean: A Swordboat Captain's Journey* by Linda Greenlaw. *Girl Cook* by Hannah McCouch is a novel about a young woman trying to succeed in the male-dominated restaurant business of Manhattan.

Luongo, Pino, and Friedman, Andrew

Dirty Dishes: A Restaurateur's Story of Passion, Pain, and Pasta. New York: Bloomsbury, 2009. 255pp. ISBN 9781596914421.

Born in Italy, Luongo decides to come to America in order to avoid serving in the Italian army. After arriving, with no English, he finds a restaurant that serves authentic Italian food that he recognizes from home. Hungry for something familiar, Luongo asks for a job and is hired as a busboy. Luongo works his way up from busboy to manager, learning the ropes of running a restaurant. Soon he opens his own restaurant with friends, and slowly builds a following of regular customers. Soon he opens another restaurant, and he becomes a favorite among the wealthy and famous. In this memoir, he recounts his various restaurants, customers, and employees. Luongo is notorious for his temper, and we see his temper flare with his staff as well as with customers. Although Luongo is not a trained chef, he does a fair bit of cooking. We get a good sense of the hectic pace of running a successful and busy restaurant, the pressure to meet high expectations, the frustrations dealing with annoying customers.

Subjects: Business, New York City, Restaurants, Restaurateurs

Now Try: Readers may be interested in checking out one of Luongo's cookbooks, such as *Two Meatballs in the Kitchen*. Sirio Maccioni recounts his immigration to New York City, his various jobs in restaurants, and finally the opening of his famously successful restaurant, Le Cirque, in *Sirio: The Story of My Life and Le Cirque*. Joe Bastianich's *Restaurant Man* is another vivid account of his struggle to become a successful restaurateur. Howard Schultz describes how he built his small Seattle company into a worldwide phenomenon in *Pour Your Heart Into It: How Starbucks Built a Company One Cup At a Time*. Danny Meyer also recounts building his business up by stellar customer service in *Setting the Table: The Transforming Power of Hospitality in Business*. Readers may also enjoy Gordon Ramsay's *Roasting in Hell's Kitchen: Temper Tantrums, F Words, and the Pursuit of Perfection*, who is famous for his volatile temper.

Meyer, Danny

Setting the Table: The Transforming Power of Hospitality in Business. New York: Harper Collins, 2006. 320pp. ISBN 9780060742751.

Danny Meyer is a New York restaurateur and the co-owner of several restaurants. Meyer begins his book with a brief description of his childhood and family, his parents' divorce, and his early development of a love of food and cooking. While in college, Meyer spent time in Italy traveling, but mostly eating at restaurants. Meyer decided that he wanted to own his own restaurant and began working in restaurants; both cooking and managing. To gain more experience, he continued traveling through Italy and France, apprenticing in restaurants. Meyer bought his first restaurant, Union Square Café and shares the important lessons he learned about business and customer satisfaction. He explains his vision of hospitality, the difference between hospitality and service, and how he set himself apart.

Subjects: Business, Restaurants, Restaurateurs

Now Try: Readers may be interested in Meyer's cookbook, *The Union Square Café Cookbook*. Other successful restaurateur's may also be of interest. Try Paul Clarke's *Lessons in Excellence From Charlie Trotter*, Isadore Sharp's *Four Seasons: The Story of a Business Philosophy*, or Joe Bastianich's *Restaurant Man*. Readers may also be interested in titles about successful businesses in other industries, such as Tony Hsieh's profile of Zappo's, *Delivering Happiness: A Path to Profits*,

Passion, and Purpose, Nuts! Southwest Airlines' Crazy Recipe for Business and Personal Success by Kevin Freiberg or *The Nordstrom Way to Customer Service Excellence* by Robert Spector.

Park, Frances, and Park, Ginger

Chocolate Chocolate: The True Story of Two Sisters, Tons of Treats, and the Little Shop That Could. 274pp. ISBN 9780312652937.

After the untimely death of their father, Frances and Ginger Park decide to go into business together, opening an upscale chocolate shop not far from the White House in Washington, DC. Never having owned a business before, they face difficulties such as an absent and negligent contractor and the early days when they ate more product than they sold. But they also delight in the joys of owning their own business, from visiting trade shows and selecting from some of the finest chocolate producers throughout the world to building a following of loyal customers. The Park sisters share the ups and downs of life, love, marriage, children, and success and infuse their writing with luscious descriptions of candy.

Subjects: Business, Chocolate, Family Relationships, Loss of a Parent, Siblings

Now Try: Gesine Bullock-Prado recounts the ups and downs of owning her own bakery in *My Life From Scratch*. Fiction readers will certainly enjoy Joanne Harris's novel *Chocolat*, about a woman who opens a decadent chocolate shop in a small French village during Lent. Fiction readers may also enjoy *Henry's Sisters* by Cathy Lamb, in which two adult sisters must return home to care for their ailing mother and run the family bakery. *DC Cupcakes* is a reality television series on TLC that features two sisters, Katherine Kallinis and Sophie Kallinis LaMontange, who own and operate their own cupcake shop in Georgetown. Their cookbook/memoir is *The Cupcake Diaries*. Buddy Valastro, another TLC star, shares stories of life in his family's bakery in *Cake Boss: Stories and Recipes from Mia Famiglia*.

Pépin, Jacques

The Apprentice: My Life in the Kitchen. Boston: Houghton Mifflin, 2003. 318pp. ISBN 9780618197378.

Pépin, one of America's most famous chefs recounts his childhood in France during World War II. After the war, Pépin's mother opened a café, and Pépin got his first taste at working in a restaurant. At age 13, he was sent to apprentice in a hotel kitchen, and thus began his long and successful career as a chef. Pépin recalls cooking for various government officials, including Charles de Gaulle, his immigration to America and employment with the Howard Johnson hotel chain, his friendships with famous food critics and chefs, such as Craig Claiborne and Julia Child, as well as his success teaching, appearing on television, and writing cookbooks.

Subjects: Chefs, Child, Julia, Claiborne, Craig, France, Pépin, Jacques, Recipes, Restaurants

Now Try: Pépin has published several cookbooks. Readers may want to start with *Essential Pépin: More Than 700 All-Time Favorites From My Life in Food*. Pépin also had a cooking show with Julia Child, *Julia and Jacques Cooking at Home*, as well as a collaborative cookbook by the same title. Readers may also want to consider Julia Child's memoir, *My Life in France*. Pierre Franey's memoir *A Chef's Tale: A Memoir of Food, France, and America* is a similar story of his childhood in France, his journey to America to cook at the 1939 World's Fair, and finally his position as a top New York chef. Marcus Samuelsson chronicles his difficult childhood, early interest in food, immigration, and his struggle to achieve success in *Yes, Chef*. Steve Lerach recounts his 30 years in the food industry, from dishwasher to chef in *Fried: Surviving Two Centuries in Restaurants*. Wolfgang Puck also immigrated to the United States and became hugely successful. One of his cookbooks may be of interest, such as *Wolfgang Puck Adventures in the Kitchen*.

Ramsay, Gordon

Roasting in Hell's Kitchen: Temper Tantrums, F Words, and the Pursuit of Perfection. New York: HarperCollins Entertainment, 2006. 287pp. ISBN 9780061191756.

Gordon Ramsay's fiery temper and popular television series have made him a household name. Whether you like him or not, Ramsay is an interesting figure and a very successful chef. In this frank memoir, Ramsay recounts his difficult childhood, living in poverty with an abusive, alcoholic father. Ramsay intended to become a soccer player, but an injury led him to a career in cooking. He openly discusses his career, relationships with other chefs, and his reputation. Readers who enjoy his television series or just want a look at the real Gordon Ramsay will enjoy this entertaining memoir.

Subjects: Chefs, Family Relationships, Marriage, Men's Lives, Profanity, Ramsay, Gordon, Restaurants, Restaurateurs

Now Try: Readers interested in more about Ramsay may want to try Neil Simpson's biography, *Gordon Ramsay: On Top of the World*. Ramsay has published a number of cookbooks that may be of interest to readers. Try *A Chef For All Seasons* or *Gordon Ramsay's Fast Food*. Early in his career, Ramsay worked for the famous chef Marco Pierre White. It is no secret that their relationship went sour, and both have their own story to tell. Try White's memoir *The Devil in the Kitchen: Sex, Pain, Madness, and the Making of a Great Chef* for his side of the story. Ramsay is the star of several television series that may also be interesting to readers. *Hell's Kitchen, Kitchen Nightmares, MasterChef*, and *The F Word* are all available on DVD. Other memoirs by men who had difficult relationships with their fathers are Andre Dubus's *Townie*, Rick Bragg's *The Prince of Frogtown*, and Joe Queenan's *Closing Time*.

Reichl, Ruth

Garlic and Sapphires: The Secret Life of a Critic in Disguise. New York: Penguin Press, 2005. 333pp. ISBN 9781594200311.

This well-known food writer, editor, and critic recounts the period she spent working as the restaurant critic for the *New York Times*. Reichl candidly talks about her ambivalence in accepting the position, as well as her sleepless nights worrying over her reviews. In an effort to remain anonymous when dining out, Reichl frequently donned elaborate disguises that involved wigs and costumes. Her adventures creating and trying out new personalities add a humorous element to her story and her detailed descriptions of the meals she ate are very gratifying. Reichl also exposes a disappointing aspect of restaurant culture when she reports the differences in the treatment she received when she was recognized.

> **Subjects:** Humor, New York City, *New York Times*, Recipes, Reichl, Ruth, Restaurant Critics, Restaurants

> **Now Try:** Readers who enjoy Reichl's humor may also enjoy her other memoirs, *Tender at the Bone: Growing Up at the Table* and *Comfort Me with Apples: More Adventures at the Table*. Memoirs from other food critics may also be appealing. Mimi Sheraton, also a critic for the *New York Times*, presents another humorous account of the life of a restaurant critic in *Eating My Words: An Appetite for Life*. *Born Round: The Secret History of a Full-Time Eater* is written by still another *New York Times* critic, Frank Bruni. Gael Greene recalls her years as a food critic for *New York* magazine in *Insatiable: Tales From a Life of Delicious Excess*. Readers who enjoy Reichl's humor may also enjoy Nora Ephron's humorous works, such as *I Feel Bad About My Neck*, or her novel *Heartburn*.

Scheib, Walter, and Friedman, Andrew

White House Chef: Eleven Years, Two Presidents, One Kitchen. Hoboken: J. Wiley, 2007. 327pp. ISBN 9780471798422.

Hired by Hilary Rodham Clinton when President Clinton was elected to office, Scheib transformed the traditional French-styled menu of the White House to more health-conscious meals featuring a more American-style menu. Staying through Clinton's presidency and the first term of George W. Bush's presidency, Scheib experienced many White House functions, interacted with the presidents and first ladies, and experienced September 11th from the White House. Scheib's unique perspective provides an inside look at the White House, the first families, and the differences between the two presidents he served. Interspersed among the stories are recipes and menus Scheib created.

> **Subjects:** Chefs, Presidents, Quick Reads, Recipes, September 11, White House

> **Now Try**: Readers who enjoy personal stories of the presidents and first families will also enjoy Roland Mesnier's memoir of his 25 years as the White House pastry chef in *All the Presidents' Pastries: Twenty-Five Years in the White House. The President's Table:*

Two Hundred Years of Dining and Diplomacy by Barry H. Landau is a fascinating, visually appealing history of food and entertaining in the White House. For fun, readers may also enjoy Julie Hyzy's mystery novel, *State of the Onion*, which features White House assistant chef Olivia Paras who is competing for the head chef position. *For the Royal Table: Dining at the Palace* by Kathryn Jones is a visually appealing look at dining with royalty. Other memoirs written by people close to the presidents may also be of interest, such as *The White House Doctor: My Patients Were Presidents* by Connie Mariano, *My First Ladies: Twenty-Five Years As the White House Chief Floral Designer* by Nancy Clarke, or *Standing Next to History: An Agent's Life Inside the Secret Service* by Joseph Petro.

Sheehan, Jason

Cooking Dirty: A Story of Life, Sex, Love and Death in the Kitchen. New York: Farrar, Straus and Giroux, 2009. 355pp. ISBN 9780374289218.

Sheehan's memoir has a lot in common with Anthony Bourdain's classic *Kitchen Confidential*. Since he was a teenager, Sheehan has worked in numerous kitchens around the country. From pizza joints to all-night diners to classier restaurants, Sheehan has seen it all. Like Bourdain, his lifestyle consists of up-all-night, sleep-all-day, 100-hour work weeks. He numbs the pain from his burns and wounds with alcohol and fuels his body with nicotine and drugs. From the moment his shift starts until the moment it ends, the pace is unrelenting and the heat (literally and figuratively) is on. This is an eye-opening, entertaining, fast-paced look at the life of a professional cook.

Subjects: Chefs, Drug Abuse, Men's Lives, Restaurants

Now Try: Fans of Sheehan's gritty, fast-paced story may want to check out Anthony Bourdain's *Kitchen Confidential: Adventures in the Culinary Underbelly* or Bill Buford's *Heat: An Amateur's Adventures as Kitchen Slave, Line Cook, Pasta-Maker, and Apprentice to a Dante-Quoting Butcher in Tuscany*. Anthony Bourdain's fiction novels are also very evocative stories about working in the kitchen. Start with *Bone in the Throat*. *Beaten, Seared, and Sauced: On Becoming a Chef at the Culinary Institute of America* by Jonathan Dixon is an entertaining account of the reality of culinary school. Readers may also enjoy Steve Dublanica's entertaining look at life in the front of the house in *Waiter Rant: Thanks for the Tip—Confessions of a Cynical Waiter*. Other work memoirs by men driven to succeed might appeal, such as Paul Austin's *Something for the Pain: One Doctor's Account of Life and Death in the ER*, Jordan Belfort's *The Wolf of Wall Street*, or Tom Breitling's and Cal Fussman's *Double or Nothing: How Two Friends Risked It All to Buy One of Las Vegas' Legendary Casinos*.

Sheraton, Mimi

Eating My Words: An Appetite for Life. New York: William Morrow, 2004. 240pp. ISBN 9780060501099.

Mimi Sheraton was the *New York Times* restaurant critic from 1975 to 1983. In addition, she has written a number of books and is a popular food writer and journalist. Sheraton candidly recounts her adventures as a critic and food writer, including meals she has eaten and places she has traveled. Comments on job-related weight gain, learning to use a computer, and her attempts to remain anonymous add humor to this entertaining memoir.

> **Subjects:** Food Writers, Humor, New York City, *New York Times*, Restaurant Critics, Restaurants, Travel

> **Now Try:** Readers will also enjoy Ruth Reichl's humorous tales of the life of a restaurant critic in *Garlic and Sapphires: The Secret Life of a Critic in Disguise*. *Fork It Over: The Intrepid Adventures of a Professional Eater* by Alan Richman and Jeffrey Steingarten's *It Must Have Been Something I Ate* are humorous accounts from other well-known food critics. Frank Bruni's *Born Round: The Secret History of a Full-Time Eater* is another memoir by a former *New York Times* critic. Jeannette Ferrary was another food writer for the *New York Times* who reminisces about her life with food in *Out of the Kitchen*. Readers may also enjoy Steven A. Shaw's inside look at restaurants, *Turning the Tables: The Insider's Guide to Eating Out*. Sheraton also wrote an interesting history of bialys, *The Bialy Eaters*.

Tramonto, Rick

Scars of a Chef: The Searing Story of a Top Chef Marked Forever by the Grit and Grace of Life in the Kitchen. Carol Stream: Tyndale House Publishers, 2011. 269pp. ISBN 9781414331621.

Although Rick Tramonto eventually became a successful chef and restaurant owner, it wasn't an easy journey for him. Enduring a difficult and sometimes violent childhood, Rick turned to drugs at an early age. After his father was imprisoned, Rick left high school to work in a Wendy's restaurant; then he paid his dues, working his way up in kitchens. His drive and dedication earned him a measure of success and he eventually created the Chicago restaurant Tru, which earned four stars. Despite his success, his personal life was suffering and his marriage fell apart. It wasn't until Tramonto heard a Christian radio program that he accepted God into his life and found peace. Like many other chefs' memoirs, the pace is quick and focused, just like Tramonto's career. However, Tramonto's focus on the spiritual aspect of his life is unique and will appeal to readers who enjoy spiritual discovery.

> **Subjects:** Chefs, Family Relationships, Marriage, Religion, Restaurants

> **Now Try:** Tramanto has a few cookbooks that may interest readers. Try *Steak With Friends* or *Tru: A Cookbook from the Legendary Chicago Restaurant*. Tyndale House Publishers has a number of inspirational memoirs by men who struggled with faith. *Quiet Strength: The Principles, Practices, and Priorities of a Winning Life* by Tony Dungy recounts his success as the first African American coach to win a Super Bowl without compromising faith and family. *Coming Back Stronger: Unleashing the Hidden Powers of Adversity* by Drew Brees tells how his faith helped him to overcome an injury that could have ended his career. Christopher Parkening recalls how despite his success as

a classical guitar virtuoso, he was unfulfilled until he accepted God into his life in *Grace Like a River*.

Wenzel, Ty

Behind Bars: The Straight-Up Tales of a Big-City Bartender. New York: St. Martin's Press, 2003. 262pp. ISBN 9780312311025.

Wenzel began her career in fashion, working for *Cosmo* magazine. Sick of the fashion scene, she quit her job to find her true calling. In need of income, she took a job bartending and stayed for 10 years. In this entertaining, eye-popping account, Wenzel gives the low down on the bar scene. She expels the myth that bartenders have a glamorous life and recounts what a typical night is really like. She regales the reader with stories of good and bad tippers, regular customers, stalkers and creeps, and sex.

Subjects: Bars, Bartenders, Career Change, New York City

Now Try: Toby Cecchini's *Cosmopolitan: A Bartender's Life* is another engaging account of life behind the bar. Debra Ginsberg also recounts stories of bad tippers and demanding customers in *Waiting: The True Confessions of a Waitress*. J. R. Moehringer's memoir, *The Tender Bar*, is a touching coming-of-age story about the life lessons learned and the friendships made with the regulars at a neighborhood bar. Readers may also enjoy Heather and Rose MacDonald's chick-lit novel *Turning Tables*, about a waitress at a chic Upper East Side restaurant.

White, Marco Pierre

The Devil in the Kitchen: Sex, Pain, Madness and the Making of a Great Chef. New York: Bloomsbury, 2007. 244pp. ISBN 9781596913615.

Before there was Anthony Bourdain or Gordon Ramsay, there was Marco Pierre White, the original bad boy chef. White was the first British chef, as well as the youngest chef, to be awarded three Michelin stars. And he didn't get those stars by being a nice guy. White recounts his rise to fame and success in this entertaining memoir. Known for his temper and demand for perfection, White is famous for giving his chefs a bollocking and tossing out customers who complain. Even with his adrenaline and nicotine-fueled lifestyle, White does not succumb to drugs and alcohol, as so many other famous chefs have admitted to. Despite his bad boy image, White comes across as a nice guy, apologizing for profanity and not speaking crudely of his trysts with women, making this a little less debauched than Bourdain's memoir.

Subject: Chefs, Men's Lives, Michelin, Restaurants

Now Try: Readers who enjoy White's bad boy image and rock-star lifestyle, will also enjoy other classic chef's memoirs such as Anthony Bourdain's *Kitchen Confidential: Adventures in the Culinary Underbelly*, Bill Buford's *Heat:*

An Amateur's Adventures as Kitchen Slave, Line Cook, Pasta-Maker, and Apprentice to a Dante-Quoting Butcher in Tuscany, and Jason Sheehan's *Cooking Dirty: A Story of Life, Sex, Love and Death in the Kitchen*. Gordon Ramsay, another chef known for his fiery temper, came up under White. Check out Ramsay's memoir, *Roasting in Hell's Kitchen*. White's cookbook, *White Heat*, includes a number of photographs of White's kitchen.

Personal Endeavor Memoirs

Today it seems that anyone who undertakes a new endeavor, project, or hobby in their life will inevitably write about it. It is increasingly easy to publish journals on the Internet, so many blog about their experiences, capturing the ups and downs of their personal and professional pursuits; many of the books in this subgenre started as blogs. This growing subgenre of memoirs has been labeled many things. Ben Yagoda, author of *Memoir: A History*, uses the term "schtick lit," meaning that the writer undertook an unusual project with the express purpose of writing about it (Yagoda 2009). In an article in *Newsweek*, Jennie Yabroff refers to these as "Year of" books, meaning the author undertakes a project for one year, whether it be living biblically, as in A. J. Jacobs's *The Year of Living Biblically* or Judith Levine's year she gave up shopping in *Not Buying It*. Yabroff traces this subgenre to Peter Mayle's 1990 book *A Year in Provence*, but Julie Powell's 2005 memoir, *Julie and Julia*, is probably the best known example and increased the interest in this subgenre. Here these titles are referred to as Personal Endeavors. Many Personal Endeavors are related to food in some way, whether it's someone's attempt to raise their own food or learn to cook. The authors typically undertake these projects or endeavors for personal reasons or to change their lives; they want to improve their cooking, learn more about where their food comes from, or grow their own food. Their intent for undertaking a Personal Endeavor usually isn't for the sole purpose of writing about it, but for their own benefit.

The Personal Endeavor Food Memoir allows the reader to experience a project he or she might not normally undertake on their own. A reader may not be interested in starting his or her own urban farm or attending culinary school, but these memoirs give him or her the chance to vicariously experience those pursuits. In some cases, the reader may be considering planning his or her own endeavor. These memoirs can provide not only inspiration, but also an idea of what to expect. Aside from facing a new challenge, many of these authors dealt with personal issues, whether it was a troubled marriage, an unhappy career, or a mid-life crisis. Through the endeavor, they often experienced growth and learned about themselves in the process. Personal Endeavors can be very illuminating, introducing readers to new information or lifestyles. Many have a lighter tone and an element of humor, as authors struggle with runaway farm animals or cooking mishaps.

Readers who enjoy Personal Endeavor food memoirs may also enjoy some of the food blogs listed in the Appendixes, as several of these titles began life as blogs. Titles from Immersion Journalism in the Investigative Food Writing chapter may also be appealing for their examinations of specific topics.

1

Alexander, William

2

52 Loaves: One Man's Relentless Pursuit of Truth, Meaning, and a Perfect Crust. Chapel Hill, NC: Algonquin, 2010. 339pp. ISBN 9781565125834.

When Alexander decided to learn to make the perfect loaf of bread, his obsession with perfection took his project to extreme levels. Alexander made one loaf of bread every week for one year, while experimenting with the various ingredients and cooking techniques until he reached perfection. Not only did he experiment with different types of flours and baking methods, he tested the pH in his water, built his own earth oven, grew his own grain, visited yeast factories and collected wild yeast, and traveled to France and Morocco to experiment with his technique. His adventures triggered some humorous events, such as breaking his oven (twice) trying to achieve the perfect temperature, and the difficulties getting his sourdough starter through airport security. Readers will enjoy the humorous aspects of his project, but also the detailed investigation of what goes into the perfect loaf of bread.

3

4

5

Subjects: Baking, Bread, Humor, Men's Lives, Recipes, Science

Now Try: Alexander's first book *The $64 Tomato: How One Man Nearly Lost His Sanity, Spent a Fortune, and Endured an Existential Crisis in the Quest for the Perfect Garden* is another humorous tale of his attempt to grow his own garden, complete with his obsession for perfection. Sara Mansfield Taber travels to France to investigate the state of contemporary French bread and the producers of its ingredients in *Bread of Three Rivers: The Story of a French Loaf.* Susan Seligson journeys around the world exploring cultural differences and methods of bread making in *Going With the Grain: A Wandering Bread Lover Takes a Bite Out of Life. The Bread Maker's Apprentice: Mastering the Art of Extraordinary Bread* by Peter Reinhart is a James Beard and IACP award-winning cookbook. Readers may also enjoy Barbara Kingsolver's memoir of her year producing her own food, *Animal, Vegetable, Miracle: A Year of Food Life.* Fiction readers may enjoy *Bread Alone* by Judith Ryan Hendricks, about a woman who takes a job as a bread maker when her husband leaves her. The Wild Yeast blog (www.wildyeastblog.com), in which the author blogs about her bread baking hobby may also be of interest.

6

7

8

Bullock-Prado, Gesine

9

My Life From Scratch: A Sweet Journey of Starting Over, One Cake At a Time. New York: Broadway Books, 2009. 226pp. ISBN 9780767932738.

Sister to the famous actress Sandra Bullock, Gesine was living in Los Angeles and working as the head of her sister's film production company. Miserable in her career, Gesine turned to baking for comfort. When friends began requesting her baked goods, Gesine decided she would make a career change. She and her husband moved to Vermont and opened a bakery. Smart-mouthed and blunt but also humorous, Gesine recounts life in rural Vermont, the unexpected difficulties and joys of running her own bakery, the fulfillment she found, and her grief over the death of her mother. Readers will enjoy this humorous and charming story, as well as the Hollywood gossip.

> **Subjects:** Bakers, Career Change, Family Relationships, Grief, Life Change, Loss of a Parent, Marriage, Recipes, Women's Nonfiction

> **Now Try:** In *Julie and Julia: 365 Days, 524 Recipes, 1 Tiny Apartment Kitchen*, Julie Powell also faces an unhappy career, which she channels into a new project that results in unexpected joy. *Chocolate Chocolate: The True Story of Two Sisters, Tons of Treats, and the Little Shop That Could* by Frances Park describes the author's and her sister's decision to open their own confectionary and the ups and downs of the business. Fran Gage, the former owner of a San Francisco patisserie, shares her love of food and baking in *Bread and Chocolate*. Readers who found their mouths watering at the descriptions of Gesine's confections may also enjoy Pascale LeDraoulec's descriptions of the pies she tastes in *American Pie: Slices of Life (and Pie) from America's Back Roads*. Fiction readers may also enjoy Joanne Harris's novel *Chocolat*, about a woman who opens a chocolate shop in a small French village. Gesine's memoir contains recipes of some of the confections described in the book, but readers longing for even more sugary confections will want to check out her cookbook *Sugar Baby: Confections, Candies, Cakes & Other Delicious Recipes for Cooking with Sugar*.

Carpenter, Novella

Farm City: The Education of an Urban Farmer. New York: Penguin Press, 2009. 276pp. ISBN 9781594202216.

Urban farming is the latest craze among foodies. Carpenter, a resident of Oakland, California, decides to become an urban farmer, squat gardening in an abandoned lot and keeping chickens, ducks, turkeys, rabbits, bees, and even pigs in her back yard. This is an entertaining and humorous tale of her attempts to create a farm amidst concrete and violence. Her farm not only served to provide her with food, but also created unlikely friendships with neighbors and a sense of community. Neighbors stopped by to help with weeding and enjoy fresh produce. Young children got a chance to see pigs and rabbits for the first time. While dumpster diving for pig food, Carpenter also met the chef of a local restaurant, who then taught her how to make salami and prosciutto from her pigs. Carpenter's entertaining endeavor is filled with interesting characters and wonderful descriptions of food and the challenges of farming.

> **Subjects:** Animal Husbandry, Beekeeping, Community Life, Gardening, Urban Farming

> **Now Try:** Manny Howard recounts his attempts at creating an urban farm in *My Empire of Dirt: How One Many Turned His Big City Backyard into a Farm*. Although he

is not as successful as Carpenter, his experiences seem to be a more realistic example of what most people would face. Janice Cole recounts her experiences keeping chickens in the city in *Chicken and Egg: A Memoir of Suburban Homesteading with 125 Recipes*. Writer Alice Walker shares her experiences raising a flock of chickens in *The Chicken Chronicles*. In *On Good Land*, Michael Ableman describes his struggle to preserve his farm as it slowly becomes surrounded by suburban sprawl. Although an older title, Judith Moffett's *Homestead Year: Back To the Land in Suburbia* chronicles her attempt to become self-sufficient on her one-acre suburban yard. *The Quarter-Acre Farm: How I Kept the Patio, Lost the Lawn, and Kept My Family Fed for A Year* by Spring Warren is another entertaining memoir of urban farming. Robin Mather describes her attempt to live on a budget by eating locally in *The Feast Nearby: How I Lost My Job, Buried a Marriage, and Found My Way By Keeping Chickens, Foraging, Preserving, Bartering, and Eating Locally (all on $40 a week)*. Readers who have been inspired by Novella's story may be interested in her how-to guide, *The Essential Urban Farmer*, which she cowrote with Willow Rosenthal. A broader guide on making one's own food (and everything else) is Mark Boyle's *The Moneyless Man: A Year of Freeconomic Living*.

Erway, Cathy

The Art of Eating In: How I Learned to Stop Spending and Love the Stove. New York: Gotham, 2010. 320pp. ISBN 9781592405251.

In New York City it is not uncommon to find apartments that are not equipped with kitchens. This is because most New Yorkers eat out for their meals. But New York is an expensive city, and eating out adds up. When Erway added up the money she spent on eating out every day, she realized she could save a lot of money just by cooking for herself. Thus, she swore off restaurant eating for two years and began a blog to chronicle her project. She experimented with new recipes and cooked meals for her friends and family. Aside from just relating her personal experiences, she looks at the effects of food on health and the increase in food waste. She is also introduced to new lifestyles, such as urban foraging, underground supper clubs, and freeganism.

Subjects: Blogs, Finance, Foraging, New York City, Recipes, Restaurants, Supper Clubs

Now Try: Interested in learning more about some of the new lifestyles Erway investigates? Jenn Garbee investigates underground supper clubs in *Secret Suppers: Rogue Chefs and Underground Restaurants in Warehouses, Townhouses, Open Fields, and Everywhere in Between*. Tristram Stuart investigates urban foraging, freeganism and dumpster diving in *Waste: Uncovering the Global Food Scandal*. *Not Buying It: My Year Without Shopping* by Judith Levine or *A Year Without "Made in China": One Family's True Life Adventure in the Global Economy* by Sara Bongiorni are both personal endeavors of the authors' attempts to reduce consumption and spend less money. Erway still maintains her blog at www.noteatingoutinny.com.

Kilmer-Purcell, Josh

The Bucolic Plague: How Two Manhattanites Became Gentlemen Farmers. New York: HarperCollins, 2010. 304pp. ISBN 9780061336980.

New Yorkers Josh, an advertising exec, and his partner Brent, a doctor turned consultant for Martha Stewart, were driving through the countryside when they found a small town. As they passed through the town they noticed a fantastic historic mansion and decided to stop and check it out. When they noticed a for-sale sign out front, they knew it must be fate. They fell in love with the house and soon became owners of the 200-year-old Beekman mansion and its surrounding 60 acres. Josh's dream of becoming a gentleman farmer is finally realized. Their weekends are spent gardening, canning, picking cherries, collecting eggs, and raising goats and turkeys. When the economy crashes, both lose their jobs, threatening the loss of their farm. After Martha Stewart hosts a segment on the Beekman's homemade goat milk soap, orders begin flying in (although the aftermath turns their idyllic life into chaos and threatens their relationship).

> **Subjects:** Blogs, Farming, GLBTQ, Goats, Job Loss, Life Change, Relationships, Stewart, Martha
>
> **Now Try:** Readers may want to watch the television series *The Fabulous Beekman Boys*, which aired on Planet Green. Brent and Josh have published *The Beekman 1802 Heirloom Cookbook* and also blog on their website, beekman1802.com. Josh's memoir, *I Am Not Myself These Days*, is about his unconventional life before becoming a gentleman farmer. Another memoir by a gay man whose relationship was tested by country living is Wade Rouse's *At Least in the City Someone Would Hear Me Scream*. Catherine Friend's *Hit By a Farm: How I Stopped Worrying and Learned to Love the Barn* is another memoir of a couple who left the city life to fulfill the dream of living on a farm. Jenna Woginrich longs for a farm of her own in *Barnheart: The Incurable Longing for a Farm of One's Own*.

Kimball, Christopher

Fannie's Last Supper: Re-Creating One Amazing Meal From Fannie Farmer's 1896 Cookbook. New York: Hyperion, 2010. 260pp. ISBN 9781401323226.

Fannie Farmer published *the Boston Cooking School Cook-Book* in 1896, which became a widely known and used cookbook. When Christopher Kimball, founder of *Cook's Illustrated* magazine, bought a historic home in Boston and began renovating the home back to its original style, he became interested in learning more about Boston in the Victorian period. Kimball describes what Boston was like in the 1890s, Victorian customs, dress, and food, as well as how food was prepared. Kimball decides to recreate a 12-coarse meal from Farmer's cookbook as authentically as possible. Readers of *Cook's Illustrated* will recognize the minute attention to detail and drive to get recipes correct, as Kimball makes various attempts at dishes such as calf's head, as well as his difficulties with traditional cooking techniques and appliances such as the coal stove.

Subjects: American History, Boston, Farmer, Fannie, Recipes, Victorian Life

Now Try: Readers may enjoy checking out the *1896 Boston Cooking School Cookbook* by Fannie Farmer. Christopher Kimball has a number of cookbooks that may also be of interest such as *The Kitchen Detective* or *The Yellow Farmhouse Cookbook*. Becky Diamond's *Mrs. Goodfellow* details the life of another important figure in American cooking, Elizabeth Goodfellow, who opened the first American cooking school in the early 1800s. Readers may also enjoy Michael Ruhlman's account of his experience renovating his Victorian home and the history of his neighborhood, *House*. Readers interested in the history of Boston during this time period may want to consider Stephen Puleo's *A City So Grand*, which details Boston's history during the second half of the 19th century. Puleo's other history of Boston, *Dark Tide*, covers the collapse of a molasses tank that killed 21 people and chronicles the importance of molasses in the U.S. war efforts. Steven Rinella's *The Scavenger's Guide to Haute Cuisine* is another entertaining account of the author's attempt to cook from an historic cookbook.

Kimball, Kristin

The Dirty Life: On Farming, Food, and Love. New York: Scribner, 2010. 276pp. ISBN 9781416551607.

Kristin Kimball was a city girl. A journalist living in New York City, she was used to the creature comforts of the city. But when she met Mark, a young farmer running a community supported farm in Pennsylvania who dreamt of a simpler life, the two fall in love. Mark hoped to own his own community-supported agriculture (CSA) farm, providing his local community with all the meat and produce needed. Kimball leaves her city life behind, moving with Mark to a 500-acre run-down farm in upstate New York, and the two begin the slow process of bringing the farm back to life. Kristin's new life with a man so different from herself is a big adjustment. Mark's dream of living off the grid as much as possible leaves Kristin learning to drive draft horses and tap maple trees for syrup. The humorous moments are interspersed with mouth-watering descriptions of the fresh foods that go straight from the ground to their plates, leaving the reader longing for the simple life.

Subjects: Farm Life, Farming, Life Change, Recipes, Relationships

Now Try: This is quickly becoming a very popular topic within food and personal endeavors and there is no shortage of similar titles. Ree Drummond also left the city life when she fell in love with a cowboy. Her memoir is *The Pioneer Woman: Black Heels to Tractor Wheels—a Love Story*. Alyssa Shelasky left her life in New York City to move to Washington, DC to be with her chef boyfriend in *Apron Anxiety: My Messy Affairs In and Out of the Kitchen*. Kurt Timmermeister's *Growing a Farmer: How I Learned to Live Off the Land*, Josh Kilmer-Purcell's *Bucolic Plague: How Two Manhattanites Became Gentlemen Farmers: An Unconventional Memoir*, Jim Minick's *The Blueberry Years: A Memoir* *of Farm and Family*, and Susan McCorkindale's *Confessions of a Counterfeit Farm Girl* are all wonderful stories of people who left their city lives behind for the farm. Although Wade Rouse does not leave his city life behind to start his own farm, his memoirs of relocating to the country, *At Least in the City Someone Would Hear Me Scream: Misadventures in Search of the Simple Life*, are quite humorous.

Kingsolver, Barbara

Animal, Vegetable, Miracle: A Year of Food Life. New York: HarperCollins, 2007. 370pp. ISBN 9780060852559.

Barbara Kingsolver is well known for her fiction writing, but here she recounts her family's experience eating locally. Concerned with the consumption of the fossil fuels required to transport out-of-season fruits and vegetables, Kingsolver and her family left their home in Phoenix and moved to a farm in Appalachia. Here, they decided that for one year, they would eat only items that they could grow themselves or that they could buy from local farmers. Kingsolver's passion for her farm and their lifestyle is inspiring. Her tales of her family's experiences planting, weeding, picking, pulling, canning, cooking, and eating bring the quiet little farm to life in the reader's mind. She provides interesting information about the food industry and examples of easy changes everyone can make to eat food that is healthier for ourselves and the planet. She also includes recipes and an illuminating chapter on turkey mating.

> **Subjects**: Animal Husbandry, Family Relationships, Farming, Gardening, Local Food, Recipes, Women's Nonfiction
>
> **Awards:** ALA Notable Book, James Beard Award
>
> **Now Try**: Alisa Smith and her husband J. B. Mackinnon chronicled their attempt to eat locally in *Plenty: Eating Locally on the 100-Mile Diet*. William Alexander's *The $64 Tomato: How One Man Nearly Lost His Sanity, Spent a Fortune, and Endured an Existential Crisis in the Quest for the Perfect Garden* is a humorous tale of the author's attempt at growing his own produce. In *Farewell, My Subaru: An Epic Adventure in Local Living*, Doug Fine shares his quest to turn his ranch into a green and sustainable environment. Readers may also be interested in some of Kingsolver's novels, such as *The Poisonwood Bible, Prodigal Summer*, or *The Bean Trees*.

Mather, Robin

The Feast Nearby: How I Lost My Job, Buried a Marriage, and Found My Way by Keeping Chickens, Foraging, Preserving, Bartering, and Eating Locally (All on Forty Dollars a Week). Berkeley, CA: Ten Speed Press, 2011. 266pp. ISBN 9781580085588.

Within a week, Robin Mather lost her job as a food writer for the *Chicago Tribune* and her husband announced he wanted a divorce. Unsure of her next move, Mather retreated to her lakeside cottage in Michigan. Due to her reduced income, she was now on a strict budget. Having eaten at some of the best restaurants, she was determined not to let her limited budget keep her from eating well. Mather decided that she would buy only foods from local growers and farmers and would stick to a budget of $40 a week. Mather's quick chapters follow the seasons and she describes the delights of eating seasonally, canning and preserving food, and raising chickens. Her choices also lead her to explore some of the issues surrounding local food, such as local versus organic, and raw milk versus pasteurized. Despite the fact that Mather's story begins with a job loss and a divorce, her story remains cheerful. Readers will enjoy the lighthearted tone, straightforward style, and luscious recipes.

Subjects: Divorce, Gentle Reads, Job Loss, Life Change, Local Food, Quick Reads, Recipes, Seasons, Women's Nonfiction

Now Try: Suzan Colon shares her experiences trying to economize on cooking after she loses her job in *Cherries in Winter*. Cathy Erway also attempted to economize her food budget by avoiding restaurants in *The Art of Eating In: How I Learned to Stop Spending and Love the Stove*. After losing her job, Dominique Browning describes how she reinvented herself and learned to find joy in other pleasures in *Slow Love: How I Lost My Job, Put on My Pajamas and Found Happiness*. Elizabeth Gilbert's *Eat Pray Love* is another memoir of a woman seeking to find herself after a divorce. Readers may also enjoy Elizabeth Berg's novel *Open House*, in which the main character transformed her home into a boarding house when her husband left her. Wade Rouse's memoir, *At Least Someone in the City Would Hear Me Scream*, is a humorous account of his move from the city to a cottage in Michigan and the adjustments he made. Louise Dickinson Rich's *We Took To the Woods* is a classic story of her and her husband's decision to live in the woods of Maine.

Mathews, Ellie

The Ungarnished Truth: A Memoir of the Pillsbury Bakeoff. New York: Berkley Books, 2007. 276pp. ISBN 9780425219454.

The world of cooking competitions is fiercely competitive and the Pillsbury Bake-off is the most coveted award. Ellie Mathews had been entering cooking competitions for several years, but in 1998, her recipe for Salsa Couscous Chicken won her the coveted Pillsbury award and $1 million. Mathews provides an inside look at the world of competitive cooking, the history of the Pillsbury Bake-Off, and her brief rise to fame after winning.

Subjects: Cooking Competitions, Investigative Stories, Recipes

Now Try: A longtime contestant and three-time finalist of the Pillsbury Bake-Off, Steve Greiger recounts his experiences on the circuit in *Baked Off!* In *Cookoff*, Amy Sutherland recounts her experiences on the competitive cooking circuit, including Pillsbury. *Knives at Dawn* by Andrew Friedman is a fascinating account of the ultimate cooking competition. In fiction, it seems that cooking competitions are ripe for intrigue and murder. *Murder of a Chocolate Covered Cherry* by Denise Swanson *or Bone Appetite* by Carolyn Haines are entertaining, light mysteries of cooking competitions gone awry. Fiction fans may also enjoy *Simply From Scratch* by Alicia Bessette, in which a widow and her nine-year-old neighbor enter a cooking competition together.

Miller, Leslie

Let Me Eat Cake: A Celebration of Flour, Sugar, Butter, Eggs, Vanilla, Baking Powder and a Pinch of Salt. New York: Simon & Schuster, 2009. 323pp. ISBN 9781416588733.

Obsessed with cake, Miller explored the history and culture of cake, examined small and large-scale bakeries, and tried her hand at cake baking and decorating. Traveling the country to meet celebrated cake bakers, Miller met Duff Goldman from Charm City Cakes, made famous from the Food Network's popular show *Ace of Cakes*. She also uncovered the histories of regional cakes, such as the Southern specialty red velvet cake, or the New Orleans classic King cake and looked at the changes in traditional wedding cakes. This is a quick, fun, light-hearted read.

> **Subjects**: Bakeries, Baking, Cake, Celebrity Chefs, Investigative Stories, Quick Reads, Recipes
>
> **Now Try**: Readers who are interested in the history and culture of cake may enjoy the short, but entertaining history *Cake: A Global History* by Nicola Humble or *Sweet Invention* by Michael Krondl. Readers who enjoyed Miller's visit to Charm City Cakes may want to check out Duff Goldman's *Ace of Cakes: Inside the World of Charm City Cakes* or Buddy Valastro's *Cake Boss: Stories and Recipes from Mia Famiglia*, another cake baker made famous from television. *Cake Wrecks: When Professional Cakes Go Hilariously Wrong* by Jen Yates is a humorous and entertaining book of cake disasters, as is the blog the book is based on. Also of interest might be one of a wide variety of food micro-histories from Humble's publisher, Reaktion Books, such as *Pie* by Janet Clarkson, *Sandwich* by Bee Wilson, or *Hamburger* by Andrew F. Smith.

Minick, Jim

The Blueberry Years: A Memoir of Farm and Family. New York: Thomas Dunne Books, 2010. 328pp. ISBN 9780312571429.

With a dream of having their own blueberry farm, the author and his wife, both schoolteachers, bought 90 acres of land in Virginia. After hours of back-breaking labor, they planted a thousand blueberry bushes. Having decided to make the farm a pick your own, once the blueberry bushes matured, they opened the farm to pickers. Despite the long days and difficult work, they found joy in their farm and the relationships they forged with their neighbors and the people who came to pick their blueberries.

Subjects: Blueberries, Community Life, Farming, Life Change, Marriage

Now Try: *Living the Good Life: How to Live Sanely and Simply in a Troubled World* by Helen and Scott Nearing is the 1954 classic that inspired the author. Other titles of leaving the city life to live on a farm are *The Wisdom of the Radish* by Lynda Browning or *The Bucolic Plague: How to Manhattanites Became Gentlemen Farmers* by Josh Kilmer-Purcell. *The Seasons on Henry's Farm* by Terra Brockman is the story of a fifth-generation farming family that practices sustainable, organic farming. In *See You in a Hundred Years: Discover One Young Family's Search for a Simpler Life . . . Four Seasons of Living in the Year 1900*, Logan Ward and his family attempted to live without modern-day conveniences.

Nabhan, Gary Paul

Coming Home to Eat: The Pleasures and Politics of Local Foods. New York: Norton, 2002. 330pp. ISBN 9780393020175.

Nabhan lives in the Southwest and decided to attempt to eat only foods that were grown or produced within 250 miles of his home. He quickly discovered the difficulties of eating locally when you live in the desert. In an attempt to eat as authentically as possible, the author focused his search for food on indigenous foods, which led him to eat prickly pear cactus and mesquite. Nabhan laments the current state of the food industry and the loss of eating locally. Although his experiment is similar to other local eating experiments, this title is unique for its focus on foods of the Southwest.

Subjects: American Southwest, Local Food

Now Try: Nabhan has written other titles, including *Chasing Chiles: Hot Spots along the Pepper Trail* and *Desert Terroir*. Other accounts of an author's attempt to eat locally may also be enjoyed. Try Barbara Kingsolver's *Animal, Vegetable, Miracle*, Robin Mather's *The Feast Nearby: How I Lost My Job, Buried a Marriage, and Found My Way By Keeping Chickens, Foraging, Preserving, Bartering, and Eating Locally (All on $40 a Week)*, or Alisa Smith's *Plenty: One Man, One Woman, and a Raucous Year of Eating Locally*. James McWilliams explores whether eating locally is a responsible choice in *Just Food: Where Locavores Get it Wrong and How We Can Truly Eat Responsibly*. Although they are not about food, Edward Abbey's and Mary Austin's environmental classics *Desert Solitaire: A Season in the Wilderness* and *The Land of Little Rain* (respectively) also provide insiders' looks at desert ecosystems.

Powell, Julie

Cleaving: A Story of Marriage, Meat and Obsession. Little, Brown and Company, 2009. 307pp. ISBN 9780316003360.

Powell follows up her best seller *Julie and Julia* (annotated below) with this story of her failing marriage. As a distraction from her troubled marriage and adulterous affair, Powell took up butchery. Between contemplating her relationship with her husband and her lover, she learned the ins and outs of butchery and discovered why butchery is a dying art. Powell also traveled throughout the world to learn about other methods of butchery, while simultaneously searching her soul. Readers looking for another charming, humorous tale like *Julie and Julia* will be disappointed. This is a much darker story with sexually explicit scenes, and readers who fell in love with Julie in the last book, may find her less appealing here. However, the details of butchery are interesting and provide a unique addition to food literature.

> **Subject:** Butchery, Explicit Sexuality, Marriage, Meat Industry, Recipes, Women's Nonfiction, World Travel

> **Now Try:** Although it has a much lighter tone, Powell's first book *Julie and Julia: 365 Days, 524 Recipes, 1 Tiny Apartment Kitchen* will appeal to those who enjoy her voice and sarcastic humor. Amy Finley shares the story of her troubled marriage in *How to Eat a Small Country*. *Eat, Pray Love* by Elizabeth Gilbert is a good suggestion for readers looking for the finding yourself aspect of Powell's memoir. Readers may also find Chelsea Handler's *My Horizontal Life: A Collection of One-Night Stands* appealing because both women are trying to understand their lives through their relationships. Readers interested in the butchery aspect may want to check out *The Butcher's Guide to Well-Raised Meat: How to Buy, Cut, and Cook Great Beef, Lamb, Pork, Poultry, and More* by Joshua and Jessica Applestone, proprietors of the butcher shop where Powell works. A novel in which a woman tries to deal with tragedy in her life through sexual experimentation is Lisa Zeidner's *Layover*.

Powell, Julie

Julie and Julia: 365 Days, 524 Recipes, 1 Tiny Apartment Kitchen. New York: Little, Brown and Company, 2005. 309pp. ISBN 9780316109697.

Julie Powell was living in New York City and working at a temp job that she didn't enjoy. When she began looking for something to do that would bring her some fulfillment, she considered cooking. She decided that she would cook all of the recipes from Julia Child's *Mastering the Art of French Cooking* in one year and record her experiment on a blog. Challenged with a tiny apartment kitchen, difficulties procuring odd ingredients such as marrow bones, and the gruesome task of killing several lobsters, Julie made her way through *MTAOFC*, even if she and her husband frequently ate well past 9 pm. Julie also recounts her relationship with her husband, the pressure she placed on herself to finish the project, and its effects on their marriage. Readers will enjoy this funny, sweet, story and the humorous mishaps.

> **Subjects:** Blogs, Child, Julia, Humor, Marriage, New York City, Recipes, September 11

> **Now Try:** Powell followed this memoir with the one annotated above, *Cleaving*, although readers should take note that book is much different in tone and subject matter from this one. Readers may enjoy reading the recipes Powell attempted in Julia Child's *Mastering the Art of French Cooking*. Readers may also be interested in learning more about Julia Child. A few good choices are Child's memoir, *My Life in France*, Joan Reardon's collection of Child's letters, *As Always, Julia: The Letters of Julia Child and*

Avis DeVoto and Noel Riley Fitch's biography *Appetite For Life*. Daniel Duane recounts his efforts to learn to cook using Alice Waters's cookbooks in *How to Cook Like a Man*. A. J. Jacobs's *The Year of Living Biblically: One Man's Humble Quest to Follow the Bible as Literally as Possible* may appeal to readers who enjoyed the humor and challenges of Powell's project.

Stark, Tim

Heirloom: Notes From an Accidental Tomato Farmer. New York: Broadway Books, 2008. 232pp. ISBN 9780767927062.

Stark was living in New York working a day job and writing at night. When he found a pile of lumber in the trash, he decided to reclaim it and build a germination rack for heirloom tomatoes. Having started a small vegetable garden on his family's Pennsylvanian land before, he decided to expand his vegetable garden. Soon he had three thousand tomato plants growing in his Brooklyn brownstone. He transported the plants to Pennsylvania for planting and ended up with a bumper crop of heirloom tomatoes that New York City chefs couldn't get enough of. Since then, Stark has made a name for himself growing tomatoes. This engaging and humorous memoir recounts his uncertainties as he embarked on this unknown path, the trials of weeds and groundhogs, the friends and family who volunteered their help, the farmer's market customers, and other farmers who offered their advice.

Subjects: Business, Farming, Humor, Men's Lives, New York City, Tomatoes

Now Try: Readers interested in tomatoes will find no shortage of titles available on that subject. Arthur Allen investigates the typical grocery store tomato and why it doesn't taste as good as it used to in *Ripe: The Search for the Perfect Tomato*. In Barry Estabrook's exposé *Tomatoland*, he reveals the mass production and chemical enhancements of the tomato industry. History buffs may enjoy *Pomodoro!: A History of the Tomato in Italy* by David Gentilcore or *The Tomato in America* by Andrew F. Smith. Historical fiction readers might consider Adam Schell's *Tomato Rhapsody*, a fictional account of the tomato's arrival in Italy and a romance between the son of a Jewish tomato farmer and a Catholic woman. Those who enjoyed the farming aspects of Stark's story should consider *Growing a Farmer* by Kurt Timmermeister and *It's a Long Road to a Tomato* by Keith Stewart. Both left their city lives behind to start their own farms. Mike Madison shares his 20 years of experience growing food and attending farmer's markets in a collection of essays, *Blithe Tomato*. William Alexander humorously recounts his experiences attempting to grow his own organic fruits and vegetables in *The $64 Tomato*.

Timmermeister, Kurt

Growing a Farmer: How I Learned to Live Off the Land. New York: W. W. Norton, 2011. 335pp. ISBN 9780393070859.

Although he built a successful career as a restaurateur in Seattle, the author's growing distaste for the highly processed foods he served led to a desire for a closer relationship to the land and his food. After selling his business, he bought a small farm on an island off Seattle. Knowing little about farming, he tried his hand at growing vegetables, beekeeping, and raising chickens, cows, sheep, and pigs. Eventually he was able to build a moderately successful and sustainable farm. Timmermeister describes the realities of farming, from difficulties such as dealing with sick animals to the joys of harvesting his own food.

Subjects: Animal Husbandry, Beekeeping, Farm Life, Farming, Life Change

Now Try: Memoirs by people who left their lives in the city to start their own farm is a hot topic now and doesn't seem to be letting up. There are a number of great memoirs readers may want to consider, such as *The Dirty Life* by Kristin Kimball, *Coop* by Michael Perry, *The Seasons on Henry's Farm* by Terra Brockman, and *The Bucolic Plague* by Josh Kilmer-Purcell. In *This Life is in Your Hands*, Melissa Coleman recalls her childhood growing up on a small farm and the effect it had on her family. Readers may also enjoy Louise Dickinson Rich's classic memoir of living the simple life, *We Took to the Woods*. One of the original American writers-turned-farmers was E. B. White; in his classic essay collection *One Man's Meat*, he describes many different aspects of farm living, and of course he fictionalized farm life with great success in his children's classic *Charlotte's Web*. Verlyn Klinkenborg also writes essay collections on the rural life; his titles include *Making Hay* and *The Rural Life*.

Weaver, Tara Austen

The Butcher and the Vegetarian: One Woman's Romp through a World of Men, Meat, and Moral Crisis. Emmaus: Rodale, 2010. 228pp. ISBN 9781605299969.

Raised as a vegetarian, Weaver had some health issues and was advised by several doctors to start eating meat. Although the meat didn't seem to improve her health, she embraced the challenge. Her experiences buying meat for the first time at the butcher shop, learning how to cook it properly, and trying to overcome her squeamishness about eating it are entertaining. She also provides a balanced look at the vegetarian/meat-eating argument, exploring ethics and nutrition. Exploring the issues of the meat industry, Weaver interviewed ranchers and farmers raising humane and ethical meat.

Subjects: Butchery, Chefs, Ethical Decisions, Farmers, Meat, Vegetarianism

Now Try: Tovar Cerulli, a vegetarian, also went back to eating meat for health reasons and explores the issues of the diet in *Mindful Carnivore*. In *Meat: A Love Story*, Susan Bourette attempts to find a way to make more ethical choices when eating meat. Catherine Friend also explores the concept of humanely raised meat in *The Compassionate Carnivore: Or, How to Keep Animals Happy, Save Old MacDondald's Farm, Reduce Your Hoofprint and Still Eat Meat*. Jonathan Safran Foer exposes the realities of the meat industry and examines the ethics of eating meat in *Eating Animals*. Readers interested in the history of vegetarianism may want to consider Tristram Stuart's *The Bloodless Revolution: A Cultural History of Vegetarianism from 1600 to Modern Times* or Karen and Michael Iacobbo's *Vegetarian America: A History*. Weaver also has her own blog, Tea and Cookies (teaandcookiesblog.com).

Foodie Memoirs

A Foodie is an informal term referring to a person with a special interest in, devotion to, or knowledge of food. There is some debate as to who was the first to coin the term. Food critic Gael Greene began using the term in the early 1980s, but the term appeared in Paul Levy's and Ann Barr's 1984 book, *The Official Foodie Handbook*. Regardless, debates abound among Foodies over the proper definition of the term. Foodie is used frequently and often interchange-ably with terms such as gourmet, gourmand, gastronome, or epicurean, and is often applied to professionals in the food industry as well as amateurs. Dave DeWitt argues that only including gourmands in the definition of Foodie does not include people who devote their lives to the agricultural aspect of food. Food producers who consider food to be an art and are constantly refining their craft should also be considered Foodies (DeWitt 2010). Currently, many Foodies don't want to be labeled as such because of the overuse of the term and its wide scope. Some also feel that the term Foodie signifies snobbery and wish to distance themselves from that characteristic. This book does not at-tempt to make a statement regarding the appropriateness of the term. For sim-plicity, in this book, the term Foodie is used to describe a person with a special interest in food, whether it be producing or consuming it, and will encompass both professionals and amateurs. Works by famous food critics and food writ-ers, as well as bloggers, home cooks, and other amateurs with special interests in food, will be included in this section.

Foodie Memoirs are the most varied of the memoirs in this chapter, in subject matter, as well as in setting and tone. Many are life stories from famous Foodies, but topics also include relationships and parenting. Their tone can range from serious to lighthearted and all points in between. Many Foodie Memoirs are written by famous figures, such as Julia Child or M.F.K. Fisher. Readers may also be interested in biographies of these figures.

> Foodie Memoirs are written by a person with a special interest in food, and encompasses both professionals and amateurs such as food critics, food writers, bloggers, and home cooks. Foodie Memoirs vary in subject matter, as well as in setting and tone. Many are life stories from famous Foodies, but topics also include relationships and parenting. Their tone can range from serious to lighthearted and all points in between.

Abu-Jaber, Diana

The Language of Baklava: A Memoir. New York: Pantheon, 2005. 330pp. ISBN 9780375423048.

With a Jordanian father and an American mother, Abu-Jaber was raised in New York but also spent brief periods living in Jordan. In this amusing coming-of-age story, Abu-Jaber recalls the influence of both cultures and cuisines in her life. Her father frequently cooked the meals of his childhood, exposing her to the exotic flavors of Middle Eastern cuisine, while her mother's Velveeta sandwiches provided the comfort of fitting in with the rest of her friends. The importance of her extended family provides amusing anecdotes and her incorporation of her favorite family recipes add charm.

> **Subjects:** Coming-of-Age, Family Relationships, Identity, Jordan, Multicultural Issues, Recipes
>
> **Now Try:** Readers who enjoy Abu-Jaber's writing style may want to try her fiction novel, *Crescent*. Bich Minh Nguyen's *Stealing Buddha's Dinner: A Memoir*, Leslie Li's *Daughter of Heaven: A Memoir With Earthly Recipes*, and Kim Sunee's *Trail of Crumbs: Hunger, Love, and the Search for Home* all capture the authors' attempts to balance the pull between their ancestral culture and cuisines and their new culture. Molly Wizenberg's *A Homemade Life* is another touching coming-of-age story about her family's love of food and their influence on her life. Readers may want to consider other multicultural coming-of-age memoirs, such as *To See and See Again* by Tara Bahrampour or *Unpolished Gem* by Alice Pung.

Amster-Burton, Matthew

Hungry Monkey: A Food-Loving Father's Quest to Raise An Adventurous Eater. Boston: Houghton Mifflin Harcourt, 2009. 260pp. ISBN 9780151013241.

When restaurant critic and food writer Amster-Burton became a stay-at-home dad, he was determined to raise his daughter to appreciate and enjoy a wide variety of foods and cuisines rather than the typical bland processed foods that children are usually given. Although feeding his child Thai food and sushi raises a few eyebrows, Amster-Burton initially finds his daughter a willing eater. As she enters her toddler years, her changing tastes turn her into the typical picky three-year-old. This humorous and touching memoir recounts the difficulties and joys the author experiences sharing his love for food with his daughter.

> **Subjects:** Family Relationships, Fathers and Daughters, Parenting, Recipes
>
> **Now Try:** *Cooking for Gracie: The Making of a Parent From Scratch* by Keith Dixon is another appealing memoir of a father struggling with his child's nutritional needs and preferences. Daniel Duane decided to learn to cook when he became a father. He shares his experiences in *How to Cook Like a Man*. *Man With a Pan: Culinary Adventures of Fathers Who Cook for Their Families* is an entertaining collection of essays from husbands and fathers who take on the responsibility of cooking. *Too Many Cooks: Kitchen Adventures with 1 Mom, 4 Kids, and 102 Recipes* by Emily Franklin is another touching and humorous account of a parent determined to instill her love of food in her children. Readers may also enjoy other fatherhood memoirs, such as *Home Game* by Michael Lewis, *How Tough Could It Be: The Trials and Errors of a Sportswriter Turned Stay-At-Home Dad* by Austin Murphy, or *Alternadad* by Neal Pollack.

Beard, James

Delights and Prejudices. Philadelphia: Running Press, 2002. 229pp. ISBN 9780762409419.

Beard is considered the father of American gourmet cooking. In his memoirs, Beard remembers his earliest taste memories. The influence of his mother is evident in his description of her life and her cooking. Beard's mother passed on her delight in cooking and the pleasure she had in eating to Beard. He recounts his childhood, holiday meals, and his exposure to cooking, markets, and canning. He also recalls his travels to other countries and the differences found in their foods. Beard's memories are heavy on food descriptions, and less on the details of his personal life, so readers who enjoy descriptive accounts of food will find much pleasure in these memoirs.

Subject: Beard, James, Family Relationships, Quick Reads

Now Try: Readers who are interested in details of Beard's personal life should try either Evan Jones's biography *Epicurean Delight* or Robert Clark's *James Beard: A Biography*. Beard published a number of cookbooks which are considered classics. Try James Beard's *American Cookery* and *Beard on Food: The Best Recipes and Kitchen Wisdom Form the Dean of American Cooking*. *Love and Kisses and a Halo of Truffles* is a collection of letters between Beard and his friend and colleague, Helen Evans Brown, which gives a personal look at Beard's friendship and feelings about food. Readers may also enjoy memoirs by some of Beard's contemporaries, such as Craig Claiborne's memoir, *A Feast Made for Laughter*, or Julia Child's *My Life in France*.

Beck, Simone

Food and Friends: Recipes and Memories from Simca's Cuisine. New York: Viking, 1991. 528pp. ISBN 9780670839346.

Simone Beck, known as Simca to her friends, was a coauthor of Julia Child's classic *Mastering the Art of French Cooking*. In this delightful memoir, Beck reminisces on her privileged childhood, World War I, her failed first marriage, and subsequent second marriage that lasted almost 50 years, World War II and the occupation of her family home by the Nazis, her interest in and love of cooking, her friendship with Julia Child and collaboration on their masterpiece.

Subject: Child, Julia, Family Relationships, France, History, Marriage, Recipes

Now Try: Julia Child's memoir, *My Life in France*, also covers Child's and Beck's friendship. *As Always, Julia* by Joan Reardon is a collection of Child's letters to her friend Avis DeVoto during her time in France and while working on *MTAOFC*. Judith Jones, a vice president of Knopf and editor of *MTAOFC*, recalls her career and the talented figures she discovered in *The Tenth Muse: My Life in Food*. Madeleine Kamman's *When French Women Cook: A Gastronomic Memoir with Over 250 Recipes* is another delightful memoir and cookbook from a French cook whose reminiscences of food and the long-gone age of rural France are quite charming. Readers may also enjoy Marcella Hazan's memoir *Amarcord: Marcella Remembers*.

Bourdain, Anthony

Medium Raw: A Bloody Valentine to the World of Food and the People Who Cook. New York: Ecco, 2010. 281pp. ISBN 9780061718946.

Much has changed for Anthony Bourdain since his best-selling memoir *Kitchen Confidential* was published. He discusses the changes in his life, such as his career change from chef to globe-trotting TV personality, as well as his marriage and fatherhood. With his biting personality and unapologetic frankness, Bourdain also offers his thoughts on the current state of cooking, the restaurant business, as well as some of the biggest names in the foodie world, offering praise for those he admires, and rants for those he doesn't, and admits that he may have been too harsh on some. Interspersed among his thoughts are humorous, and often vulgar, stories and bits of food porn.

Subjects: Bourdain, Anthony, Chefs, Essays, Fatherhood, Humor, Marriage, Parenting, Profanity, Restaurants, Travel, Waters, Alice

Now Try: Bourdain's *The Nasty Bits: Collected Varietal Cuts, Usable Trim, Scraps, and Bones* as well as his illustrated book, *No Reservations*, offer more of his thoughts on cooking and travelling. A. A. Gill's *Previous Convictions: Assignments From Here and There* is a collection of essays about his travels and family with similar humor. Although completely different topics, Justin Halpern's *Sh*t My Dad Says* also has a similar tone and humor. Readers may also want to consider other collections of essays about food, such as Jeffrey Steingarten's *The Man Who Ate Everything*, Stefan Gates's *Gastronaut*, and Jim Harrison's *The Raw and the Cooked*. Another caustic essayist who might appeal to Bourdain fans is comedian Lewis Black, frequent commentator on *The Daily Show* and author of *Nothing's Sacred* and *Me of Little Faith*.

Bruni, Frank

Born Round: A Story of Family, Food, and a Ferocious Appetite. New York: Penguin Press, 2009. 354pp. ISBN 9781594202315.

Bruni, a restaurant critic for the *New York Times*, recounts his lifelong issues with food and weight. Food played a big role in Bruni's Italian American family. During childhood, his mother and grandmother plied him with heaping portions of food, and Bruni, who loved food, never refused. But as he got older, he became more self-conscious about his weight and developed a love–hate relationship with food. Bruni admits his problems with bulimia and laxative abuse. When Bruni is hired as the food critic for the *New York Times*, he realizes he must face his life-long struggle with food.

Subjects: Bruni, Frank, Eating Disorders, Family Relationships, Men's Lives, New York City, *New York Times*, Restaurant Critics

Awards: *New York Times* Notable Book

Now Try: Bruni was a journalist before his career as a food critic. Readers may want to consider his nonfiction titles, including *Ambling Into History: The Unlikely Odyssey of George W. Bush* and *A Gospel of Shame: Children, Sexual Abuse, and the Catholic Church*. Other memoirs in which authors explore their relationships with food and their families include Judith Moore's *Fat Girl: A True Story*, Ruth Reichl's *Tender at the Bone*, and Nigel Slater's *Toast: The Story of a Boy's Hunger*. Memoirs by other well-known restaurant critics may also be of interest, such as Craig Claiborne's *A Feast Made for Laughter*, Gael Greene's *Insatiable*, or Mimi Sheraton's *Eating My Words*.

Child, Julia, and Prud'homme, Alex

My Life in France. New York: Alfred A. Knopf, 2006. 317pp. ISBN 9781400043460.

Recently married, Julia and her new husband Paul Child moved to Paris in 1948 where he was assigned with the United States Foreign Service. Julia spoke little French and had few cooking skills. In this entertaining memoir, Julia describes the years she spent living in France, her discovery of the food, customs, and people that she came to love. It was here that she entered Le Cordon Bleu, the famous culinary school, where she learned the tenets of French cuisine and cooking. She recalls the early years of her marriage, the friendships she formed and the creation of her masterpiece, *Mastering the Art of French Cooking*. Julia's unique voice presents a humorous, lighthearted story filled with her unique descriptions of foods and the joy she found in life. Child says that "the pleasures of the table, and of life, are infinite" which comes across in this book.

Subjects: Child, Julia, Cookbooks, Culinary School, France, Le Cordon Bleu, Life Change, Marriage

Award: IACP Award

Now Try: Readers who enjoy Julia's voice will want to read the collection of letters exchanged between herself and longtime friend Avis DeVoto: *As Always, Julia: The Letters of Julia Child and Avis DeVoto* by Joan Reardon. Readers who want to know more about Julia's life should try the definitive biography, *Appetite for Life* by Noel Riley Fitch. Bob Spitz has also written a new biography of Child, *Dearie: The Remarkable Life of Julia Child*. Nancy Verde Barr recounts her years working with Julia in *Backstage with Julia: My Years with Julia Child*. Jennet Conant's *A Covert Affair: Julia Child and Paul Child in the OSS* may also be appealing. Julie Powell's *Julie & Julia* is the memoir that reawakened popular interest in Child's classic tome, *Mastering the Art of French Cooking*.

Claiborne, Craig

A Feast Made for Laughter. Garden City: Doubleday, 1982. 414pp. ISBN 9780385157001.

Although this is an older title, Craig Claiborne was a famous American food writer, restaurant critic, prolific cookbook author, and former food editor of the *New York Times*. In his memoir, Claiborne describes his early childhood in Mississippi and the southern food he was raised on. After his entrance in the Navy, his travels exposed him to foreign foods and he developed a love of food and cooking. He recalls his time living in France, attending culinary school, his career and his friendships with other culinary greats.

> **Subject:** Claiborne, Craig, Cookbooks, Family Relationships, Food Writers, Friendships, Recipes, Restaurant Critics

> **Now Try:** Thomas McNamee's biography of Claiborne, *The Man Who Changed the Way We Eat*, offers readers intimate details of Claiborne's life. Readers may also enjoy the memoirs of another well-known southern food writer, *Between Bites: Memoirs of a Hungry Hedonist* by James Villas. Frank Bruni's *Born Round* is another memoir by a *New York Times* food writer and critic. Claiborne had relationships with many other culinary greats, such as Julia Child, James Beard, and Pierre Franey. Memoirs by these figures may be good suggestions: *My Life in France* by Julia Child, *Delights and Prejudices* by James Beard, and *A Chef's Tale: A Memoir of Food, France, and America* by Pierre Franey.

Epstein, Jason

Eating: A Memoir. New York: Alfred A. Knopf, 2009. 174pp. ISBN 9781400042968.
In this short memoir, publishing editor Epstein recounts his love for food and its importance in his life. He begins with his childhood summers in Maine and his grandmother's cooking, the summers he spent cooking during college, and the early days of his marriage and career. He recounts some of his most memorable meals with famous writers and chefs and also remembers his first meal after 9/11. Epstein includes his favorite recipes, which are written in a more conversational style, rather than the typical formulaic recipe.

> **Subjects:** Men's Lives, Quick Reads, Recipes, September 11, Travel

> **Now Try:** Epstein also wrote about his life in publishing in *Book Business: Publishing Past, Present, and Future*. Readers may also enjoy Kenny Shopsin's quick memoir/cookbook, *Eat Me: The Food and Philosophy of Kenny Shopsin* or Adam Roberts's *The Amateur Gourmet*. Laurie Colwin's *Home Cooking* and works by M.F.K. Fisher, such as *The Art of Eating*, also employ a conversational style with warm descriptions of meals.

Escoffier, Auguste

Memories of My Life. New York: Van Nostrand Reinhold, 1997. 252pp. ISBN 9780442023966.
One of the most famous chefs in modern history, Auguste Escoffier shares the details of his life beginning with his childhood and apprenticeship to a cook at the age of 13 (in this book based on his journals, and originally published by

his grandson in 1985). During the Franco Prussian war, he served as an army cook. After the war, he went on to work in a number of restaurants and hotels and cook for famous celebrities and royal figures, finally partnering with Cesar Ritz. His renowned cookbook, the *Guide Culinaire* cemented his place in culinary history. Escoffier's short chapters and easy-to-read style make this a quick read. His accounts of celebrities and royalties are entertaining, and the menus and recipes he includes provide a look at typical French cuisine of the time.

> **Subjects:** Chefs, Cookbooks, Escoffier, Auguste, France, Restaurants

> **Now Try:** Readers who want to know more about Escoffier should check out Kenneth James's definitive biography *Escoffier: The King of Chefs*. Although most readers will not be interested in cooking the recipes in Escoffier's *The Escoffier Cookbook and Guide to the Fine Art of Cookery: For Connoisseurs, Chefs, Epicures, Complete with 2973 Recipes*, some readers may enjoy reading the recipes. Steve Rinella's attempts to create a feast from Escoffier's cookbook, *The Scavenger's Guide to Haute Cuisine* is an entertaining, modern look at this classic cookbook. Ian Kelly's *Cooking for Kings: The Life of Antonin Carême, the First Celebrity Chef* is another fascinating biography of one of the most famous French chefs in history. Fiction readers may want to try N. M. Kelby's *White Truffles in Winter*, a fictional account of Escoffier and his love for two women: his wife and his mistress, Sarah Bernhardt.

Fisher, M.F.K.

The Gastronomical Me. New York: Duell, Sloan & Pearce, 1943. 295pp. ISBN 9789110014404.

> Mary Frances Kennedy Fisher is considered one of the most well-known and prolific food writers in American history. In this memoir, Fisher's memories are tied to food. From the first time she cooked for herself as a child, to the first oyster she ate, cooking for men she loved, her travels and life abroad, and the various changes she faced throughout her life, food always played a big role in her life. Her short chapters are thoughtful and full of humor. Fisher is known for her literary style of writing and will be appreciated by fans of good prose.

> **Subjects:** Fisher, M.F.K., Food Writers, France, Living Abroad, Quick Reads

> **Now Try:** Fisher has written over 20 books. *Serve it Forth* was Fisher's first book, published in 1937. In Fisher's literary style, this book presents her musings on culinary history from the ancient Greeks to Catherine de Medici. Readers who enjoy Fisher's literary style mixed with humor may also enjoy *Blue Trout and Black Truffles: The Perigrinations of an Epicure* by Joseph Wechsberg and *Between Meals: An Appetite for Paris* by A. J. Liebling. Roy Andries de Groot's classic narrative cooking, *The Auberge of the Flowering Hearth* may also be appealing. Although not about food, Mary McCarthy's *Memories of a Catholic Girlhood*, is another writer from Fisher's era and writes in a similar style.

Fussell, Betty

My Kitchen Wars: A Memoir. New York: North Point Press, 1999. 238pp. ISBN 9780865475779.

Betty Fussell is a well-known food writer, although food is not the primary focus of this candid, and sometimes shocking, memoir. Fussell recounts the suicide of her mother, and the subsequent influence of her grandparents in her life. Her father's quick remarriage to her harsh stepmother left her eager to escape to college; there, finally on her own, Fussell quickly became a wild girl. She recalls meeting Paul, who became her husband, and their marriage. Paul expected her to take on the traditional role of wife and mother, which she did for a time, but her desire to have a career of her own led her back to school for an advanced degree. This began the crack in the marriage that led to affairs, and eventually divorce. Fussell does mention cooking sporadically throughout the book, but she didn't begin seriously cooking until her divorce.

> **Subjects:** Coming-of-Age, Divorce, Explicit Sexuality, Family Relationships, Food Writers, Marriage, Women's Nonfiction

> **Now Try:** Fussell's other titles may also be of interest. *Raising Steaks: The Life and Times of American Beef* and *The Story of Corn* both examine the history of these foods as well as their current state. She profiles the great culinary figures in *Masters of American Cookery: M.F.K. Fisher, James Beard, Craig Claiborne, and Julia Child*. In her memoir, Fussell writes candidly of her sexual appetite and her lovers. Gael Greene is also very frank with regards to the sexual revolution and her sexual relations in her memoir *Insatiable: Tales From a Life of Delicious Excess*. *Cleaving: A Story of Marriage, Meat, and Obsession* by Julie Powell is another memoir about a rocky marriage that may be of interest. Women's Fiction novels that share the subject matter of divorce and self-discovery are Elizabeth Berg's *Open House* and Diane Johnson's *Le Divorce*.

Greene, Gael

Insatiable: Tales From a Life of Delicious Excess. New York: Warner Books, 2006. 368pp. ISBN 9780446576994.

The Insatiable Critic for *New York* magazine recalls her functional family and childhood, growing up eating Mac & Cheese and Jell-O. Despite knowing little about gourmet food and never having written a restaurant review, Greene eagerly accepted the position as critic for *New York* magazine in 1968. This opened a new world to Greene, who had a front seat at the best tables when haute cuisine was just gaining popularity in America. Greene lusciously describes the meals she ate while traveling the world. Also gaining popularity in America at the time was the sexual revolution, and Greene is very frank about indulging her sexual appetite as well, recounting lovers she has had over the years. The gossipy tone and luscious descriptions make this an engrossing, entertaining read.

> **Subjects:** Explicit Sexuality, Greene, Gael, Relationships, Restaurant Critics, Restaurants, Travel, Women's Nonfiction

Now Try: Ruth Reichl's memoir *Tender at the Bone: Growing Up at the Table* also recalls the mediocre foods she ate as a child and her awakening to gourmet food which led to a job as a food writer. Jeannette Ferrary, another food writer, shares her memoirs in *Out of the Kitchen*. Greene published her first novel in 1976, *Blue Skies, No Candy*, an erotic novel that garnered a lot of attention. Chelsea Handler also writes candidly about her sexual encounters in *My Horizontal Life*.

Hazan, Marcella

Amarcord: Marcella Remembers. New York: Gotham Books, 2008. 307pp. ISBN 9781592403882.

Marcella Hazan is a well-known cookbook writer who is credited with bringing traditional Italian cooking techniques to the United States. In her memoir, Hazan describes her childhood in a small provincial town in Italy, the deprivations caused by World War II, and the country cooking they relied on for survival. After meeting her American husband, Hazan moved to America, where she didn't know anyone or even speak the language. At the time, she didn't know how to cook, but to occupy herself she began experimenting in the kitchen. Soon she began teaching Italian cooking to other women, which eventually blossomed into a career teaching and writing cookbooks. Her career, travels, and relationship with her husband make for an engaging and touching memoir.

Subjects: Cookbooks, Hazan, Marcella, Italy, Italian Cuisine, Marriage, Multicultural Issues, Relationships

Now Try: *The Essentials of Classic Italian Cooking* is Hazan's classic cookbook. Anna Del Conte also grew up in Italy, left during World War II, and began writing Italian cookbooks in England. She shares her life story in *Risotto With Nettles*. Jacques Pépin recalls his immigration to the United States and building his career in cooking in his memoir, *The Apprentice: My Life in the Kitchen*. Laura Schenone tracks down her distant Italian relations to find an authentic Italian family recipe in *Lost Ravioli Recipes of Hoboken: A Search for Food and Family*. *Cooking With Italian Grandmothers: Recipes and Stories From Tuscany to Sicily* by Jessica Theroux provides authentic, traditional Italian recipes along with personal stories from the women Theroux met. Readers may also enjoy *How Italian Food Conquered the World* by John Mariani, which traces the history of Italian food and how many Italian dishes have become household dishes in the United States.

Hesser, Amanda

Cooking for Mr. Latte: A Food Lover's Courtship, With Recipes. New York: W. W. Norton & Company, 2003. 336pp. ISBN 9780393051964.

For Amanda Hesser, food writer for the *New York Times* and author of several cookbooks, food is a big part of her life. But when she began dating a man for whom food was not important, she wonders if this relationship can work. This lighthearted and humorous memoir recounts Hesser's courtship and her attempts to introduce her partner to the joys of food. She also shares stories of her adventures as a food writer, including some interesting meals with other famous foodies.

Subjects: Dating, Food Writers, Hesser, Amanda, Humor, New York City, *New York Times*, Quick Reads, Recipes, Relationships

Awards: IACP Award

Now Try: Readers who enjoy Hesser's writing style may want to try her narrative cookbook *The Cook and the Gardener: A Year of Recipes and Writings for the French Countryside*. Giulia Melucci's *I Loved, I Lost, I Made Spaghetti: A Memoir of Good Food and Bad Boyfriends* is a lighthearted and humorous account of Melucci's dating life, even though she does not find her own Mr. Latte. Elizabeth Bard recalls how she fell in love, moved to Paris, and discovered the joy of French food in *Lunch in Paris: A Love Story With Recipes*. Ree Drummond left her city life when she fell in love with a cowboy; try her memoir, *Pioneer Woman*. Amy Finley recounts how she moved her family to France where she and her husband first fell in love to try to save their marriage in *How to Eat a Small Country: A Family's Pursuit of Happiness, One Meal at a Time*.

Jaffrey, Madhur

Climbing the Mango Trees: A Memoir of a Childhood in India. New York: Alfred A. Knopf, 2006. 297pp. ISBN 9781400042951.

Madhur Jaffrey is a noted cookbook writer of Indian cuisine. In her memoir, Jaffrey recalls her childhood in Delhi, living with her extended family in her grandfather's large home. Her vivid descriptions illuminate the exotic setting, the sounds, smells and flavors of India. She traces her family's history and emphasizes the importance of her extended family. The culture and traditions of her Hindu upbringing, as well as the important events and large family gatherings, were centered around food. She also details India's independence and partition, and the upheaval that followed.

Subjects: Coming-of-Age, Family Relationships, India, Indian Cuisine, Multicultural Issues, Recipes

Now Try: Some of Madhur Jaffrey's cookbooks include *At Home With Madhur Jaffrey* and *Madhur Jaffrey's World Vegetarian*. Both Shoba Narayan's *Monsoon Diary: A Memoir with Recipes* and Colette Rossant's memoir *Apricots on the Nile: A Memoir with Recipes* are vivid accounts of exotic flavors and settings. Chitrita Banerji explores the exotic and diverse cuisines of India in *Eating India: An Odyssey Into the Food and Culture of the Land of Spices*. Thrity Umrigar's *First Darling of the Morning* is another memoir of a childhood in India. Fiction readers may also enjoy *The Hundred-Foot Journey* by Richard Morais, about a boy from Mumbai who grows up to open a restaurant in France.

Jones, Judith

The Tenth Muse: My Life in Food. New York: Alfred A. Knopf, 2007. 290pp.
ISBN 9780307264954.

A long-time editor for Knopf, Jones has edited the works of many famous writers and noted cookbook authors. Most notably, Jones took a chance on a cookbook that many publishers wouldn't touch: Julia Child's *Mastering the Art of French Cooking*. In her memoir, Jones remembers that growing up, food was not a subject that was discussed. Meals were comprised of disappointing, bland foods. Her aunt introduced her to the pleasures of cooking at the age of 11, and after moving to France after college, Jones was introduced to French cuisine. She fell in love with French cuisine, as well as the man who would become her husband. Jones describes the beginning of her career, and working with Julia Child, as well as the 1960s, when immigrants' pride in their culinary heritage led to her work on cookbooks for Chinese, Middle Eastern, Italian, and Indian cuisine.

> **Subjects:** Chefs, Cookbooks, France, Marriage, Recipes
>
> **Now Try:** Jones has also written a cookbook, *The Pleasures of Cooking for One*. Readers who enjoy Jones's experience working with Julia Child may also enjoy Nancy Verde Barr's *Backstage with Julia: My Years with Julia Child*. Memoirs by authors Jones worked with may also be of interest, such as Julia Child's *My Life in France*, Marcella Hazan's *Amarcord*, and Madhur Jaffrey's *Climbing the Mango Trees: A Memoir of a Childhood in India*. Another Foodie author who worked in publishing is Jason Epstein; his memoirs are *Eating* and *Book Business*.

Melucci, Giulia

I Loved, I Lost, I Made Spaghetti. New York: Grand Central Publishing, 2010. 284pp. ISBN 9780446534413.

In this lighthearted memoir, Melucci chronicles her attempts to find love and her string of failed relationships. Although she is a successful young woman living in New York City, her boyfriends read like a Who's Who of losers. Cooking is a big part of Melucci's life; Italian food in particular. She cooks to entice men and to soothe her broken heart. Scattered among her simple, yet elegant recipes are the frustrating, yet entertaining stories of her relationships.

> **Subjects**: Dating, New York City, Quick Reads, Recipes, Relationships
>
> **Now Try**: Elizabeth Gilbert's *Eat, Pray, Love: One Woman's Search for Everything Across Italy, India, and Indonesia* is another memoir of a woman who finds solace in food while healing from a failed relationship. Readers may also enjoy other memoirs of food and love such as Amanda Hesser's *Cooking for Mr. Latte*, *Julie and Julia* by Julie Powell, *Lunch in Paris* by Elizabeth Bard, and *A Homemade Life: Stories and Recipes From My Kitchen Tabl*e by Molly

Wizenberg. Susan Shapiro shares stories of her heartbreaks in *Five Men Who Broke My Heart*. *My Boyfriend Wrote a Book about Me* by Hilary Winston is a humorous tell-all about the author's exes.

Narayan, Shoba

Monsoon Diary: A Memoir With Recipes. New York: Villard, 2003. 223pp. ISBN 9780375507564.

In this animated memoir, Narayan describes her childhood growing up in small village in India, surrounded by her extended family. She provides insightful details of the culture, customs, and rituals of her upbringing. Her family's love of food and its importance in their lives is evident in her charming stories. Her descriptions of various villagers, such as the milk man and the flower woman, bring the small village to life. When Narayan agrees to an arranged marriage and moves to New York City with her husband, her attempts at cooking fail until she returns to the traditional Indian cooking of her childhood. This touching and tender story provides the reader with a vivid portrait of rural India, as well as Hindu customs.

Subjects: Coming-of-Age, Family Relationships, Hindu, India, Indian Cuisine, Marriage, Multicultural Issues

Now Try: *Climbing the Mango Trees: A Memoir of a Childhood in India* by Madhur Jaffrey and *Eating India: An Odyssey into the Food and Culture of the Land of Spices* by Chitrita Banerji also paint vivid portraits of India. In *The Lost Ravioli Recipes of Hoboken: A Search For Food and Family* by Laura Schenone and *A Tiger in the Kitchen: A Memoir of Food and Family* by Cheryl Lu-lien Tan, the authors attempt to learn the traditional cooking of their ancestors. Fiction readers may enjoy Anne Cherian's novel *A Good Indian Wife* or Amulya Malladi's novel *The Mango Season*.

Reichl, Ruth

Tender at the Bone: Growing Up at the Table. New York: Random House, 1998. 282pp. ISBN 9780679449874.

Reichl, who has been a restaurant critic for the *LA Times* and the *New York Times*, and an editor for *Gourmet* magazine, remembers the beginnings of her interest in food. Reichl became interested in food at an early age, when it was clear her mother (known as the "Queen of Mold" and prone to giving guests food poisoning) had none. Neither mother nor grandmother were interested in cooking, so Reichl's instruction came from housekeepers. As she got older, her parents left her alone frequently, so she experimented and found food to be a comfort and a way to please her friends. Reichl relives her adolescent and teen years, college, travels abroad, marriage, and relocation to Berkley. Her relationship with her mother, while always strained, looms large.

Subjects: Coming-of-Age, Family Relationships, Food Writers, Mothers and Daughters, Recipes, Reichl, Ruth

Now Try: Reichl has written other memoirs, including *Comfort Me with Apples: More Adventures at the Table* and *Not Becoming My Mother: And Other Things She Taught Me Along the Way*. Patricia Volk's *Stuffed: Adventures of a Restaurant Family* is a humorous account of her upbringing in a restaurant family. Louise De-Salvo recalls her family's relationships with food and each other in *Crazy in the Kitchen: Food, Feuds, and Forgiveness in an Italian American Family*. Nigel Slater also remembers his childhood and enjoyment of food in his memoir *Toast: The Story of a Boy's Hunger*. The relationships between daughters and their mothers have been the focal point of many character-driven novels, including Kate Long's *The Bad Mother's Handbook* and Rae Meadows's aptly titled *Mothers and Daughters*.

Reynolds, Jonathan

Wrestling With Gravy: A Life With Food. New York: Random House, 2006. 335pp. ISBN 9781400062744.

This former columnist for the *New York Times Magazine* presents a humorous coming-of-age memoir filled with fond memories of food and family. He recounts his parents' divorce, his mother's depression, and the first time his uncle took him to a fancy hotel restaurant. Despite some of the serious situations, he infuses his stories with humor. Holiday meals are also a source of fond memories and wit, evident in his naming of one chapter on Thanksgiving "Alice Waters Cooks Her Turkey Too Long." Reynolds also recalls the years he spent studying acting and working with Hollywood directors and offers tips for seducing a woman with cooking.

Subjects: Coming-of-Age, Family Relationships, Humor, Men's Lives, Recipes

Now Try: *Toast* by Nigel Slater is another coming-of-age memoir about a man with fond memories of food. Frank Bruni's *Born Round: A Story of Family, Food, and a Ferocious Appetite* recalls his childhood, relationship with his family, and his obsession with food. Other coming-of-age memoirs in which men recall the difficult relationships with their families might appeal to these readers, such as Tobias Wolff's *This Boy's Life* or Bernard Cooper's *The Bill From My Father*.

Roberts, Adam D.

Amateur Gourmet: How to Chop, Shop, and Table Hop Like a Pro. New York: Bantam, 2007. 216pp. ISBN 9780553804973.

Although he was a law student, Roberts found enjoyment in cooking and eating and decided to expand his knowledge. Roberts began a blog to chronicle his adventures in pursuit of becoming a gourmet which has culminated in this humorous and entertaining book. Each chapter reads like a brief essay and encourages readers that they can cook like a gourmet even if they aren't a trained chef. Roberts describes the simplicity and joy in preparing pasta, goes out to eat with restaurant critic Ruth Reichl, goes grocery shopping with food writer Amanda Hesser, takes knife lessons from a chef, and visits an upscale French restaurant by himself. Roberts's enthusiastic and witty voice makes this an engaging, quick read.

> **Subjects:** Blogs, Essays, Hesser, Amanda, Men's Lives, Quick Reads, Recipes, Reichl, Ruth, Restaurants

> **Now Try:** Roberts continues to write about his adventures in food on his blog, www.amateurgourmet.com. Julie Powell's *Julie & Julia* and Cathy Erway's *The Art of Eating In* both began as blogs and might appeal for their similar styles. Readers may also enjoy other titles of essays such as Laurie Colwin's *Home Cooking*, Simon Hopkinson's *Roast Chicken and Other Stories*, or John Thorne's *Outlaw Cook*.

Rossant, Colette

The World in My Kitchen: The Adventures of a (Mostly) French Woman in New York. New York: Atria Books, 2006. 227pp. ISBN 9780743490283.

Rossant has published a number of cookbooks, starred in a PBS television cooking series for children, and written for a number of publications, including the "Underground Gourmet" for *New York* magazine. In this memoir, she recounts her marriage in 1955 to an American architect and her move from France to the United States. As she adapted to life in America, she was also introduced to new foods. Some, such as bagels, she loved. Others, like American vegetables, she felt could use some improvement. As she began to cook and experiment with American ingredients, this led to her career as a cookbook writer and friendships with famous culinary figures.

> **Subjects:** Cookbooks, France, Immigrants, Marriage, New York City, Recipes

> **Now Try:** Rossant has written two earlier memoirs. In *Apricots on the Nile: A Memoir with Recipes* she recalls her childhood in Egypt during World War II. In *Return to Paris: A Memoir*, she continues with her return to Paris from Egypt as a teenager to live with her grandmother. Marcella Hazan came to America after she was married and slowly fell into a career of cooking, teaching, and writing, which she recalls in *Amarcord: Marcella Remembers*.

Schenone, Laura

The Lost Ravioli Recipes of Hoboken: A Search for Food and Family. New York: W. W. Norton & Co., 2008. 331pp. ISBN 9780393061468.

While writing her James Beard award-winning book *A Thousand Years Over a Hot Stove*, Schenone spent a lot of time researching the history of women and cooking. Wanting to create a connection to her own ancestors, Schenone wanted to find, and perfect, her own authentic family recipe. Her father remembers eating his grandmother's homemade raviolis as a child, so Schenone settled on his side of the family, which hailed from Genoa. Setting out to learn to make the ravioli, she reconnects with lost family members and travels to Genoa to meet distant relations and learn her family's history. She also discovers that over time, the ravioli recipe had become Americanized, so attempts to find the authentic recipe. Schenone travels to Italy several times, getting to know her distant relations and receiving lessons in proper ravioli-making techniques. Along the way, cooking provides a way to bond with her family and resolve old family issues.

Subjects: Family Relationships, Italy, Recipes, Travel

Now Try: *Cooking With Italian Grandmothers: Recipes and Stories from Tuscany to Sicily* by Jessica Theroux is filled with traditional Italian recipes and personal stories. David Gentilcore's *Pomodoro!: A History of the Tomato in Italy* provides a history of Italian cuisine. Readers may enjoy other memoirs about an author's quest to learn to cook the foods of his or her ancestors. Cheryl Lu-Lien Tan returned to Singapore to learn to create the traditional foods of her family in *A Tiger in the Kitchen: A Memoir of Food and Family*. In *Serve the People: A Stir-Fried Journey Through China* by Jen Lin-Liu, the American-born author moves to China to attend cooking school. Linda Murray Berzok presents a collection of essays and recipes from multicultural families in *Storied Dishes: What Our Family Recipes Tell Us About Who We Are and Where We've Been*. Readers may also enjoy Ann Mah's *Kitchen Chinese: A Novel About Food, Family, and Finding Yourself*. Schenone's other book *A Thousand Years Over a Hot Stove*, is a detailed, fascinating history of women's roles in cooking.

Silver, Charlotte

Charlotte au Chocolate: Memories of a Restaurant Girlhood. New York: Riverhead Books, 2012. 258pp. ISBN 9781594488153.

The Hasty Pudding Club, founded in 1770, is the oldest student society at Harvard. In 1982, the club was having financial problems and agreed to rent the upstairs of its building to Silver's parents, who opened the restaurant Upstairs at the Pudding. Silver, who was born right as the restaurant opened, grew up surrounded by the wealthy clients and the hectic pace of the kitchen. Her father, the chef, managed the back of the house, while her mother prepared the desserts and delighted in schmoozing with the guests. Silver's mother dressed her in party dresses and instilled in her the importance of proper manners. After several years, her father tired of working in the restaurant and left his family, leaving her mother to run the restaurant by herself. With her mother constantly engaged at the restaurant, Silver knew her only option for a good meal would be at the restaurant. Despite the restaurant's precarious financial situation, her mother managed to keep the restaurant going for a number of years until its doors finally closed.

Subjects: Childhood, Family Relationships, Restaurants

Now Try: Patricia Volk's *Stuffed: Adventures of a Restaurant Family* is another memoir in which food and the family restaurant are a big part of the author's life. Ruth Reichl recounts her mother's tenuous relationship with food in

Tender at the Bone: Growing up at the Table. Readers who enjoy Silver's literary writing style may also enjoy Gabrielle Hamilton's memoir *Blood, Bones and Butter*. Other childhood memoirs that might be of interest are Annie Dillard's *An American Childhood*, Donald Davis's Tales from a *Free-Range Childhood*, Jeannette Walls's *The Glass Castle* or Frank McCourt's *Angela's Ashes*.

Simmons, Gail

Talking With My Mouth Full: My Life as a Professional Eater. New York: Hyperion, 2012. 270pp. ISBN 9781401324506.

Top Chef judge, food writer and project director at *Food & Wine* magazine, Simmons covers the steps in her life that led her to her dream career. Growing up in Canada, Simmons had a fairly normal childhood. Her mother was a gifted cook and taught cooking classes out of their home. Although not much of a cook, her father had a few specialties that he was known for: pickles and applesauce. After college, Simmons was adrift, uncertain of what to do with her life. When a friend suggested she write down the things she enjoyed most, her answer was: eat, write, travel, cook. Using this as her guide, she began writing some small food pieces for a local newspaper. After deciding to attend culinary school, she worked in some prestigious New York City restaurants and as an assistant to *Vogue* food writer Jeffrey Steingarten, until she landed a job at *Food & Wine* magazine, and later became a judge for the television series *Top Chef*. Simmons's upbeat, conversational tone make this a quick and entertaining read.

> **Subjects:** Boulud, Daniel, Chefs, Family Relationships, *Food & Wine*, Food Writers, New York City, Recipes, Steingarten, Jeffrey, *Top Chef*

> **Now Try:** NPR commentator Bonny Wolf has a narrative cookbook by the same title, which covers regional foods in America. Jenna Weber also left college uncertain of her future, and after following her true passions, ended up attending culinary school and writing her memoir, *White Jacket Required: A Culinary Coming-of-Age Story*. Readers may enjoy other memoirs with a similar conversational, upbeat tone such as Guilia Melucci's *I Loved, I Lost, I Made Spaghetti* or Amanda Hesser's *Cooking for Mr. Latte*. Readers may also want to check out one of the *Top Chef* cookbooks, such as *How to Cook like a Top Chef*.

Slater, Nigel

Toast: The Story of a Boy's Hunger. New York: Gotham, 2004. 238pp. ISBN 9781592400904.

British food columnist and cookbook author, Slater recounts the foods he associates with important memories, people, and events from his childhood. Slater was very close to his mother, who was not a very good cook. But her early death during his youth prompted him to remember the foods she prepared for him as comfort foods. His father, who was distant and often physically abusive, seldom prepared proper meals for Slater and he relished the various candies he was given. His father's remarriage to an unpleasant woman, Slater's discovery of the pleasures of cooking, his early start working, and his father's death are all recounted amongst favorite foods.

Subjects: Childhood, Coming-of-Age, Family Relationships, Loss of a Parent, Slater, Nigel

Now Try: Slater has a number of other books that may be of interest. In *Eating for England*, Slater explores British foods. In *The Kitchen Diaries: A Year in the Kitchen With Nigel Slater*, the author chronicles his meals for an entire year and includes recipes. Ruth Reichl's memoir *Tender at the Bone: Growing Up At the Table* is another coming-of-age memoir focused around food. Frank Bruni's *Born Round: A Story of Family, Food, and a Ferocious Appetite* recalls his childhood, relationship with his family, and his obsession with food. *Fair Shares For All: A Memoir of Family and Food* by John Haney recounts his childhood in England and the quintessential British foods of his childhood. Readers may also want to consider other coming-of-age memoirs in which men recall the difficult relationships with their families such as Tobias Wolff's *This Boy's Life* or Bernard Cooper's *The Bill From My Father*; a slightly more upbeat British coming-of-age memoir is Michael Frayn's *My Father's Fortune: A Life*.

Tan, Cheryl Lu-Lien

A Tiger in the Kitchen: A Memoir of Food and Family. New York: Hyperion, 2011. 296pp. ISBN 9781401341282.

Tan was born in Singapore, but immigrated to the United States at the age of 18. In her 30s, living and working in New York City, Tan realized that she had become westernized. She had fully adapted to western cuisine and didn't know how to prepare any of her native dishes. Tan returns to Singapore with the intention of learning to create traditional Singaporean dishes in order to connect with her family and her heritage. She recalls her fondest memories of childhood, which include special family meals and her grandmother's cooking. While in Singapore, Tan reconnects with her family and learns much of her family's history. Her touching family story and exotic recipes create an engaging and enjoyable memoir.

Subjects: Family Relationships, Multicultural Issues, Recipes, Singapore

Now Try: Readers may enjoy *Cradle of Flavor: Home Cooking from the Spice Islands of Indonesia, Singapore, and Malaysia* by James Oseland which provides anecdotes of the author's travels and explanations of ingredients, techniques, and eating traditions. Jen Lin-Liu's *Serve the People: A Stir-Fried Journey Through China* is a memoir of a Chinese American who returns to her homeland to rediscover the foods of her ancestors. Diana Abu-Jaber describes the influence of two cultures in her life; her Arab and American families, in *The Language of Baklava*. In *Tastes Like Cuba: An Exile's Hunger for Home*, Eduardo Machado reminisces about the foods of his home country. In *Daughter of Heaven: A Memoir With Earthly Recipes*, Chinese American Leslie Li connects with her heritage through traditional Chinese cuisine.

Fiction readers may also enjoy Ann Mah's *Kitchen Chinese: A Novel About Food, Family, and Finding Yourself.*

Villas, James

Between Bites: Memoirs of a Hungry Hedonist. New York: J. Wiley, 2002. 296pp. ISBN 9780471214205.

A food writer and editor for over 40 years, Villas chronicles his escapades in food in this engaging and humorous memoir. Villas begins with his discovery of the delights of French food when he unknowingly stumbles into one of the most famous restaurants in France. After returning to America, his increasing love for food inspired him to leave his teaching career and begin writing about food. Villas recalls his career writing for *Town & Country, Gourmet,* and *Esquire,* attending cooking school in France, and working undercover as a waiter in an upscale restaurant. He also remembers his friendships with Craig Claiborne, James Beard, and Paul Bocuse, and his embarrassment of getting sick from oysters during his first interview with M.F.K. Fisher.

> **Subjects:** Beard, James, Claiborne, Craig, Fisher, M.F.K., Food Writers, Humor, Investigative Stories, Travel, Villas, James
>
> **Now Try:** Readers may want to consider checking out one of Villas's cookbooks, such as *The Glory of Southern Cooking* or *Pig: King of the Southern Table.* British wine writer Hugh Johnson recounts his career and travels in *Wine: A Life Uncorked.* Food writer Jeannette Ferray recalls her career and acquaintance with culinary greats such as Alice Waters and M.F.K. Fisher in *Out of the Kitchen.* The writings of M.F.K. Fisher are also a good suggestion for readers who enjoy Villas; *The Measure of Her Powers* is a selection of Fisher's writings throughout her career. Other Investigative works in which men throw themselves into their subjects include David Grann's *The Lost City of Z* and Richard Preston's *The Wild Trees: A Story of Passion and Daring.*

Volk, Patricia

Stuffed: Adventures of a Restaurant Family. New York: Alfred A. Knopf, 2001. 242pp. ISBN 9780375411069.

In this witty and entertaining memoir, Volk describes her family as "feeding people." From her great-grandfather who invented pastrami to her grandfather who owned several restaurants, her family has always had a connection with food. Each chapter is devoted to a particular family member, with memorable, unique, quirky relatives, their stories and the life of the Jewish immigrant in New York. Volk's descriptions are vivid and her stories humorous and memorable.

> **Subjects:** Family Relationships, Humor, Judaism, New York City, Quick Reads, Recipes
>
> **Now Try:** Readers who enjoyed Volk's unique and quirky relatives will also enjoy Frank Bruni's stories of his relatives and their love of food in *Born Round: A Story of Family, Food, and a Voracious Appetite.* Ruth Reichl's *Tender at the Bone: Growing Up At the Table* is a humorous memoir of the author's relationship with her mother and food. Charlotte Silver's *Charlotte Au Chocolat: Memories of a Restaurant Girlhood* is another

memoir by someone who grew up in the family restaurant. Readers may also want to consider some of the Expatriate stories in the Travel section for the unique and quirky locals, such as *The Reluctant Tuscan: How I Discovered My Inner Italian* by Phil Doran or Peter Mayle's *A Year in Provence*. Other humorous memoirs about family may also be of interest, such as David Sedaris's *Dress Your Family in Corduroy and Denim*. Volk has also written a fiction novel, *To My Dearest Friends*.

Wizenberg, Molly

A Homemade Life: Stories and Recipes From My Kitchen Table. New York: Simon & Schuster, 2009. 320pp. ISBN 9781416551058.

> The author of the popular food blog "Orangette" pens a narrative of her family life and a remembrance of her father. Her parents enjoyed cooking and homemade meals and passed that love on to the author. Many of the author's memories of her family, and especially of her father, involve food, and she reminisces on their relationship and some of his favorite recipes. After her father's death, Wizenberg turns to cooking for comfort and soon begins blogging. After she begins communicating with one of her readers, the two begin a relationship, which eventually leads to marriage.
>
> **Subjects:** Blogs, Family Relationships, Loss of a Parent, Marriage, Recipes, Women's Nonfiction
>
> **Now Try:** Readers may want to check out Wizenberg's award-winning blog Orangette (orangette.blogspot.com). Readers may also be interested in titles by other authors who began by blogging, such as Julie Powell's *Julie & Julia*, Cathy Erway's *The Art of Eating In*, or Adam D. Roberts's *The Amateur Gourmet*. Elizabeth Bard's *Lunch In Paris: A Love Story With Recipes*, she recounts how she fell in love and married a Frenchman and also turned to cooking after the death of a loved one. Matt McAllester recalls how he began cooking his mother's recipes after her death to deal with his grief in *Bittersweet: Lessons From My Mother's Kitchen*. Other narratives that include stories of grieving are Roger Rosenblatt's *Making Toast* and Calvin Trillin's *About Alice*.

Comfort Food

A recurrent topic of memoirs is overcoming adversity. Sarah Statz Cords also refers to these as "personal triumph" or "recovery" stories (Cords 2006). Both Cords and Rosalind Reisner include memoirs about overcoming adversity in their readers' advisory guides. These stories describe the personal hardships the author endured and the struggles she overcame. The author usually exhibits some form of growth that evolves from her struggles and overcomes her situation. Cords points out that these stories are often harsh, graphic, dark in tone, and can be overwhelming in subject matter and level of detail. In both

Cords's and Reisner's guides, these stories are often about drug use, illnesses, disabilities, abuse, crime, or danger.

Overcoming adversity is also a common theme in Food Memoirs; however, these titles tend not to be as harsh or as dark as those included in Cords's and Reisner's guides. The titles in this subgenre do include stories of hardship such as illnesses, disabilities, or death; however, their overall style and tones tend to be gentler and less graphic than Overcoming Adversity memoirs. The authors of these titles coped with their struggles by turning to food or cooking for comfort, which lends a lighter tone to the stories. In order to indicate the lighter tone of these titles, this subgenre will be referred to as Comfort Food rather than overcoming adversity, as it has been used in other guides.

Comfort Food titles are appealing because readers can often identify with the challenges faced by the author. Readers may have experienced similar obstacles, and reading about another's experiences can be cathartic or inspiring. Readers who have not faced such obstacles can also find these titles inspiring. Because the subject matter can be more personal, readers may also find that Comfort Food titles have a more intimate voice. Readers who enjoy these titles may also want to consider the traditional Overcoming Adversity memoirs.

Comfort Food Memoirs are stories in which the authors struggle with hardships such illness, disabilities, or death, and turn to food or cooking for comfort. These tend to be gentle titles with an intimate voice.

Colon, Suzan

Cherries in Winter: My Family's Recipe for Hope in Hard Times. New York: Doubleday, 2009. 202pp. ISBN 9780385532525.

When Colon is laid off from her job, she must look for ways to cut back on spending, and decides that she will save money by cooking at home more often. She pulls out her grandmother's recipe file and begins to use the recipes her grandmother used during the Great Depression. Colon moves back and forth between her own story and the difficulties she faces living in the current depression, to that of her grandmother's life and experiences. Although her grandmother has already passed away, using her grandmother's recipes gives her a feeling of connection to her grandmother. She includes her grandmother's tips for saving money and offers her own tips as well.

Subjects: Family Relationships, Finance, Gentle Reads, Quick Reads, Recipes

Now Try: Robin Mather learns to eat well within a budget in *The Feast Nearby*. In *Bittersweet: Lessons From My Mother's Kitchen*, Matt McAllester turns to his mother's recipes after her death to connect with her and deal with his grief. In *The Lost Ravioli Recipes of Hoboken*, Laura Schenone connects with long-lost family members to find a traditional family recipe in order to connect with her heritage. *At My Grandmother's Knee: Recipes and Memories Handed Down By Women of the South* by Faye Porter is a collection of southern recipes interspersed with brief, touching memories of the grandmothers who made them. Novelist Adriana Trigiani remembers her grandmothers in *Don't Sing at the Table: Life Lessons From My Grandmothers*. Other titles for women on saving money may also be appealing; try *The Frugalista Files* by Natalie McNeal or *A Purse of Your Own* by Deborah Owens. Novels in which characters have strong connections to their parents or grandparents might also appeal, such as Jo Ann Mapson's *The Owl and Moon Café* or Cathy Lamb's *Henry's Sisters*.

Deen, Paula

It Ain't All About the Cookin. New York: Simon & Schuster, 2007. 287pp. ISBN 9780743292856.

Most people recognize Paula Deen as the sassy, cheerful Southern Food Network celebrity. In her memoir, Deen's sassy personality comes across on every page, but she also candidly remembers her Southern upbringing and family, her grief over her parents' deaths, and shares the intimate details of her troubled first marriage and struggles with panic attacks and agoraphobia. She tells of the difficulties she faced starting her own catering company and her rise to successful restaurant owner, cookbook author, and celebrity. Deen's intense devotion and love for her family comes through, as well as her drive to persevere. Readers will find Deen's writing very casual, with incorrect grammar and a strong southern twang; but her honest, and sometimes bawdy, language adds flavor and humor.

> **Subjects:** American South, Agoraphobia, Deen, Paula, Family Relationships, Humor, Marriage, Recipes

> **Now Try:** Readers may be interested in one of Deen's numerous cookbooks. Try *The Lady & Sons Savannah Country Cookbook*. Deen's sons have also published their own cookbooks. Start with *The Deen Bros. Cookbook* by Jamie Deen. Deen finally found happiness in her second marriage to Michael Groover; readers may be interested in his memoir, *My Delicious Life with Paula Deen*. Sandra Lee, another popular Food Network celebrity describes her struggles for success in *Made From Scratch: A Memoir*. Readers may enjoy other memoirs by Southerners, such as Rick Bragg's *All Over But the Shoutin*, Janisse Ray's *Ecology of a Cracker Childhood*, or Jill Connor Browne's *Sweet Potato Queens' Book of Love*. Women's fiction set in the South may also be appealing, such as Rebecca Wells's *Divine Secrets of the Ya-Ya Sisterhood*, Fannie Flagg's *Fried Green Tomatoes*, or Sarah Addison Allen's *The Sugar Queen*. Martha Hall Foose's *Screen Doors and Sweet Tea* is a charming narrative cookbook about the south.

Kane, Adrienne

Cooking and Screaming: Finding My Own Recipe for Recovery. New York: Simon Spotlight Entertainment, 2008. 272pp. ISBN 9781416587972.

Shortly before she was due to graduate college, Kane suffered a stroke that left her paralyzed and barely able to speak. She had to relearn basic tasks, such as walking and eating. To help with her rehab, Kane turned to cooking. Food became her pastime: something that challenged her but also gave her pleasure. Through the basics of learning to chop and stir, Kane strengthened her body and found comfort. In this humorous and touching memoir, Kane recounts her struggle to recover, as well as the support she received from her family and her budding relationship.

> **Subjects:** Health Issues, Quick Reads, Recipes, Recovery/Rehabilitation, Relationships
>
> **Now Try:** In *Keeping the Feast: One Couple's Story of Love, Food, and Healing*, Paula Butturini describes how she and her husband turned to their shared love of food to heal the mental and physical injuries from a shooting. Food critic Cecily Ross recounts her husband's heart attack and how they had to change their eating habits in *Love in the Time of Cholesterol*. Grant Achatz's memoir *Life On the Line: A Chef's Story of Chasing Greatness, Facing Death, and Redefining the Way We Eat* is an amazing memoir of his battle with tongue cancer while becoming a leading chef. Molly Bimbaum recounts her dreams to be a chef until an accident left her without her sense of smell in *Season to Taste: How I Lost My Sense of Smell and Found My Way*. Jon Reiner, an award-winning food writer, recounts how his battle with Crohn's disease left him unable to eat in *The Man Who Couldn't Eat*. Elisabeth Tova Bailey's *The Sound of a Wild Snail Eating* is also a memoir by a woman learning to deal with serious health issues by taking joy in simple pleasures. Sarah Manguso's *The Two Kinds of Decay* is another memoir about a young woman facing serious health issues. Suzy Becker's *I Had Brain Surgery, What's Your Excuse?* is a touching story about the author's recovery from brain surgery.

Lee, Sandra

Made From Scratch: A Memoir. Des Moines: Meredith Books, 2007. 271pp. ISBN 9780696239199.

On TV, Sandra Lee exudes style, professionalism and success. But this popular Food Network personality and cookbook author overcame many obstacles to achieve her success. In this candid memoir, Sandra Lee recounts the challenges she has faced throughout her life. Her abusive and neglectful mother forced Lee to leave home at an early age. Bouncing from home to home, Lee moved around a lot. She eventually started her own company, which became a huge success, only to lose everything and have to start over. This quick read shows Lee's tenacity and determination to overcome the challenges in her life, as well as the strong love she has for her family.

> **Subjects:** Abuse, Family Relationships, Lee, Sandra, Quick Reads, Women's Nonfiction
>
> **Now Try:** Lee has made a name for herself with her Semi-Homemade line of cookbooks. Try *Sandra Lee Semi-Homemade Cooking*. Paula Deen's *It Ain't All About the Cookin'* is another memoir from a Food Network celebrity that overcame challenges to find success. Readers may enjoy other memoirs from women about overcoming adversity, such as Kelly Corrigan's *The Middle Place*, Laura Flynn's *Swallow the Ocean*, or *The Girl's*

Guide to Homelessness by Brianna Karp. Novels featuring strong women characters that might appeal to these readers include Jennifer Weiner's *Then Came You*, Deborah Rodriguez's *Cup of Friendship*, or Ann Hood's *The Red Thread*.

McAllester, Matt

Bittersweet: Lessons From My Mother's Kitchen. New York: The Dial Press, 2009. 214pp. ISBN 9780385342186.

McAllester, a Pulitzer Prize winning journalist, finds himself overcome with grief when his mother passes away unexpectedly. In this touching memoir, McAllester recalls the loving mother of his childhood, but when his mother began to descend into mental illness and alcoholism, their relationship struggled, and at times was nonexistent. After her death, McAllester requests his mother's medical records and truly sees the depths of her illness. McAllester turns to his mother's collection of cookbooks and begins cooking her recipes in order to connect with her and work through his grief. When he is stressed or trying to overcome his sorrow, McAllester turns to the kitchen, heeding his mother's advice to read Elizabeth David. Creating cassoulets, omelets, and strawberry ice cream, he recreates the positive memories he shared with his mother.

> **Subjects:** Family Relationships, Loss of a Parent, Mental Illness, Mothers and Sons, Recipes

> **Now Try:** Diane Tye pieces together her mother's life through her recipe collection in *Baking as Biography*. In *Life, Death & Bialys: A Father/Son Baking Story*, Dylan Schaffer recalls his attempts to come to terms with his father before his death by spending a week together at the French Culinary Institute. In *Toast: The Story of a Boy's Hunger*, Nigel Slater recalls his mother's early death and his solace in food. Other nonfiction titles about mothers and sons may be appealing, such as Tobias Wolff's *This Boy's Life* or Rick Bragg's *All Over But the Shoutin'*. Fiction titles about mothers and sons may also be suggested, such as Greg Ames's *Buffalo Lockjaw* or David Lipsky's *The Art Fair*.

Moore, Judith

Fat Girl: A True Story. New York: Hudson Street Press, 2005. 196pp. ISBN 9781594630095.

As Moore says, "This is a story about an unhappy fat girl who became a fat woman who was happy and unhappy." In this frank, candid memoir, Moore recalls her childhood, which was marked by physical and sexual abuse, bullying, and obesity. Trying to escape the pain and unhappiness of her childhood, Moore found solace and comfort in food. Her obsessions over food led to obesity and feelings of self-loathing. As an adult, she continued to struggle with her weight, relationships, and sense of belonging.

Subjects: Abuse, Dieting, Obesity, Women's Nonfiction

Now Try: Moore has also written *Never Eat Your Heart Out*, in which she recalls the foods that are linked with her childhood memories. Frank Bruni shares his obsession with food and struggles with weight growing up in *Born Round: The Secret History of a Full-Time Eater*. In *Moose: A Memoir of Fat Camp* by Stephanie Klein, the author recounts her struggles with weight and self-acceptance. Betsy Lerner describes her lifetime struggle with an eating disorder in *Food and Loathing: A Lament*.

Nguyen, Bich Minh

Stealing Buddha's Dinner: A Memoir. New York: Viking, 2007. 256pp. ISBN 9780670038329.

In this vivid coming-of-age memoir, which won a PEN/Jerard award, Nguyen recounts her family's decision to leave Vietnam in 1975, and settle in Grand Rapids, Michigan. Nguyen aptly conveys her feelings as an outsider as she remembers being pulled between her family's traditions and her desire to fit in with her friends and classmates. Her conflicts specifically relate to food, as she loves her family's traditional food, but also wants to fit in by eating the typical American junk foods that the rest of her friends eat. Her story is peppered with 1980s pop culture references and provides an engaging account of the immigrant experience.

Subjects: Coming-of-Age, Immigration, Multicultural Issues, Vietnam

Now Try: Nguyen has also written a fiction novel, *Short Girls*, about two estranged Vietnamese sisters. Other nonfiction food titles about the author's conflict between family traditions and a desire to fit into American life are Diana Abu-Jaber's *The Language of Baklava* and Linda Furiya's *Bento Box in the Heartland: My Japanese Girlhood in White Bread America*. In the travel memoir *Catfish and Mandala*, author Andrew Pham also investigates his Vietnamese family's history. The ALA-Notable novel *Midnight at the Dragon Café* by Judy Fong Bates is a novel about immigration and food; Jean Kwok's *Girl in Translation* also examines the cultural difficulties faced by children of immigrants.

Schaffer, Dylan

Life, Death & Bialys: A Father/Son Baking Story. New York: Bloomsbury, 2006. 264pp. ISBN 9781596911925.

Schaffer's father left his family when Schaffer was only five years old, leaving him with a mother who suffered from mental illness. As a result, Schaffer's relationship with his father was strained. But when his father develops terminal lung cancer and asks Schaffer to spend a week in New York City taking a bread baking class at the French Culinary Institute with him, Schaffer reluctantly agrees. During their time in New York, Schaffer attempts to come to terms with his father, asking the questions he needs answered. Schaffer's father can be both obnoxious and charismatic, which makes him a very entertaining character.

Schaffer recounts their experiences learning to bake bread, along with the classmates and teachers they meet.

> **Subjects:** Baking, Family Relationships, Fathers and Sons, Loss of a Parent, New York City, Quick Reads

> **Now Try:** Although Kathryn Borel's father is not suffering from an illness, they suffer from a strained relationship and his difficult personality makes their trip through France together a challenge. Readers may enjoy her memoir, *Corked: A Memoir*. Other memoirs of complicated father–son relationships may be appealing, such as Andre Dubus's *Townie*, Bernard Cooper's *The Bill From My Father*, Nick Flynn's *Another Bullshit Night in Suck City*, or Rick Bragg's *The Prince of Frogtown*. A novel with a complex father–son relationship at its heart is Jonathan Tropper's *The Book of Joe*.

Severson, Kim

Spoon Fed: How Eight Cooks Saved My Life. New York: Riverhead, 2010. 242pp. ISBN 9781594487576.

> In this frank and touching memoir, Severson, a food writer, pays tribute to the women who not only taught her to cook, but served as a source of inspiration and strength during difficult moments of her life. Severson battled alcoholism and struggled with accepting her own homosexuality. Without knowing it, Marion Cunningham, Alice Waters, Leah Chase, Edna Lewis, Ruth Reichl, Rachel Ray, and Marcella Hazan taught Severson life lessons when she most needed them. With the constant comfort of the kitchen and the inspirational figures in her life, Severson was able to achieve sobriety, mature, and start a family of her own.

> **Subjects:** Alcoholism, Coming-of-Age, Family Relationships, Hazan, Marcella, Homosexuality, Inspirational, Quick Reads, Ray, Rachel, Reichl, Ruth, Waters, Alice

> **Now Try:** Readers may be interested in titles by, or about the women who influenced Severson. Try Ruth Reichl's *Comfort Me With Apples*, Marcella Hazan's *Amarcord*, or *Alice Waters and Chez Panisse* by Thomas McNamee. In *A Year by the Sea*, Joan Anderson recalls how she found peace by moving to a cottage by the sea and connecting with nature. *The Women Who Raised Me* is Victoria Rowell's story of her childhood in foster care with a variety of strong, loving women who served as role models and mentors.

Sunee, Kim

Trail of Crumbs: Hunger, Love, and the Search for Home. New York: Grand Central Publishing, 2008. 374pp. ISBN 9780446579766.

> Abandoned at age three in South Korea, Sunee was adopted by an American couple and raised in New Orleans in a community where she was

one of only two Asians. Constantly feeling lost and searching for a home, she moves to Europe in her 20s and begins an affair with a wealthy French business-man. Although she lives a lavish life, she is frequently lonely and finds solace in cooking elaborate gourmet meals. Her sensuous descriptions and mouthwater-ing recipes bring together her Korean heritage, New Orleans upbringing, and her life in France.

Subjects: Coming-of-Age, France, Identity, Multicultural Issues, Recipes, Relationships

Now Try: *Bento Box in the Heartland: My Japanese Girlhood in Whitebread America* by Linda Furiya and *Stealing Buddha's Dinner: A Memoir* by Bich Minh Nguyen are both coming-of-age memoirs about the authors' attempts to balance their heritage with their American lives. Other coming-of-age memoirs that may be appealing are Elena Gorokhova's *A Mountain of Crumbs* and Marie Arana's *American Chica*. Anne Tyler's fiction novel, *Digging to America*, is a story of two Korean daughters adopted into American families.

Consider Starting With . . .

The following titles are considered benchmarks of Food Memoirs and represent the Working Life, Personal Endeavors, and Foodie subgenres. Readers new to the genre may want to start with one of these titles.

Bourdain, Anthony. *Kitchen Confidential: Adventures in the Culinary Underbelly.*

Child, Julia. *My Life in France.*

Powell, Julie. *Julie and Julia: 365 Days, 524 Recipes, 1 Tiny Apartment Kitchen.*

Reichl, Ruth. *Tender at the Bone.*

References

Cords, Sarah Statz. 2006. *The Real Story: A Guide to Nonfiction Reading Interests.* Westport, CT: Libraries Unlimited.

DeWitt, Dave. 2010. *Founding Foodies: How Washington, Jefferson, and Franklin Revo-lutionized American Cuisine.* Naperville: Sourcebooks.

Minzesheimer, Bob. 2008. "Everybody Has a Story to Tell, So Memoirs Sell." *USA Today* (February 27).

Muhlke, Christine. 2009. "Heartburn: Food Memoirs With Recipes." *New York Times* (May 31).

Reisner, Rosalind. 2009. *Read On . . . Life Stories: Reading Lists for Every Taste.* Santa Barbara, CA: ABC-CLIO.

Shapiro, Laura. 1998. "Memories of Meals Past: Sex Still Sells Biographies, but Cookery is Catching Up." *Newsweek* 131 (15): 68.

Vidal, Gore. 1995. *Palimpsest: A Memoir*. New York: Random House.

Waxman, Barbara Frey. 2008. "Food Memoirs: What They Are, Why They Are Popular, and Why They Belong in the Classroom." *College English* 70 (4): 363.

Wyatt, Neal. 2007. *The Readers' Advisory Guide to Nonfiction*. Chicago: American Library Association.

Yabroff, Jennie. 2007. "A Year of Selling Books." *Newsweek* (September 28).

Yagoda, Ben. 2009. *Memoir: A History*. New York: Riverhead Books.

1

2

3

4

5

6

7

8

9

Chapter 2

Food Biographies

Definition of Food Biographies

One of the oldest forms of literary expression, biography is simply defined as the written story of a life; a detailed account of an individual's life written by another person (Liers 2005). Biographies typically cover the subject's life from birth to death, and draw upon all available evidence, including written accounts, correspondences, and interviews. Biographies tend to be lengthier and more formal than memoirs or autobiographies. However, there are some biographies that are shorter and less formal with a chatty (and sometimes even gossipy) tone. These may focus on a particular period of the subject's life, rather than the subject's entire life. Many biographies are written posthumously; increasingly, however, many are written while the subject is still living. Some critics dismiss biographies of living figures as having a lack of data or perspective, but in *Biography: A User's Guide* (Rollyson 2008), Carl Rollyson states that these accounts should not be dismissed because contemporary witnesses can provide a familiarity with the subject that a later biographer may not be able to accomplish.

The earliest forms of biography were the narrative carvings found on Egyptian tombs and temples meant to record the lives of kings, found as early as 1300 BC. The ancient Greeks wrote biographies to profile important philosophers and influential figures. During the Middle Ages, biographies recorded the lives of the saints. During the Renaissance, biographies were written to record the lives of artists and monarchs. Many of these early forms of biography probably bypassed factual evidence in favor of glorification of the subject (Columbia Electronic Encyclopedia 2007). American biography began with Cotton Mather's *Magnalia Christi Americana* in 1702, which was a classic work of Puritan biography extolling the lives of New England's governing officials. It omitted personal details and the subjects' flaws. This was typical of the time—biographies were meant to show the exemplary lives the subjects lived (Rollyson 2008). James Boswell is credited with setting a new standard for biography with his monumental biography of Samuel Johnson in *Life of Johnson* in 1791 (Hamilton 2007). Boswell included letters, diaries, interviews, chronicles of conversations, and detailed the minutiae of Johnson's life, including his dress, eating habits, and activities. This comprehensive biography is considered the first definitive biography and has shaped the modern biography.

Biographies remain as popular as ever. Biographies frequently grace the best-seller lists with subjects ranging from historical figures to political leaders, monarchs, inventors, artists, and celebrities. Televised biographies are also a popular format for biography. Television channels such as A&E, The History Channel, Biography, and even E! frequently air short biographies of historical figures and popular celebrities. Feature films are another popular format for biography, as evident with recent award-winning biopics such as *Capote*, *John Adams*, and *The Aviator*.

In Food Lit, there has not been an abundance of biographies, historically speaking. While written cookbooks can be found from as early as the first century, there are not many details available of the lives of the cooks and chefs who produced them. This may be because cooks were often viewed as servants and society held little esteem for the profession. Chefs began to earn some distinction in the 18th and 19th centuries, as we see in Ian Kelly's biography of Antonin Carême *Cooking for Kings: The Life of Antonin Carême, the First Celebrity Chef*. In addition, until recently, food and cooking were viewed as in the woman's domain. Since biography is historically a male genre, there might not have been much interest in biographies of culinary figures. However, the sexual division of labor is equalizing and cooking is no longer seen as only the woman's responsibility. Men comprise 35 percent of the Food Network's audience, and many popular chefs and TV food personalities are male (Levine 2011). Now that popular interest in cooking and food is increasing with both men and women, there may be increased interest in biographies of culinary figures.

Biographies are a detailed account of an individual's life written by another person. Biographies typically cover the subject's life from birth to death, and draw upon all available evidence, including written accounts, correspondences, and interviews. However, there are some biographies that are shorter and less formal with a chatty (and sometimes even gossipy) tone.

Appeal of Food Biographies

On his Ricklibrarian blog, author Rick Roche explains why people read biographies: to discover fascinating people, to rediscover people we think we know, to reassess infamous characters, to get the story behind the legendary characters, to "get the dirt," to find a hero, and to learn history through the life of an individual (Roche 2009b). All of these reasons point to one common appeal factor: character. Food Biographies have very high character appeal (Wyatt 2007). Readers enjoy reading about other people's lives: their successes and failures, conflicts, and reactions to life's events. They want to know the subject, to get a sense of his or her personality. With the easy accessibility of the Internet and sites such as Wikipedia, basic facts are readily available, but readers enjoy getting the dirt or the inside scoop on their heroes, such as what he or she wore or ate, his or her relationships, etc. Samuel Johnson said that the "petty detail is often the most revealing" (Rollyson 2008). Food Biographies provide the intimate details that readers crave.

Food Biographies also appeal to readers with an interest in history. Details and descriptions can give the reader a sense of the time in which the subject lived, the customs, historical events, and politics of the time. The inclusion of such items as recipes and menus can illustrate period customs. The vivid sense of time and place, the frame of the subject's life, can bring historical events to life for the reader.

Food Biographies offer variety, and readers of all tastes can usually find something in it to like. Subjects and settings vary from figures like the chef who created Napoleon's wedding cake to a forgotten food writer from Kansas. Styles and formats also vary, offering readers the opportunity to choose between a more formal, in-depth book or a shorter, more casual read. Readers who enjoy biography for its character appeal may also enjoy memoirs and autobiographies. Readers who enjoy the historical aspect of biographies may find history titles of interest.

Organization of the Chapter

In *The Real Story*, Sarah Statz Cords organizes her Biography chapter into subsections that include creative figures such as artists, entertainers, and writers; figures who are outstanding in their fields and best known for their careers; figures who were activists and change-makers; and historical figures (Cords 2006). Because there are fewer biographies in the food literature genre, this chapter is not broken down into subsections based on subject. It could be said that all of the figures found in this chapter were creative, outstanding in their fields, and change-makers. All of the single-subject biographies are presented together and a brief subsection for group biographies follows.

Alexander, Kelly, and Harris, Cynthia

Hometown Appetites: The Story of Clementine Paddleford, the Forgotten Food Writer Who Chronicled How America Ate. New York: Gotham, 2008. 318pp. ISBN 9781592403899.

Although her name is not widely known today, from 1936 to 1966, Clementine Paddleford was a food writer for the *New York Herald Tribune* and was one of the best known food writers of the day. This book traces Paddleford's life from her childhood in Kansas, her early interest in reporting and writing, to her education in New York and her ground-breaking career in food writing. Rather than writing typical recipes, Paddleford was one of the first to begin writing engaging articles about food that were intensely researched and filled with vivid descriptions and details. This was a departure from the typical food articles that were printed at the time and quickly gained popularity for Paddleford. She was also the first to define regional American food. Throughout her career she traveled the United States, sampling and reporting on the differences in regional cuisines. In 1960 she published *How America Eats*, which was groundbreaking for the time. This little-known figure is illuminated in this well-researched book.

Subjects: Food Writers, Journalism, Paddleford, Clementine, Recipes, Regional Cuisines, Women's Nonfiction

Now Try: Readers who are able to track down a copy may enjoy reading Paddleford's *How America Eats*. In 2011, Rizzoli press released *The Great American Cookbook* by Clementine Paddleford, which is a culmination of her research on regional American food, revised for today's cook. Mark Kurlansky's *Food of a Younger Land: A Portrait of American Food Before the National Highway System, Before Chain Restaurants, and Before Frozen Food, When the Nation's Food Was Seasonal* and Pat Willard's *America Eats!: On the Road with the WPA—the Fish Fries, Box Supper Socials, and Chitlin Feasts That Define* both feature the Works Progress Administration's project America Eats, which examined regional cuisines. One of the road food books by Jane and Michael Stern, such as *Two for the Road*, may also be of interest. Readers may also enjoy biographies of other ground-breaking female food writers and cooks, such as Noel Riley Fitch's biography of Julia Child, *Appetite for Life*, or Joan Reardon's biography of M.F.K Fisher, *Poet of the Appetites*.

Andrews, Colman

Ferran: The Inside Story of El Bulli and the Man Who Reinvented Food. New York: Gotham, 2010. 301pp. ISBN 9781592405725.

A well-known figure to most foodies, Ferran Adrià is the chef and owner of the famous restaurant El Bulli. Ferran is considered to be one of the best chefs in the world, as well as one of the most influential and revolutionary chefs of this century. El Bulli, which was located in Spain, closed its doors in 2011. The restaurant was awarded three Michelin stars and was considered to be one of the best restaurants in the world. Aside from detailing Ferran's life and career, this book explains why Ferran is such an influential figure in culinary history. The author describes what Ferran has done for the world of avant-garde cuisine (and what that is), and the new techniques he pioneered. The book also explores Catalan cuisine and describes the experience of eating at the mythical El Bulli. Andrews breaks away from the typical biography format to include conversations with the chef and meals Adrià prepared for him.

Subjects: Adrià, Ferran, Chefs, El Bulli, Molecular Gastronomy, Restaurants

Now Try: Ferran Adrià provides an inside view of his famous restaurant in *A Day at El Bulli*. Readers are treated to vivid photographs of the restaurant, and descriptions of the menu. Adrià's *The Family Meal* is his first cookbook meant for the home cook. Lisa Abend follows Adrià and his army of 35 stagiaires as they bring Adriàs vision to life in *The Sorcerer's Apprentices: A Season in the Kitchen at Ferran Adrià's El Bulli*. In *Everything But the Squeal*, John Barlow travels around Spain partaking in the various preparations of the hog. *Spain: A Culinary Road Trip* by Mario Batali and Gwenyth Paltrow, as well as Batali's DVD series *Spain: On the Road Again* might also be of interest. Readers may also enjoy other biographies or memoirs of chefs known for their culinary vision, such as Grant Achatz's *Life, on the Line: A Chef's Story of Chasing Greatness, Facing Death, and Redefining the Way We Eat*, another chef known for his culinary vision. *The Fat Duck Cookbook* by Heston Blumenthal is a compilation of recipes from Blumenthal's famous restaurant, as well as a history of his rise to success. Thomas McNamee details another influential figure in American cuisine in *Alice Waters and Chez Panisse*.

Chelminski, Rudolph

The Perfectionist: Life and Death in Haute Cuisine. New York: Gotham, 2005. 354 pp. ISBN 9781592401079.

Bernard Loiseau was a celebrated French chef, and owner of La Côte d'Or restaurant, which was awarded three Michelin stars. In 2003, Loiseau shocked the culinary world by committing suicide. Chelminski, who knew Loiseau for many years, recounts his life beginning with his decision to become a chef at age 17, his apprenticeship, and his rise to become a three-star chef. He describes the pressure and demands of the job as well as Loiseau's workaholic personality. Chelminski speaks with Loiseau's family, friends, and colleagues about his struggles with bipolar disorder, and explores what drove this talented chef to take his life. Readers will also find a knowledgeable account of modern French cuisine and other important French chefs, as well as a history of the Michelin family and its coveted rating system.

> **Subjects:** Business, Chefs, France, Loiseau, Bernard, Men's Lives, Michelin Guide, Mental Illness, Restaurants, Suicide

> **Now Try:** William Echikson describes Louiseau's hectic campaign to earn three Michelin stars in *Burgundy Stars: A Year in the Life of a Great French Restaurant*. Readers may also enjoy other titles about the pressures of working in an award-winning restaurant, such as Leslie Brenner's *The Fourth Star: Dispatches from Inside Daniel Boulud's Celebrated New York Restaurant* and Lisa Abend's *The Sorcerer's Apprentices: A Season in the Kitchen at Ferran Adrià's El Bulli*. *Ferran: The Inside Story of El Bulli and the Man Who Reinvented Food* by Colman Andrews is another biography of a chef known for his exacting standards. Michael Ruhlman seeks to understand what causes chefs to seek perfection in *The Soul of a Chef: The Journey Toward Perfection*. Readers may also want to consider Chelminski's history of Beaujolais wine, *I'll Drink to That: Beaujolais and the French Peasant Who Made It the World's Most Popular Wine*.

Cooper, Artemis

Writing at the Kitchen Table: The Authorized Biography of Elizabeth David. New York: Ecco Press, 2000. 364pp. ISBN 9780060198282.

Elizabeth David was a popular British food and cookbook writer. While living in France, Italy, and Greece, she developed a love of Mediterranean food and cooking, which she introduced to the English home. She did not favor haute European cuisine, but promoted traditional farmhouse food. She was critical of typical British fare, and encouraged cooks to adopt flavorful ingredients that were uncommon at the time. Although she was a household name, David was very private and not much was known about her. This balanced biography presents a detailed account of David's life, from her privileged upbringing to her world travels, relationships, and her cooking and writing career and offers insight into David's true personality.

Subjects: Cookbooks, David, Elizabeth, Food Writers

Now Try: Elizabeth David wrote a number of cookbooks. Two of her most well-known and well-loved are *Italian Food* and *French Provincial Cooking*. Readers may also enjoy reading her collection of essays and recipes, *An Omelette and a Glass of Wine*. *Finding Betty Crocker: The Secret Life of America's First Lady of Food* by Susan Marks sheds light on another figure whose identity was closely guarded. Elizabeth Lawrence is another woman who captivated readers by writing about her interest in gardening; fans of this title might also consider her biography *No One Gardens Alone: A Life of Elizabeth Lawrence* by Emily Herring Wilson.

D'Antonio, Michael

Hershey: Milton S. Hershey's Extraordinary Life of Wealth, Empire, and Utopian Dreams. New York: Simon and Schuster, 2006. 305pp. ISBN 9780743264099.

This extensively researched biography provides an objective look at the creator of the famous candy. D'Antonio traces Hershey's childhood and his perseverance despite his early failures, and the creation of his company, the first popular and inexpensive chocolate bar in the United States, and the charming town Hershey, Pennsylvania. This is an intimate look at Hershey's unique personality and generosity.

Subjects: American History, Business, Candy Industry, Community Life, Hershey, Milton

Now Try: Both *The Emperors of Chocolate: Inside the Secret World of Hershey and Mars* by Joel Glenn Brenner and *Chocolate Wars: The 150-Year Rivalry Between the World's Greatest Chocolate Makers* by Deborah Cadbury provide in-depth details of some of the greatest names in candy making, as well as their struggles to succeed. Profiles of other businesses and leaders may also be of interest, such as Mark Kurlansky's *Birdseye: The Adventuers of a Curious Man*, a profile of Clarence Birdseye, the man who invented the method for fast-freezing and revolutionized the food industry. Other titles that may be of interest are T. J. Stiles's *The First Tycoon: The Epic Life of Cornelius Vanderbilt*, Ron Chernow's *The House of Morgan: An American Banking Dynasty and the Rise of Modern Finance*, and Hardy Green's *The Company Town: The Industrial Edens and Satanic Mills That Shaped the American Economy*.

Fitch, Noel Riley

Appetite for Life: The Biography of Julia Child. New York: Doubleday, 1997. 569pp. ISBN 9780385483353.

This is a comprehensive and extensive biography of one of the most well-known and well-loved figures in the American culinary field. Julia Child was born in 1912 in California and went on to publish several cookbooks, including *Mastering the Art of French Cooking*, as well as starring in several television cooking series. The book begins with background on Child's grandparents and parents, and details her birth and childhood, education, and travels. Her work with the OSS, marriage to Paul Child, life in France, attendance at the famous Cordon Bleu culinary school, the process of writing and publishing her cookbook, settling down in Cambridge, and her television career are all covered in depth. Excerpts from letters and diaries, as well as numerous sources, make this a complete look at the life of a woman who made French cuisine accessible to Americans and changed the way we cook and eat.

> **Subjects:** Child, Julia, France, French Cuisine, Women's Nonfiction

> **Now Try:** Readers who are interested in Julia Child's life but are daunted by the length of Fitch's biography should try Laura Shapiro's *Julia Child: A Life*. Although shorter in length and less focused on details, this is an entertaining, quick read that provides a good overview of Child's life. Bob Spitz has also written a new biography of Child, *Dearie: The Remarkable Life of Julia Child*. Readers may also enjoy Julia's memoirs *My Life in France* as well as Joan Reardon's collection of Julia Child's letters to Avis DeVoto, *As Always, Julia: The Letters of Julia Child and Avis DeVoto*. Fans of Julia Child's cookbooks may enjoy Julie Powell's memoir *Julie & Julia: 365 Days, 524 Recipes, 1 Tiny Apartment Kitchen: How One Girl Risked Her Marriage, Her Job and Her Sanity to Master the Art of Living*, as well as the movie based on this book. Readers who appreciate the extensive research and detailed biography written by Fitch, may be interested in Fitch's other detailed biography, *Anais: The Erotic Life of Anais Nin*.

Fried, Stephen

Appetite for America: How Visionary Businessman Fred Harvey Built a Railroad Hospitality Empire That Civilized the Wild West. New York: Bantam, 2010. 518pp. ISBN 9780553804379.

This detailed history recounts the life of Fred Harvey, the founding father of the nation's service industry. Born in Britain, Harvey arrived in America just before the Civil War. He began working as a dishwasher in New York City, but eventually moved to the Midwest and became involved in the expanding railroad. Harvey saw an opportunity and created a chain of railway restaurants called the Harvey House. The superior food and high standards of customer service made Harvey's restaurants a huge success. Harvey was also known for his innovative marketing and progressive employment practices. Aside from the comprehensive coverage of Harvey's life, the author also provides a fascinating look at changes occurring in the United States, such as racial tensions and relations with Native Americans.

Subjects: American History, Business, Harvey, Fred, Railroads, Restaurants

Now Try: Readers may enjoy checking out *The Harvey House Cookbook: Memories of Dining Along the Santa Fe Railway* by George H. Foster. *The Harvey Girls: Women Who Opened the West* by Lesley Poling-Kempes includes interviews, historical research, and photos of the women who came to the west to work as Harvey Girls, but many stayed and settled, founding cattle and mining towns. James D. Porterfield's *Dining By Rail: The History and Recipes of America's Golden Age of Railroad Cuisine* illustrates the history of train dining. Larry Tye's *Rising from the Rails: Pullman Porters and the Making of the Black Middle Class* is another interesting history of the railroad and American social history. Readers may also enjoy *The First Tycoon: The Epic Life of Cornelius Vanderbilt* by T. J. Stiles, a biography of another visionary businessman. Stephen Fried has also written on other topics, including an inside look at Conservative Judaism in *The New Rabbi*.

Himelstein, Linda

The King of Vodka: The Story of Pyotr Smirnov and the Upheaval of an Empire. New York: Harper, 2009. 384pp. ISBN 9780060855895.

Vodka has been a fixture of daily life in Russia for centuries. Monks were distilling their own vodka as far back as the 1500s. Easy and cheap to produce, vodka was used for medicinal purposes, as a form of payment, and in a variety of rituals. Pyotr Smirnov was born in a rural Russian village in 1831. A poor, nearly illiterate serf, Pyotr rose to create a successful empire. When he died in 1898, his company was the leading producer of vodka that was favored by Russians and European royalty. His success was not easy however. He faced opposition from temperance societies, supported by Tolstoy and Dostoyevski, rogue and counterfeit distillers, political uprisings, labor strikes, and the creation of a state vodka monopoly. Smirnov left 3 wives and 10 children when he died, whose infighting almost led to the downfall of Smirnov's legacy.

Subjects: Business, Russian History, Smirnov, Pyotr, Spirits, Vodka

Now Try: *Bacardi and the Long Fight For Cuba: The Biography of a Cause* by Tom Gjelten and *The Sugar King of Havana: The Rise and Fall of Julio Lobo, Cuba's Last Tycoon* by John Paul Rathbone are both detailed accounts of figures that became fixtures of a country's history. *The Business of Spirits: How Savvy Marketers, Innovative Distillers, and Entrepreneurs Changed How We Drink* by Noah Rothbaum examines the liquor industry and the large companies that have dominated it. *The Match King: Ivar Kreuger, The Financial Genius Behind a Century of Wall Street Scandals* by Frank Partnoy is another good title that looks at a complex businessperson. Readers interested in Russian history and culture might consider Ian Frazier's *Travels in Siberia*, Rachel Polonsky's *Molotov's Magic Lantern: Travels in Russian History*, or Sharon Hudgins's *The Other Side of Russia: A Slice of Life in Siberia*.

Hughes, Kathryn

The Short Life and Long Times of Mrs. Beeton. New York: Knopf. 2006. 480pp. ISBN 9780307263735.

Isabella Beeton was born in London in 1836. Her husband, Samuel Beeton, was a publisher and editor of the *Englishwoman's Domestic Magazine*. Shortly after their marriage in 1856, Isabella began writing cooking columns for the magazine. In 1861 she published *The Book of Household Management*, which covers an array of household subjects including cooking, child-rearing, and the management of servants. The book became a huge success and went on to become a must have for newly married Victorian women. Although she died at a young age, the book was updated several times and the name "Mrs. Beeton" went on to become a brand in itself. This book provides details of Isabella's and Samuel's families, details of Isabella's childhood, her marriage, and the creation of the book that made Mrs. Beeton a household name. The author's access to the Beeton family archives makes this a well-researched book that will delight readers who enjoy details of Victorian life.

> **Subjects:** Beeton, Isabella, Cookbooks, Family Relationships, Victorian Period, Women's Nonfiction

> **Now Try**: *Mrs. Beeton's Book of Household Management* is still available and while readers may not find these tips particularly useful today, it is still an interesting read. *Inside the Victorian Home: A Portrait of Domestic Life in Victorian England* by Judith Flanders is an entertaining, insightful look at daily Victorian life. Kathryn Hughes's *George Eliot: The Last Victorian* and Linda Lear's *Beatrix Potter: A Life in Nature* are other in-depth accounts of well-known women who lived during the Victorian period. Another woman who references Mrs. Beeton's cookbook is Margaret Powell, in her classic memoir (which served partially as a basis for the popular TV programs *Upstairs Downstairs* and *Downton Abbey*), *Below Stairs*. Although he's not very complimentary about it, Bill Bryson refers to Mrs. Beeton's book frequently in *At Home: A Short History of Private Life*. Becky Diamond recounts the life of Elizabeth Goodfellow, a woman who opened the first cooking school in America, in *Mrs. Goodfellow: The Story of America's First Cooking School*.

James, Kenneth

Escoffier: The King of Chefs. London; New York: Hambledon and London, 2002. 319pp. ISBN 9781852853969.

Auguste Escoffier is one of the most famous chefs in modern history. Born in France in 1846, he became a cook's apprentice at the age of 13.

He rose to become a noted chef, working in well-respected and famous restaurants. In 1884, he accepted a position from Cesar Ritz to run the kitchens of the Grand Hotel in Monte Carlo. Escoffier's influence led to reforms in French cuisine, in both taste and presentation. He also reformed restaurant service, and he and Ritz's partnership led to new standards in modern luxury hotels. This is a detailed look at a very important historical culinary figure. Sample menus are provided throughout the book, helping the reader imagine life at the time, and a glossary is provided at the back which proves helpful.

> **Subjects:** Chefs, Escoffier, Auguste, France, French History, Menus, Restaurants, Ritz, Cesar

> **Now Try:** Readers may enjoy Escoffier's personal memoirs, *Memories of My Life* or his masterpiece, *Le Guide Culinaire*, which contains over five thousand recipes and has been translated into English. Steve Rinella humorously attempts to recreate a 45 course banquet from the recipes found in *Le Guide Culinaire* in *Scavenger's Guide to Haute Cuisine*. Ruth Brandon follows the extraordinary career of the first celebrity chef in 19th-century England in *The People's Chef: The Culinary Revolution of Alexis Soyer*. Ian Kelly details the life of the first celebrity chef in France in *Cooking for Kings: The Life of Antonin Carême, the First Celebrity Chef*. *White Truffles in Winter* by N. M. Kelby is a fictionalized account of Escoffier's life. Other historical fiction set in 19th-century France might also appeal, such as Susan Vreeland's *Luncheon of the Boating Party* or Louis Bayard's *The Black Tower*.

Jones, Evan

Epicurean Delight: The Life and Times of James Beard. New York: Knopf, 1990. 366pp. ISBN 9780394574158.

Julia Child once said, "In the beginning there was Beard." Born in Portland, Oregon in 1903, Beard became a cook and a prolific writer of cookbooks, and is considered the father of American gourmet cooking. Evan Jones, husband of Beard's editor Judith Jones, knew Beard for many years. Jones recounts Beard's early life and the huge influence of his mother, his early love for food, Beard's early desire for a career in opera and theater, and his decision to turn to cooking when his dream did not materialize. He traces Beard's career from his beginning as a caterer to his cooking school and writing career. Jones's personal relationship with Beard provides an intimate perspective that sheds light on this culinary giant.

> **Subjects:** Beard, James, Food Writers, Men's Lives

> **Now Try:** Robert Clark's *James Beard: A Biography* (later retitled *The Solace of Food*) chronicles Beard's life in conjunction with the changes occurring at the time with food and the development of the modern food industry. Clark also explores some of Beard's more personal issues, such as his weight, personality, and homosexuality that are not fully explored in Jones's biography. Beard's own memoirs *Delights and Prejudices* will also appeal to fans wanting to get a better picture of Beard's personality. Beard published a number of cookbooks during his career that may be of interest to readers. Try *Beard on Food, James Beard's Theory and Practice of Good Cooking*, or *James Beard's American Cookery*.

Kelly, Ian

Cooking for Kings: The Life of Antonin Carême, the First Celebrity Chef. New York: Walker & Company, 2003. 310pp. ISBN 9780802714367.

Antonin Carême was born in 1783 in the Paris slums. Abandoned by his father at a young age, he was taken in by a cook and began working as a kitchen apprentice. He went on to work as a pastry-maker, experimenting with sugar and creating spectacular creations. He was noticed by the Duc de Talleyrand, one of Napoleon's counselors, and soon began working as a freelance chef for many of the Paris elite, as well as other royalty throughout the world. Although other chefs had published cookbooks, these were essentially collections of recipes. Carême was the first to publish a book that detailed culinary principles and a culinary system. This detailed history not only sheds light on the life of this famous chef, but also recounts the politics of France during this time period, details the extravagance of the elite, as well as the difficulties in cooking and serving such lavish and elaborate meals. Carême's illustrations and menus are provided.

Subjects: Carême, Antonin, Chefs, Cookbooks, France, French History, Menus

Now Try: Readers interested in the history of French cuisine may want to try *A Revolution in Taste: The Rise of French Cuisine, 1650–1800* by Susan Pinkard. Kathryn Jones's *For the Royal Table: Dining at the Palace* is a behind-the-scenes look at three hundred and fifty years of royal dining in England. *All the King's Cooks: The Tudor Kitchens of King Henry VIII at Hampton Court Palace* by Peter Brears is a fascinating history of the massive royal kitchens. Anne Willan's *The Cookbook Library: Four Centuries of the Cooks, Writers, and Recipes That Made the Modern Cookbook* is an illustrated guide through the history of European and American cuisine. Readers intrigued by the pomp of royalty and Carême's elaborate creations of the time may enjoy the elaborate descriptions of royal life in *Queen of Fashion: What Marie Antoinette Wore to the Revolution* by Caroline Weber. Readers may also want to consider *A Scented Palace: The Secret History of Marie Antoinette's Perfumer* by Elisabeth de Feydeau and Jane Lizop.

Mazzeo, Tilar J.

The Widow Clicquot: The Story of a Champagne Empire and the Woman Who Ruled It. New York: Collins, 2008. 265pp. ISBN 9780061288562.

At the beginning of the 19th century producing champagne was a small-time enterprise. But when Barbe-Nicole Clicquot Ponsardin was widowed at age 27, she transformed her struggling, small-time family wine brokerage into the most important champagne house of the 19th century. With no formal business training, her technical innovations in the cellars allowed for the creation of modestly priced champagne, which made champagne accessible to more people. Barbe-Nicole became one of the wealthiest and most successful entrepreneurs in a time when men dominated this industry. This fascinating, brief history provides a look at the history of champagne, French history and the political unrest of the time, as well as an interesting character, which makes this a highly readable choice.

> **Subjects:** Business, Champagne, French History, Wine, Women's Nonfiction

> **Now Try:** Don Kladstrup provides another fascinating account of French wine in *Champagne: How the World's Most Glamorous Wine Triumphed Over War and Hard Times*. *Women, Work & the Art of Savoir Faire: Business Sense & Sensibility* by Mireille Guiliano is an enjoyable business memoir by the former CEO of Veuve Clicquot. Readers may also enjoy Mazzeo's other title, *The Secret of Chanel No. 5: The Intimate History of the World's Most Famous Perfume*. Fiction readers may enjoy Sarah Kate Lynch's novel *House of Daughters*, which features three half-sisters who inherit their father's fledgling champagne vineyard and set about bringing it back to life as they mend their fragile relationship.

McCoy, Elin

The Emperor of Wine: The Rise of Robert M. Parker, Jr. and the Reign of American Taste. New York: Ecco, 2005. 342pp. ISBN 9780060093686.

Robert Parker is known throughout the world as the most influential and the most controversial wine critic. His 100-point rating scale exerts enormous influence on consumers' wine buying habits and also impacts the way wine is being made and sold. McCoy traces Parker's life from his unfulfilling law career to his introduction to wine, which turned from a hobby into a passionate career. The criteria for judging wines, and ways in which wine critics agree and disagree is also explained. McCoy also discusses the controversies surrounding Parker. Many wine producers and critics argue that Parker has reshaped tastes in wine to suit his own preference, caused prices to soar, and is ruining the tradition of wine.

> **Subject:** Men's Lives, Parker, Robert M., Wine, Wine Critics

> **Now Try:** Alice Feiring makes an argument against Parker's influence and the use of his wine scoring system in *The Battle for Wine and Love: or How I Saved the World from Parkerization*. *Judgment of Paris: California vs. France and the Historic 1976 Paris Tasting That Revolutionized Wine* by George Taber details a blind wine taste-test in which French judges chose unknown California wines to be superior to French wines. Tyler Colman examines the politics behind the wine industry in *Wine Politics: How Governments, Environmentalists, Mobsters, and Critics Influence the Wines We Drink*. Readers may also want to consider titles about major winemakers, such as *The House of Mondavi: The Rise and Fall of an American Wine Dynasty* Julia Flynn Siler.

McNamee, Thomas

Alice Waters and Chez Panisse: The Romantic, Impractical, Often Eccentric, Ultimately Brilliant Making of a Food Revolution. New York: Penguin Press, 2007. 380pp. ISBN 9781594201158.

Alice Waters is a chef and owner of the famous restaurant Chez Panisse. Waters opened Chez Panisse in Berkley, California in 1971 and since then it has become one of the most renowned restaurants in the country. One of the first voices promoting fresh, local, and seasonal eating, Waters is considered to be one of the most influential people in food. This book traces her life and the experiences that inspired her to open her own restaurant, as well as her creation of the Edible Schoolyard program. The early days of the restaurant's existence and its evolution are chronicled, as well as the changes in American farms, processed foods, and chain restaurants.

1

2

> **Subjects:** Business, Chefs, Local Food, Menus, Recipes, Restaurants, Waters, Alice, Women's Nonfiction
>
> **Now Try:** Waters has published a number of cookbooks. Readers may want to consider *The Art of Simple Food. Forty Years of Chez Panisse: The Power of Gathering* by Waters details the history of the restaurant and its rise to success and the creation of the Chez Panisse Foundation, as well as photographs and menus from the restaurant's history. David Kamp traces the changes in American cuisine, as well as Waters's influence, in *The United States of Arugula: How We Became a Gourmet Nation.* Carlo Petrini's *Slow Food: Collected Thoughts on Taste, Tradition, and the Honest Pleasures of Food* explains the principles of the Slow Food movement, of which Waters is a vocal member. Readers may also want to consider *Diet for a Small Planet* by Frances Moore Lappé, an influential title from the 1970s' food movement. The blog Lettuce Eat Kale (lettuceeatkale. com) is written by Sarah Henry, a food writer from Berkeley, California, who shares stories about local food artisans and covers food issues, such as school food, food security, and cultural food trends.

3

4

5

McNamee, Thomas

6

The Man Who Changed the Way We Eat: Craig Claiborne and the American Food Renaissance. New York: Free Press, 2012. 352pp. ISBN 9781439191507.

> In 1957 Craig Claiborne became the first man to hold the position of food editor of the *New York Times*. When his first major article criticized the state of New York City restaurants, the readership was stunned. Articles about restaurants were always polite; criticism of food and restaurants was not done. But Claiborne was determined to teach America about good food, and went on to become one of the most influential voices on American food. McNamee provides an intimate look at Claiborne's life, from his childhood in Mississippi through his distinguished career. Before moving to New York City, Claiborne studied cooking and hospitality at the famous École Hôtelière in Lausanne, Switzerland. Once in New York, Claiborne formed relationships with famous chefs, such as Pierre Franey and Jacques Pépin, enjoyed lavish meals at the best restaurants, hosted extravagant dinners, and traveled around the world. But his private life was often troubled: his strained relationship with his

7

8

9

mother haunted him for years; he ate and drank to excess and to the detriment of his health; he had trouble handling his finances; and in his later years, his erratic personality distanced him from many of his friends. Readers will appreciate McNamee's extensive research and intimate level of detail of Claiborne's life, as well as the coverage of the New York City food scene and other famous names in the food scene.

> **Subjects:** Alcohol Abuse, Chefs, Family Relationships, Food Writers, Franey, Pierre, New York City, Pépin, Jacques, Restaurant Critics

> **Now Try:** Claiborne tells his own story in his memoir *A Feast Made for Laughter.* Readers may also want to consider the memoirs of Claiborne's closest friends, Pierre Franey's, *A Chef's Tale: A Memoir of Food, France, and America,* and Jacques Pépin's *The Apprentice: My Life in the Kitchen.* David Kamp traces the rise in popularity of gourmet food in *The United States of Arugula.* Readers may also appreciate more details on the history of the New York City food scene found in Michael Batterberry's *On the Town in New York: The Landmark History of Eating, Drinking, and Entertainments from the American Revolution to the Food Revolution.* Claiborne published a number of cookbooks; readers may be interested in checking out his most famous work, the *New York Times Cookbook.* McNamee has also written the detailed biography *Alice Waters and Chez Panisse.*

Mendelson, Anne

Stand Facing the Stove: The Story of the Women Who Gave America The Joy of Cooking. New York: Holt, 1996. 474pp. ISBN 9780805029048.

In this thorough and detailed account, Mendelson chronicles the lives of Irma Rombauer and her daughter, Marion Rombauer Becker, and their creation of one of the most popular cookbooks in history, *The Joy of Cooking.* The book begins with Irma Rombauer's young life in St. Louis, her marriage, and family. When Irma's husband committed suicide in 1930, Irma decided to write a cookbook which she self-published. The modest success of the cookbook caught the attention of a publisher, Bobbs-Merrill. Irma signed a contract with the publisher; however, she did not understand that the contract gave the publisher the copyrights of the original version as well as any new editions. Mendelson describes the shocking behavior of the publisher and the legal battles and a strained relationship that were a result. When Rombauer began a revised edition, Marion became a coauthor and added more recipes that featured healthier and fresher ingredients. Mendelson traces the subsequent editions of *The Joy of Cooking,* illustrating the evolution of American cooking and eating habits.

> **Subjects:** Becker, Marion Rombauer, Business, Cookbooks, Publishing, Rombauer, Irma, Women's Nonfiction

> **Now Try:** In 2006, *The Joy of Cooking* celebrated its 75th anniversary with a new, updated edition from Irma Rombauer's grandson, Ethan Becker. Like Julia Child's cookbook, *Mastering the Art of French Cooking,* this is a classic. Readers may also enjoy titles about Julia Child, such as her biography, *Appetite for Life* by Noel Riley Fitch, or *As Always, Julia: The Letters of Julia Child and Avis DeVoto* by Joan Reardon, which showcases

Julia's frustrations with her coauthors. Harry Haff describes the lives and careers of some of America's first influential cooks in *The Founders of American Cuisine*. Mendelson has also written a fascinating micro-history, *Milk: The Surprising Story of Milk through the Ages*.

Reardon, Joan

Poet of the Appetites: The Lives and Loves of M.F.K. Fisher. New York: North Point Press, 2004. 509pp. ISBN 9780865475625.

Mary Frances Kennedy Fisher is one of the most well-known food writers of the 20th century. This detailed biography traces Fisher's life from her birth in Michigan and childhood in California to her education at boarding schools and college, to her early interest in journalism. Fisher began writing and published her first article in 1934. She became interested in cooking, and published her first book in 1937, which was a collection of food-related essays. Reardon goes on to cover her marriages, birth of her daughter, family life, life in France, travels, and the success of her career. This is a comprehensive look at Fisher's life and gets behind some of the myths that Fisher perpetuated about her life.

> **Subjects:** Family Relationships, Fisher, M.F.K., Food Writers, France, Marriage, Travel, Women's Nonfiction
>
> **Awards:** IACP Award
>
> **Now Try:** Readers may be interested in reading Anne Zimmerman's recent biography of Fisher, *An Extravagant Hunger: The Passionate Years of M.F.K. Fisher*. For readers who want to read some of Fisher's titles, there are plenty. *The Art of Eating, With a Bold Knife and Fork, The Gastronomical Me,* and *How to Cook a Wolf* are some of her most well-known titles. *Writing at the Kitchen Table: The Authorized Biography of Elizabeth David* by Artemis Cooper is the biography of another well-known food figure who kept her private life secret. Reardon has also written *M.F.K. Fisher, Julia Child, and Alice Waters: Celebrating the Pleasures of the Table*, a profile of these three influential women. Reardon recently published Julia Child's letters to her friend Avis DeVoto in *As Always, Julia: The Letters of Julia Child and Avis DeVoto*. Readers may also enjoy the writings of Mary McCarthy, a contemporary of Fisher's. Try her memoir, *Memories of a Catholic Girlhood* or her novel *The Group*.

Simpson, Neil

Gordon Ramsay: The Biography. London: John Blake, 2006. 282pp. ISBN 9781844542185.

This engaging biography covers the public and private life of one of Britain's most famous chefs. Although relatively short compared to other biographies, Simpson touches on Ramsay's youth, his promising soccer career, and the injury that led him to leave soccer and become a chef.

Despite Ramsay's quick rise to success as a restaurateur and television star, he faced criticism and controversy, as well as difficulties in his personal life, such as his troubled relationship with his father and his brother's drug addiction. The reader is also given an intimate look at Ramsay as a husband and family man, which is not often seen. Simpson's quick pace and intimate details will appeal to readers who enjoy gossipy tell-alls.

Subjects: Chefs, Family Relationships, Marriage, Quick Reads, Restaurants

Now Try: Readers may want to read Ramsay's own memoir, *Roasting in Hell's Kitchen*. His television series may also be of interest; suggest *Kitchen Nightmares* or *Hell's Kitchen*. Gilly Smith has written quick biographies of other famous British chefs including *Nigella Lawson* or *Jamie Oliver: Turning Up the Heat*. Marco Pierre White was Ramsay's mentor and boss for a time. Readers may want to try his memoir, *Devil in the Kitchen*. Nigel Slater is another famous British foodie; his memoir *Toast* or *Eating for England* may be suggested.

Collective Food Biographies

Arndt, Alice.

Culinary Biographies: A Dictionary of the World's Great Historic Chefs, Cookbook Authors and Collectors, Farmers, Gourmets, Home Economists, Nutritionists, Restaurateurs, Philosophers, Physicians, Scientists, Writers, and Others Who Influenced the Way We Eat Today. Houston: Yes Press, 2006. 418pp. ISBN 9780971832213.

The title of this book really says it all. This lengthy tome is an almost-comprehensive collection of brief biographies of culinarians, which for this book's purpose essentially means anyone who ever had anything to do with food in any capacity. The collection is arranged alphabetically and only includes deceased figures. The collection reaches as far back as the sixth-century BC, including the philosopher Pythagoras for his views on vegetarianism, and concludes with Julia Child, whose death in 2004 was the most recent of this collection. Figures from all over the world are included such as Epicurus and James Beard and not so well-known figures such as Minekichi Akabori. Subjects are indexed by category and geographical location and subjects' texts are listed chronologically. This is a quick read with fascinating details and facts.

Subjects: Chefs, Food Writers, History, Philosophers, Quick Reads, Reference

Now Try: Readers may enjoy other food reference titles, such as *The Oxford Companion to Food* by Alan Davidson, *The Atlas of Food: Who Eats What, Where, and Why* by Erik Millstone, or even for fun, *The Devil's Food Dictionary: A Pioneering Culinary Reference Work Consisting Entirely of Lies* by Barry Foy. Readers may want to consider collective biographies on other topics, such as *The Scientists: A History of Science Told Through the Lives of Its Greatest Inventors* by John Gribbin, or compendiums like *1001 Days That Shaped the World* by Peter Furtado and *1001 Inventions That Changed the World* by Jack Challoner.

Rogov, Daniel

Rogues, Writers and Whores: Dining with the Rich and Infamous. London: Toby Press, 2007. 335pp. ISBN 9781592641727.

1

> Rogov provides short biographies of many famous epicures stretching all the way back to the Roman period, including kings, queens, courtesans, politicians, writers, artists, and of course, chefs. Many created or inspired famous dishes that are still eaten today. Rogov's juicy tidbits of these famous figures' lives and his descriptions of historical food customs make this a quick, entertaining look at the history of food.

2

>> **Subjects**: Artists, Chefs, Famous Figures, Food Habits, Gastronomy, History, Quick Reads, Recipes, Royalty

>> **Now Try**: Readers may be interested in food trivia titles such as *Schott's Food and Drink Miscellany* by Ben Schott or *Who Put the Devil in Deviled Eggs?: A Food Lover's Guide to America's Favorite Dishes* by Ann Treistman. Other group biographies that contain juicy personal details may also be appealing, such as *Sex with Kings: 500 Years of Adultery, Power, Rivalry, and Revenge* by Eleanor Herman, *A Treasury of Great American Scandals: Tantalizing True Tales of Historic Misbehavior by the Founding Fathers and Others Who Let Freedom Swing* by Michael Farquhar, or *The Greatest Stories Never Told: 100 Tales from History to Astonish, Bewilder, and Stupefy* by Rick Beyer.

3

4

Consider Starting With . . .

5

Readers just getting started in Food Biographies may want to begin with some of these popular titles about well-known figures in food.

Arndt, Alice. *Culinary Biographies: A Dictionary of the World's Great Historic Chefs, Cookbook Authors and Collectors, Farmers, Gourmets, Home Economists, Nutritionists, Restaurateurs, Philosophers, Physicians, Scientists, Writers, and Others Who Influenced the Way We Eat Today.*

6

Fitch, Noel Riley. *Appetite for Life: The Biography of Julia Child.*

Jones, Evan. *Epicurean Delight: The Life and Times of James Beard.*

7

McNamee, Thomas. *Alice Waters and Chez Panisse: The Romantic, Impractical, Often Eccentric, Ultimately Brilliant Making of a Food Revolution.*

Reardon, Joan. *Poet of the Appetites: The Lives and Loves of M.F.K. Fisher.*

8

References

9

The Columbia Electronic Encyclopedia. 2007. *Biography.* New York: Columbia University Press.

Cords, Sarah Statz. 2006. *The Real Story: A Guide to Nonfiction Reading Interests.* Westport: Libraries Unlimited.

Hamilton, Nigel. 2007. *Biography: A Brief History.* Cambridge: Harvard University Press.

Levine, D. M. 2011. "Getting Food Right: Brooke Johnson, President of the Food Network and Cooking Channel, on the Shift from Cooking to Watching." *Adweek* (September 21). Available at: http://www.adweek.com/news/television/getting-food-right-134922 (accessed February 2, 2012).

Liers, Frederic. 2005. "Biography." In *The New Dictionary of the History of Ideas*, ed. by Maryanne Cline Horowitz, 217–20. New York: Charles Scribner's Sons.

Roche, Rick. 2009a. *Real Lives Revealed: A Guide to Reading Interests in Biography.* Santa Barbara: Libraries Unlimited.

Roche, Rick. 2009b. "Reasons to Read Biography," *Ricklibrarian* (blog) (June 23). http://ricklibrarian.blogspot.com.

Rollyson, Carl. 2008. *Biography: A User's Guide.* Chicago: Ivan R. Dee.

Wyatt, Neal. 2007. *The Readers' Advisory Guide to Nonfiction.* Chicago: American Library Association.

Part II

Nonfiction Genres

Chapter 3

Food Travel

Definition of Food Travel

Travel has been a common human activity for thousands of years. People have traveled for purposes of migration, pilgrimage, trade, exploration, and colonization. It is only natural then, that travel should be a common subject of writing. Travel was an important element of biblical narratives as well as Greek and Roman epics. Herodotus, who is considered the father of history, includes travel in his fifth-century BC writings. One of the most famous travel narratives was from Marco Polo, a Venetian who traveled back and forth to China between 1271 and 1295. Petrarch's description of his ascent of Mount Ventoux in 1336 is one of the earliest records of travel for the sake of pleasure. In early modern Europe, travel writing was the second best-selling genre, behind history. European audiences were enthralled by explorers' narratives of customs and manners of indigenous populations. As the British Empire expanded, the public was eager for stories of Native Americans as well as the Opium Wars with China. Travel literature remains popular today. Simon Winchester points out that there is a wealth of travel literature available in America. Besides books, there are a number of monthly journals and magazines that include literary travel writing, from *National Geographic* to *GQ*, to the *Virginia Quarterly Review* (Winchester 2009). Travel writing has become so popular that Robert Burgin will publish a guide, *Going Places: A Guide to Travel Narratives*, in January 2013.

Travel literature chronicles a journey, although Jason Wilson, editor of *The Best American Travel Writing* series, recalls Paul Theroux's comment that travel writing is not just about a particular country, but about the person who is doing the traveling (Winchester 2009). In her readers' advisory guide, Neal Wyatt states that travel literature can include titles that are solely focused on a destination, as well as titles that use the destination to expand on a broader range of topics (Wyatt 2007). Wyatt also says travel literature combines landscape, history, and culture with aspects of memoir (Wyatt 2008). Sarah Statz Cords points out that current travel literature incorporates a memoir-like style with recreated dialogue and memories, drama, and selective organization of events that adds to its appeal (Cords 2006).

In recent years, food has become a common element incorporated into travel literature. Food and travel are natural pairings. When you travel, you have to eat. Eating in new places can provide memorable moments of discovering new foods and connecting with people. In Food Travel literature, food becomes the primary focus of the trip, as the author travels to a particular destination in order to experience the food. The author paints a vivid picture of his or her travels and provides insight into the location's history and culture, as well as local food traditions. Many writers have made very successful careers describing novel foods eaten in foreign lands, such as Frances Mayes's *Under the Tuscan Sun*, which is probably the most well-known travel title focused on food. *Booklist* editor Brad Hooper believes that Travel and Food Literature are popular for the same reason: both appeal to our senses (Hooper 2010). We experience food and travel with our senses. We taste the food, smell the coffee, see an historic ruin, and feel the sand beneath our feet. Food and Travel writing both satiate our sensory desires.

Appeal of Food Travel

Food Travel Lit allows readers the vicarious experience of armchair travel. Readers can visit faraway places without having to leave their homes. Some readers enjoy revisiting places they have already been. Others may want to read about a place before they go. Some readers simply want to read about a place they know they will never visit. Food Travel Lit allows the reader to experience a new location, its history, culture, people, and food. These stories inspire a sense of exploration, discovery, and adventure.

The best Food Travel Lit makes readers feel as if they are actually there with the author. Readers want to feel like they can taste the food the writer is eating, or, for example, smell the aromas of an Asian food court. Therefore, elements of setting, style, and tone are important appeal factors. Rich, detailed descriptions and evocative language create a strong sense of place. Pacing tends to be somewhat leisurely; some of the Expatriate titles are even more slowly paced and reflective. Tone is often upbeat, although some narratives where the author is traveling to escape something or come to terms with something can be more reflective or contemplative. Creating a vivid setting is important to these narratives; however, Wyatt also states that the actual location of the travel is another important factor to consider (Wyatt 2008). Some readers search out books set in particular places they wish to read about, such as France, Italy, or Asia.

Character is another important appeal factor in Food Travel Lit. As mentioned before, the writing is not just about the place, but also about the person doing the traveling. The author becomes an important character and his or her voice and personality should be considered. Many authors also include stories of locals they meet during their travels. The Expatriate titles in particular often include stories of local residents and neighbors that add color and appeal to the story.

Story also plays a part in Food Travel Lit's appeal. Aside from the overarching travel story, readers also enjoy stories and anecdotes of the mishaps and difficulties the author experiences along the way. In some of the narratives the author also faces some kind of personal struggle: a midlife crisis, the ending of a relationship, or starting a new life. These stories can have the feel of a memoir, although the travel theme is still the main focus.

Finally, Food Travel Lit appeals to readers who enjoy learning. These titles provide insight into local cultures and often detail the history of a location. Readers gain a sense of exploration as well as a new understanding of a place.

Readers who enjoy Food Travel Lit may want to consider titles from the Food Adventure Lit chapter. These titles are also enjoyable for the vicarious experiences, sense of exploration, exotic settings, and details. Food Memoirs may also be appealing for the strong character element. Outside of Food Lit, readers may enjoy other nonfiction travel titles. There are also a number of television series that feature food and travel, which readers may enjoy. A number of food blogs also incorporate stories of travel that readers may also enjoy.

Organization of the Chapter

This chapter begins with traditional **Food Travel** titles. These titles chronicle an author's experiences traveling to various places and savoring the local foods. In **Expatriate Life** titles, the author shares her experiences living in a foreign country.

Food Travel

The titles in this section are traditional Food Travel stories. The author paints a picture of his or her travels to various places, savoring local foods. The stories often provide insight into the location's people, history, and culture. Vivid settings, rich descriptions, and evocative language are essential. The author may also include anecdotes of mishaps and difficulties along the way as well as portraits of colorful local characters.

> In Food Travel Literature the author travels to a particular destination to experience the food. These titles incorporate a memoir-like style and details about the landscape, history, and culture of the location. They tend to have rich, detailed descriptions and evocative language, a leisurely pace, and upbeat tone.

Apple, R. W., Jr.

Far Flung and Well Fed: The Food Writing of R. W. Apple, Jr. New York: St. Martin's Press, 2009. 410pp. ISBN 9780312325770.

Apple, who died in 2006, was a popular columnist for the *New York Times* who wrote primarily of his food-centered travels. This compilation includes over 50 of his essays on his travels throughout the United States, Europe, Australia, and Asia. Softshell crabs, Philly cheesesteak, Italian buffalo mozzarella, and Vietnamese pho are just a few of the foods to which Apple turns his attention. Besides rich descriptions of food, Apple also conveys vivid portraits of the cities and countries he visits. Humorous and lively, the short essays will appeal to readers who appreciate a rich sense of place and good food.

> **Subjects:** Essays, Humor, *New York Times*, Quick Reads
>
> **Now Try:** Calvin Trillin's humorous short essays of his adventures with food and travel may also appeal to readers who enjoy Apple's writing. Trillin's *The Tummy Trilogy* contains his most well-known food and travel essays. M.F.K. Fisher's *The Art of Eating*, Joseph Wechsberg's *Blue Trout and Black Truffles*, and Anthony Bourdain's *A Cook's Tour* are also good suggestions that include a rich sense of place and food. Actor and comedian Stephen Fry humorously recounts his travels through America, often describing the food, in *Stephen Fry in America*.

Banerji, Chitrita

Eating India: An Odyssey into the Food and Culture of the Land of Spices. New York: Bloomsbury, 2007. 265pp. ISBN 9781596910188.

Most westerners who have sampled Indian cuisine have likely been exposed to Punjabi cuisine; however, India has a vast range of distinctive regional cuisines besides Punjabi. Throughout history, India has seen waves of immigrants and conquerors, from Persians, Middle Eastern Jews, to Mongols, Arabs, and Europeans. All of these cultures have influenced India's cuisines. Banerji journeys across India to introduce readers to India's various regions, traditional dishes, comfort foods, celebratory dishes, sweets, and even roadside foods. Her lush descriptions of exotic foods and discussion of how outside influences have shaped India's cuisines presents a fascinating look into Indian culture, history, and cuisine.

> **Subjects:** Immigrants, India, Indian Cuisine
>
> **Now Try:** Readers who would like a more personal view of Indian cuisine and culture may enjoy Shoba Narayan's *Monsoon Diary: A Memoir with Recipes* and Madhur Jaffrey's *Climbing the Mango Trees: A Memoir of a Childhood in India*. Readers interested in the distinction between the various regional cuisines may enjoy Fuschia Dunlop's exploration of China and its regional cuisines in *Shark's Fin and Sichuan Pepper: A Sweet and Sour Memoir of Eating in China*. Readers looking for a simple, straightforward introduction to Indian cooking may want to check out Neeta Saluja's *Six Spices: A Simple Concept of Indian Cooking*. Richard C. Morais's fiction novel *The Hundred-Foot Journey* contains rich descriptions of India and its cuisine. Padma Viswanathan's fiction novel *The Toss of a Lemon* provides an evocative look at Indian life and culture.

Borel, Kathryn

Corked: A Memoir. New York: Grand Central Publishing, 2009. 262pp. ISBN 9780446409506.

Borel's French-born father Philippe, a wine aficionado, tried to instill his passion for wine in his daughter. But Borel had no interest in wine and paid little attention. When she realizes that her time with her father may be short and she knows so little of his passion, she invites her father on a wine-tasting trip through France. Hoping that they can improve their dysfunctional relationship and seeking solace after the breakup of a serious relationship, Borel begins the trip with high hopes. But her father's constant demand for perfection and quick temper quickly lead to frustration. As the two make their way through France, they begin to get to know each other as adults. Although Philippe is quite the curmudgeon, the reader cannot help but forgive him. This is a humorous and touching father–daughter story, filled with interesting tidbits about wine.

> **Subjects:** Family Relationships, Fathers and Daughters, France, Wine, Women's Nonfiction
>
> **Now Try:** Those who enjoyed reading about the relationship between the author and her father may also enjoy Lucy Knisley's *French Milk*, a vivid travelogue of her trip to Paris with her mother, or Sue Monk Kidd's *Traveling With Pomegranates*, as she attempts to reconnect with her daughter while traveling through Europe. Roy Cloud recounts his travels through France with his brother, in *To Burgundy and Back Again: A Tale of Wine, France, and Brotherhood*. Readers who enjoyed the struggles and joys of the father–daughter relationship, may also enjoy Gabrielle Hamilton's memoir *Blood, Bones and Butter: The Inadvertent Education of a Reluctant Chef*, which explores her struggles with her relationship with her mother. Husband and wife wine columnists Dorothy J. Gaiter and John Brecher recall their life together and the wines they have shared in *Love By the Glass*. Readers may also enjoy Sarah Kate Lynch's fiction novel *House of Daughters*; set in the lush French countryside, three estranged sisters come together to rebuild the family vineyard.

Castagno, Dario

Too Much Tuscan Sun: Confessions of a Chianti Tour Guide. Guilford, CT: Globe Pequot Press, 2004. 268pp. ISBN 9780762736706.

There is an abundance of memoirs written about Tuscany; however, most are from the perspective of the American who has moved abroad and purchased a run-down home with the intent of restoring it to its former glory. This lighthearted, unique memoir is not that kind of story. Castagno was born in England to Italian parents and has been living in Tuscany for many years. Wanting to share the love of his country, he began his own business as a tour guide of the Tuscan region. Castagno humorously recalls some of his more memorable clients, from the exasperating to the amusing and endearing. The book is organized by month, and Castagno describes the festivities, foods, and the changing landscape of each month. He also includes some history of Tuscany, as well as Chianti, the famous wine region.

> **Subjects:** Chianti, Humor, Italy, Tuscany, Wine

> **Now Try:** Readers will want to continue with Castagno's *A Day in Tuscany: More Confessions of a Chianti Tour Guide* and *Too Much Tuscan Wine. Ciao America!: An Italian Discovers the U. S.* by Beppe Severgnini is a humorous account of an Italian's year living in America. Phil Doran humorously recalls his move to Tuscany in *The Reluctant Tuscan: How I Discovered My Inner Italian.* Matthew Fort recounts his travels through Italy in *Sweet Honey, Bitter Lemons: Travels in Sicily on a Vespa.*

Ciezadlo, Annia

Day of Honey: A Memoir of Food, Love, and War. New York: Free Press, 2011. 382pp. ISBN 9781416583936.

In 2003, Ciezadlo, a reporter, newly married, spent her honeymoon in Baghdad. Her husband, also a reporter, had been posted to Iraq. For the next several years, they lived in Baghdad and Beirut. The author was quick to set up her kitchen. She cooked foods that were familiar to provide comfort and foods that seemed strange in order to understand her new surroundings. While war raged around her, the author focused on civilian life: how civilians went about their lives amidst the hardships of war. Believing that food allows a visitor to experience a country and its people in a more intimate way, Ciezadlo ate with Iraqi women, tribal sheikhs, warlords, and militiamen. Ciezadlo creates a touching account with vivid and evocative descriptions and thoughtful writing.

> **Subjects:** Iraq, Lebanon, Marriage, Multicultural Issues, Recipes, War

> **Now Try:** A section of Anthony Bourdain's illustrated travel book *No Reservations* details the time period Bourdain and his television show's staff spent trapped in Beirut while it was being bombed by the Israelis in 2006 (his travel show *No Reservations* also featured two episodes spent there, during and after the conflict). Other nonfiction accounts of life in war zones might be suggested to these readers, including Deborah Copaken Kogan's *Shutterbabe: Adventures in Love and War*, Sandy Tolan's *The Lemon Tree: An Arab, a Jew, and the Heart of the Middle East*, and Anthony Shadid's *Night Draws Near: Iraq's People in the Shadow of America's War* (Shadid's own memoir, *House of Stone: A Memoir of Home, Family, and a Lost Middle East*, published posthumously in 2012, might also appeal). TV news correspondent Linda Ellerbee takes a break from news to recall the many meals she has eaten all over the world in *Take Big Bites: Adventures Around the World and Across the Table.* Although not set in a war zone, Judith Matloff's *Home Girl: Building a Dream House on a Lawless Block* also showcases the author's determination to make a house a home, even in the middle of a dangerous neighborhood.

Dunlop, Fuchsia

Shark's Fin and Sichuan Pepper: A Sweet and Sour Memoir of Eating in China. New York: W. W. Norton & Company, 2008. 320pp. ISBN 9780393066579.

An award-winning food writer, Dunlop vividly recalls the time she spent in China as a student. Fascinated with China, the culture, and the cuisine, Dunlop vowed to eat everything that was offered to her. This practice opened her up to new tastes and was the start of her love for Sichuan cuisine. Dunlop went on to attend China's premier Sichuan cooking school where she was introduced to exotic ingredients and new cooking techniques. Dunlop describes the delights of her travels and culinary experiences throughout China, including Sichuan, the Forbidden City, and remote areas of west China. Evocative and vivid, Dunlop's writing captures the beauty of China and its cuisine.

Subjects: China, Chinese Cuisine, Culinary School, Women's Nonfiction

Awards: IACP Award

Now Try: Readers may be interested in Dunlop's cookbooks, which highlight the foods she discovered in China, including *Land of Plenty: A Treasury of Authentic Sichuan Cooking*. Jen Lin-Liu's *Serve the People: A Stir-Fried Journey Through China* is another absorbing adventure where the author attends culinary school in a foreign country. In *The Fortune Cookie Chronicles: Adventures in the World of Chinese Food*, Jennifer 8 Lee travels far and wide exploring the history of Chinese food. Polly Evans's *Fried Eggs with Chopsticks* is an entertaining account of the author's adventures traveling through China. Peter Hessler's *Country Driving: A Chinese Road Trip* is an exciting journey through China that provides an inside look at a rapidly changing country.

Fay, Kim

Communion: A Culinary Journey through Vietnam. San Francisco: Things Asian Press, 2010. 293pp. ISBN 9781934159149.

Fay spent several years during the 1990s living in Vietnam, and fell in love with the culture, food, and landscape. Several years later, Fay decided to return to Vietnam in order to learn Vietnamese cooking. She embarks on a culinary journey through Vietnam, visiting restaurants, farms, and markets, meeting chefs, and attending cooking classes. She samples a variety of foods, from street vendors to upscale restaurants, and recounts the vibrant culture. She also explores Vietnam's history of Communism and war, and the current political climate.

Subjects: Recipes, Vietnam, Vietnamese Cuisine

Now Try: Kim Fay has also written a travel guide to Vietnam, *To Vietnam with Love: A Travel Guide for the Connoisseur*. *Secrets of the Red Lantern: Stories and Vietnamese Recipes from the Heart* by Pauline Nguyen is the story of the author's family's escape from war-torn Vietnam to Australia, where they opened the popular Red Lantern restaurant. Other books with a focus on Asian cuisine are *Wild, Wild East: Recipes and Stories from Vietnam* by Bobby Chinn, a chef who opened a restaurant in Hanoi; *Hot Sour Salty Sweet* by Jeffrey Alford and Naomi Duguid; and *Serve the People: A Stir-Fried Journey Through China* by Jen Lin-Liu. Anthony Bourdain is very vocal about his love of Vietnamese food and culture. His book *Medium Raw* contains a chapter about Vietnam. Andrew Pham's classic travel title about searching out his Vietnamese roots, *Catfish and Mandala: A Two-Wheeled Voyage through the Landscape and Memory of Vietnam* may also be suggested.

Fieri, Guy

Diners, Drive-Ins, and Dives: An All-American Road Trip . . . With Recipes! New York: William Morrow/Harper Collins, 2008. 250pp. ISBN 9780061724886.

Food Network personality Guy Fieri takes readers on a trip across America, showcasing some of the country's best local diners. From classic diner fare like burgers, meatloaf, and coconut cream pie to more creative dishes like mojito glazed duck and Cap'n Crunch encrusted French toast, Guy samples them all. The histories of the restaurants, backgrounds of the owners, and behind-the-scenes look lend a personal feel to the book. His descriptions of the foods will have readers planning their next road trip.

Subjects: American Cuisine, Diners, Drive-In Restaurants, Restaurants, Road Trips

Now Try: Fieri has a follow-up book, *More Diners, Drive-Ins, and Dives*, as well as a cookbook, *Guy Fieri Food: Cookin' It, Livin' It, Lovin' It.* Jane and Michael Stern are also well known for their road food books. Try *Roadfood: The Coast-to-Coast Guide to 800 of the Best Barbecue Joints, Lobster Shacks, Ice Cream Parlors, Highway Diners, and Much, Much More.* Adam Richman is another TV personality, known for his show *Man vs. Food.* Readers may enjoy his book *America the Edible: A Hungry History From Sea to Dining Sea.* Other road trips featuring food are *Hamburger America: One Man's Cross-Country Odyssey to Find the Best Burgers in the Nation* and *American Pie: Slices of Life (and Pie) from America's Back Roads* by Pascale LeDraoulec. Other road trip stories may also be appealing, such as Pete Jordan's *Dishwasher: One Man's Quest to Wash Dishes in All Fifty States* and Mike Walsh's *Bowling Across America: 50 States in Rented Shoes.*

Finley, Amy

How to Eat a Small Country: A Family's Pursuit of Happiness, One Meal at a Time. New York: Clarkson Potter, 2011. ISBN 9780307591388. 280pp.

Finley met her French husband when he was visiting the United States. After three dates, she moved to France with him and enrolled in culinary school. After several years of marriage, Finley found herself back in the United States, with two children. She was no longer cooking and felt unfulfilled. When she entered a Food Network cooking challenge and won, her husband declared that he did not want to be married to a television star and would leave the marriage if she accepted the network's contract for a show. Finley gave up the show and moved her family to France for a year in an attempt to repair the strained marriage and find happiness again. From their home base in Brianny, they traveled throughout France exploring regional cuisines such as bouilliabasse and Bresse chicken, as well as other more traditional meals like tete de veul. In between descriptions of France and tales of their travels and meals, Finley recounts the circumstances that led them to leave their lives in San Francisco and move to France. Finley's conversational tone, humor, and personal stories all bring the reader into their family. The only thing missing are the recipes to the mouth-watering foods she describes.

> **Subjects:** Family Relationships, France, French Cuisine, Marriage

> **Now Try**: *The Food of France* by Waverly Root is one of the first books Finley read when beginning her love affair of French cooking. Although Julie Powell's *Cleaving* has a darker tone and is more sexually explicit, this is also a story of a troubled marriage and the author's attempt to find herself and fix her marriage through food. In *Keeping the Feast: One Couple's Story of Love, Food, and Healing*, Paula Butturini describes how she and her husband turned to Italy and their shared love of food to heal after an unexpected injury. In *Halfway to Each Other: How a Year in Italy Brought Our Family Home*, Susan Pohlmanand her husband move their family to Italy in an attempt to save their marriage. David Lebovitz finds happiness again when he moves to Paris after the death of his partner in *The Sweet Life in Paris*.

Haller, James

Vie de France: Sharing Food, Friendship, and a Kitchen in the Loire Valley. New York: Berkley Books, 2002. 270pp. ISBN9780425184721.

> When he turned 60, award-winning chef and restaurateur Haller was contemplating the next phase of his life. Having always wanted to rent a house for an extended stay in Europe, when a friend offered to set it up, he agreed, on the condition that he did not have to lift a pot for the entire vacation. Haller and a group of friends rented a 17th-century house in the Loire Valley in France for a month. But the abundance of fresh foods he found in the marketplace, the quality meats from the local butcher, and the abundance of cheeses and wines were too tempting to keep him out of the kitchen for long. Soon he was creating luscious meals with fresh, local ingredients. He and his friends also explore the French countryside, local chateaux, antique stores, and cafes.

> **Subjects:** Chefs, France, Friendships, Men's Lives, Recipes, Retirement

> **Now Try:** Other male perspectives on life in France are Mark Greenside's *I'll Never Be French No Matter What I Do*, Tony Hawk's *A Piano in the Pyrenees*, and Peter Mayle's *A Year in Provence*. *A Year in the World* by France Mayes and *Hot Sun, Cool Shadow* by Angela Murrills may also be appealing for their descriptions of food and the French countryside. Kimberley Lovato's *Walnut Wine and Truffle Groves: Culinary Adventures in the Dordogne* is vivid culinary travel guide of southwestern France.

Hodgson, Moira

It Seemed Like a Good Idea at the Time: My Adventures in Life and Food. New York: Nan A. Talese/Doubleday, 2008. 334pp. ISBN 9780767912709.

As a result of her father's career, Hodgson lived abroad for much of her childhood. From Switzerland and Germany to more exotic locations like Vietnam and Egypt, the author was introduced to the local customs, culture, and foods of her host country and developed a love and appreciation for travel and food. As an adult, she settled down in New York City, but found enjoyment in entertaining and hosting elaborate dinner parties. Her travels continued when she began writing for travel and food magazines, taking her to more exotic locations such as Mexico and Morocco. Hodgson combines her charming reminiscences of her childhood and exotic travels with tempting recipes that connect her to the people and places in her life.

> **Subjects:** Coming-of-Age, Family Relationships, Memoirs, Recipes, Women's Nonfiction

> **Now Try:** Julia Child's *My Life in France* is a charming story of her travels in France and her discovery of her love of French food. Readers may also enjoy other coming-of-age memoirs tied to food, such as Kate Moses's *Cakewalk* or Ruth Reichl's *Tender at the Bone*. Alexandra Fuller's memoirs may appeal to readers who enjoy exotic settings. Start with *Don't Let's Go to the Dogs Tonight*. Colette Rossant has also written memoirs of her world travels throughout her life and her love of food; try her title *The World in My Kitchen*. Gail Simmons, who grew up to be a judge on the television show *Top Chef* and food writer, also traveled a lot and her family life revolved around food. Her memoir is *Talking with My Mouth Full*.

Jamison, Bill, and Cheryl Alters Jamison

Around the World in 80 Dinners: The Ultimate Culinary Adventure. New York: William Morrow, 2008. 258pp. ISBN 9780060878955.

For their anniversary, the Jamisons decided to take a three-month trip around the world, stopping in 10 countries, including Bali, Thailand, India, China, and South Africa. Determined to eat authentically local food at each destination, they tasted dishes from food stalls, street vendors, mom and pop restaurants, and five-star restaurants. Aside from eating, the Jamisons visited several wineries and attended a few local cooking classes. The third-person narration can be a little jarring, but this travelogue provides great descriptions of the various foods and flavors, as well as contact information of the restaurants they visited, and a recipe from each particular region they visited.

> **Subjects:** International Cuisine, Marriage, Quick Reads, Recipes

> **Now Try:** Readers may want to check out one of the several cookbooks the Jamisons have written, such as *American Home Cooking: Over 300 Spirited Recipes Celebrating Our Rich Tradition of Home Cooking*. Readers who enjoy the Jamisons' adventures may also like *Two for the Road: Our Love Affair With American Food* by Michael and Jane Stern. Readers may also enjoy Nan Lyons' adventures around the world in *Around the World in 80 Meals*. Frances Mayes's *A Year in the World: Journeys of a Passionate Traveler* will appeal to readers who enjoy wonderful descriptions of places and food. Amy Finley's *How to Eat a Small Country* is her story of her attempt to save her marriage by travelling through France with her husband and children, experiencing its cuisine.

Calvin Trillin's *Travels With Alice* and Doreen Orion's *Queen of the Road* may also be appealing to readers who enjoy husband and wife travel stories.

Liebling, A. J.

Between Meals: An Appetite for Paris. San Francisco: North Point Press, 1986. 185pp. ISBN 9780865472365.

An American journalist who wrote for the *New Yorker* until his death in 1963, Liebling spent a year in Paris, ostensibly studying at the Sorbonne. Rather than apply himself to his studies, Liebling used this time to educate himself in the fine art of food and spent much of his time enjoying French cuisine. In this humorous, novel-like narrative, Liebling recounts his time in Paris and the rich, elaborate meals and wine he consumed.

Subjects: France, Humor, Journalism, Men's Lives

Now Try: Readers who enjoy Liebling's style may want to read some of his other writings on other subjects, such as sports, politics, or World War II. *The Sweet Science* and *Just Enough Liebling* are good places to start. M.F.K. Fisher, Calvin Trillin, and Joseph Wechsberg (*Blue Trout and Black Truffles: The Perigrinations of an Epicure*) all have similar writing styles, incorporating a literary style, novel-like narratives, and humor. Ernest Hemingway's memoir, *A Moveable Feast*, of his time living in Paris in the 1920s, may also appeal to readers who enjoy Liebling's writing. Joseph Mitchell was another American journalist who told real stories in his writing; consider his title *Up in the Old Hotel* or *The Bottom of the Harbor*.

Lin-Liu, Jen

Serve the People: A Stir-Fried Journey Through China. Orlando: Harcourt, 2008. 341pp. ISBN 9780151012916.

Lin-Liu is a Chinese American born in America, who decides to move to China as an adult. When she wants to learn to cook in the traditional Chinese way, she signs up at a local cooking school. One of only a few women there, Lin-Liu discovers the vast cultural differences between Americans and Chinese. After completing cooking school, she takes various jobs with a noodle maker and at a dumpling restaurant, discovering that making a living in China as a cook is very difficult. She also explores the differences between cooking and eating in the city and the country, as well as upscale restaurants and street stalls.

Subjects: China, Chinese Cuisine, Culinary School, Recipes, Women's Non-fiction

Now Try: Readers may also enjoy other accounts of authors who attend culinary school, such as Kathleen Flinn's *The Sharper Your Knife the Less You Cry*. Alice Steinbach's memoir *Educating Alice* is another entertaining combination of learning and travel. Readers who enjoy glimpses of life in China may want to try Linda Furiya, who describes her adventures living and eating in China in *How to Cook a Dragon: Living, Loving, and Eating in China*. J. Maarten Troost recounts his off-the-beaten-path adventures through China in *Lost on Planet China: One Man's Attempt to Understand the World's Most Mystifying Nation*. Yan Lianke's fiction novel by the same name, *Serve the People!* portrays an illicit love affair between a commander's wife and a lowly household servant and offers a glimpse at life under Mao's regime. Readers fascinated by the cultural issues in this book might also consider Amy Chua's controversial memoir *Battle Hymn of the Tiger Mother*, about raising her American children in what she considers the more traditional Chinese way.

Mayes, Frances

A Year in the World: Journeys of a Passionate Traveler. New York: Broadway, 2006. 420pp. ISBN 9780767910057.

Mayes, best known for her memoir of her life restoring an Italian villa, *Under the Tuscan Sun*, decides to explore more of the world and sets out on a new adventure. Although she doesn't actually travel the entire world, her typical compelling prose brings the reader with her. Mayes visits Spain, Portugal, Greece, Crete, Turkey, Sicily and Naples, and Scotland. Uninspired by tourist hotels and guided tours, Mayes and her husband frequently rent apartments so they can interact with local residents and shop in local markets. Food is always a cornerstone of Mayes's focus, and she explores the region's cuisines throughout her travels. The seafood in Sicily, the pizza in Naples, lamb in Crete, and Scottish shortbread are just a few of the sumptuous foods Mayes recalls.

> **Subjects:** Gentle Reads, Greece, Italy, Local Food, Marriage, Portugal, Scotland, Spain, Turkey

> **Now Try:** Readers who enjoy Mayes's writing style will want to read her popular memoir, *Under the Tuscan Sun* as well as her other memoirs, *Bella Tuscany* and *Every Day in Tuscany*. Marlena de Blasi has a similar writing style with compelling prose and vivid, luscious descriptions of food. Start with *A Thousand Days in Venice*. Sue Monk Kidd also infuses her literary writing style in her travelogue, *Traveling With Pomegranates*. The blog Kiss My Spatula (kissmyspatula.com) incorporates literary musings on food, unique recipes, and stunning photography that may appeal to fans of Mayes's writing.

Mayle, Peter

French Lessons: Adventures with Knife, Fork, and Corkscrew. New York: Alfred A. Knopf, 2001. 227pp. ISBN 9780375405907.

Mayle, who chronicled his move to Provence in *A Year in Provence*, leaves his home base and travels throughout France to experience the vast pleasures of French cuisine. He visits both small restaurants and Michelin starred restaurants, as well as food festivals and celebrations. Experiencing the revered black truffles, various French cheeses, frogs, escargots, and the famous Bresse chickens are some of the highlights of his trip. He also searches for the perfect omelet, witnesses a wine marathon through Bordeaux, and investigates the qualifications for the Michelin guide. Mayle is a lively narrator who infuses his humorous prose with vivid descriptions of colorful locals and savory meals.

Subjects: France, French Cuisine, Humor, Michelin Guide

Now Try: Readers who have not read Mayle's *A Year in Provence* will be rewarded with a humorous account of Mayle's first year living in Provence. Mayle's *Confessions of a French Baker: Breadmaking Secrets, Tips, and Recipes* is also a quick, entertaining, and interesting account of French bread. Mayle has also written a number of fiction titles that are set in France and have his characteristic humor and light tone. Readers may also want to try David Lebovitz's *The Sweet Life in Paris,* a humorous account of adapting to French customs. Chris Stewart's *Driving Over Lemons* is another lighthearted story of the author's adventures getting to know his adopted country, Spain. Roy Cloud's *To Burgundy and Back Again* is another humorous tale of his travels through France with his brother.

Roahen, Sara

Gumbo Tales: Finding My Place at the New Orleans Table. New York: W. W. Norton, 2008. 293pp. ISBN 9780393061673.

When Roahen's boyfriend moved to New Orleans for medical school, Roahen, a line cook, came along. When she got a job as a restaurant critic, she immersed herself in New Orleans cuisine. Wanting to feel like an authentic New Orleanian, her first task was to understand gumbo. From gumbo, she moved on to Sazerac, a rye whiskey drink, sno-balls, muffuletta, po-boys, turducken, beignets, and crawfish. She also explains the traditional celebrations of New Orleans, such as Carnival and Mardi Gras. Roahen brings the people of New Orleans to life when she recalls Hurricane Katrina and the experiences of friends, neighbors, and proprietors. The detailed and intimate descriptions of the food and people of New Orleans provide a very strong sense of place.

Subjects: Hurricane Katrina, Local Food, New Orleans, Recipes

Now Try: Tom Fitzmorris's *Hungry Town: A Culinary History of New Orleans, the City Where Food Is Almost Everything* is an entertaining and comprehensive account of traditional New Orleans food. Readers may also be interested in John Besh's IACP award-winning cookbook, *My New Orleans.* Readers looking for a brief but rich description of New Orleans may want to try Roy Blount Jr.'s *Feet on the Street.* Jerry Strahan recounts his bizarre adventures as a hot dog vendor in New Orleans's French Quarter in *Managing Ignatius.* Poppy Z. Brite's novel *Liquor* is an absorbing page-turner centered around the New Orleans food scene. *Zeitoun* by Dave Eggers is a disturbing account of one New Orleans's experiences in the aftermath of Hurricane Katrina. Dan Baum's *Nine Lives: Mystery, Magic, Death, and Life in New Orleans* or Julia Reed's *The House on First Street: My New Orleans Story* may also be suggested.

Spitz, Bob

The Saucier's Apprentice: One Long, Strange Trip Through the Great Cooking Schools of Europe. New York: W. W. Norton, 2008. 323pp. ISBN 9780393060591.

On the brink of a mid-life crisis and facing problems in his current relationship, Spitz decides to travel to Europe to learn to cook. Although he already enjoys cooking, he feels as if he is just trying to replicate the recipes without really understanding *how* to cook. Spitz travels across France and Italy, attending a variety of cooking schools. Some are professional cooking schools, some are in the kitchens of famous chefs, and some are in the homes of amateur cooks. Spitz eats and cooks quite a few wonderful meals, which are described in great detail. The chefs and the other participants in his classes make for interesting, and sometimes humorous, tales.

> **Subjects**: Culinary School, France, French Cuisine, Humor, Italy, Italian Cuisine, Men's Lives, Recipes

> **Now Try**: There are several memoirs by authors who turned to travel to deal with struggles in their lives. When Kathleen Flinn's job was eliminated, she took a chance on a lifelong dream and moved to Paris to study at the famous Le Cordon Bleu cooking school in *The Sharper Your Knife the Less You Cry*. Elizabeth Gilbert's best seller *Eat Pray Love* turned to travel and food to heal from a broken relationship. When Mike Walsh struggles with a midlife crisis and the death of his father, he sets out to bowl in all 50 states in *Bowling Across America*. Some of the science of cooking books may be possible suggestions, as this author didn't feel he really knew the *how* of cooking. Try *Cooking for Geeks* by Jeff Potter, which also has a humorous tone. Spitz has also written biographies of the Beatles and Bob Dylan, as well as a new biography of Julia Child, *Dearie: The Remarkable Life of Julia Child*, which may also be of interest.

Stern, Jane, and Stern, Michael

Two for the Road: Our Love Affair with American Food. Boston: Houghton Mifflin, 2006. 292pp. ISBN 9780618329632.

Just out of graduate school, this couple was uncertain of what they would do with their lives. One thing they knew was that they shared a love for food. When they proposed a book on truck-stop dining to a publisher and were accepted, they hit the road. Since then, the Sterns have crisscrossed the United States eating road food from pie to cheese curds, maple candy, fried chicken, and barbeque, to name just a few. Along the way they encounter unusual restaurants and unforgettable people, endure some humorous mishaps, and struggle with the extra poundage that comes with eating several meals a day (Amish bloomers are useful). The passionate food descriptions and humorous adventures make this an endearing read.

> **Subjects**: Humor, Local Food, Marriage, Road Trips

> **Now Try:** Readers who enjoy stories of couples traveling together and discovering new foods may also want to try Bill and Cheryl Jameson's *Around the World in 80 Dinners*, Margaret Hathaway's *The Year of the Goat*, Ann Vanderhoof's *The Spice Necklace*, and

Calvin Trillin's *Alice, Let's Eat*. Readers who enjoyed the Sterns's encounters with unforgettable characters may also enjoy Pascale Le Draoulec's *American Pie*. George Motz travels through America in search of the best burger in *Hamburger America*. Although unrelated to food, readers may be interested in Jane Stern's memoirs, *Ambulance Girl*, which describes her attempt to overcome her depression and numerous phobias by becoming an emergency medical technician; or her latest title, *Confessions of a Tarot Reader*, in which she describes another of her skills, reading tarot cards and fortunes (which she has done for over 40 years).

Stevens, Stuart

Feeding Frenzy: Across Europe in Search of the Perfect Meal. New York: Atlantic Monthly Press, 1997. 265pp. ISBN 9780871136879.

> Stevens jets off to Europe with his friend Rachel "Rat" Kelly on a tour of tour of Europe's Michelin three-star restaurants. The two drive across Europe in an unreliable 1965 Ford Mustang, visiting 29 restaurants in 29 days. England, France, Germany, Belgium, Monaco, and Italy are all on their itinerary. The two indulge in elaborate meals prepared by some of Europe's greatest chefs. Stevens infuses his account with luscious descriptions of their meals and recounts their humorous misadventures.
>
> > **Subjects**: Europe, Friendships, Restaurants, Road Trips
> >
> > **Now Try:** Readers may want to consider one of Stevens's other travelogues such as *Malaria Dreams: An African Adventure*, *Night Train to Turkistan: Modern Adventures Along China's Ancient Silk Road*. Peter Mayle's *French Lessons* is a humorous account of his travels through France. *Lost on Planet China* by J. Maarten Troost is another humorous account of the author's adventures traveling in a foreign country. Ferran Adrià's *A Day at El Bulli* provides a look at the inner workings of a three-star restaurant. Other books featuring road trips, such as Hunter S. Thompson's classic *Fear and Loathing in Las Vegas*, or friends traveling together, like Ewan McGregor's and Charley Boorman's motorcycle travel accounts, *Long Way Round* and *Long Way Down*, may also be suggested.

Trillin, Calvin

The Tummy Trilogy. New York: Farrar, Straus, and Giroux, 1994. 386pp. ISBN 9780374279509.

> Calvin Trillin is a journalist and writer for the *New Yorker*. Travel and food are often popular themes of his writing. This compendium is comprised of three of his books of travel and food: *Alice, Let's Eat*, *American Fried*, and *Third Helpings*. Travelling throughout the United States, Trillin dined in a variety of restaurants and sampled many regional cuisines, his wife Alice a frequent accomplice. Trillin prefers everyday, average restaurants to the more upscale establishments and seeks out everyday foods such as

hamburgers, chili dogs, barbecue, and pizza. Although the foods he consumes are not fancy, the writing makes everyday foods enticing. Trillin's humor and charm and the short chapters make this an entertaining read.

Subjects: Food Writers, Humor, Journalism, Marriage, Quick Reads

Now Try: Other works by Trillin, such as *Messages from My Father: A Memoir* or *About Alice*, his memories of his wife Alice, who passed away from cancer, may also be suggested. Readers who enjoy Trillin's humor may also enjoy A. J. Liebling's *Between Meals: An Appetite for Paris*. Readers open to materials in other formats might want to try the documentary films *A Hot Dog Program* and *Sandwiches You Will Like*.

Vanderhoof, Ann

The Spice Necklace: My Adventures in Caribbean Cooking, Eating and Island Life. Boston: Houghton Mifflin Harcourt, 2010. 459pp. ISBN 9780618685370.

Vanderhoof and her husband left their jobs in magazine publishing in the 1990s to sail around the Caribbean for two years, which she chronicled in her first memoir, *An Embarrassment of Mangoes*. Faced with having to return to life on land, they decide to continue their journey sailing the eastern side of the Caribbean, visiting Grenada, the Dominican Republic, St. Lucia, and Trinidad. Intent on seeing real island life rather than tourist areas, the Vanderhoofs get to know many of the islands' residents. Their new friends introduce them to authentic island cuisine, from wild goat to tropical fruits and vegetables, seafood, nutmeg, and other spices the islands are known for. Vanderhoof combines vivid details and exotic settings, mouth-watering recipes, and interesting local characters.

Subjects: Caribbean, Marriage, Recipes, Sailing

Now Try: Readers will want to read the beginning of the Vanderhoof's journey, *An Embarrassment of Mangoes*. Readers may also enjoy *The Motion of the Ocean* by Janna Cawrse Esarey, who recounts the adventure she took with her husband when they left their stress-filled lives to sail across the Pacific. Melinda and Robert Blanchard also capture the exotic setting and foods of the Caribbean in *A Trip to the Beach*, their account of leaving behind their lives in Vermont to open a restaurant on Anguilla. Chris Stewart shares his humorous account of his adventures skippering a boat around the Greek Islands in *Three Ways to Capsize a Boat*; other Travel books which feature sailing as a mode of transportation include Kevin Patterson's *The Water in Between: A Journey at Sea* and Pamela Stephenson's *Treasure Islands: Sailing the South Seas in the Wake of Fanny and Robert Louis Stevenson*. Anu Lakhan's *Trinidad: Caribbean Street Food* and Peter Laurie's *Barbados: Caribbean Street Food* bring to life the flavors of the Caribbean.

Expatriate Life

Frances Mayes's best seller, *Under the Tuscan Sun*, made the Expatriate Life subgenre one of the most popular of Food Literature. In these stories, the author decides to move to a foreign country, either to join a loved one or simply for a change of scenery. The author usually struggles with adapting to a new culture and language. Often the author purchases a home that is in need of repair, which provides insight into the local culture as well as entertaining anecdotes. While some authors made this move for the purposes of learning to cook or starting a farm, food was not the primary reason for most authors' relocation. However, food plays a prominent role in these stories. Expatriate Life stories include vivid descriptions and abundant details of the foods and the setting, as well as interesting local characters that bring the surroundings to life. The pacing is typically slower than other travel titles.

1

2

> Expatriate Life titles are stories of the author's experience moving to a foreign country. They tend to include vivid descriptions and abundant details of the foods and the setting, insight into the local culture, and entertaining stories of local characters.

3

Bard, Elizabeth

4

Lunch in Paris: A Love Story, With Recipes. Little, Brown and Co., 2010. 324pp. ISBN 9780316042796.

An American journalist, Bard met and fell in love with a Frenchman while working in London. Soon she decided to move to Paris to be with him and the two planned to marry. In Paris, Bard discovers that life moves a little slower. Parisians enjoy life, love, and especially food. Bard begins shopping in the French markets and learns to cook French cuisine in her tiny Parisian kitchen. She cooks romantic meals for her fiancé, hearty meals for cold winter nights, and comforting meals when her father-in-law passes away. She also experiences difficulties adjusting to living in a foreign country, but as time goes on, she discovers the wonders of Paris and falls in love with her adopted country.

5

6

Subjects: France, French Cuisine, Life Change, Paris, Relationships

Now Try: Sarah Turnbull's *Almost French* is another story of a woman who moves to Paris after falling in love with a Frenchman. *Marcus of Umbria: What an Italian Dog Taught an American Girl About Love* by Justine van der Leun is an enjoyable memoir of the author's decision to relocate to Italy when she falls in love. When John Baxter moved to Paris to be with the woman he loved, he was put in charge of cooking the Christmas feast for her entire French family. His memoir is *Immoveable Feast: A Paris Christmas*. While Amanda Hesser doesn't relocate to a foreign country, her memoir *Cooking for Mr. Latte: A Food Lover's Courtship, with Recipes* is an entertaining story of love and food. Amy Thomas marvels at all the delicious sweets she discovers when she moves to Paris in *Paris, My Sweet: A Year in the City of Light (and Dark Chocolate)*. Readers may also enjoy Vanina Marsot's novel *Foreign Tongue: A Novel of Life and Love in Paris*, about an American woman who comes to Paris to mend her broken heart, and falls in love with the city's culture and food, as well as a Frenchman.

7

8

9

Anthony Capella's novel *The Food of Love*, features an American woman traveling in Rome who falls in love with an Italian who woos her with sumptuous food.

Brennan, Georgeanne

A Pig in Provence: Good Food and Simple Pleasures in the South of France. San Francisco: Chronicle Books, 2007. 223pp. ISBN 9780811852135.

Seeking a simpler life, Brennan moved to Provence in 1970. She began her dream of starting a farm by acquiring a herd of goats and learned to make fresh goat cheese. She also began cooking Provençal cuisine and learned to forage for wild mushrooms. While her adventures in the kitchen and with the goats are entertaining, the details of her small community make this a charming read. Descriptions of the meals and picnics she shares with her friends and neighbors, and community feasts illustrate how food brings the community together.

Subjects: Community Life, France, French Cuisine, Friendships, Life Change, Gentle Reads, Goats

Now Try: Patricia Atkinson recounts her decision to move to France to establish a vineyard and live closer to the land in *La Belle Saison: Living Off the Land in Rural France*. Carol Drinkwater also left her life in England to move to southern France with her husband and start an olive vineyard, which she recalls in *The Olive Farm*. In *I'll Never Be French (No Matter What I Do)*, Mark Greenside describes how he fell in love with life in a small village in Brittany. Readers may also enjoy Bridget Asher's novel *The Provence Cure for the Brokenhearted*. Karen Wheeler left her city life for rural France in *Tout Sweet: Hanging Up My High Heels for a New Life in France*. Margaret Hathaway's and Karl Schatz's account of their dream of goat farming, *The Year of the Goat: 40,000 Miles and the Quest for the Perfect Cheese*, may also be suggested.

Carreiro, Suzanne

The Dog Who Ate the Truffle: A Memoir of Stories and Recipes from Umbria. New York: Thomas Dunne Books, 2010. 372pp. ISBN 9780312571405.

An American food critic, Carreiro vividly recalls the year and a half she spent living in Umbria, Italy. She develops friendships with her colorful neighbors, learns to speak Italian, and learns to cook the regional foods from the local cooks and Italian grandmothers. Her newfound friendships with a truffle hunter (whose dog will often eat the prized truffles), an asparagus hunter, and a baker lead to some entertaining and delicious adventures. She also participates in cheese making and harvesting olives. The descriptions of daily life in Umbria and authentic recipes create a vivid picture of this region.

Subjects: Community Life, Friendships, Italian Cuisine, Italy, Local Customs, Recipes, Umbria

Now Try: Marlena De Blasi's *A Thousand Days in Tuscany* also recounts her colorful new neighbors and adventures learning about and preparing regional specialties. Readers may also enjoy *Cooking with Italian Grandmothers* by Jessica Theroux which contains recipes and stories about traditional Italian comfort food. *Pomodoro!: A History of the Tomato* in Italy by David Gentilcore is an interesting history of Italian cuisine. In Sarah-Kate Lynch's novel *Dolci di Love*, a woman travels to Italy when she discovers her husband has a secret life and ends up finding happiness. Elizabeth Adler's novel *Summer in Tuscany* features an American who travels to Italy and becomes caught up in the drama of a small village.

De Blasi, Marlena

A Thousand Days in Tuscany: A Bittersweet Adventure. Chapel Hill, NC: Algonquin Books, 2004. 325pp. ISBN 9781565123922.

De Blasi is a chef and a writer who met her husband in Venice. After several years living in Venice, she and her husband decide to pack up their lives and move to the Tuscan countryside. They purchase an old farmhouse, which they discover has no heat, no telephone, and antiquated electric wiring. Although they are complete strangers, the local villagers quickly pull them in, offering them friendship and food. Life revolves around food and the villagers take much pleasure in their food, and De Blasi frequently describes sumptuous meals and feasts, as well as participating in grape and olive harvesting, truffle hunting, bread baking, and mushroom foraging.

> **Subjects:** Community Life, Gentle Reads, Italy, Italian Cuisine, Marriage, Recipes

> **Now Try:** Frances Mayes has a very similar writing style to De Blasi. Readers will enjoy her memoirs of life in Tuscany, beginning with *Under the Tuscan Sun*. Readers may also enjoy De Blasi's *A Thousand Days in Venice*, which begins her story of moving to Italy after meeting her husband or *The Lady in the Palazzo*, her story of buying a 15th-century palazzo in Umbria. De Blasi also brings her characteristic vivid prose to her fiction novel, *Amandine*. Angela Murrills also describes a life revolving around food in their southern French village in *Hot Sun, Cool Shadow*.

Doran, Phil

The Reluctant Tuscan: How I Discovered My Inner Italian. New York: Gotham Books, 2005. 306pp. ISBN 9781592401185.

Doran is a successful Hollywood television writer, but the pressures of his career leave him plagued with stress and insomnia. Unbeknownst to Doran, while traveling in Italy his wife purchases an ancient rundown farmhouse in Tuscany, hoping to create an oasis from their hectic Hollywood life. Knowing the difficulties he faces when restoring a home, Doran is reluctant about this purchase. Typical of the Italian expatriate tale, Doran has his share of difficulties with the locals: the mayor, police, landlords, workmen, and so on but soon he begins to find enjoyment in his new life. Lunch, which had previously been inhaled from a fast-food drive thru, was now a two-hour long event, followed by a refreshing siesta. The beauty of Italy, the luscious food, and the slower pace of life bring Doran around. Doran humorously recounts his new life in Italy, adjusting to the slower pace and the difficulties he faces living in Italy, with no heat and bureaucracy.

Subjects: Humor, Italy, Life Change, Men's Lives, Tuscany

Now Try: Michael Tucker, another Hollywood expatriate humorously recalls his unexpected move to Italy in *Living in a Foreign Language: A Memoir of Food, Wine, and Love in Italy*. Ferenc Máté describes his adopted home with lush descriptions of scrumptious meals, rich wines, and friendly natives in *The Hills of Tuscany: New Life in an Old Land*. Readers may also enjoy Tony Hawks's humorous adventures owning a home in the French Pyrenees in *A Piano in the Pyrenees*. Readers interested in expatriate life outside of Europe may enjoy Tahir Shah's account of renovating a run-down palace in Casablanca in *The Caliph's House*. Peter Mayle's novel *A Good Year* is also a humorous story of a man who relocates to France when he inherits a run-down vineyard.

Lebovitz, David

The Sweet Life in Paris: Delicious Adventures in the World's Most Glorious and Perplexing City. New York: Broadway Books, 2009. 282pp. ISBN 9780767928885.

Lebovitz, an American pastry chef, cookbook author, and blogger, decided to move to Paris after the unexpected death of his partner. This humorous, lively memoir is Lebovitz's account of his experiences as an expatriate in Paris. From the beginning he was challenged by cultural differences. Adapting to life in a new country was not easy, but it does provide comic fodder. Lebovitz first struggles with the size of his tiny apartment and kitchen. He is confused by the rules of etiquette and hygiene and frustrated by the bureaucracy and slow workmen. Although he pokes fun at Parisian culture, it is good-natured. His tales truly provide an insider's look at life in Paris. He also recounts the sumptuous meals he eats, as well as the delicious recipes and dinners he creates in his tiny apartment kitchen, despite its size.

Subjects: France, GLBTQ, Grief, Humor, Life Change, Loss of a Partner, Men's Lives, Paris, Recipes

Now Try: After reading Lebovitz's tempting recipes, readers may want to check out one of his cookbooks. *Ready for Dessert*, a compilation of Lebovitz's best recipes, is a good place to start. Lebovitz also writes a blog, which was awarded *Saveur's* Best Culinary Travel Blog of 2011, at www.davidlebovitz.com. Adam Gopnik recounts his years living in Paris with his family in *Paris to the Moon*. *Lunch in Paris: A Love Story with Recipes* by Elizabeth Bard is an entertaining, delightful account of life in Paris from the expatriate's point of view. Sarah Turnbull's *Almost French: Love and a New Life in Paris* is another humorous account of the author's struggles to adapt to the Parisian culture. Alan Epstein moved to Rome and fell in love with the vibrant city in *As the Romans Do*. Readers who enjoy stories of men starting their lives over may want to try John Grisham's novel *Playing for Pizza*, which features a washed-up NFL player who finds a new start playing football in Italy.

Máté, Ferenc

A Vineyard In Tuscany: A Wine Lover's Dream. New York: W. W. Norton, 2007. 273pp. ISBN 9780920256565.

Mate had always dreamt of owning his own vineyard. Against the advice of friends, he and his wife purchase a run-down vineyard that includes a 13th-century friary, 15 acres of vines, olive trees, and wooded land. Before he can return the house and vineyard to its former glory, he must deal with Italian bureaucracy: the legal documents, applications, and permits that must be acquired, and pass a test in order to become recognized as a farmer. Once that is done, he must hire a crew of Italians to help with the work, which leads to some entertaining episodes. As work progresses, he discovers the remains of an Etruscan village on his land and learns the secrets to growing the best grapes and making wine. Readers will savor the beauty of the Italian landscape, the delectable meals, and the charming characters.

Subjects: Humor, Italy, Men's Lives, Wine, Winemaking

Now Try: Mate has also written *The Hills of Tuscany* and *The Wisdom of Tuscany*. Against his better judgment, Phil Doran and his wife buy a house in Tuscany in *The Reluctant Tuscan*. Carol Drinkwater buys a run-down olive farm in the south of France in *The Olive Farm*. Peter Mayle's novel *A Good Year* features a Londoner who inherits a vineyard in Provence. Three estranged sisters inherit their father's champagne vineyard and attempt to bring it back to life in Sarah-Kate Lynch's novel, *House of Daughters*.

Mayes, Frances

Every Day in Tuscany: Seasons of an Italian Life. New York: Broadway Books, 2010. 306pp. ISBN 9780767929820.

Frances Mayes became a best-selling writer with her popular memoir, *Under the Tuscan Sun*, which was made into a popular movie. In *Under the Tuscan Sun*, Mayes and her husband buy an old Tuscan villa, Bramasole, and set about bringing it back to life. Since then Mayes has continued writing about her life in Italy. In her latest account, she celebrates the 20th anniversary of her move to Italy. She and her husband have bought a second home in the mountains, where they escape to when they receive a bomb threat at Bramasole. With descriptive prose she describes everyday life in Italy: the people, the landscape, the wine, and most especially, the food. Food is a big part of her life, and she recounts the sumptuous meals she creates for friends and family. The detailed descriptions make the reader feel as if they are a guest in her home.

Subjects: Gentle Reads, Italian Cuisine, Italy, Recipes

Now Try: While readers don't have to start with *Under the Tuscan Sun*, it is Mayes's most well-known book and probably the most well-known example of ex-pat story. She has also written *Bella Tuscany* and *In Tuscany*. In *A Year in the World: Journeys of a Passionate Traveler*, Mayes decides to travel outside of Italy. Marlena De Blasi's descriptive, lush prose is reminiscent of Mayes's style. Readers may enjoy *A Thousand Days in Venice* or *A Thousand Days in Tuscany*. Although not focused on food, Sally and Carl Gable's *Palladian Days: Finding a New Life in a Venetian Country House* is a divine expatriate story of living in a Venetian villa. Readers may also enjoy other expatriate stories of moving abroad and renovating ancient homes such as *Castles in the Air* by Judy Corbett or Jeffrey Greene's *French Spirits*.

Mayle, Peter

A Year in Provence. New York: Vintage Books, 1991. 207pp. ISBN 9780679731146.
Living in England, Mayle and his wife often dreamed of leaving rainy England behind and moving to sunny Provence. Their dreams finally come true with the purchase of a 200-year-old farmhouse in Provence. Mayle recounts their first year in Provence, month by month, including their frustrations with making repairs and installing central heating, and the uninvited summer guests that never seem to stop arriving. The usual characters are all here: the eccentric neighbors and colorful locals, grocers, butchers, and farmers. Mayle claims that "one of the characteristics . . . about the French is their willingness to support good cooking" which he supports by recalling wonderful meals, trips to the market and vineyards, and hunting for truffles.

> **Subjects:** Community Life, France, French Cuisine, Gentle Reads, Life Change, Provence
>
> **Now Try:** Readers may also enjoy Mayle's fiction, such as *A Good Year* or *A Vintage Caper*, which are also humorous stories about expatriate life in France. Jeffrey Greene's *French Spirits: A House, a Village, and a Love Affair in Burgundy* and Susan Hermann Loomis's *On Rue Tatin: Living and Cooking in a French Town* are both stories of the authors' experiences purchasing old homes in France, their frustration with renovations and the joys they discover in new friendships and good meals. Although set in Wales, readers may enjoy Judy Corbett's *Castles in the Air*, about her adventures restoring an ancient castle. A humorous novel based loosely on Jen Lancaster's life, in which the main character and her husband renovate a house, is *If You Were Here*.

Tardi, Alan

Romancing the Vine: Life, Love, & Transformation in the Vineyards of Barolo. New York: St. Martin's Press, 2006. 348pp. ISBN 9780312357948.
Tardi was the chef and owner of a popular Italian restaurant in Manhattan. In 2001, he decided to close his restaurant, leave the big city behind, and move to a small village in the Piedmont district of Italy, known for Barolo wine. Tardi recounts his first year in Italy as he adjusts to a different way of life, meets the locals, and learns to cultivate his own grapevines. When he falls in love with a local woman, Ivana, he spends much of his time in her brother's vineyards. Tardi introduces readers to the charming local characters, local customs and history,

and lore and descriptions of wine production. Culinary specialties of the region, including authentic recipes, are also included.

Subjects: Italian Cuisine, Italy, Life Change, Recipes, Relationships, Wine, Winemaking

Awards: James Beard Award

Now Try: Matthew Gavin Frank also recounts how he came under the spell of the famous wine in *Barolo*. In *A Vineyard in Tuscany*, Ferenc Máté describes how he turned a Tuscan ruin into a winery. Australian Isabella Dusi and her husband left their lives behind to move to a Tuscan Village in *Bel Vino: A Year of Sundrenched Pleasure Among the Vines of Tuscany*. Readers may also enjoy Annie Hawes's charming account of her life among olive growers on the Italian Riviera in *Extra Virgin: A Young Woman Discovers the Italian Riviera, Where Every Month Is Enchanted* by Annie Hawes. Readers may also enjoy Kimberly Kafka's novel *Miranda's Vines*, in which a successful chef leaves her promising career in San Francisco to return to Oregon to take over her family's endangered vineyard.

Tucker, Michael

Living in a Foreign Language: A Memoir of Food, Wine, and Love in Italy. New York: Atlantic Monthly Press, 2007. 255pp. ISBN 9780871139627.

Tucker and his wife Jill Eikenberry are best known for their roles on the television show *L. A. Law*. While between jobs, the couple was vacationing in Italy and fell in love with a 350-year-old home in Umbria. After purchasing the home, they fell in love with the slower-paced, simpler way of life, and decided to sell their home on the West Coast and divide their time between Italy and New York. They explore the region, savoring the local cuisine, and Tucker befriends the local butchers, shopkeepers, and farmers, and finds joy in creating his own Italian meals.

Subjects: Community Life, Italian Cuisine, Italy, Life Change, Marriage, Wine

Now Try: Readers may also want to check out Tucker's other title, *I Never Forget a Meal*, which chronicles his life, marriage, and love affair with food. *The Reluctant Tuscan* by Phil Doran is another memoir by a Hollywood native who fell in love with life in Italy. Alan Tardi is a New York chef who recounts his move to a colorful Italian village in *Romancing the Vine*. Tim Parks is an American who describes his experiences living in an Italian neighborhood in Verona in *Italian Neighbors*. Betsy Draine and her husband, Michael Hinden recall searching for a summer home in France and the joys of finding their new home in *A Castle in the Backyard*. Readers may also enjoy *An Embarrassment of Mangoes*, in which Ann Vanderhoof describes how she and her husband left their busy lives behind to sail around the Caribbean, delighting in the local cuisines.

Wells, Patricia, and Wells, Walter

We've Always Had Paris . . . and Provence: A Scrapbook of Our Life in France. New York: Harper, 2008. 317pp. ISBN 9780060898618.

Patricia Wells is a well-known, award-winning author of several cookbooks on French food. In this charming memoir, she and her husband recall how they met and reminisce about their early careers, their decision to go to France, and the years they spent living and traveling through France. Alternating between Patricia and Walter, each recounts the memorable moments and flavors they have savored. Their time in France began in Paris as Patricia researched the city's restaurants, tea parlors, pastry shops, boulangeries, and chocolatiers for her books. They experience the lifestyle, fashions, and food of Paris. After they tire of the bustle of the city life, they leave Paris behind and settle in a home in the Provence countryside.

Subjects: France, French Cuisine, Marriage, Multiple Narrators, Recipes

Now Try: Readers may want to check out one of Wells's cookbooks. *The Provence Cookbook*, *Patricia Wells at Home in Provence*, and *Simply French* were all James Beard Award winners. Other titles featuring married couples and their expat experiences might also appeal to readers. Try Betsy Draine's *A Castle in the Backyard*, Frances Mayes's *Under the Tuscan Sun*, or Marlena De Blasi's *A Thousand Days in Tuscany*. Other books written by husbands and wives that might be appealing are Jane and Michael Stern's *Two for the Road: Our Love Affair With American Food* and Bill and Cheryl Jamison's *Around the World in 80 Dinners*. Another possibility is *The Company We Keep: A Husband and Wife True Life Spy Story*, in which CIA agents Robert and Dayna Baer share the story of how they fell in love during a mission. Novels that feature love stories with multiple perspectives may also be enjoyed. Try *The Time Traveler's Wife* by Audrey Niffenegger or *Stupid and Contagious* by Caprice Crane.

Consider Starting With . . .

These popular titles are good suggestions for readers new to the Food Travel genre.

Bourdain, Anthony. *A Cook's Tour: In Search of the Perfect Meal.*

De Blasi, Marlena. *A Thousand Days in Venice.*

Dunlop, Fuchsia. *Shark's Fin and Sichuan Pepper: A Sweet and Sour Memoir of Eating in China.*

Mayes, Frances. *Under the Tuscan Sun.*

Mayle, Peter. *A Year in Provence.*

Trillin, Calvin. *The Tummy Trilogy.*

References

Cords, Sarah Statz. 2006. *The Real Story: A Guide to Nonfiction Reading Interests.* Westport, CT: Libraries Unlimited.

Hooper, Brad, and Barry Trott. 2010. "Food and Travel: Twin Readers' Advisory Pleasures." *Reference & User Services Quarterly* 50 (2): 122.

Winchester, Simon. 2009. *The Best American Travel Writing* Boston: Houghton Mifflin Harcourt.

Wyatt, Neal. 2008. "Getting up to Speed in Travel Writing." NoveList. Available at www.ebscohost.com/novelist (paid subscription, see your local library).

Wyatt, Neal. 2007. *The Readers' Advisory Guide to Nonfiction.* Chicago: American Library Association.

1

2

3

4

5

6

7

8

9

Chapter 4

Food Adventure

Definition of Food Adventure

An adventure is defined as an unusual and exciting, typically hazardous, experience or activity calling for enterprise and enthusiasm. Readers' advisor and author Diana Tixier Herald suggests that adventure stories are the oldest recorded genre. She cites *The Epic of Gilgamesh*, which was chronicled on clay tables in 3,000 BC and told of adventures of Gilgamesh and his quest for immortality (Herald 2006). Librarian Tina Frolund agrees that adventure stories may be the oldest genre; however, she believes its beginnings date even further back in time. She imagines adventure stories evolved from the tradition of oral storytelling as far back as the cavemen who probably told stories of their adventures hunting prey (Frolund 2007).

Library Journal columnist Neat Wyatt states that the adventure genre is one of the most compulsively readable genres (Wyatt 2007). Adventure writing includes stories of survival, exploration, travel, and suspense. The protagonist is typically a larger-than-life character and forgoes his or her own safety to venture out into unknown, often dangerous, situations. Challenges and obstacles are common themes. Sarah Statz Cords references a few well-known nonfiction titles that fit the adventure genre: Jon Krakauer's *Into Thin Air*, Sebastian Junger's *The Perfect Storm*, and Mark Bowden's *Black Hawk Down* (Cords 2006).

Within Food Literature, adventure writing differs somewhat from other nonfiction genres. Exploration, travel, and unknown situations are common themes in Food Adventure Literature. However, Food Adventure stories do not contain as much suspense as other nonfiction genres. The protagonist is typically involved in unusual and exciting experiences, although rarely is danger involved, unless you consider possible intestinal ailments, attacks of gout, or a sliced finger. In Food Adventure Lit, the author travels in order to explore specific foods. These are stories of adventure, travel, and discovery where the protagonist is involved in exciting experiences in exotic or foreign settings and faced with unknown situations.

Appeal of Food Adventure

Sarah Statz Cords tells us that adventure stories are often page-turners (Cords 2006). Page-turners are a combination of exciting stories, brisk pacing, and exotic settings. While Food Adventure stories may not have the edge-of-your-seat pacing of Bowden's *Black Hawk Down*, the pacing is still quick. Food Adventure stories are entertaining, exciting, and compelling stories that unfold in exotic or foreign settings. There is often an element of uncertainty, whether that be traveling to far-flung locations or indulging in strange local delicacies. This uncertainty adds to the feeling of adventure.

Character is another strong appeal element of Food Adventure stories. Most Food Adventure is told from the first-person point of view, which helps the reader identify with the narrator. The narrator(s) takes risks and faces challenges, which readers enjoy observing. The authors also have a personal interest or passion in the foods they are exploring, and often elements of the authors' personal lives are included in the story.

Diana Tixier Herald requires that a successful adventure story allow the reader to experience the adventure vicariously (Herald 2006). This is a common element of appeal in Food Adventure. Many of these stories take place in foreign settings where the reader may not have a chance to go, or the stories describe unique experiences such as sampling an exotic delicacy, that the reader may not have a chance to experience. The details and descriptions in Food Adventure bring the story alive and allow the reader the opportunity to experience the event with the author.

Organization of the Chapter

In **Food Adventures and Explorations**, the author travels in order to investigate a specific culinary subject, such as cheese or pie that he or she has a particular interest or passion for. Some authors seek out strange or unusual foods. These titles are included in **Extreme Cuisine**.

Food Adventures and Explorations

In Food Adventures and Explorations, the author travels in order to investigate a specific culinary subject, such as cheese or pie. The author has a personal interest or passion in the foods he or she is exploring, and often elements of the author's personal life are included in the story. Every destination is chosen for its opportunities to learn more about the subject. Setting is an important element. Authors include details and descriptions of the place as well as local history and traditions. Readers are also often introduced to the local personalities the authors meet while on their travels.

Travel is a common element in Food Adventures and Explorations, therefore readers who enjoy these titles may also enjoy titles from the Food Travel Lit chapter. Readers may also enjoy the Immersion Journalism titles from the Investigative Food Writing chapter, which also investigate specific topics. Personal Endeavor Memoirs may also be appealing for the character appeal and the authors' personal inter-est in the subject.

In Food Adventures and Explorations, the author travels in order to explore a specific culinary subject. These are stories of adventure, travel, and discovery and incorporate a strong sense of place.

Barlow, John

Everything But the Squeal: Eating the Whole Hog in Northern Spain. New York: Farrar, Straus & Giroux, 2008. 306pp. ISBN 9780374150105.

In Galacia, a region in the northwest part of Spain, pork reigns supreme. The pig is the favored food of this region and residents consume all parts of it, head to tail. Intrigued by this, Barlow decides to travel throughout Galacia tasting every part of the pig, much to the chagrin of his vegetarian wife. While on his quest, Barlow introduces readers to the history and traditions of this little known area of Spain, while getting to know the local personalities.

Subjects: Local Food, Pork, Spain, Travel

Now Try: Peter Kaminsky visits some pork-loving locations around the world in *Pig Perfect: Encounters with Remarkable Swine and Some Great Ways to Cook Them*. Stéphane Reynaud shares his appreciation for all things pork in *Pork and Sons*, introducing readers to farmers and butchers as well as providing a number of recipes. Fergus Henderson's *The Whole Beast: Nose to Tail Eating* is a popular cookbook that celebrates using the entire animal. Readers may enjoy Claudia Roden's cookbook *The Food of Spain*. Lighthearted, humorous travel narratives may also be appealing, such as Tony Hawks's *Round Ireland with a Fridge* or *A Piano in the Pyrenees*, Bill Bryson's *A Walk In the Woods*, or Bill and Cheryl Jamison's *Around the World in 80 Dinners*. Readers may also want to try the DVD series *Spain: On the Road Again*, featuring Mario Batali's and Mark Bittman's road trips through Spain.

Beahrs, Andrew

Twain's Feast: Searching for America's Lost Foods in the Footsteps of Samuel Clemens. New York: Penguin Press, 2010. 323pp. ISBN 9781594202599.

Mark Twain chronicled his travels in Europe in *A Tramp Abroad*. In it, he reminisces about the American foods he misses while he is away. Twain traveled extensively throughout the United States and his favored foods represented a variety of regional American cuisine. Some of these foods are still a part of our modern cuisine, however many have been forgotten. Beahrs attempts to find out if some of Twain's favorite foods are still eaten. His travels take him to Illinois in search of endangered prairie hens, New Orleans for croakers, San Francisco for oysters, and Arkansas for raccoon. Beahrs explores the changes that have occurred in the landscape and local ecosystems, as well as culture, that have caused many of these foods to go out of favor. The historical culinary details, highlights of Twain's life and literary works, and investigation of the current state of wild, local foods will appeal to fans of history as well as investigative writing.

> **Subjects:** American Cuisine, American History, Food Habits, History, Travel, Twain, Mark

> **Now Try:** Readers may enjoy checking out the work that inspired this title, Twain's *A Tramp Abroad* or even *The Autobiography of Mark Twain* or Ron Powers biography, *Mark Twain: A Life*. In *America Eats!: On the Road with the WPA*, Pat Willard travels through America to see if the culinary traditions documented in the original Federal Writers' Project America Eats still exist. Readers may also enjoy other road trips through America such as Stephen Fry's *Stephen Fry in America*, Bill Bryson's *Lost Continent*, or Michael Paterniti's *Driving Mr. Albert* about his travels across the country with Albert Einstein's brain.

Hathaway, Margaret

The Year of the Goat: 40,000 miles and the Quest for the Perfect Cheese. Guilford, Conn.: Lyons Press, 2007. 204pp. ISBN 9781599210216.

Hathaway and her fiancé live in New York City but dream of leaving their city life behind for the peace of the country. Their dream is to own a goat farm and produce goat cheese. But when they discover the cost of starting a farm and the risks involved, they think their dreams are sunk. On the advice of a therapist, they decide to take a year off to travel the country researching goat farming to determine if this is truly the life they want. Hathaway and her fiancé spend a year crossing the country, visiting goat farms, breeders, cheese makers, and attend goat auctions, slaughters, festivals, and conventions.

> **Subjects:** Animal Husbandry, Cheese, Farming, Goats, Marriage, Travel

> **Now Try:** Readers interested in learning whether Hathaway's dream of having her own goats came true will be pleased to see her next book *Living With Goats: Everything You Need To Know to Raise Your Own Backyard Herd*. In *The Cheese Chronicles: A Journey Through the Making and Selling of Cheese in America, From Field to Farm to Table*, Liz Thorpe travels America visiting farms and factories and profiling American cheese makers. *Goat Song: A Seasonal Life, A Short History of Herding, and the Art of Making Cheese* by Brad Kessler and *Hay Fever: How Chasing a Dream on a Vermont Farm Changed My Life* by Angela Miller are entertaining stories of people who left the city life to farm goats. *The Dirty Life* by Kristin Kimball is another story of an author who left her city life to move to a farm in the country. Readers may also enjoy Sarah Kate Lynch's fiction novel, *Blessed are the Cheesemakers*, a heartwarming story of aging cheese makers in Ireland.

Hopkins, Kate

99 Drams of Whiskey: The Accidental Hedonist's Quest for the Perfect Shot and the History of the Drink. New York: St. Martin's Press, 2009. 308pp. ISBN 9780312381080.

What makes whiskey so popular? Hopkins, author of The Accidental Hedonist blog (accidentalhedonist.com), decides to find the best whiskey on the market and learn what makes the various whiskies different. She begins with a history of early forms of distillation and the evolution of the spirit, and then travels to the countries best known for their production of it: Scotland, Ireland, Canada, and the United States. Visiting distilleries, pubs, and corporations, she recounts the various processes used in making whiskies and samples a wide variety of them. She meets historians, pub owners, and whiskey aficionados; she also discovers the historical context of whiskey in the various countries, including Scotland and Ireland's conflicts with the English, the Whiskey Rebellion in Pennsylvania, and the effects of Prohibition on the United States' whiskey industry. Part history and part travelogue, Hopkins provides an entertaining narrative.

Subjects: Blogs, History, Spirits, Whiskey, World Travel

Now Try: Jason Wilson's *Boozehound: On the Trail of the Rare, the Obscure, and the Overrated in Spirits*, and Max Watman's *Chasing the White Dog: An Amateur Outlaw's Adventures in Moonshine* are both entertaining travel adventures about spirits. Andrew Jefford investigates the whiskey distilleries on the Scottish Isle of Islay in *Peat Smoke and Spirit*. Zane Lamprey travels the world sampling local spirits, from Irish whiskey to Japanese sake in *Three Sheets: Drinking Made Easy*. Tom Standage's *A History of the World in Six Glasses* provides an interesting cultural history of alcohol. Steve Almond's *Candyfreak* and Taras Grescoe's *The Devil's Picnic: Around the World in Pursuit of Forbidden Fruit* may be of interest to readers who enjoy travel and explorations of a particular food. Peter Krass profiles the life of the famous whiskey maker in *Blood and Whiskey: The Life and Times of Jack Daniel*. Hopkins also recounts her travels through the United States and Europe investigating the history of candy in *Sweet Tooth: The Bittersweet History of Candy*.

Le Draoulec, Pascale

American Pie: Slices of Life (and Pie) From America's Back Roads. New York: Harper Collins Publishers, 2002. 353pp. ISBN 9780060197360.

What could be more American than pie? When Pascale Le Draoulec decided to leave San Francisco to take a job as a food writer in New York City, the move presented an opportunity for food writing fodder. Instead of flying, Le Draoulec decided to drive across the country, in search of the quintessential American dessert: pie. Setting out with no definite itinerary, she meanders through back roads and small towns in search of the best pies and the people who make them. Her practice was to stop in a small town and ask the locals for recommendations. Many people had pie stories, remembering pies they used to eat as a child or someone who made memorable pies. She tasted huckleberry, shoofly, sweet potato, cherry, and even Olallieberry pies. The mouthwatering descriptions of the pies (recipes included!) are enough to entice any reader, but the personal stories of the warm, friendly people she meets on her journey will appeal to readers who enjoy interesting characters.

Subjects: Local Food, Pie, Recipes, Travel, United States

Now Try: Readers may want to try Janet Clarkson's *Pie: A Global History*, a quick read on all things pie. Readers who enjoy the personal stories of the friendly people Le Draoulec met on her journey may also enjoy Michael and Jane Stern's *Two for the Road: Our Love Affair with American Food* or their cookbook, *Road Food*. Alton Brown's *Feasting on Asphalt* is another entertaining account of his quest to find the best roadside food and get to know the people who make it. Peter Reinhart captures his quest to find the perfect pie—pizza pie—in *American Pie*. George Motz travels across the United States in search of the perfect hamburger in *Hamburger America*.

LeMay, Eric

Immortal Milk: Adventures in Cheese. New York: Free Press, 2010. 242pp. ISBN 9781439153048.

LeMay and his wife Chuck are cheese enthusiasts. In an effort to immerse themselves in their favorite food, they set out to learn more about cheese. Traveling to France, Italy, Wisconsin, and San Francisco, they seek out familiar and untried cheeses, determined to understand how something that can be so stinky can elicit so much desire and pleasure. The passionate cheese makers they meet on their journey school them in the art of making cheese and explain how cheese can have such vastly different flavors. They explore the differences between raw milk cheeses and pasteurized cheeses, aging, rinds and curds, and visit the Slow Food International Cheese Festival, where they sample cheeses from around the world.

Subjects: Cheese, Quick Reads, World Travel

Now Try: Liz Thorpe's *The Cheese Chronicles: A Journey Through the Making and Selling of Cheese in America, From Field to Farm to Table* and Gordon Edgar's *Cheesemonger: A Life on the Wedge* both explore the wonders of cheese, from farm to table. *Goat Song: A Seasonal Life, A Short History of Herding, and the Art of Making Cheese* by Brad Kessler and *Hay Fever: How Chasing a Dream on a Vermont Farm Changed My Life* by Angela Miller are entertaining stories of people who left the city life to farm goats and make cheese. Carlo Petrini's *Slow Food* is a compilation of articles about the Slow Food movement and introduces readers to exotic foods from around the world. Sara Mansfield Taber is as passionate about bread as LeMay is about cheese. Try her book *Bread of Three Rivers: The Story of a French Loaf.*

MacLean, Natalie

Red, White and Drunk All Over: A Wine-Soaked Journey from Grape to Glass. New York: Bloomsbury, 2006. 279pp. ISBN 9781582346489.

MacLean's passion for wine comes across in this lively account of all things wine that will appeal to novices, casual wine lovers, and aficionados. MacLean travels from Burgundy to Sonoma, learning how wine is made, tasting various wines, and interviewing wine growers. She explores various grape-growing philosophies, the cork versus screwcap debate, and the ongoing feuds between wine critics. Back at home, she goes undercover as a sommelier in a five-star restaurant, works in a wine shop, and hosts a wine-tasting party in her home. Her vivid descriptions and the colorful personalities of the people she meets during her research make this an enjoyable quick read.

Subjects: Quick Reads, Travel, Wine

Now Try: Lawrence Osborne's *The Accidental Connoisseur* and Mike Weiss's *A Very Good Year* are other good choices for in-depth accounts of winemaking and the wine industry. Kate Hopkins's *99 Drams of Whiskey: The Accidental Hedonist's Quest for the Perfect Shot and the History of the Drink* is another passionate adventure where the author explores all aspects of her subject, meeting colorful personalities along the way. Alice Feiring argues against the influence of wine critics in *The Battle for Wine and Love: or How I Saved the World from Parkerization*. George Taber explores the issue of corking in *To Cork or Not to Cork*. John and Erica Platter's *Africa Uncorked* is a fascinating account of their travels through Africa tasting wine.

Riccardi, Victoria Abbott

***Untangling My Chopsticks: A Culinary Sojourn in Kyoto**. New York: Broadway Books, 2003. 282pp. ISBN 9780767908511.

Always fascinated by stories of Japan, Riccardi left her job, apartment, and boyfriend to spend a year living in Kyoto, Japan. Having studied at Le Cordon Bleu, Riccardi had a deep interest in Japanese cuisine and kaiseki, the ritualized cuisine that accompanies the formal Japanese tea ceremony. While in Kyoto, Riccardi lives with a Japanese couple and attends a school of kaiseki. Riccardi recounts the fascinating history of the tea ceremony and kaiseki and gives elaborate details of the foods that are prepared. Her Japanese family teaches her about typical modern-day Japanese cuisine and she vividly recounts trips to the markets and grocery stores and describes typical Japanese home cooking as well as holiday foods. Riccardi's unique experience provides an intimate look at a culture that is often impenetrable to Americans, and her descriptions of exotic foods and elaborate food rituals are highly interesting.

Subjects: Culinary School, Japan, Japanese Cuisine, Kaiseki, Recipes, Tea Ceremony, Travel

Now Try: Readers who are interested in learning more about kaiseki may want to check out *Kaiseki: The Exquisite Cuisine of Kyoto's Kikunoi Restaurant* by Yoshihiro Murata. Holly Hughes's *Best Food Writing 2010* features an essay about Kyoto and its tofu. Karin Muller's *Japanland: A Year in Search of Wa* describes her year living in Japan experiencing traditional customs and culture. Readers may also enjoy Sarah Marx Feldner's vivid cookbook *A Cook's Journey Through Japan*. Pico Iyer's *The Lady and the Monk* is a vivid account of his time spent living in a monastery in Kyoto. Fiction novels such as Arthur Golden's *Memoirs of a Geisha* and Ellis Avery's *The Teahouse Fire* may also appeal to readers who enjoy the vivid depictions of traditional tea ceremonies and life in Kyoto. Cathy Yardley's romantic/chick lit novel *Turning Japanese* features an American who moves to Japan to follow her dream of creating manga.

Walsh, Robb

Sex, Death, and Oysters: A Half-Shell Lover's World Tour. Berkeley: Counterpoint, 2009. 267pp. ISBN 9781582434575.

Food writer Walsh's obsession with oysters began with his investigation of a local Texas species of oyster being passed off as Blue Points. His investigation sparked his interest and led to a journey that took him across the United States and throughout the world. Walsh travels from Texas to New Orleans and New York City, Ireland, England, France, and Canada. Visiting oyster reefs and oyster bars, he samples and compares the differences between species of oysters. Walsh learns how to shuck an oyster, discovers why oysters aren't eaten in the summer months, and investigates the folklore of the oyster's aphrodisiac properties. Fascinating facts about oysters, the history of oyster consumption, and the current state of the oyster industry and regulations are all included.

> **Subjects:** Folklore, Micro-Histories, Oysters, Travel

> **Now Try:** Rowan Jacobsen covers all things oyster in his quick, easy-to-read guide, *A Geography of Oysters: The Connoisseurs' Guide to Oyster Eating in North America*. Mark Kurlansky's *The Big Oyster: History on the Half Shell* is a detailed micro-history that will appeal to readers who are interested in the history of the oyster's popularity. Erin Byers Murray went to work on an oyster farm to understand modern oyster farming in *Shucked: Life on a New England Oyster Farm*. Readers may also enjoy investigations of other foods, such as *Chasing Chiles: Hot Spots Along the Pepper Trail* by Kurt Michael Friese, Kraig Kraft, and Gary Paul Nabhan.

Watman, Max

Chasing the White Dog: An Amateur Outlaw's Adventures in Moonshine. New York: Simon & Schuster, 2010. 292pp. ISBN 9781416571780.

Watman chronicles America's long history of producing moonshine, from the Whiskey Rebellion in the 1790s through Prohibition up to today. Interspersed with interesting stories of rebellions, criminal trials, and outlaws, Watman includes his humorous experiments attempting to distill his own hooch and his acquaintances with other moonshiners.

> **Subjects:** American History, Investigative Stories, Moonshine, Prohibition, Spirits, Travel

> **Now Try:** Charles D. Thompson Jr.'s *Spirits of Just Men* traces the history of moonshine in the 1930s and chronicles the Great Moonshine Conspiracy Trial of 1935. Readers may also enjoy *Last Call: The Rise and Fall of Prohibition* by Daniel Okrent. *The Wettest*

County in the World by Matt Bondurant is a fictional story of a family of boot-leggers. Fans of television may enjoy the Discovery Channel series *Moonshiners*. Readers may also enjoy immersion histories on other topics such as Tony Horwitz's *Confederates in the Attic* or Sarah Vowell's *Assassination Vacation*. Max Watman also wrote Race *Day*, the story of American horse racing.

Willard, Pat

America Eats!: On the Road with the WPA: the Fish Fries, Box Supper Socials, and Chitlin Feasts That Define Read American Food. New York: Bloomsbury, 2008. 305pp. ISBN 9781596913622.

In the 1930s, the Works Progress Administration created the Federal Writers' Project for unemployed writers. Writers were asked to contribute to a project called America Eats. The plan was to produce a book of compiled essays and recipes that would describe the various traditional foods eaten throughout the United States. Unfortunately, the project was abandoned when the United States entered World War II and the essays and recipes were archived in the Library of Congress. Willard uses these unpublished essays written by writers such as Eudora Welty, Ralph Ellison, and Saul Bellow, to travel around the country to see if the traditions captured in the 1930s still exist today. Willard combines pieces from the original project along with her contemporary experiences, and traditional recipes as well as updated versions.

Subjects: Food Habits, Travel, U.S. History

Now Try: Mark Kurlansky's *The Food of a Younger Land* is a compilation of the original essays and recipes from the Federal Writers' Project. *American-Made: The Enduring Legacy of the WPA: When FDR Put the Nation to Work* by Nick Taylor details the history of the Works Progress Administration and the jobs it created. Readers may also enjoy the biography of an early food writer: *Hometown Appetites: The Story of Clementine Paddleford, the Forgotten Food Writer Who Chronicled How America Ate* by Kelly Alexander and Cynthia Harris. *Two for the Road: Our Love Affair With American Food* by Jane and Michael Stern offers a more modern take on American food.

Extreme Cuisine

In Extreme Cuisine, authors seek out experiences with strange or unusual foods. Often they travel to exotic or foreign locations in order to experience local delicacies that are considered strange in our culture. Exploration and a sense of discovery are strong appeal factors. Vivid details and descriptions give the readers a sense of the foods that are completely foreign in their own culture. The authors also include descriptions of the local cultures and food traditions. These titles tend to be exciting and entertaining, and often somewhat humorous, as authors navigate foreign cultures and suffer intestinal ailments from ingesting these exotic foods. Readers who enjoy the Extreme Cuisine titles may also enjoy some of the popular television series that also feature extreme cuisine and travel.

In Extreme Cuisine, authors travel to exotic or foreign locations in order to experience unusual local delicacies. These titles tend to be exciting and entertaining, have a quick pace, and are rich in details and descriptions.

Bourdain, Anthony

A Cook's Tour: In Search of the Perfect Meal. New York: Bloomsbury, 2001. 274pp. ISBN 9781582341408.

> After the success of his memoir *Kitchen Confidential*, Bourdain takes a break from the kitchen and goes on a trip around the world in search of the perfect meal. Portugal, Russia, Morocco, Tokyo, Cambodia, Vietnam, and Scotland are just a few of the stops on his trip. With his typical sarcastic wit, Bourdain entertains with stories of exotic foods, cultural differences, and the connections he makes through food with the people he meets. Fans of Bourdain's popular Travel Channel show *No Reservations* will enjoy Bourdain's willingness to try anything and his love for discovering new cultures and food.

> **Subjects:** Bourdain, Anthony, Chefs, Food Habits, Humor, Local Food, Profanity, World Travel

> **Now Try:** Readers may also want to look at Bourdain's illustrated journal *No Reservations: Around the World on an Empty Stomach*, which contains pictures and tidbits from his many travels. Andrew Zimmern is also known for his Travel Channel show, *Bizarre Foods*. His love of discovering other cultures and opening one's mind to new experiences will appeal to Bourdain's fans. Try Zimmern's *The Bizarre Truth: How I Walked Out the Door Mouth First . . . And Came Back Shaking My Head*. Readers may also enjoy Jerry Hopkins's *Extreme Cuisine: The Weird & Wonderful Foods that People Eat*. Adam Richman is another host from the Travel Channel, with his show *Man vs. Food*. His travelogue of American cuisine, *America the Edible: A Hungry History, from Sea to Dining Sea* may be of interest.

Bowles, Tom Parker

The Year of Eating Dangerously: A Global Adventure in Search of Culinary Extremes. New York: St. Martin's Press, 2007. 374pp. ISBN 9780312373788.

> Having grown up on the typical English diet of bland foods, Parker Bowles travels the world from New Mexico to Asia, sampling some of the world's most diverse cuisines and dangerous foods, and experiencing local food cultures. Eel, chilis, barbeque, dog, cobra, and puffer fish are just a few of the exotic and strange foods Parker Bowles samples. His humorous and strange adventures, as well as his detailed descriptions of local delicacies, allow readers the vicarious experience of extreme cuisine.

Subjects: Local Food, World Travel

Now Try: Readers may also be interested in Bowles's book *Full English: A Journey Through the British and Their Food*, which explores British food traditions. Jerry Hopkins's *Extreme Cuisine: The Weird & Wonderful Foods that People Eat* is another entertaining look at exotic foods. Steve Rinella's *The Scavenger's Guide to Haute Cuisine* is a humorous account of the author's attempt to track down exotic foods. John Barlow's *Everything But the Squeal* recounts his quest to eat every part of the hog. Readers may also enjoy titles from the Personal Endeavor Memoirs, in which the authors set out to attempt a challenge, such as Manny Howard's *My Empire of Dirt* or William Alexander's *52 Loaves*. Other personal challenges may also be appealing, such as A. J. Jacobs's *Drop Dead Healthy*.

Gates, Stefan

Gastronaut: Adventures in Food for the Romantic, the Foolhardy, and the Brave. Orlando: Harcourt, 2005. 257pp. ISBN 9780156030977.

This quick read is a collection of brief, humorous, and sometimes disgusting, stories of Gates's experiences eating and making strange foods. Gates is willing to eat anything, from insects to guinea pigs to bodily fluids. He also enjoys experiments making his own cheese, margarine, and smoked meats, but also tries strange experiments such as guilding foods. Gates describes some of the memorable meals he has created, such as a bacchanalian orgy and cooking a whole pig in an underground fire pit. Most recipes will not tempt readers to try this at home, but readers will enjoy Gates's humor and daring.

Subjects: Essays, Experiments, Humor, Quick Reads, Recipes

Now Try: Jerry Hopkins's *Extreme Cuisine: The Weird & Wonderful Foods That People Eat* is an entertaining look at some of the foods people will eat. Andrew Zimmern frequently samples strange foods on his travels. Try his memoir *The Bizarre Truth: How I Walked Out the Door Mouth First . . . and Came Back Shaking My Head*. Steven Rinella recounts the elaborate feast he prepared using some strange and uncommon ingredients in *The Scavenger's Guide to Haute Cuisine*.

Hopkins, Jerry

Extreme Cuisine: The Weird and Wonderful Foods That People Eat. North Clarendon, VT: Tuttle Publishing, 2004. 320pp. ISBN 9780794602550.

Hopkins has traveled the world sampling a wide variety of regional specialties that are uncommon to Americans. In this book he examines eating habits around the world and explores how foods that are considered acceptable in one region are rejected and even abhorred in others. He details local foods and their history in a culture's diet. The book is divided into sections: mammals, reptiles, birds, insects, plants, and leftovers. We see everything from dogs, rats, bats, snakes, roaches, butterflies, termites, spiders, bark, grass, seaweed, durian fruit, blood, gold, road kill, dirt, and dumpster diving.

Subjects: Food Habits, World Travel

Now Try: Christa Weil's *Fierce Food: The Intrepid Diner's Guide to the Unusual, Exotic, and Downright Bizarre* also features foods that are considered extreme to Americans. Marvin Harris examines the diversity of human food habits in *Good to Eat: Riddles of Food and Culture*. Lonely Planet's *Extreme Cuisine: Exotic Tastes from Around the World* is a quick, intriguing read with photographs. Anthony Bourdain's *A Cook's Tour* and Andrew Zimmern's *The Bizarre Truth* both share their experiences sampling uncommon regional cuisines throughout the world. Margaret Visser illuminates the cultural differences in table manners and eating rituals around the world in *The Rituals of Dinner: The Origins, Evolution, Eccentricities, and Meaning of Table Manners*. Readers willing and interested in trying some new foods without going too extreme may enjoy Fergus Henderson's cookbook *The Whole Beast: Nose to Tail Eating*.

Marcone, Massimo Francesco

In Bad Taste? The Adventures and Science behind Food Delicacies. Toronto: Key Porter Books, 2007. 198pp. ISBN 9781552638828.

Marcone journeys to remote regions of the world to learn the secrets behind bizarre variations of mainstream foods that are considered delicacies. In Ethiopia and Indonesia, Marcone inspects Kopi Luwak coffee, or civet coffee, the world's most expensive coffee that is made from beans that have passed through a civet's digestive tract. In Morocco, he explores argan oil from nuts harvested from goat dung. In Italy, he finds a cheese that is notable for being riddled with insect larvae. Birds' nests used for soup in Malaysia, insects in Thailand, and morels in North America are a few other bizarre delicacies that are featured. Marcone faces smugglers, warlords, corrupt officials, and dangerous wildlife to find out if these foods are measurably better than their conventional counterparts. Aside from the travel and adventure, Marcone takes his finds into the laboratory for scientific investigation.

Subjects: Food Habits, Local Food, Science, World Travel

Now Try: Marcone follows up this book with *Acquired Tastes: On the Trail of the World's Most Sought-After Delicacies*, investigating shark-fin soup, ant eggs, scorpions, and fried grasshoppers. *Extreme Cuisine* by Jerry Hopkins is a similarly adventurous title, as is *Fierce Food* by Christa Weil. Another author who traveled to discover what goes into his food (even his junk food) is Steve Ettlinger, in his title *Twinkie Deconstructed*. *Unmentionable Cuisine* by Calvin Schwabe, although an older title, looks at food prejudices and why we eat certain foods and reject others. Jonathan Deutsch compiles extreme cuisines in *They Eat That?: A Cultural Encyclopedia of Weird and Exotic Food from around the World*. Rachel Herz looks at why cultures differ in their views of what is considered disgusting in *That's Disgusting: Unraveling the Mysteries of Repulsion*. Readers may also want to check out the blog Deep End Dining (www.deependdining.com), which is dedicated to seeking out uncommon foods and exotic cuisines.

Majumdar, Simon

Eat My Globe: One Year to Go Everywhere and Eat Everything. New York: Free Press, 2009. 279pp. ISBN 9781416576020.

Simon Majumdar's family has an obsession with food. All of the events of his life have centered around food. With a photographic memory for foods, he can recall meals he has eaten over his lifetime. Having turned 40, working in a career that was no longer fulfilling, the author reflects on the goals he set for himself. One of his goals was to go everywhere, eat everything. One day, having had enough of the daily grind, he submits his resignation and begins planning his world tour of eating. His plan is to sample traditional dishes of each location. Starting in the UK with Britain and Ireland he samples black pudding, pork pie, and cheese. In Tokyo, he experiences sumo stew, cod sperm, Hida beef (the cousin of Kobe beef) and learns to make miso soup, tempura, and sushi. China brings one of his worst experiences: rat. Mongolia features horse meat and fermented mare's milk. In Iceland he tries sheep's head and shark meat (another terrible experience). His travels also take him to Australia, Russia, Argentina, Thailand, Vietnam, India, Morocco, Chicago, New Orleans, and many other places. Majumdar's humor and short chapters make this a quick, fun read.

Subjects: Food Habits, Humor, Local Food, Quick Reads, World Travel

Now Try: Other travel stories of exploring exotic foods are *The Man Who Ate Everything* by Jeffrey Steingarten and *Then Man Who Ate the World: In Search of the Perfect Dinner* by Jay Rayner. Other titles of men taking on a life change might be appealing as well. Try A. J. Jacobs's *Drop Dead Healthy*, Doug Fine's *Farewell, My Subaru: An Epic Adventure in Local Living* or Mark Boyle's *The Moneyless Man: A Year of Freeconomic Living.*

Rinella, Steve

The Scavenger's Guide to Haute Cuisine. New York: Miramax Books/Hyperion, 2006. 319pp. ISBN 9781401352370.

Since his childhood, Rinella has hunted, fished, and foraged for food. When he comes across Escoffier's classic 1903 *Le Guide Culinaire*, which utilized what would now be considered bizarre and exotic ingredients, Rinella decides to recreate a 45-course banquet using Escoffier's recipes. Intending to procure the necessary ingredients himself, either by hunting, fishing, or raising the animals, he embarks on a year-long quest, which takes him across the United States and Canada. Hunting for antelope and rabbit and fishing for blue trout may not be so strange, but catching a stingray, eels, and a turtle, and foraging for pigeon eggs and swallows' nests are not the usual activities of most hunters and make for some humorous adventures. The resulting three-day banquet he prepares showcases some interesting recipes and provides a look at historical haute cuisine. Readers who may be turned off by the hunting aspect may be surprised to read of Rinella's deep respect and appreciation for the land and the animals he hunts.

Subjects: Escoffier, Auguste, Fishing, Foraging, Humor, Hunting, Recipes, Travel

Now Try: While lengthy, readers may be interested in perusing Escoffier's *Le Guide Culinaire*, the inspiration for this work. Readers interested in doing their own scavenging may want to check out *Hunt, Gather, Cook: Finding the Forgotten Feast* by Hank Shaw or Lily Raff McCaulou's account of her attempt to hunt her own food, *Call of the Mild: Learning to Hunt My Own Dinner*. Those who enjoyed Rinella's adventures may want to try his book *American Buffalo: In Search of a Lost Icon* where he explores the history of American buffalo and embarks on a buffalo hunt in Alaska. Guy Grieve recounts his adventures in the wilderness of Alaska in *Call of the Wild: My Escape to Alaska*. Michael Perry's memoir *Coop: A Year of Poultry, Pigs, and Parenting* may appeal to readers who enjoy Rinella's humorous personality and low-key writing style. New York chef Georgia Pellegrini attempts to hunt the ingredients for her recipes in *Girl Hunter: Revolutionizing the Way We Eat, One Hunt at a Time*. Langdon Cook attempts to connect with the land through foraging in *Fat of the Land: Adventures of a 21st Century Forager*. Hunter Angler Gardner Cook is a blog written by a man who hunts, fishes, gardens, and forages for his food. It can be found at honest-food.net.

Walsh, Robb

Are You Really Going to Eat That?: Reflections of a Culinary Thrill Seeker. New York: Counterpoint, 2003. 268pp. ISBN 9781582432786.

Walsh is food writer, restaurant critic, and commentator for NPR's Weekend Edition. This title is a collection of his essays written over the past 10 years. In these essays Walsh recounts his world travels, focusing on food as a window into other cultures. Walsh has traveled to Jamaica's Blue Mountains to sample coffee, Bresse to see the famed blue-footed chickens, Trinidad for the world's hottest hot sauce, Thailand to experience the notoriously stinky durian fruit. Spam, oysters, Creole gumbo, and Texas barbeque are a few of the other foods he seeks out. As Walsh explores the history and origins of these foods, he provides insights into the local culture as well.

Subjects: Essays, History, Local Food, Recipes, World Travel

Now Try: Readers should consider some of Walsh's other titles, such as *Sex Death and Oysters: A Half-Shell Lover's World Tour*. *Legends of Texas Barbecue Cookbook: Recipes and Recollections from the Pit Bosses* explores the history of Texas Barbecue and the cultural influences. In *Save the Deli*, David Sax travels the country investigating the history and culture of delis in America. Jeffrey Steingarten's *The Man Who Ate Everything* is another entertaining collection of stories about the author's experiments with novel foods.

Zimmern, Andrew

The Bizarre Truth: How I Walked Out the Door Mouth First . . . and Came Back Shaking My Head. New York: Broadway Books, 2009. 271pp. ISBN 9780767931298.

Zimmern is best known for his Travel Channel show, *Bizarre Foods*. He travels to exotic locations and samples local delicacies that are often considered extreme cuisine to most of his viewers. To Zimmern, food is the easiest way to bridge gaps and build friendships and sampling local cuisines is the best way to see and understand a culture. In this humorous account, Zimmern recounts some of his more memorable trips including puffin hunting in Iceland, lung fishing in Uganda, and other exotic locations such as Paris, Spain, and Nicaragua. His hope is to raise awareness of global cultures and encourage people to travel and experience other cultures.

Subjects: Food Habits, Local Food, World Travel

Now Try: Zimmern is known for his willingness to try foods that many would find strange. Readers who enjoy the vicarious experience of eating strange foods may also enjoy Jerry Hopkins's *Strange Foods: Bush Meat, Bats, and Butterflies: An Epicurean Adventure Around the World.* Zimmern's fans will also enjoy Anthony Bourdain's *A Cook's Tour: Global Adventures in Extreme Cuisines* for his interest in experiencing new and unfamiliar cuisines. Robb Walsh's *Are You Really Going to Eat That?* is another entertaining collection of extreme cuisine adventures. Stefan Gates's odd experiments with food in *Gastronaut: Adventures in Food for the Romantic, the Foolhardy, and the Brave* may also be appealing.

Consider Starting With . . .

The following titles are excellent choices for readers new to Food Adventure Literature, encompassing both Food Adventures and Explorations and Extreme Cuisine.

Bourdain, Anthony. *A Cook's Tour: In Search of the Perfect Meal.*

Le Draoulec, Pascale. *American Pie: Slices of Life (and Pie) From America's Back Roads.*

Riccardi, Victoria Abbott. *Untangling My Chopsticks: A Culinary Sojourn in Kyoto.*

Rinella, Steve. *The Scavenger's Guide to Haute Cuisine.*

References

Cords, Sarah Statz. 2006. *The Real Story: A Guide to Nonfiction Reading Interests*. Westport, CT: Libraries Unlimited.

Frolund, Tina. 2007. *Genrefied Classics: A Guide to Reading Interests in Classic Literature*. Westport, CT: Libraries Unlimited.

Herald, Diana Tixier. 2006. *Genreflecting: A Guide to Popular Reading Interests*. Westport, CT: Libraries Unlimited.

Wyatt, Neal. 2007. *The Readers' Advisory Guide to Nonfiction*. Chicago: American Library Association.

Part III

Nonfiction Subject Interests

Chapter **5**

History of Food

Definition of History of Food

History, simply defined, is a record or description of events that happened in the past. In the fifth century BC, the Greek historian Herodotus was the first to record the conflicts of the Greeks and Persians with the purpose of explaining the past to a wider audience, earning him the designation as the "father of history." Since then, historians and scholars have written histories to chronicle the lives of famous leaders and important events, explain events, illustrate the strengths and weaknesses of governments, and persuade readers to embrace certain behaviors and ways of living. The writing of history was also used to illustrate truths about human behavior and the natural world that would allow people to understand the present (Messer 2006). Although the styles of recording history have changed over time, it has always served to bring the past to life. Today, histories are written about a wide variety of events and figures. Histories of nations, wars, and famous leaders are still popular, but many readers also enjoy focused histories of single objects or ideas called micro-histories.

John Arnold states that "part of thinking about 'history' is to think about what—or who—history is for" (Arnold 2000). We know that history can explain important events, tell us where we came from and who we are now. But what is the purpose of studying the history of food? Because food is a universal commonality, it provides us with a common ground to our past. In *Near a Thousand Tables*, Felipe Fernandez-Armesto states that the history of food is part of world history and is inseparable from all other interactions between humans and nature (Fernandez-Armesto 2002). Jennifer Cognard-Black and Melissa A. Goldthwaite also point out that studying the foods and food habits of the past also gives us insight into historical societies and cultures. The practice of preparing, eating, and sharing food conveys human interactions (Cognard-Black and Goldthwaite 2008). Thomas Jefferson said that if you want to understand the workings of a society, you have to look into their kettles and eat their bread (Gdula 2007). Mark Kurlansky points out that food can illuminate the nature of humans and provide insight into individual's lives (Kurlansky 2002). Histories like *97 Orchard: An Edible History of Five Immigrant Families in One New York Tenement* by Jane Ziegelman examine the immigrant experience in America from the elemental perspective of food, which gives readers a very personal look into the lives of immigrants.

Appeal of History of Food

A typical fan of food history will often look for a book on a certain subject, event, or time period. The opportunity for learning or understanding a specific topic is generally the main appeal factor for readers of history. But as Neal Wyatt observes, there is a limit to books on any given subject; therefore librarians should think about connections between books beyond subject (Wyatt 2007). Besides subject, history is appealing for its variety. History covers a wide variety of topics and time periods. Some are highly fact-based and scholarly, while some are focused more on story.

Story is often an important element for the history reader. A rich, story-filled narrative can bring the events of the past to life and help the reader to make sense of events. Details and descriptions such as setting, customs, everyday life, or correspondences, are therefore important in creating a more engaging story. Character can be another strong appeal factor in history. Strong character development creates a sense of connection with the reader and provides a better sense of understanding of the time period.

Readers of History of Food titles may also enjoy broader titles of history. For example, readers who enjoy Donald Kladstrup's *Wine and War: The French, the Nazis, and the Battle for France's Greatest Treasure,* may also enjoy other histories of World War II and Nazi looting. Or readers who enjoy histories of influential food companies may want to consider one of the many histories of other influential companies. There is also a wide array of micro-histories outside the subject of food that may be appealing as well. Biographies of famous culinary figures may also be appealing to fans of food histories.

Organization of the Chapter

The titles in this chapter range from lengthy, broad histories, to shorter titles focused on a single subject or time period. **Epic Food Histories** cover longer periods of history, usually spanning multiple centuries. **Defining Times** offer chronological retellings of significant time periods. **Influential Food Enterprises** feature histories of companies that have had a significant, lasting impact on the food industry. **Micro-Histories** are in-depth studies focused on a narrow topic.

Epic Food Histories

In *The Real Story,* Sarah Statz Cords refers to Epic Histories as the kind of books people usually think of when they think of history books (Cords 2006). Epic Food Histories cover broad periods of history and world-changing events. The titles found here span several centuries or even thousands of years and focus on the evolution of human culture and civilizations in relation to food. Epic Food Histories tend to be lengthier works. Although the page numbers on these titles don't come as close to Epic Histories on other subjects, these titles feel lengthy. They are very detailed, well-researched, and dense. Readers who enjoy Epic Food Histories may enjoy reading broader Epic Histories for even more detail on a specific time period.

> Epic Food Histories cover broad periods of history, spanning several centuries, and focus on the evolution of human culture and civilizations in relation to food. These titles tend to be lengthy, and are well-researched and detailed.

Colquhoun, Kate

Taste: The Story of Britain through its Cooking. New York: Bloombsury, 2007. 460pp. ISBN 9781596914100.

British cuisine is often a source of mockery, but this history of Britain through its cooking is a fascinating story filled with facts. Beginning with the pre-Roman period, Colquhoun moves through the Norman conquest, the Middle Ages, the Tudor reign, the influence of the East and the New World, up to the rationing during World War II, the birth of convenience foods, and the current celebrity chefs. Colquhoun traces the evolution of culinary techniques, equipment, and ingredients, explains the creation of well-known dishes, and explores food fads and changes in manners and morals. Colquhoun uses food to examine greater issues such as politics, social and cultural values, conflicts, advances, and patriotism.

Subjects: British Cuisine, British History, Food Habits, Great Britain

Now Try: *British Food: An Extraordinary Thousand Years of History* by Colin Spencer explores the eating habits of the rich and poor throughout British history. *Spicing up Britain: The Multicultural History of British Food* by Panikos Panayi looks at the impact of immigration on British cuisine. Cookbooks illustrating cooking methods throughout British history may also be appealing, such as *Tudor Cookery* by Peter C. D. Brears, *Food and Cooking in Victorian England* by Andrea Broomfield, or *Georgian Cookery: Food and History* by Jennifer Stead. Readers may enjoy Nigel Slater's entertaining observations on British food and eating habits in *Eating for England*. Another book about the history of homes and domesticity, told from a British perspective is Bill Bryson's *At Home*. Anglophile readers might also consider works covering British history more broadly, such as Simon Schama's multivolume *A History of Britain* series. Colquhoun also just published a historical true crime title, *Murder in the First-Class Carriage*, which combines historical details of the Victorian period with a murder mystery.

Fernandez-Armesto, Felipe

Near a Thousand Tables: A History of Food. New York: Free Press, 2002. 258pp. ISBN 9780743226448.

Fernandez-Armesto asserts that food history is an inseparable part of world history. He argues that the evolution of human culture can be traced to major revolutions in the history of food. Beginning with the origins of cooking, to the development of eating rituals, the invention of agriculture and herding, the development of long-range food trade, the beginnings of ecological exchanges, and finally to the industrialization of food. Although the text is lengthy and dense, the author nonetheless delivers a vivid, thought-provoking history of food filled with fascinating facts and historical details.

> **Subjects:** Civilization, Culture, Food Habits, Scholarly, World History
>
> **Awards:** IACP Award
>
> **Now Try:** Readers who enjoyed Fernandez-Armesto's vivid and detailed writing may also enjoy his book *Civilizations*, for an overview of the world's civilizations. Readers may also want to check out other titles about broader world history and cultural development such as Jared Diamond's *Guns, Germs, and Steel* or Jacques Barzun's *From Dawn to Decadence*. Paul Freedman's *Food: A History of Taste* is another satisfying comprehensive history of food and the evolution of human culture.

Fraser, Evan D. G., and Rimas, Andrew

Empires of Food: Feast, Famine and the Rise and Fall of Civilizations. New York: Free Press, 2010. 302pp. ISBN 9781439101896.

Throughout history, civilizations have been founded on the production and exchange of food. Surpluses, transportation, trade, and storage allow societies to support large populations. But when populations become too large and tax the system or a change in climate causes crop failure, the system will collapse and cause a shift in power. Societies face famine, poverty, and often, war. Fraser and Rimas argue that the current food empire is headed for collapse. They argue that the mistakes being made in the modern food empire reflect the belief that the Earth is fertile, the unwillingness to accept that the climate is changing, and the continuing production of large amounts of few commodities. The authors examine societies over the past 12,000 years to illustrate the patterns, including ancient Egypt, the Roman Empire, the Mayans, and medieval Europe.

> **Subjects:** Agriculture, Civilization, Current Affairs, Economics, Society, World History
>
> **Now Try:** Readers may also want to read Felipe Fernandez-Armesto's *Near a Thousand Tables* for its examination of food on the development of civilizations. Richard Manning's *Against the Grain* is another compelling examination of the issues facing the current agricultural system. Readers may also be interested in Wendell Berry's *The Unsettling of America*, in which Berry examines the modern agricultural system and American culture. Although Fraser and Rimas examine food in large civilizations, readers may also enjoy Ben Hewitt's *The Town that Food Saved*, which examines food within a

much smaller society. Some of the titles from Investigative Writing chapter may also be a good choice. Anna Lappé's *Diet for a Hot Planet* and Thomas Pawlick's *The End of Food: How the Food Industry is Destroying Our Food Supply—and What We Can Do About It* examine the issues caused by the current state of the food industry.

Freedman, Paul

Food: The History of Taste. Berkeley: University of California Press, 2007. 368pp. ISBN 9780520254763.

Freedman provides a chronological history of taste from prehistory to the present. Freedman begins with early humans' development of a fondness for sweets. The ancient Greeks and Romans were noted for their diets with an excess of rich foods. Imperial China delighted in procuring and savoring the best and rarest foods. The foods of Islamic civilizations were influenced by a combination of Arabian, Persian, Indian, and Byzantium cultures. Medieval Europe developed a passion for spices, however after the Renaissance, New World resources, such as coffee, tea, maize, and chocolate were desired. In more modern times, French cuisine became the height of taste. Freedman's fascinating history of food throughout civilization will appeal to readers who enjoy comprehensive and detailed accounts.

> **Subjects:** Food Habits, Scholarly, World History
>
> **Awards:** IACP Award
>
> **Now Try:** Felipe Fernandez-Armesto's *Near a Thousand Tables: A History of Food* is another comprehensive and detailed account of the role food played in the evolution of civilization. Readers may enjoy exploring one of the many micro-histories of foods such as Wolfgang Schivelbusch's *Tastes of Paradise*, Mark Kurlansky's *Salt*, Patricia Rain's *Vanilla*, Sophie Coe's *The True History of Chocolate*, or Linda Civitello's *Cuisine and Culture: A History of Food and People*. A comprehensive look at the rise of one culture's cuisine may also be appealing, such as Susan Pinkard's *A Revolution in Taste: The Rise of French Cuisine*.

Murray, Sarah

Moveable Feasts: From Ancient Rome to the 21ˢᵗ Century, the Incredible Journeys of the Food We Eat. New York: St. Martin's Press, 2007. 256pp. ISBN 9780312355357.

The transportation of food over hundreds of miles has been a common practice for centuries. Murray details the history of food transportation systems from the Silk Road to the transportation of olive oil throughout the ancient Roman empire to the creation of the barrel, which revolutionized the transportation of wine. She also explores some contemporary food transportation systems, such as the complex lunch delivery service found in Mumbai, or the shipping of frozen salmon to China for processing before returning it to the United States for sale. Murray argues that while eating locally produced foods is admirable, the transportation of food is often more economical.

Subjects: Local Food, Transportation, World History

Now Try: Readers who are interested in the current debate about local foods may also enjoy James McWilliams's *Just Food: Where Locavores Get It Wrong and How We Can Truly Eat Responsibly*. Readers interested in the other side of the argument might consider J. B. MacKinnon's and Alisa Smith's *Plenty: Eating Locally on the 100-Mile Diet* or Barbara Kingsolver's *Animal, Vegetable, Miracle*. Another fascinating look at transportation and issues pertaining to it is John McPhee's investigative title *Uncommon Carriers*. Two of Burt Wolf's travel/food series, *What We Eat* and *Travels and Traditions*, available on DVD, might also appeal to these readers.

Schenone, Laura

A Thousand Years Over a Hot Stove: A History of American Women Told Through Food, Recipes and Remembrances. New York: W. W. Norton and Co., 2003. 412pp. ISBN 9780393016710.

Schenone traces the broad history of women's responsibility for cooking back to the first people in North America. With rich descriptions, she illustrates women's cooking methods from the Native Americans to the pioneer women and the slave women, to the development of urban life and technology's effects on cooking. A well-researched and detailed history, the book also includes excerpts and recipes from old cookbooks, housewife guides, old drawings, and advertisements.

Subjects: American History, Recipes, Women's Nonfiction

Awards: James Beard Award

Now Try: While researching this book, Schenone became interested in researching her own family history which she recounts in *The Lost Ravioli Recipes of Hoboken: A Search for Food and Family*. Janet Theophano also explores women's history through cookbooks in *Eat My Words: Reading Women's Lives Through the Cookbooks They Wrote*. Laura Shapiro's *Perfection Salad* chronicles the women who served as culinary reformers at the turn of the twentieth century. Other titles about women who were important early culinary figures may also be of interest, such as Becky Diamond's *Mrs. Goodfellow: The Story of America's First Cooking School* or Kathryn Hughes's *The Short Life and Long Times of Mrs. Beeton: The First Domestic Goddess*. Readers may also want to consider broader women's history titles such as Gail Collins's *America's Women: Four Hundred Years of Dolls, Drudges, Helpmates, and Heroines* or Barbara Ehrenreich's *For Her Own Good: 150 Years of the Experts' Advice to Women*.

Standage, Tom

An Edible History of Humanity. New York: Walker & Company, 2009. 269pp. ISBN 9780802715883.

Throughout history hunger has been the driving force behind social change, political organization, competition, industrial development, military conflicts, and economic expansions. Standage illustrates this in his comprehensive history of food and civilization. Trade in exotic spices spawned the age of exploration and led to the colonization of the New World. The ability to feed armies played a major role in the outcome of several wars. The production of food surpluses led to the creation of major societies. Food trade routes led to cultural exchange and the dramatic expansion of food supplies led to a surge in world population. Standage also explores which foods have done the most to shape the world, including corn, cereal grains, spices, tropical fruits, sugar, and potatoes.

> **Subjects:** Civilization, Exploration, Society, Trade, World History

> **Now Try:** Readers may also enjoy Standage's other title *A History of the World in Six Glasses*. Readers interested in more specifics about the foods that drove change may want to try a micro-history such as Jack Turner's *Spice: The History of a Temptation* or Larry Zuckerman's *The Potato: How the Humble Spud Rescued the Western World*. Richard Wrangham's *Catching Fire: How Cooking Made Us Human* explores how the discovery of fire and its use for cooking led to the evolution of the human species. Penny Le Couteur's *Napoleon's Buttons: How 17 Molecules Changed History* explains how the discovery of certain molecules influenced the course of civilization.

Standage, Tom

A History of the World in 6 Glasses. Westminster: Anchor Books, 2006. 311pp. ISBN 9780385660877.

> Standage purports that six beverages have had a great influence on the course of history and explores the impact of each. In ancient Mesopotamia and Egypt, the adoption of farming and the domestication of cereal grains led to the creation of beer. In ancient Greece, wine was the basis of a vast sea trade that spread Greek influence. The Colonial period was an age of exploration, which prompted the development of a compact, durable drink that was ideal for sea transportation, which led to the development of spirits. During the Age of Reason, coffee became a popular drink because it was thought to promote clarity of thought and was favored by philosophers and scientists. The popularity of tea in Britain opened lucrative trade routes with the East and led to its rise at the first global superpower. When Coca-Cola became popular in America, it became the most widely known and distributed product and a symbol for globalization and capitalism.

> **Subjects:** Beer, Coca-Cola, Coffee, Economics, Globalization, Micro-Histories, Spirits, Tea, Wine

> **Now Try:** Readers may also want to check out Standage's other history, *An Edible History of Humanity*. Micro-histories of the drinks profiled in this book may be of interest, such as *Man Walks into a Pub: A Sociable History of Beer* by Pete Brown, *Wine: The 8,000 Year Old Story of the Wine Trade* by Thomas Pellachia, *And a Bottle of Rum: A History of the New World in Ten Cocktails* by

Wayne Curtis, *Coffee: A Dark History* by Antony Wild, *Liquid Jade: The Story of Tea from East to West* by Beatrice Hohenegger, and *For God, Country, and Coca-Cola* by Mark Pendergrast. Histories of other popular beverages may also be suggested, such as *Cognac: The Seductive Saga of the World's Most Coveted Spirit* by Kyle Jarrard or *Bitters: A Spirited History of a Classic Cure-All, with Cocktails, Recipes, and Formulas* by Brad Thomas Parsons and Ed Anderson. Readers may also enjoy *Seeds of Change: Six Plants that Transformed Mankind* by Henry Hobhouse. A broader history that may be of interest is *A History of the World in 100 Objects* by Neil MacGregor.

Defining Times

Defining Times cover significant historical food events or time periods. The time periods are usually briefer than those found in Epic Food Histories. Story is an important factor in these titles, as are details. Character becomes an appeal factor in many of these titles, as they often focus on specific figures who played a role in the evolution of cuisine. Readers who enjoy titles from Defining Times may also enjoy biographies or memoirs of the characters found in these titles.

> Defining Times cover significant historical food events or time periods. These titles are detailed and story and character are important appeal factors.

Adamson, Melitta Weiss

Food in Medieval Times. Westport: Greenwood Press, 2004. 256pp. ISBN 9780313321474.

This detailed work provides a history of the origin and migration of foodstuffs during the medieval period. Adamson examines how foods were prepared and preserved, and how social hierarchy determined what people ate. Eating habits and customs, as well as concepts of diet and nutrition are also explored. Quotes are taken from medieval cookbooks, and cuisines are broken down by region.

Subjects: Food Habits, Medieval Period, Society, World History

Now Try: *Food in the Ancient World* by Joan P. Alcock and *Food in Early Modern Europe* by Ken Albala are part of the *Food through History* series and provide detailed histories of the culinary traditions of the time. Readers may also enjoy *The Medieval Kitchen* by Olide Redon, Francoise Sabban, and Silvano Serventi, a collection of original medieval recipes, translated and adapted for the modern cook. Ian Mortimer's *The Time Traveler's Guide to Medieval England* is a compelling history that details everyday life during the 14th century. Barbara Tuchman's *A Distant Mirror* chronicles the events of the 14th century. Although a young adult title, *What Life Was Like in the Age of Chivalry* from the Time Life series is nonetheless a vivid and comprehensive history of the period. *All the King's Cooks: The Tudor Kitchens of King Henry VIII at Hampton Court Palace* by Peter C. D. Brears is a fascinating history of food in a royal court.

Brenner, Leslie

American Appetite: The Coming of Age of a Cuisine. New York: Avon
Books, 1999. 370pp. ISBN 9780380973361.

> When it comes to its cuisine, America's reputation has not been highly re-
> garded. Brenner traces the course of American cuisine, from the arrival of
> the Puritans and the influence of the Native Americans to the emergence
> of industrial canning, the decline in American cooking, and the focus on
> nutritional values instead of the pleasure of food. A number of factors led
> to changes and developments in American cuisine, such as the influence
> of immigrants from many countries, including Thailand, China, Japan,
> Mexico, and Italy. The food movement in California, led by Alice Waters,
> led to a desire for local, fresh foods and gourmet foods such as chante-
> relles and foie gras. Attempts to define American cuisine are difficult, as
> it continues to evolve.

> > **Subjects:** American Cuisine, American History, Child, Julia, Claiborne, Craig,
> > Food Habits, Immigrants, Local Food, Waters, Alice

> > **Now Try:** Brenner's bibliography references a wide range of titles, including
> > classics such as Clementine Paddleford's *How America Eats* and Waverly Root's
> > *Eating in America*. Anne Vileisis explains how Americans became removed
> > from their food in *Kitchen Literacy*. Thomas McNamee's *Alice Waters and Chez
> > Panisse* chronicles Waters's role in the American food movement. David Kamp
> > considers the beginning of America's obsession with gourmet eating in *United
> > States of Arugula*. Anne Willan traces the history of European and American
> > cuisine through cookbooks in *The Cookbook Library: Four Centuries of the Cooks,
> > Writers, and Recipes That Made the Modern Cookbook*.

Collins, Kathleen

Watching What We Eat: The Evolution of Television Cooking Shows. New
York: Continuum Pub., 2009. 278pp. ISBN 9780826429308.

> Cooking shows were originally intended for housewives but now ap-
> peal to all demographics. Collins traces the beginning of cooking shows
> from radio to television and suggests that cooking shows are a unique so-
> cial barometer, illustrating the transition of women from home to work,
> the changes in gender roles and the move from cooking as a necessity to
> cooking as a leisure activity. Collins also focuses on famous cooks such
> as Betty Crocker, James Beard, Julia Child and the Galloping and Frugal
> Gourmets, and the development of the Food Network and celebrity chefs.

> > **Subjects:** American History, Beard, James, Celebrity Chefs, Child, Julia,
> > Crocker, Betty, Mass Media, Television

> > **Now Try:** Susan Marks explores the changing image of one of America's most
> > famous cooks in *Finding Betty Crocker: The Secret Life of America's First Lady of
> > Food*. Readers may also enjoy Nancy Verde Barr's memoir of her time working

with Julia Child, *Backstage with Julia*. Readers may also enjoy memoirs of other famous television cooks such as Paula Deen's *It Ain't All About the Cookin'* or Sandra Lee's *Made From Scratch*. Another accessible social history is Stephanie Coontz's *The Way We Never Were: American Families and the Nostalgia Trap*. Cooking shows abound on TV and may appeal to readers who enjoyed this book. Bravo channel's *Top Chef*, Food Network's *Iron Chef America* and Fox's *Kitchen Nightmares* are a few popular shows.

DeWitt, Dave

The Founding Foodies: How Washington, Jefferson, and Franklin Revolutionized American Cuisine. Naperville: Sourcebooks, 2010. 317pp. ISBN 9781402217869.

DeWitt argues that the first colonists and leaders of the United States were the first true Foodies. Their devotion to agricultural experimentation allowed them to produce better crops and sustain the country in its infancy. The colonists learned much about hunting and farming from the Native Americans, and their acceptance of corn as a staple became the key to their survival. The colonists also relied on the abundance of Cod they discovered in the New World, as well as salt, rum, and pork. These foods prevented the colonists from starving, supported the country's growth and its ability to produce its own crops, such as tobacco. DeWitt specifically focuses on George Washington, Thomas Jefferson, and Benjamin Franklin who were lovers of food and wine and understood the importance of farming, as well as brewing. Despite containing quite a bit of interesting historical information, this is a quick read.

> **Subjects:** Agriculture, American History, Colonists, Farming, Founding Fathers, Franklin, Benjamin, Jefferson, Thomas, Native Americans, Quick Reads, Recipes, Washington, George
>
> **Now Try:** Readers who enjoy DeWitt's entertaining style may also enjoy his study of the eating habits of 15th- and 16th-century Italy in *Da Vinci's Kitchen: A Secret History of Italian Cuisine*. In *Founding Gardeners*, Andrea Wulf also examines the founding fathers' interest in agriculture. Readers may also enjoy *The Billionaire's Vinegar* by Benjamin Wallace, which explores Thomas Jefferson's love for wine. Mark Kurlansky's microhistories *Salt* and *Cod* may also be of interest to readers looking for more in-depth detail of specific foods. Also of interest to these readers might be a variety of popular biographies of the Founding Fathers, including Joseph Ellis's *American Sphinx*, about Thomas Jefferson, and Walter Isaacson's *Benjamin Franklin: An American Life*. Harry Haff profiles some of the early influential cooks and cookbooks of American cuisine in *The Founders of American Cuisine: Seven Cookbook Authors, with Historical Recipes*.

Diner, Hasia R.

Hungering for America: Italian, Irish, and Jewish Foodways in the Age of Migration. Cambridge: Harvard University Press, 2001. 292pp. ISBN 9780674006058.

From 1820 to 1920 over 30 million Europeans immigrated to the United States in search of work, better pay, and better lives. The culinary traditions of these immigrants greatly influenced American culture. Diner focuses on three of the major immigrant groups: Italian, Irish, and Jewish to examine how their culinary traditions were incorporated into American life. The Italians found that they could afford better food in America and created a culture that centered around food and led to many culinary businesses. The Irish, who fled famine, did not have much in the way of food culture. Many of the Irish women who became cooks and servants for the wealthy became familiar with the food and customs of the upper classes. For the Jews, food was sacred and tightly controlled by religious law, which became a way to assert their identity and distinctiveness. Diner includes a variety of sources, from memoirs, literature, archives, government reports, and cookbooks to examine the backgrounds and conditions of the immigrant experience.

> **Subjects:** American History, Food Habits, Immigrants, Scholarly

> **Now Try:** 97 *Orchard: An Edible History of Five Immigrant Families in One New York Tenement* by Jane Ziegelman is a similar history that focuses on the culinary traditions of the Italian, Irish, and Jewish immigrants. Readers should also consider Diner's other title, *The Jews of the United States*, which traces the history of Jews from the small community in colonial America to the present. Other titles from Harvard University Press that might be of interest are Donna Gabbacia's *We Are What We Eat: Ethnic Food and the Making of Americans*, which traces the effects of immigrant culinary traditions on American cuisine or Rebecca Spang's *The Invention of the Restaurant*.

Gdula, Steven

The Warmest Room in the House: How the Kitchen Became the Heart of the Twentieth-Century American Home. New York: Bloomsbury USA, 2007. 238pp. ISBN 9781582343556.

> Thomas Jefferson said that if you want to understand the workings of a society, you have to look into their pots and eat their bread. Gdula attempts to do just that: provide a history of American culture during the 20th century by focusing on the kitchen. This detailed but easy-to-read history explores trends in food, innovations in technology and appliances, changes in kitchen design, and changes in cultural attitudes over the course of the 20th century. Broken down by decade, the author illustrates how the kitchen evolved from workroom to the center of family life. He describes the development of new approaches to cooking and the emergence of refrigeration, microwaves, and Tupperware. The effects of national and worldwide events such as the Depression and World Wars I and II are also explored. Famous cookbooks as well as influential food figures such as Julia Child are also included.

> **Subjects:** American History, Child, Julia, Kitchens, Micro-Histories, Technology

> **Now Try:** Mark Kurlansky's *The Food of a Younger Land: A Portrait of American Food Before the National Highway System, Before Chain Restaurants, and Before Frozen Food, When the Nation's Food Was Seasonal* and Pat Willard's *America Eats!:*

On the Road with the WPA: The Fish Fries, Box Supper Socials, and Chitlin Feasts That Define are both entertaining and accessible histories of American food culture of the 20th century. Bill Bryson's *At Home: A Short History of Private Life* is an entertaining history of the specific rooms in the home. Novels in which cooking environments and food play an integral part of the plot are Judith Ryan Hendricks's *Bread Alone* and Aimee Bender's *The Particular Sadness of Lemon Cake*.

Haber, Barbara

From Hardtack to Home Fries: An Uncommon History of American Cooks and Meals. New York: Free Press, 2002. 244pp. ISBN 9780684842172.

In this lively history, Haber turns to memoirs, diaries, oral histories, and cookbooks to examine major events in American history through the lens of food. Haber covers the mass immigration of the Irish as a result of the Potato Famine, the Civil War diet kitchens, the role of the Harvey Girls in settling the West, the austere diet of food reformers, the notably bad food served in Franklin D. Roosevelt's White House, and the foods served to American prisoners of war during World War II. Short chapters with firsthand accounts and recipes make this an entertaining and accessible overview of American history.

> **Subjects:** American History, Immigrants, Oral History, Quick Reads, Recipes

> **Now Try:** Readers interested in some of the specific periods covered by Haber may want to try *Starving the South: How the North Won the Civil War* by Andrew F. Smith, which examines the fight for food during the Civil War. *Appetite for America* by Stephen Fried details the life of Fred Harvey and his creation of the Harvey House empire. Bob Greene's *Once Upon a Town: The Miracle of the North Platte Canteen* describes how a town turned its train depot into a place for World War II servicemen to get a home-cooked meal. General nonfiction titles on American history might also be of interest. Try Paul Johnson's *A History of the American People* and Howard Zinn's *A People's History of the United States*.

Harris, Jessica B.

High on the Hog: A Culinary Journey from Africa to America. New York: Bloomsbury USA, 2011. 291pp. ISBN 9781596913950.

Harris's detailed history traces the influence of African cuisine to the United States. When African slaves were brought to America, they brought with them their own foods, cooking techniques, and food rituals, which have become a part of America cuisine, specifically in the south. Harris focuses on several foods that have become an important part of African American culture and identity, such as okra, watermelon, black-eyed peas, chitlins, and fried chicken. A number of talented African American cooks, from slaves of large plantations to cooks for the presidents, are profiled.

> **Subjects:** African American Cuisine, American History, Recipes, Slavery

> **Now Try:** Readers may also be interested in checking out one of Harris's cookbooks, such as *The Welcome Table* or *Iron Pots and Wooden Spoons*. Judith Carney explores the

foods brought to America by slaves which have become part of American cuisine in *In the Shadow of Slavery*. Frederick Douglass Opie also examines the origins of African American cuisine in *Hog and Hominy*. Readers may also want to consider *The Warmth of Other Suns* by Isabel Wilkerson, which chronicles the migration of African Americans who fled the South in search of a better life and changed the face of America.

Kamp, David

The United States of Arugula: How We Became a Gourmet Nation. New York: Broadway Books, 2006. 392pp. ISBN 9780767915793.

Kamp traces the evolution of American cuisine, from its modest beginnings through the rise of gourmandism and its acceptance in popular culture. Initially food was viewed as fuel and few cared about taste, and as industry grew, processed foods proliferated. But a few figures stand out in history as those who tried to show Americans that food could be better and easy to make: James Beard, Julia Child, M.F.K. Fisher, and Craig Claiborne. In the 1970s, the hippie movement began to promote fresh, local, and seasonal foods. Soon, a desire for gourmet foods made upscale products and grocery stores popular. As Americans began to take an interest in their food, chefs became celebrities, television shows and books made food and eating a form of entertainment.

Subjects: American Cuisine, Beard, James, Celebrity Chefs, Child, Julia, Claiborne, Craig, Fisher, M.F.K., Food Movements, Gourmet, Television, Waters, Alice

Awards: *New York Times* Notable Book

Now Try: Readers may want to check out Kamp's other works, such as *The Food Snob's Dictionary* or *The Wine Snob's Dictionary*. There are plenty of biographies available to readers who would like more details on any of the figures found in this book, such as *An Extravagant Hunger: The Passionate Years of M.F.K. Fisher* by Anne Zimmerman or *The Solace of Food: A Life of James Beard* by Robert Clark. *Alice Waters and Chez Panisse* by Thomas McNamee is a good suggestion for readers interested in more information about one of the leaders of the movement for local, seasonal foods. In *The Art of Eating*, Edward Behr explores the origins and history of various ingredients in his quest for finding good food. The continuing evolution of America's food tastes is also revealed in such Investigative works as Mark Caro's *The Foie Gras Wars* and Michael Pollan's *In Defense of Food*.

Kladstrup, Donald, and Kladstrup, Petie

Wine and War: The French, the Nazis, and the Battle for France's Greatest Treasure. New York: Broadway Books, 2001. 279pp. ISBN 9780767904476.

During World War II, the Nazis looted art and wine from France. Although Hitler did not take an interest in wine, he understood the prestige and profit to be had from French wines and was determined to obtain the best French wines for Germany. When the French army found Hitler's cave of looted wines, they found thousands of bottles including some of the finest wines ever made. This intriguing narrative details the methods of subterfuge and sabotage that the French citizens, winemakers, and restaurateurs attempted to save their wine, from creating hidden rooms to burying bottles under gardens and sabotaging Nazi trains.

Subjects: France, French History, Nazis, Wine, World War II

Now Try: Readers who are interested in the topic of Nazi looting may want to try *The Monuments Men: Allied Heroes, Nazi Thieves and the Greatest Treasure Hunt in History* by Robert M. Edsel and Bret Witter, *Rescuing Da Vinci: Hitler and the Nazis Stole Europe's Great Art—America and Her Allies Recovered It* by Robert M. Edsel, or *The Venus Fixers: The Remarkable Story of the Allied Soldiers Who Saved Italy's Art During World War II* by Ilaria Dagnini Brey. Other titles about France and its food and wine may also be of interest, such as *Au Revoir to All That: Food, Wine, and the End of France* by Michael Steinberger, *Corked* by Kathryn Borel, *The Food of France* by Waverly Root, and *Corkscrewed* by Robert Camuto.

Kuh, Patric

The Last Days of Haute Cuisine: America's Culinary Revolution. New York: Viking, 2001. 241pp. ISBN 9780670891788.

When Henri Soulé opened the restaurant Le Pavillon in New York in 1941, it was the height of haute cuisine. Kuh traces the creation of Le Pavillon from the 1939 World's Fair and the evolution of the restaurant business in post-World War II America. As figures such as James Beard and Julia Child brought French cooking to a more mainstream level, Americans began to reject the elitist haute cuisine. The use of credit cards in restaurants also made fine dining accessible to more Americans. Kuh also traces the beginnings of a number of famous French restaurants that were born out of this evolution, such as Chez Panisse, Le Cirque, and Spago. This fascinating and well-researched history will appeal to fans of history as well as readers who enjoy inside tales of the restaurant business.

Subjects: American History, Business, French Cuisine, Restaurants

Awards: James Beard Award

Now Try: Readers interested in the background of French cuisine may want to consider Susan Pinkard's *A Revolution in Taste*, which details the history of French cuisine or *Haute Cuisine: How the French Invented the Culinary Profession* by Amy B. Trubek. Pierre Franey's memoir *A Chef's Tale* is an account of his experiences cooking at the 1939 World's Fair and as a top chef at Le Pavillon. Readers may also want to consider David Kamp's account of the American food revolution in *The United States of Arugula* or Thomas McNamee's biography *Alice Waters and Chez Panisse*. Danny Meyer's *Setting the Table*, while not a book on history, nonetheless provides an inside look at the modern restaurant business.

Kurlansky, Mark

The Food of a Younger Land: A Portrait of American Food—Before the National Highway System, Before Chain Restaurants, and Before Frozen Food, When the Nation's Food Was Seasonal. Riverhead, 2009. 416pp. 9781594488658.

In the 1930s, the Works Progress Administration created the Federal Writers' Project for unemployed writers. Writers were asked to contribute to a project called America Eats. The plan was to produce a book of compiled essays and recipes that would describe the various traditional foods eaten throughout the United States. Unfortunately, the project was abandoned when the United States entered World War II and the essays and recipes were archived in the Library of Congress. Kurlansky has compiled these documents, adding his own commentary. This compilation illustrates the many food traditions found throughout the various regions in the United States, shows how people made do with the few ingredients they had during the Depression, and the beginnings of convenience foods.

> **Subjects:** American History, Essays, Federal Writers' Project, Food Habits, Great Depression, Local Food

> **Now Try:** Readers interested in the Federal Writers' Project and the stories they collected during the Depression may want to try *Soul of a People: The WPA Writers' Project Uncovers Depression America* by David A. Taylor. Pat Willard chronicles her recent travels through America to see if the culinary traditions documented in the original America Eats project still exist in *America Eats!: On the Road with the WPA*. Readers looking for more stories about changes in American cooking and diet may enjoy *Revolution at the Table: The Transformation of the American Diet* by Harvey Levenstein or *Finding Betty Crocker: The Secret Life of America's First Lady of Food* by Susan Marks. Readers may also want to try some of Kurlansky's micro-histories, such as *Salt*, *Cod*, or *The Big Oyster*. Another book which examines American culture, state by state, is *State by State: A Panoramic Portrait of America*, edited by Matt Weiland and Sean Wilsey.

Landau, Barry

The President's Table: Two Hundred Years of Dining and Diplomacy. New York: Collins, 2007. 292pp. ISBN 9780060899103.

This engaging and highly visual history provides a chronicle of the American presidency from the perspective of food. Landau begins with George Washington and the founding fathers and continues through George W. Bush, describing favorite foods of each president and how each president entertained from informal gatherings to large state banquets. Photographs of original invitations and menus, as well as the china patterns chosen by each president are included. Political highlights of each presidency are covered, but the overall tone remains light. The personal details such as Franklin D. Roosevelt's incompetent cook, the introduction of French cuisine during John F. Kennedy's presidency, Jimmy Carter's love for peanut butter waffles, and the distaste of broccoli by both Presidents Bush Sr. and Jr. are entertaining and enjoyable.

> **Subjects:** American History, American Presidents, Dining, Politics
>
> **Now Try:** Readers may also be interested in memoirs of White House chefs. Walter Scheib's memoir *White House Chef: Eleven Years, Two Presidents, On Kitchen* and Roland Mesnier's memoir *All the Presidents' Pastries: Twenty-Five Years in the White House* are wonderful inside stories of the food lives of the presidents. Readers interested in the founding fathers' food preference may want to try Dave DeWitt's *The Founding Foodies: How Washington, Jefferson, and Franklin Revolutionized American Cuisine*. For a look at royal dining, try Kathryn Jones's *For the Royal Table: Dining at the Palace*. Also of interest might be Robert Hardman's beautifully illustrated book *A Year with the Queen*, which also includes many details of the lavish entertaining and dining events attended and hosted by the British royal family. Fiction readers may enjoy Julie Hyzy's White House Chef mysteries. The first in the series, *State of the Onion*, features White House assistant chef Olivia Paras, who competes for the top chef position and takes on the role of amateur sleuth after she catches a mysterious intruder at the White House.

Levenstein, Harvey

Revolution at the Table: The Transformation of the American Diet. New York: Oxford University Press, 1988. 275pp. ISBN 9780195043655.

Between 1880 and 1930 a revolution occurred in the American diet. In the 19th century, Americans wanted to eat a lot. Plumpness was considered ideal. Today, Americans are obsessed with calories, diets, and maintaining thin figures. Levenstein examines the forces and figures that incited this transformation. Prohibition, war, urbanization, nutritional science, changes in technology, and the development of the industrial food system, as well as changes in women's roles in the home all led to changes in the way Americans prepared foods. Home economists and social workers who attempted to make positive dietary changes, the scientist who discovered vitamins, Dr. John Harvey Kellogg, who invented cornflakes as a vegetarian health food, and the giant food corporations, were all instrumental in this revolution.

> **Subjects:** American History, Diets, Food Industry, Kellogg, John Harvey, Scholarly
>
> **Now Try:** Readers may want to continue with Levenstein's *Paradox of Plenty*, which details the continued changes from the 1930s to the present that shaped America's diet. Levenstein will also release his book *Fear of Food: A History of Why We Worry about What We Eat* in 2012. Susan Yager's *The Hundred Year Diet* is another well-researched book about America's obsession with weight. Readers may also enjoy Mark Kurlansky's compilation of essays written for the Federal Writers' Project America Eats in the 1930s, *The Food of a Younger Land*, which illustrates the changes in American diets; also of interest might be Michael Pollan's more global title, *The Omnivore's Dilemma*. T. C. Boyle's historical novel *The Road to Wellville* is an entertaining satire about a couple that visit John Harvey Kellogg's health spa.

Lovegren, Sylvia

Fashionable Food: Seven Decades of Food Fads. New York: MacMillan Publishing Company, 1995. 455pp. ISBN 9780025757059.

This entertaining book provides a history of American eating fads throughout the 20th century. The book is broken down by decade and describes the major events and changes in society and technology occurring at the time and how that affected what people were eating and how food was prepared. The introduction of classic foods such as Jell-O and marshmallows, descriptions of once typical concoctions such as the frosted sandwich loaf, and the descriptions of entertaining styles make this a fun read for readers who want a quick overview.

Subjects: American History, Food Habits, Humor, Recipes, Technology

Now Try: Carolyn Wyman's *Better Than Homemade* highlights the packaged foods that have changed the way we eat and have become a part of pop culture. James Lileks has a number of entertaining reads. *The Gallery of Regrettable Foods* is a humorous, quick read of popular foods and recipes between the 1940s and 1970s. *Mommy Knows Worst: Highlights from the Golden Age of Bad Parenting Advice* is also quite amusing. Readers may also enjoy *Mental Hygiene: Better Living Through Classroom Films* by Ken Smith. Wendy McClure's diet memoir *I'm Not the New Me* also provides a personal and humorous take on dieting; her illustrated humor book *The Amazing Mackerel Pudding Plan* also pokes gentle fun at diet recipes from the 1970s.

McWilliams, James

A Revolution in Eating: How the Quest for Food Shaped America. New York: Columbia University Press, 2005. 386pp. ISBN 9780231129923.

This well-researched and thorough history of colonial America examines the important role of food in shaping the identity of the nation. When the colonists came to America, the distance from their homeland forced an intimacy with the land and food. With no markets or shops to acquire goods, colonists had to produce their own food. The influence of Native American agricultural practices allowed for their survival. Regional foodways began to develop with the growing ethnic diversity from other settlers, such as the Dutch, German, and French. These regional habits began to converge when the consumption of alcohol, specifically rum, led to intercoastal trade. The impact of slavery on culinary traditions is also explored.

Subjects: Agriculture, American History, Colonists, Native Americans, Slavery

Now Try: Keith Stavely's and Kathleen Fitzgerald's *America's Founding Food* is an interesting chronicle of the origins of the food of New England from the first settlers in the 17th century. Readers who are interested in early American cuisine may also enjoy Dave DeWitt's *The Founding Foodies: How Washington,*

Jefferson, and Franklin Revolutionized American Cuisine. Readers may also enjoy perusing *The First American Cookbook: A Facsimile of "American Cookery"* by Amelia Simmons, which was the first known American cookbook, published in 1796. David Kamp's *The United States of Arugula* is an entertaining history of the evolution of modern American cuisine. Burt Wolf's series of documentary films, titled *What We Eat*, also focus on the history of food and the influence on worldwide cuisines of different nationalities.

Pinkard, Susan

A Revolution in Taste: The Rise in French Cuisine, 1650–1800. New York: Cambridge University Press, 2009. 317pp. ISBN 9780521821995.

France has long been known for its fine cuisine. Pinkard provides an in-depth history of the evolution of French cuisine. Medieval cooking methods emphasized a liberal use of spices, resulting in a singular flavor. But by the 1600s, cooks began incorporating more fruits and vegetables. Fresh food and simple preparations were favored and an emphasis was placed on taste and texture. The sauces that are considered part of classic French cooking were developed during this time. Pinkard examines the social changes that occurred that led to France's culinary revolution. She also describes the evolution of the dinner party and various culinary techniques, debunks common myths, and provides authentic historical recipes.

> **Subjects:** France, French Cuisine, French History, Recipes, Scholarly

> **Now Try:** Another history of French cuisine is Priscilla Parkhurst Ferguson's *Accounting for Taste: The Triumph of French Cuisine.* Amy B. Trubek explores how France became the center of the culinary world in *Haute Cuisine: How the French Invented the Culinary Profession.* Anne Willan traces the history of European and American cuisine through cookbooks in *The Cookbook Library: Four Centuries of the Cooks, Writers, and Recipes That Made the Modern Cookbook.* Readers may enjoy Ian Kelly's *Cooking for Kings*, the biography of France's most famous chef, Antonin Carême, and his influence on French haute cuisine. Waverly Root's classic *The Foods of France* explores not only the food of France, but also its history, landscape, and culture. *The Essence of Style* by Joan DeJean chronicles the French influence on not only cuisine, but also high fashion and interior design.

Rose, Sarah

For All the Tea in China: How England Stole the World's Favorite Drink and Changed History. New York: Viking, 2010. 261pp. ISBN 9780670021529.

In the 18th and 19th centuries, Europe's thirst for tea was unquenchable. China was the only country to grow and manufacture tea. In order to afford to buy China's tea, the British East India Company grew opium in India, sold the opium to China, and used the proceeds to buy tea. However, the sale of opium was banned in China in 1729, which led to illegal smuggling. But the British East India Company worried that China would begin to produce its own opium, leaving them with no product to trade for tea. The British East India Company decided to begin growing its own tea in India, but first needed healthy specimens of tea plants, thousands of seeds, and the knowledge that was only possessed by the accomplished tea manufacturers. So the Company hired a spy. Robert Fortune, a Scottish gardener and botanist, was hired to secretly enter China and steal the secrets of the Chinese tea manufacturers. This enthralling account follows Fortune's journey deeper into China than any other foreigner had ever gone.

Subjects: British East India Company, Business, China, Tea, Travel

Now Try: *Nathaniel's Nutmeg: Or the True and Incredible Adventures of the Spice Trader Who Changed the Course of History* by Giles Milton is another history of an Englishman hired by the British East India Company to defend its interests in the Spice Islands. *Merchant Kings: When Companies Ruled the World, 1600–1900* by Stephen R. Bown chronicles the history of the major companies that dominated commercial trade, including the British East India Company. *Bananas: How the United Fruit Company Shaped the World* by Peter Chapman is a history of the United Fruit Company's exploitation of Central America. Readers may also be interested in other histories about the obsessive quests for prized items, such as *A Perfect Red: Empire, Espionage, and the Quest for the Color of Desire* by Amy Butler Greenfield, *Flower Hunters* by Mary Gribbin, and *Tulipomania: The Story of the World's Most Coveted Flower & the Extraordinary Passions It Aroused* by Mike Dash.

Yager, Susan

The Hundred Year Diet: America's Voracious Appetite for Losing Weight. New York: Rodale Books, 2010. 260pp. ISBN 9781605290119.

Dieting is a hot topic in America and there is always a steady stream of diet books being published. Dieting is not a recent fad though. Americans have been dieting since the early 1800s. In this well-researched book, Yager chronicles America's obsession with weight and the never-ending struggle to find the perfect diet. The famous diets that have been popular throughout America's history are covered: John Harvey Kellogg's diet, Inuit diet, liquid diets, no meat and all meat diets, no carbs and all carb diets, the champagne diet, the Atkins diet, Pritikin, Kempner, Weight Watchers, Ornish, Scarsdale, and the Beverly Hills diet are just a few of the diets Americans have subjected themselves to over the past two centuries. The weight loss contests and reducing salons that were popular, the invention of diet soda and risky diet drugs, and the abundance of artificial sweeteners used today are all covered. Yager also discusses the rise in obesity and increase in gastric bypass weight loss surgery.

Subjects: American History, Diets, Food Habits, Kellogg, John Harvey

Now Try: Readers might want to consider *Rethinking Thin* by Gina Kolata, who examines various food fads throughout history, traces the changes in society's standards for the ideal body and explains the scientific causes of obesity. A. J. Jacobs humorously recounts his investigation into a number of fad diets in *Drop Dead Healthy*. There is certainly no shortage of weight-loss and weight issue memoirs. A few to try may be Wendy McClure's *I'm Not the New Me*, Jennette Fulda's *Half-Assed*, Jen Lancaster's *Such a Pretty Fat*, and Edward Ugel's *I'm With Fatty*. Readers may also be interested in some of the investigative titles that examine the food industry and the current obesity issue, such as Eric Schlosser's classic *Fast Food Nation*, Hank Cardello's *Stuffed: An Insider's Look at Who's (Really) Making America Fat*, or Barry Popkin's *The World is Fat: The Fads, Trends, Policies, and Products That Are Fattening the Human Race*.

Ziegelman, Jane

97 Orchard: An Edible History of Five Immigrant Families in One New York Tenement. Smithsonian Books, 2010.

Ziegelman traces the culinary contributions of immigrants in America by studying five immigrant families that lived in one Lower East Side New York City tenement from 1863 to 1935. Each family represents the major nationalities that immigrated to America during this time: German, Irish, Italian, German Jewish, and Lithuanian Jewish. Life for the immigrants in New York City is vividly described, living in cramped tenements and navigating the teeming streets of the city. She examines how each family adapted to life in America, how they attempted to preserve their culinary traditions by incorporating their native foods, how they improvised when necessary, and how these native foods in turn came to be part of American food culture. The vivid descriptions and personal stories of each family will appeal to readers who enjoy a strong sense of place, unique narrative, and personal connection.

Subjects: American History, Food Habits, Immigrants, New York City, Recipes

Now Try: *Hungering for America: Italian, Irish, and Jewish Foodways in the Age of Migration* by Hasia R. Diner is a similar history of the immigrant influence on American cuisine. *Chop Suey* by Andrew Coe is a wonderful history of the influence of Chinese cuisine in America. *Taco USA* by Gustavo Arellano looks at the influence of Mexican cuisine in America. *Breaking Bread* by Lynne Christy Anderson compiles personal stories and recipes from immigrant kitchens. Readers may also enjoy the fiction novel *Up From Orchard Street* by Eleanor Widmer, which follows three generations of a Russian Jewish immigrant family who live on Orchard Street with a matriarch who is known for cooking and operates a restaurant out of their tenement apartment.

Influential Food Enterprises

Throughout history there have been a number of companies that have affected the course of food in some way. Most of these companies are still in existence today, and are known as leaders in their market. Others, such as the United Fruit Company, may no longer be in existence, but have had a lasting impact on countries around the world. These titles are very detailed and often character-focused, chronicling the lives of the founder(s) of these companies. Readers may also enjoy biographies of the figures profiled in some of these titles. There are also a wide variety of histories of companies outside of food, which may also be of interest to readers.

Influential Food Enterprises are titles that trace the history of companies that have affected the course of food and have had a lasting impact. These titles tend to be very detailed and character-focused.

Brenner, Joel Glenn

The Emperors of Chocolate: Inside the Secret World of Hershey and Mars. New York: Random House, 1999. 366pp. ISBN 9780679421900.

In the competitive candy industry, Hershey and Mars dominate the market. Brenner looks at the evolution of chocolate production and the two men who turned their small candy companies into empires. While very successful, the two had very different personalities. Hershey was known for his kindness and philanthropy, while Mars was short-tempered and extremely frugal. Brenner also describes the fierce competition of the industry, the secrecy, marketing fights, and corporate espionage. This detailed and well-researched history provides a behind the scenes look at a dramatic story and two very different, but very interesting characters.

Subjects: Business, Candy Industry, Chocolate, Hershey, Mars

Now Try: Readers may also want to try Deborah Cadbury's history of the major chocolate makers, *Chocolate Wars: The 150-Year Rivalry Between the World's Greatest Chocolate Makers*. *Hershey: Milton S. Hershey's Extraordinary Life of Wealth, Empire, and Utopian Dreams* by Michael D'Antonio is a detailed biography of the famous candy maker. *Company Town* by Hardy Green is a history of companies that have created communities for their workers, such as Hershey. *Crisis in Candyland: Melting the Chocolate Shell of the Mars Family Empire* by Jan Pottker is another examination of the Mars family and its intense secrecy. *Bitter Chocolate* by Carol Off traces the history of chocolate. Readers may also be interested in other titles about competition between two similar companies, such as *Sneaker Wars* by Barbara Smit or John Newhouse's *Boeing Versus Airbus*.

Cadbury, Deborah

Chocolate Wars: The 150-Year Rivalry Between the World's Greatest Chocolate Makers. New York: Public Affairs, 2010. 348pp. ISBN 9781586488208.

Although a history of chocolate and some of the world's greatest chocolate makers including Fry, Rowntree, Cadbury, Lindt, Nestle, Hershey, and Mars, the author focuses mainly on the Cadbury company, of which she is a descendant. The Cadbury chocolate dynasty was created by a family of Quakers. The author details the Cadbury family history, traces the beginning of the company and how the family's Quaker values influenced the way the business was run. Cadbury also covers how the Quaker values influenced the family's use of their wealth, their involvement in social issues, and their attempts to improve society with their business. Other competing chocolate dynasties are chronicled, along with the changes throughout the 19th and 20th centuries, and the 2010 takeover of the Cadbury company by Kraft.

Subjects: Business, Cadbury, Candy Industry, Chocolate, Quakers

Now Try: Readers interested in the Cadbury company may want to try John Bradley's *Cadbury's Purple Reign*. For a quick history of chocolate, readers should consider Sarah Moss's *Chocolate: A Global History*, part of the Edible series by Reaktion Books. In *Candyfreak*, Steve Almond traces the histories of his favorite candies and how they are made. Elizabeth Candler Graham and Ralph Roberts provide a history of the Coca-Cola company and personal stories of the family dramas in *The Real Ones: Four Generations of the First Family of Coca-Cola*. Another company history that is bound up with family history is Barbara Smit's *Sneaker Wars: The Enemy Brothers Who Founded Adidas and Puma and the Family Feud that Forever Changed the Business of Sports*.

Chapman, Peter

Bananas: How the United Fruit Company Shaped the World. New York: Canongate, 2007. 224pp. ISBN 9781841958811.

The United Fruit Company was formed in 1899 and traded in tropical fruit, particularly bananas. The company became a global corporation that wielded enormous power and influence, controlled millions of acres of land, and was involved in many violent incidents in Latin America. In this brief work, Chapman provides a history of the company, from its inception to its rise to power and finally, to its fall in the 1970s. He describes the shocking practices of political deceit, bribery, and violence, as well as the company's role in the destruction of native lands and the creation of poverty and homelessness. Chapman also touches on the biology of the banana and the current threat the banana faces today.

Subjects: Bananas, Business, Latin American History, Quick Reads, United Fruit Company.

Now Try: Readers who are interested in the current threat to bananas may enjoy Dan Koeppel's *Banana: The Fate of the Fruit that Changed the World*. Koeppel does touch on the United Fruit Company, but his main focus is the threat facing the banana. Virginia Scott Jenkins's *Bananas: An American History* explores the history of the banana's popularity in America, as well as the banana companies who affected Latin America. Rich Cohen's *The Fish That Ate the Whale: The Life and Times of America's Banana King* profiles Samuel Zemurray, a banana peddler who battled the United Fruit Company. Adam Gollner's *The Fruit Hunters* investigates major food corporations and their role in the international fruit trade. Michael Krondl's *The Taste of Conquest* chronicles the history of the spice trade and how the desire for spices led to the conquest of foreign lands. Readers may also enjoy titles that explore the effects of our food choices, such as *How Bad Are Bananas?* by Mike Berners-Lee and Michael Pollan's *The Omnivore's Dilemma*.

Clark, Taylor

Starbucked: A Double Tall Tale of Caffeine, Commerce, and Culture. New York: Little, Brown and Company, 2007. 297pp. ISBN 9780316013482.

Starbucks has become an American institution and world phenomenon. Clark traces the rise of coffee's popularity in America and the factors that made coffee a trendy luxury in the 1990s. Starbucks' early beginnings, its rise to fame and fortune, and the methods it has used to become one of the most effective brands in the world are covered. Despite being seen as a forward-thinking business, Clark argues that Starbucks presents some ethical issues, including the homogenization of our country and its exploitation of third-world coffee farmers.

Subjects: Business, Coffee, Starbucks

Now Try: There are a number of books about this popular icon. Readers may want to read Starbucks' CEO Howard Schultz's narrative *Onward: How Starbucks Fought for Its Life without Losing Its Soul*. A Starbucks employee tells his story in *How Starbucks Saved My Life: A Son of Privilege Learns to Live Like Everyone Else*. Michael Weissman's *God in a Cup: The Obsessive Quest for the Perfect Coffee* is an interesting investigation into the socioeconomic impacts of coffee. Readers may also enjoy titles about other companies that have risen to become world phenomenon, such as David Kirkpatrick's *The Facebook Effect: The Inside Story of the Company That Is Connecting the World* by or Leander Kahney's *The Cult of iPod*.

Marks, Susan

Finding Betty Crocker: The Secret Life of America's First Lady of Food. New York: Simon & Schuster, 2005. 274pp. ISBN 9780743265010.

Betty Crocker has been a household name since the 1920s. From her birth in 1921 in an effort to convince women to try new technologies and products in the kitchen, to her role in encouraging the shift toward processed convenience foods, Betty Crocker has been instrumental in the changes in America's cooking and eating habits. Marks sets out to find out the history behind the face of what has been one of the most successful branding campaigns. She details the people responsible for inventing and shaping Crocker's persona, as well as the women who worked in the Betty Crocker test kitchens. Also included are original Betty Crocker recipes, advertisements, fan letters, and portraits, which will be popular with readers who enjoy primary historical sources.

Subjects: American History, Business, Crocker, Betty, Great Depression, Marketing, Recipes, Women's Nonfiction, World War II

Now Try: Harvey Levenstein's *Revolution at the Table* and *Paradox of Plenty* trace the changes in the American diet throughout the 20th century. *Something From the Oven: Reinventing Dinner in 1950s America* by Laura Shapiro examines the new technologies and changes in women's roles that began after World War II. Readers may also enjoy *Watching What We Eat: The Evolution of Television Cooking Shows* by Kathleen Collins. Stephanie Coontz traces the history of the American family and dispels a number of myths about the ideal family life in *The Way We Never Were*.

Pacult, F. Paul

A Double Scotch: How Chivas Regal and The Glenlivet Became Global Icons.
Hoboken: John Wiley & Sons, 2005. 290pp. ISBN 9780471662716.

The Scottish people have been producing whiskey for more than five centuries. Pacult details the histories of the men behind the creation of the two brands that most exemplify Scotch whiskey: Chivas Regal and The Glenlivet. Beginning with a brief history of the Scottish people, the origins of whiskey, and a description of how whiskey is made, Pacult then moves on to the Chivas brothers and the father–son partnership of George and John Gordon Smith who created The Glenlivet. One, grocers from Aberdeen and the other Highland farmers, although they took different routes to achieve success, both focused on quality, authenticity, and customer service which set them apart from the rest. The difficulties and dangers of the whiskey trade, including taxation and legislative interference, illicit distilling and smuggling provide an entertaining portrait of the turbulent whisky industry of the 19th century.

> **Subjects:** Business, Chivas Regal, Glenlivet, Scottish History, Scotland, Spirits, Whiskey

> **Now Try:** Kevin Kosar's *Whiskey: A Global History* provides a brief, but informative history of whiskey. *Barrels and Drams: The History of Whisk(e)y in Jiggers and Shots* by Dowd M. William is a collection of essays about whiskey history, production, and collecting. Pacult's *American Still Life: The Jim Beam Story and the Making of the World's #1 Bourbon* provides a look at the Beam family and 19th- and 20th-century America. Kate Hopkins's *99 Drams of Whiskey* is an entertaining history of whiskey in Ireland, Scotland, America, and Canada, interspersed with her travels tasting various whiskies. Andrew Jefford investigates the whiskey distilleries on the Scottish Isle of Islay in *Peat Smoke and Spirit*. *Bad Whisky* by Edward Burns recounts the Victorian scandal of adulteration of whisky in public houses in the United Kingdom. Readers may also enjoy other histories of famous spirits, such as *The King of Vodka* by Linda Himelstein or *Bacardi and the Long Fight for Cuba* by Tom Gjelten.

Perman, Stacy

In-N-Out Burger: A Behind-the-Counter Look at the Fast-Food Chain that Breaks All the Rules. New York: Collins Business, 2009. 345pp. ISBN 9780061346712.

In-N-Out Burger is a family-owned burger chain found mostly in Southern California that has achieved a cult-like following. The chain is untraditional in that the owners refuse to sell the company or franchise. The author traces the history of the restaurant and offers an inside look at the secretive family that founded it, highlighting their struggles to maintain the business, the tensions and lawsuits, and refusal to give in to the fast-food industry. The story is interspersed with the details of the evolution of the fast-food industry and how In-N-Out Burger managed to become a cultural institution.

> **Subjects:** Business, Fast Food Industry, In-N-Out Burger, Restaurants

> **Now Try:** Kirk Kazanjian's *Making Dough* provides a look at another popular American chain that has achieved the cult-like following similar to In-N-Out Burger: Krispy

Kreme doughnuts. *The Real Ones: Four Generations of the First Family of Coca-Cola* by Elizabeth Candler Graham and Ralph Roberts or Deborah Cadbury's *Chocolate Wars: The 150-Year Rivalry Between the World's Greatest Chocolate Makers* may also be appealing. Readers may also enjoy Eric Schlosser's *Fast Food Nation* for its examination of the fast-food industry.

Rothfeder, Jeffrey

McIlhenny's Gold: How a Louisiana Family Built the Tabasco Empire. New York: Collins, 2007. 251pp. ISBN 9780060721848.

Before the Civil War, Edmund McIlhenny owned a prosperous sugar plantation on Avery Island in Louisiana's gulf. Having fled Union troops during the war, he returned to find his plantation destroyed. Penniless, he began clearing his garden to begin replanting. One plant that survived were the red pepper plants. McIlhenny began creating a pepper sauce from these plants, which evolved into Tabasco sauce. This is the story that the company has perpetuated. Rothfeder proposes that much of this story is a fable and attempts to shed light on the true McIlhenny success. The author traces the history of the McIlhenny family, which has always been very secluded and secretive. Their brand is jealously guarded and continually refused to sell shares or accept buyout offers. Did Edmund McIlhenny really invent the pepper sauce that became Tabasco? Rothfeder attempts to get to the truth in this entertaining history.

> **Subjects:** American History, Business, Tabasco

> **Now Try:** Readers may enjoy Paul McIlhenny's *The Tabasco Cookbook: 125 Years of America's Favorite Pepper Sauce.* Joel Glen Brenner's *The Emperors of Chocolate* details the histories of two of the biggest, most secretive chocolate makers. *The House of Mondavi: The Rise and Fall of an American Wine Dynasty* by Julia Flynn Siler is a history of a family wine empire full of rivalry and drama. *Dethroning the King: The Hostile Takeover of Anheuser-Busch, An American Icon* by Julie MacIntosh is a dramatic account of the takeover of one of America's most well-known brands. *First in Thirst: How Gatorade Turned the Science of Sweat into a Cultural Phenomenon* by Darren Rovell is a history of the development and branding of the sports drink that dominates the market.

Siler, Julia Flynn

The House of Mondavi: The Rise and Fall of an American Wine Dynasty. New York: Gotham, 2007. 452pp. ISBN 9781592402595.

This extensively researched history of America's preeminent wine empire is chocked with sibling rivalry, greed, and drama. Siler begins with the immigration of Cesare Mondavi from Italy in 1906. Cesare purchased a derelict Napa winery in 1943, which he left to his two sons after his death. A fallout between the brothers led Robert Mondavi to build his own business that ended up making Mondavi number one in American wine. After Robert's sons were made co-CEOs, efforts to expand created a feud between the brothers as well as the breakup and forced sale of the company. Based on over five hundred hours of interviews, including interviews with Robert Mondavi and his sons, Siler's history is as thorough as it is captivating.

Subjects: Business, Family Relationships, Mondavi, Wine

Now Try: Readers may be interested in Robert Mondavi's memoir, *Harvests of Joy: How the Good Life Became Great Business. Napa: The Story of an American Eden* by James Conway traces the history of winemaking in Napa Valley and the emergence of winemaking empires, such as the Mondavis and the Gallos. *Gallo be Thy Name* by Jerome Tuccille traces the history of the famous Gallo winemaking family, also chocked full of intrigue and drama. *Citizen Coors: A Grand Family Saga of Business, Politics, and Beer* by Dan Baum traces the history of the Coors' family empire and the company's infamous business practices. Readers may also enjoy *Dynasties: Fortunes and Misfortunes of the World's Great Family Businesses* by David Landes, which profiles some of the great family businesses throughout the world.

Food Micro-Histories

Micro-histories are a popular subgenre of Food History. On the surface, Micro-histories focus on a single, narrow topic. Readers' Advisor Nancy Pearl refers to them as "one-word wonders" for their titles and focus (Renee and Pearl 2005). However, most Micro-histories use the single, narrow topic to view a bigger picture of history. Harvard history professor Jill Lepore defines Micro-histories as stories about a single person, place, or event that reveal a society's broader structures (Lepore 2002). Micro-histories are in-depth, well-researched histories that are highly narrative. These titles are very detailed and descriptive and provide an intimate feel for the time period. Although they are quite detailed, many of these titles are much shorter than most history titles. Micro-histories cover a wide range of topics, but one of the most common is food. Why is this? Perhaps because to the average reader, broader, lengthier titles about history may seem boring, or even intimidating. But food is something everyone can relate to and enjoy, which may make the history more appealing. In addition, as more people are questioning where our food comes from, historical details of the origins of our foods may be of interest. Readers who enjoy Food Micro-histories may certainly enjoy Micro-histories on subjects outside of food, but readers may also enjoy contemporary investigations of a particular food. Titles in Food Adventures and Explorations may be appealing as the authors explore a specific food. Many of the Food Micro-histories also include shocking histories of the exploitation of people and struggles to dominate a particular industry. Readers who enjoy these stories may also find some of the titles in the Investigative Food Writing chapter appealing, for the shocking aspects of current practices in the food industry.

Micro-Histories focus on a single, narrow topic in order to view a bigger picture of history. These titles are in-depth, well-researched, detailed, and highly narrative.

Abbott, Elizabeth

Sugar: A Bittersweet History. New York: Duckworth Overlook, 2009. 453pp. ISBN 9781590202975.

1

Abbott traces the history of sugar from its discovery to the present day and the profound affects it has had on the world. When sugar emerged as the favored sweetener over honey, it was considered a luxury of the rich. The desire for sugar fueled slavery and the destruction of indigenous tribes, and Abbott details what daily life was like for sugar slaves. The Industrial Revolution made sugar more affordable to other classes and also created technology that brought about new foods made out of sugar. Sugar has also been integral in the creation of the fast-food culture, and Abbott explores the health issues that have developed due to excessive consumption of sugar. Although lengthy and detailed, Abbott includes vivid details about slave life, as well as life during the Industrial Revolution.

2

3

Subjects: Fast-Food Industry, Industrial Revolution, Slavery, Sugar

Now Try: Peter Macinnis's *Bittersweet: The Story of Sugar* is another micro-history of sugar. *The Sugar King of Havana* by John Paul Rathbone is the history of a wealthy Cuban sugar baron. *The Sugar Barons* by Matthew Parker chronicles the history of the sugar trade. Henry Hobhouse's *The Seeds of Change* traces the histories of six plants, including sugar, which changed the course of history. Readers may also want to consider Abbott's other micro-history, *The History of Celibacy*.

4

5

Allen, Stewart Lee

In the Devil's Garden: A Sinful History of Forbidden Food. New York: Ballantine Books, 2002. 315pp. ISBN 9780345440150.

6

Throughout history, many foods have been feared for their association with sin and even forbidden. Allen explores the reasons that foods such as tomatoes, potatoes, matzo balls, and chocolate have been forbidden over the centuries, categorizing them with one of the seven deadly sins. Included are a number of historical recipes and menus featuring the forbidden foods. Allen also travels to exotic locations to investigate some of the few remaining food taboos.

7

Subjects: Recipes, Taboos, Travel

Now Try: Readers who appreciate Allen's writing style and thorough research may also enjoy his micro-history of coffee: *The Devil's Cup: A History of the World According to Coffee*. Other micro-histories of sinful indulgences may also be of interest, such as Iain Gately's *Drink: A Cultural History of Alcohol*, *Tobacco: A Cultural History of How an Exotic Plant Seduced Civilization*, or Bennet Alan Weinberg's and Bonnie K. Bealer's *The World of Caffeine: The Science and Culture of the World's Most Popular Drug*. Readers may also want to consider Taras Grescoe's *The Devil's Picnic: Travels Through the Underworld of Food and Drink*, which chronicles his travels seeking forbidden foods. Novels that emphasize

8

9

the more mystical side of food, like Laura Esquivel's *Like Water for Chocolate*, or Aimee Bender's *The Particular Sadness of Lemon Cake* may also be appealing.

Bruce, Scott

Cerealizing America: The Unsweetened Story of American Breakfast Cereal. Boston: Faber and Faber, 1995. 312pp. ISBN 9780571198511.

In this fascinating history of American history and pop culture, the author traces the history of breakfast cereals from its beginnings as a health food to its evolution to a sugar-sweetened food for children. The first cereals in America came about in the 1800s and were touted by religious leaders like Sylvester Graham and health crusaders like Harvey Kellogg. Originally used for invalids and dyspeptic patients, cereals eventually became everyday food for all Americans. Readers will enjoy the historical details of their favorite cereals such as Cheerios, Rice Krispies, Grape Nuts, and Cream of Wheat.

Subjects: American History, Cereal, Kellogg, John Harvey

Now Try: Harvey Levenstein's *Revolution at the Table* traces the changes in the American diet, including the invention of cereals. Susan Yager's *The Hundred Year Diet* also looks at America's obsession with dieting, also touching on cereals as a health food. *The Great American Cereal Book: How Breakfast Got Its Crunch* by Martin Gitlin is a history of the most famous cereal brands. Readers may also enjoy the fiction novel *The Road to Wellville* by T. C. Boyle, about a couple that visits John Harvey Kellogg's health spa in 1907 Michigan in search of better health. This novel also inspired a motion picture by the same title. Readers may also be interested in a history of medicine. Try *Seeking the Cure: A History of Medicine in America* by Ira Rutkow.

Coe, Andrew

Chop Suey: A Cultural History of Chinese Food in the United States. New York: Oxford University Press, 2009. 303pp. ISBN 9780195331073.

The first American trade expedition to China in 1784 introduced Americans to Chinese food, however most of the merchants stuck to western food while in China and it was many years before Chinese food became popular with Americans. Coe begins this fascinating history with the beginnings of trade with China and the life of the merchants while living in China. He also describes the Chinese cuisine of the time for both rural and royal Chinese. When the Chinese began to immigrate to the United States in large numbers to work on the transcontinental railroad, they brought their cuisine with them and Chinese restaurants began popping up in areas heavily populated by Chinese immigrants, particularly San Francisco. Although racism against Chinese immigrants was common, the cheap prices of Chinese restaurants attracted many Americans, who quickly took a liking to westernized Chinese dishes, such as Chop Suey.

Subjects: China, Chinese Cuisine, Immigrants, Scholarly

Now Try: *97 Orchard: An Edible History of Five Immigrant Families in One New York Tenement* by Jane Ziegelman is an account of the other major immigrant cultures who brought their cuisine to America. *Taco USA* by Gustavo Arellano is a history of the influence of Mexican cuisine in America. Jennifer 8 Lee explores the history of Chinese food in America in her entertaining investigation *Fortune Cookie Chronicles: Adventures in the World of Chinese Food*. Iris Chang's *The Chinese in America* is a dramatic history of Chinese immigration. Lisa See's biography of her Chinese American family, *On Gold Mountain*, is an engaging history of one Chinese family's immigration to the United States. Readers may enjoy novels centered on Chinese cuisine and culture, such as Nicole Mones's *The Last Chinese Chef*, Ann Mah's Kitchen Chinese, or Judy Fong Bates's *Midnight at the Dragon Café*.

Collingham, Lizzie

Curry: A Tale of Cooks and Conquerors. New York: Oxford University Press, 2007. 352pp. ISBN 9780195320015.

In this well-researched history, Collingham traces the origins of Indian cuisine and the influences that transformed it into what it is today. India has a long history of invasions. Each culture that has ruled over India has influenced the country and shaped its culture, including its cuisine. From the Mughal Empire of the 1600s to the Portuguese and British, each culture brought their own ingredients and cooking styles that transformed Indian cuisine and gave birth to almost every well-known Indian dish such as biryani, vindaloo, and curry. Collingham also explores the spread of Indian cuisine and its impact on the West, particularly in Britain. Although extensively researched, this is an accessible and vivid history of Indian cuisine.

> **Subjects:** India, Indian Cuisine, Recipes, Scholarly
>
> **Now Try:** Readers interested in titles about the history of the spice trade and its affect on India may want to consider *The Taste of Conquest: The Rise and Fall of Three Great Cities of Spice* by Michael Krondl and *Spice: The History of a Temptation* by Jack Turner. *For all the Tea in China: How England Stole the World's Greatest Drink and Changed History* by Sarah Rose is a history of how England's desire for tea changed India. *Eating India: An Odyssey Into the Food and Culture of the Land of Spices* by Chitrita Banerji takes readers on a vivid journey through the various regional Indian cuisines. Collingham also wrote a history of the effects of food on World War II, *The Taste of War: World War II and the Battle for Food*.

Curtis, Wayne

And a Bottle of Rum: The History of the New World in 10 Cocktails. New York: Crown Publishers, 2006. 294pp. ISBN 9781400051670.

Curtis traces the history of America from the 18th century through the perspective of rum. He argues that rum was a drink invented by the colonists and was a vital part of the economic and cultural life. In the 19th century rum was eclipsed by other drinks, but made a comeback in the 20th century. Each era of America had its particular rum drink, from the Kill-Devil drink of pirates, to Grog, Planter's Punch, daiquiris, rum and Cokes, up to the sophisticated Mojitos popular today. Curtis examines the political, economic, and cultural environments of the time that allowed the particular drink to come about.

Subjects: American History, Caribbean, Colonists, Rum, Spirits

Now Try: Ian Williams provides another look at this subject in *Rum: A Social and Sociable History of the Real Spirit of 1776*. Readers who enjoyed the stories behind the classic cocktails may enjoy David Wondrich's *Imbibe! From Absinthe Cocktail to Whiskey Smash, a Salute in Stories and Drinks to "Professor" Jerry Thomas, Pioneer of the American Bar*. Histories of other drinks may also be of interest, such as *Cognac: The Seductive Saga of the World's Most Coveted Spirit* by Kyle Jarrard or *Bitters: A Spirited History of a Classic Cure-All, with Cocktails, Recipes, and Formulas* by Brad Thomas Parsons and Ed Anderson. Tom Standage's *A History of the World in Six Glasses* is a broader history of the world told through other popular drinks. Food travel titles that investigate the history and making of spirits may also be of interest. Try Jason Wilson's *Boozehound* or Kate Hopkins's *99 Drams of Whiskey*. *A History of the World in 100 Objects* by Neil MacGregor may appeal to readers who enjoy history told through the lens of a particular subject.

Ellis, Richard

Tuna: A Love Story. New York: Alfred A. Knopf, 2008. 334pp. ISBN 9780307267153. The Bluefin Tuna is the most popular food fish in the world and is on the brink of extinction due to overfishing. In this thorough and impassioned account, Ellis describes the various species of tuna and its biology. The history of commercial fishing and the tuna's popularity, particularly in Japanese cuisine are covered. Ellis also explains how tunas are caught, gathered up in huge pens out at sea and kept until they are fattened enough for market. Vividly describing how the tuna are killed when it comes time for slaughter, Ellis argues that most people don't consider the brutality of their death.

Subjects: Aquaculture, Fishing, Japan, Overfishing, Tuna

Now Try: In *The Empty Ocean* Ellis explores other areas of the oceans that are in danger besides commercially important fish. Ellis also writes about the destruction of other species in *Tiger Bone & Rhino Horn: The Destruction of Wildlife for Traditional Chinese Medicine* and *On Thin Ice: The Changing World of the Polar Bear*. Paul Greenberg explores the current state of the main commercial fish—salmon, tuna, cod, and sea bass, and their current state in *Four Fish: The Future of the Last Wild Food* by Paul Greenberg. Douglass Whynott takes readers through two seasons of Bluefin tuna harpoon fishing off the New England coast in *Giant Bluefin*. H. Bruce Franklin explores another fish that is nearly extinct in *The Most Important Fish in the Sea: Menhaden and America*. William Langewiesche's *The Outlaw Sea*, while not about fishing, is about the vastness and wildness of the world's oceans.

Ferrieres, Madeline

Sacred Cow, Mad Cow: A History of Food Fears. New York: Columbia University Press, 2006. 399pp. ISBN 9780231131926.

> Issues regarding food safety are frequently in the news, but fear for food safety is not a recent phenomenon. This extensively researched work explores fears of food safety going back to the Middle Ages. Some fears were valid, however some were the result of myths and cultural prejudices. Regulations of meat butchery passed during the Middle Ages helped to address fears of rotten or impure meat. Later, the discovery of the New World led to fears of many of the new foods that were discovered. These fears led to beliefs that newly discovered plants, such as the tomato, were poisonous. When the conditions of the Chicago stockyards were exposed, fears for food safety led to new laws. Although scholarly, the fascinating historical details will appeal to readers.

> **Subjects:** Food Safety, Scholarly, Science, World History

> **Now Try:** Bee Wilson's *Swindled: The Dark History of Food Fraud, From Poisoned Candy to Counterfeit Coffee* is a history of the foods that have been altered throughout history, which also led to food safety laws. Marion Nestle's *Food Safety: The Politics of Food Safety* explores the current issues of food safety laws. Colm Kelleher examines the link between Mad Cow and Alzheimer's Disease in *Brain Trust: The Hidden Connection Between Mad Cow and Alzheimer's Disease*. Eric Schlosser exposes health concerns with fast-food in *Fast Food Nation*. Readers may also want to consider Upton Sinclair's novel, *The Jungle*, which was based on the conditions in the Chicago stockyards.

Fisher, Carol

American Cookbook: A History. Jefferson: McFarland & Company, 2006. 260pp. ISBN 9780786423422.

> Cookbooks can be more than a simple collection of recipes. Cookbooks can be a valuable resource for historical and sociological studies. Over time we can see the changes in the role of women in the home, the influence of political events and social movements, the availability of foods and products, and advances in technology. Fisher examines the history of the printed cookbook from the first American cookbook by Amelia Simmons in 1796. The cookbook revolution that began in the 1800s brought about a multitude of cookbooks and the first cooking schools in America. The first charity cookbooks, regional and ethnic cookbooks, health cookbooks, and cookbooks produced by the U.S. Department of Agriculture (USDA) are documented, as well as the creation of America's most well-known cook, Betty Crocker. Readers will appreciate the detailed history of the lives of American women, as well as the original recipes, personal accounts, and pictures.

Subjects: American History, Cookbooks, Crocker, Betty, Recipes, Women's Nonfiction

Now Try: Laura Schenone's *A Thousand Years Over a Hot Stove: A History of American Women Told Through Food, Recipes and Remembrances* and Janet Theophano's *Eat My Words: Reading Women's Lives Through the Cookbooks They Wrote* are also exceptional histories of women's lives as told through cooking. Harry Haff's *The Founders of American Cuisine* looks at the early cooks and cookbooks of American cuisine. Anne Willan traces the history of European and American cuisine through cookbooks in *The Cookbook Library: Four Centuries of the Cooks, Writers, and Recipes That Made the Modern Cookbook*. Readers may also enjoy Yvonne Schofer's *A Literary Feast: Recipes and Writings by American Women Authors from History*. Christopher Kimball's *Fannie's Last Supper* is an engaging account of his attempt to cook an entire meal from Fannie Farmer's 1896 cookbook. Although it may be difficult to find, Amelia Simmons's cookbook, *The First American Cookbook* is interesting to examine. Fiction readers may also enjoy J. Lynne Hinton's novel, *Friendship Cake*, about a women's church group that decides to create a cookbook.

Fletcher, Nichola

Charlemagne's Tablecloth: A Piquant History of Feasting. New York: St. Martin's Press, 2005. 256pp. ISBN 9780312340681.

Fletcher explores the custom of feasting throughout history and across several cultures. Feasts have been held to celebrate events and holidays, to enhance or display one's power or social standing, and as a form of generosity. Fletcher begins with the origins of feasting in ancient Persia, moving through the Romans, medieval Europe, the Renaissance, and Victorian periods. Famous traditional feasts are described, such as the imperial Chinese banquets and Japanese tea ceremonies, as well as feasts for Thanksgiving, Mardi Gras, and the Day of the Dead. The descriptions of smells, décor, and foods, as well as period recipes and menus make this an accessible and entertaining history.

Subjects: Feasting, Food Habits, Recipes, World History

Now Try: Roy Strong presents another perspective on this topic in *Feast: A History of Grand Eating*. Martin Jones examines why humans have turned eating into a ritual in *Feast: Why Humans Share Food*. Readers may also enjoy histories of other rituals such as Greg Tobin's *Holy Holidays!: The Catholic Origins of Celebration* or Craig Harline's *Sunday: A History of the First Day From Babylonia to the Super Bowl*.

Gentilcore, David

Pomodoro! A History of the Tomato in Italy. New York: Columbia University Press, 2010. 254pp. ISBN 9780231152068.

Today, Italian cuisine is synonymous with tomatoes. Italy is the main producer of tomatoes in Europe and accounts for a $2.2 billion market. But tomato hasn't always been popular in Italy. Introduced in the 16th century, tomato was initially thought to be poisonous and was avoided. It took three hundred years before the tomato became part of mainstream Italian consumption. Gentilcore traces the changes in Italian attitudes and food habits that allowed tomato to become a national symbol. Using the changes in attitudes towards tomatoes as a lens, Gentilcore also examines the changes in Italian values, beliefs, and society over several centuries.

Subjects: Italian Cuisine, Italian History, Tomatoes

Now Try: For an American perspective on the history of tomato, try *The Tomato in America* by Andrew F. Smith. Barry Estabrook examines the current state of tomato and the changes that have been made to it by the industrialized food system in *Tomatoland: How Modern Industrial Agriculture Destroyed Our Most Alluring Fruit*. Readers may also enjoy the fiction novel *Tomato Rhapsody* by Adam Schell, about a Jewish tomato farmer in 16th-century Italy who falls in love with a Catholic girl. *How Italian Food Conquered the World* by John F. Mariani is another comprehensive history of the Italian cuisine. *Extra Virginity: The Sublime and Scandalous World of Olive Oil* by Tom Mueller is an investigation into the adulteration of another product that is synonymous with Italian cuisine. Other books in the series Perspectives on Culinary History may be of interest: *French Gastronomy: The History and Geography of a Passion* by Jean-Robert Pitte, *Pasta: The Story of a Universal Food* by Silvano Serventi, *Italian Cuisine: A Cultural History* by Alberto Capatti, and *British Food: An Extraordinary Thousand Years of History* by Colin Spencer. An entire book display could almost be created using books with tomato in the title; consider William Alexander's *The $64 Tomato*, Mike Madison's *Blithe Tomato: An Insider's Wry Look at Farmers' Market Society*, Annabelle Gurwitch's *You Say Tomato, I Say Shut Up: A Love Story*, Tim Stark's *Heirloom: Notes from an Accidental Tomato Farmer*, and even Jayne Pupek's novel *Tomato Girl*. Not to mention *The Attack of the Killer Tomatoes*—a humorous film from the late 1970s and somewhat of a cult classic.

Grimes, William

Appetite City: A Culinary History of New York. New York: North Point Press, 2009. 368pp. ISBN 9780865476929.

In this entertaining history of one of America's greatest food cities, Grimes gives an historical tour of New York City's dining culture from the chophouses to the oyster bars, to the abundance of restaurants that have populated the city since the 1800s. He traces the changes in food preferences over the years and the effect that immigration, Prohibition, and the various wars have had on the city. Photos, drawings, and original menus enhance the vivid details.

Subjects: American History, New York City, Restaurants

Now Try: Readers may also want to check out Michael Batterberry's *On the Town in New York: The Landmark History of Eating, Drinking, and Entertainments from the American Revolution to the Food Revolution* or John Mariani's *America Eats Out: An Illustrated History of Restaurants, Taverns, Coffee Shops, Speakeasies, and Other Establishments That Have Fed Us for 350 Years*. *97 Orchard: An Edible History of Five Immigrant Families in One New York Tenement* by Jane Ziegelman is a fascinating in-depth look at the immigrant influence on New York City's culinary history. A. E. Hotchner's *Everyone Comes to Elaine's* provides the inside story of this famous New York City restaurant's 40-year history. Readers may also enjoy New York cook and restaurateur Kenny Shopsin's *Eat Me: The Food and Philosophy of Kenny Shopsin*. For readers interested in the history of New York, try David McCullough's *The Great Bridge: The Epic Story of the Building of the Brooklyn Bridge* or *Triangle: The Fire That Changed America* by Dave Von Drehle.

Hohenegger, Beatrice

Liquid Jade: The Story of Tea from East to West. New York: St. Martin's Press, 2006. 320pp. ISBN 9780312333287.

The origins of tea are strongly rooted in Eastern culture. In ancient China, tea was used as a remedy. Buddhist Japan used tea as part of their spiritual practices. When tea was discovered by Western merchants, tea became a coveted commodity that led to smuggling, espionage, trade wars, and the creation of the English East India Company. The English demand for tea brought about the importation of opium to China, the creation of large tea plantations in India, and supported the slavery of sugar plantations. Hohenegger details early tea lore and culture of the East, the clash of cultures between the East and the West, and the introduction of tea to Europe. She also explores contemporary issues of tea production such as the social inequalities that were created by colonialism and still exist today, the physical aspects of tea production and its effect on the soil, and Fair Trade practices. Various miscellaneous facts about tea such as the discovery of the tea plant, the creation of the tea bag, differences in types of tea, and the job of a tea taster add to this lively and entertaining history.

> **Subjects:** Tea, Trade, World History

> **Now Try:** *For All the Tea in China* by Sarah Rose is a fascinating history of the lengths Britain went to secure their supplies of tea. *Tea: Addiction, Exploitation and Empire* by Roy Moxham focuses on the dark side of the tea trade and includes his description of his experience working on a tea estate. *Merchant Kings: When Companies Ruled the World, 1600–1900* by Stephen Bown traces the history of the most famous monopolies that ruled commerce, including the British East India Company. Readers may want to consider other micro-histories of beverages and foods that established international trade routes, such as *Salt* by Mark Kurlansky, *Uncommon Grounds* by Mark Pendergrast, or *Nathaniel's Nutmeg* by Giles Milton.

Humble, Nicola

Cake: A Global History. London: Reaktion Books, 2010. 144pp. ISBN 9781861896483.

This short volume traces the consumption of cake throughout history, from the earliest cakes discovered in the remains of Neolithic villages in Switzerland, to the transformation of cakes in the 1700s with the removal of yeast, to the evolution of modern cakes using chemical rising agents. Humble examines the culture of cake around the world and how it earned its place in rituals and celebrations, and illustrates how cakes differ by country. A collection of famous cakes,

including Queen Elizabeth II's wedding cake, adds an element of entertainment as does the inclusion of recipes for a variety of cakes found
throughout history.

Subjects: Cake, Quick Reads, Recipes

Now Try: This book is part of Reaktion Books' Edible series, which may be
appealing to readers. The series consists of brief, easy-to-read volumes on a
variety of foods, including chocolate, cheese, caviar, pie, pizza, pancakes, and
whiskey. Michael Krondl's *Sweet Invention* looks at desserts, throughout the
past and present, and across several cultures. Cake baking is a popular theme
for television shows today. Readers may be interested in books by some of
the stars of these shows, such as *Cake Boss* by Buddy Valastro or *Ace of Cakes*
by Duff Goldman. Leslie Miller's *Let Me Eat Cake* is an entertaining memoir of
her attempt at learning to decorate cakes. Melissa Gray, producer of NPR's All
Things Considered presents *All Cakes Considered*, an enticing collection of cake
recipes and the stories of their origins. Krystina Castella's *A World of Cakes* is a
vivid collection of recipes, color photographs, and cultural histories of cakes
from around the world. For fun, try *Cake Wrecks: When Professional Cakes Go
Hilariously Wrong* by Jen Yates.

Iacobbo, Karen, and Iacobbo, Michael

Vegetarian America: A History. Westport, CT: Praeger Publishers, 2004.
267pp. ISBN 9780275975197.

When thinking of the vegetarian movement in America, most people picture its beginnings with the hippies of the 1960s and 1970s. But vegetarian movements have actually been a part of American history since
the 1700s. The authors trace the history of the vegetarian movement in
America, the major proponents of the vegetarian diet, and the ways the
vegetarian movement have affected the mainstream American diet. Early
proponents of vegetarianism were Christians who followed the Bible's
command not to eat flesh. Sylvester Graham, a Presbyterian temperance
reformer in the early 19th century, became the father of the American
vegetarian movement. Graham believed that health was directly con-
nected to diet and that abstinence from meat was essential to health.
Dr. John Harvey Kellogg was also a proponent of the vegetarian diet and
revolutionized the breakfast cereal industry. The authors also explore
how the vegetarian movement was also linked to the abolitionist movement, the feminist movement, and the Seventh Day Adventists.

Subjects: American History, Diets, Graham, Sylvester, Health Issues, Kellogg,
John Harvey, Seventh Day Adventists, Vegetarianism

Now Try: For a broader history, readers should try Tristram Stuart's *The Bloodless Revolution: A Cultural History of Vegetarianism: From 1600 to Modern Times*.
Readers may want to consider *The Ethics of What We Eat* by Peter Singer. In
Diet for a Small Planet, Frances Moore Lappé argues that eating a meat-based
diet contributes to global hunger. Lierre Keith argues that vegetarianism is

not necessarily the answer to saving our planet in *The Vegetarian Myth: Food, Justice, and Sustainability*. Tara Austen Weaver's *The Butcher and the Vegetarian* and Tovar Cerulli's *The Mindful Carnivore* are both memoirs in which the authors explore the health and ethical aspects of both vegetarian and meat diets.

Kindstedt, Paul S.

Cheese and Culture: A History of Cheese and Its Place in Western Civilization. White River Junction, Vt.: Chelsea Green Publishing, 2012. 256pp. ISBN 9781603584111.

Detailed, yet still accessible, food scientist Kindstedt incorporates archaeology, religion, literature, and food politics into this extensively researched and comprehensive history of cheese and its place in the development of Western civilization. Beginning with the ancient origins of cheese making and moving through the classical, medieval, and Renaissance periods to the modern era, the author examines the traditional cheeses that came about during each period and how they were tailored to the environment and culture of the time. Finally, he explores the friction that has developed between the United States and the European Union over issues surrounding cheese making and trade, such as protecting traditional product names, food safety regulation, and the use of new agricultural technologies such as genetically modified organisms (GMOs) and hormones.

Subjects: Cheese, World History

Now Try: *Cheese: A Global History* by Andrew Dalby is a briefer, yet interesting history of cheese. Eric LeMay recounts his travels investigating the various flavors of cheese in *Immortal Milk: Adventures in Cheese*. The PBS documentary, *The Cheese Nun*, features a Benedictine nun who is in charge of cheese making at her convent. The history of one of France's most famous cheeses is detailed in Pierre Boisard's *Camembert: A National Myth*. Gordon Edgar shares his experiences selling cheese in *Cheesemonger*. Sarah-Kate Lynch's novel *Blessed are the Cheesemakers* is a charming story of Irish cheese makers.

Koeppel, Dan

Banana: The Fate of the Fruit That Changed the World. Hudson Street Press, 2007. 304pp. ISBN 9781594630385.

The banana is the most popular fruit in the United States. This book chronicles the history of the banana's evolution and migration from Southeast Asia to the United States in the 15th century, as well as the rise of the United Fruit Company and its impact on Central America. The complicated, but fascinating, reproductive system of the banana is also explained, as well as the threats facing the future survival of this favorite fruit.

Subjects: Banana, Botany, Endangered Species, Investigative Stories, United Fruit Company

Now Try: For more details on the United Fruit Company, readers may want to try Peter Chapman's *Bananas: How the United Fruit Company Shaped the World*. Rich Cohen's

The Fish That Ate the Whale: The Life and Times of America's Banana King profiles Samuel Zemurray, a banana peddler who battled the United Fruit Company. Readers who enjoy detailed food histories may also like *Citrus: A History* by Pierre Laszlo. Michael Pollan's *The Botany of Desire: A Plant's-Eye View of the World* will appeal to readers who enjoy not only the history of human desire for a particular plant, but also the various aspects of genetically engineered food. Readers who are astonished by the possibility of the disappearance of bananas may also enjoy *Fruitless Fall: The Collapse of the Honey Bee and the Coming Agricultural Crisis* by Rowen Jacobsen.

Kurlansky, Mark

The Big Oyster: History on the Half Shell. New York: Ballantine Books, 2006. 307pp. ISBN 9780345476388.

Kurlansky is well known for his entertaining micro-histories. In this book he traces the oyster's influence on the economy, ecology, and gastronomy of New York City. Enjoyed as a delicacy by the Native Americans, Dutch settlers were delighted to find the trove of oysters in New York harbor, and New York quickly became the leading American city for oyster consumption. By the late 19th century, both the rich and the poor ate oysters frequently. Kurlansky details the growth of New York City and the problems that arose, including the pollution that led to the decline of oyster populations and the eventual shutting down of the oyster fields.

> **Subjects**: American History, Maps, New York City, Oysters, Recipes

> **Now Try:** Eleanor Clark won a National Book Award in 1965 for *The Oysters of Locmariaquer*, a portrait of a French town on the coast of Brittany, famous for its cultivation of Belon oysters. Readers may also want to check out Rowan Jacobsen's *A Geography of Oysters* and Robb Walsh's *Sex, Death, and Oysters*. Erin Byers Murray recalls her firsthand experience on an oyster farm in *Shucked*. Readers interested in the history of New York City may want to consider Russell Shorto's *The Island at the Center of the World*, a history of the Dutch settlers and the founding of New Netherland or even Edward Rutherfurd's historical fiction novel, *New York*. Kurlansky's other micro-histories include *Cod: A Biography of the Fish that Changed the World* or *Salt: A World History*. His most recent *Birdseye: The Adventures of a Curious Man*, profiles Clarence Birdseye, the man who invented the method for fast-freezing and revolutionized the food industry. Kurlansky's fiction, *Edible Stories,* may also be of interest.

Mendelson, Anne

Milk: The Surprising Story of Milk Through the Ages. New York: Alfred A. Knopf, 2008. 336pp. ISBN 9781400044108.

Milk has been a favored beverage for thousands of years, but the milk we find in American grocery stores is quite bland compared to the rest of the world. Historically, cows were not the only animal that humans used for milk.

Mendelson's detailed account traces the history of milking traditions from Asia and Europe and the animals that have been raised for milk. Turning her focus to the changes in the production of milk in modern Western societies, she illustrates how modern industrial farming and processing have diluted milk. She explores the arguments for raw versus pasteurized milk; organic versus conventional milk. The chemistry of milk is also explained and she includes a number of narrative recipes for dishes with milk as the main focus, such as cheese and yogurt.

Subjects: Industrial Agriculture, Milk, Recipes

Now Try: Other histories of milk that may be considered are *Milk: A Global History* by Hannah Velten or *Milk: A Local and Global History* by Deborah Valenze. David E. Gumpert investigates raw milk in *Raw Milk Revolution*. Melanie Dupuis also examines the effects of industrialized farming on the quality of today's milk in *Nature's Perfect Food*. Readers interested in additional recipes may want to consider *The Home Creamery* by Kathy Farrell-Kingsley. Eric LeMay and his wife travel the globe seeking out various cheeses and learning about making cheese in *Immortal Milk*. *Blessed are the Cheesemakers* by Sarah-Kate Lynch is a charming novel about a dairy farm that produces its own cheese. Mendelson also wrote a history of the classic *Joy of Cooking*: *Stand Facing the Stove*.

Milton, Giles

Nathaniel's Nutmeg: The True and Incredible Adventures of the Spice Trader Who Changed the Course of History. New York: Farrar, Straus and Giroux, 1999.

In 17th-century Europe, nutmeg was the most coveted luxury, said to have powerful medicinal properties. However, no one was certain where nutmeg came from. The London merchants bought nutmeg from Venice merchants, who bought it from Constantinople merchants. It was known that nutmeg came from the East Indies, but exactly where was unknown. The race between the Dutch East India Company and Britain to find the treasured spice was heated. The English, determined to win the race, sent Nathaniel Courthope to hold off the Dutch, which led to a brutal showdown. Milton infuses this comprehensive and detailed history with the excitement of the rivalry and race.

Subjects: Exploration, Nutmeg, Spices, Trade, World History

Now Try: Histories of the spice trade may be of interest, such as *Spice: The History of a Temptation* by Jack Turner or *The Taste of Conquest: The Rise and Fall of the Three Great Cities of Spice* by Michael Krondl. Readers may want to checkout Jane Lawson's *The Spice Bible* for recipes and information about a number of spices. *For All the Tea in China: How England Stole the World's Favorite Drink and Changed History* by Sarah Rose is the history of the man sent by Britain to secure Britain's tea interests in China. *Merchant Kings: When Companies Ruled the World, 1600–1900* by Stephen R. Bown profiles the companies that raced to discover and exploit resources for their countries all over the world. While not about food, Amy Butler Greenfield's *A Perfect Red: Empire, Espionage, and the Quest for the Color of Desire* is another history about the desire for foreign goods.

Mullins, Paul R.

Glazed America: A History of the Doughnut. Gainsville: University Press of Florida, 2008. 200pp. ISBN 9780813032382.

This popular American treat evolved from the influence of the sweet fried pastries of the Dutch, Chinese, French, German, and Latin American, to the inventor of the doughnut hole. Mullins traces the history of doughnut production, consumption and marketing and looks at consumer loyalties to different doughnut brands. The impact of the doughnut on our health is also discussed.

Subjects: Doughnuts, Health Issues, Scholarly

Now Try: John T. Edge is known for his exploration of iconic American foods. In *Donuts: An American Passion*, he combines a cultural history of doughnuts with recipes. *Making Dough* by Kirk Kazanjian is the history of Krispy Kreme doughnuts and their secrets to success. William Rosenberg, the founder of Dunkin' Donuts, shares his path to success in *Time to Make the Donuts*. Sally Levitt Steinberg, the granddaughter of the inventor of the doughnut-making machine, compiles history, trivia, and recipes in *The Donut Book*. What goes perfectly with a good doughnut? A cup of coffee. *Starbucked* by Taylor Clark may also appeal to readers, as might Howard Shcultz's business histories about Starbucks, *Pour Your Heart Into It* and *Onward*. The history of another popular American treat may also be suggested: *Crunch!: A History of the Great American Potato Chip* by Dirk E. Burhans. For fun, fiction fans may enjoy Jessica Beck's Donut Shop mystery series. Start with *Glazed Murder*.

Off, Carol

Bitter Chocolate: The Dark Side of the World's Most Seductive Sweet. New York: New Press, 2008. 328pp. ISBN 9781595583307.

This absorbing history and investigative account traces the love affair people have had with chocolate since its discovery by the Olmecs over three thousand years ago, despite the injustices it has caused. A coveted drink of the Mayans and Aztecs, cocoa was served only to the elite or for religious purposes. Once discovered by Spanish conquistadors, it became popular with European royalty, however the modification of adding sugar to cocoa helped fuel slavery. The Industrial Revolution made mass production possible, making cocoa accessible to even the working class and led to the creation of chocolate giants, such as Hershey, Mars, and Cadbury. The author also investigates the shocking corruption, exploitation, and violence occurring today in the Ivory Coast over coveted coca groves.

Subjects: Chocolate, Economics, Industrial Revolution

Now Try: Mort Rosenblum's *Chocolate* traces the history of chocolate and profiles current growers and producers. Maricel Priscilla's *The New Taste of*

Chocolate is an extensive history of chocolate and includes recipes. *Sugar: A Bittersweet History* by Elizabeth Abbott may also appeal to readers. Listed in Off's bibliography, readers may want to consider *King Leopold's Ghost: A Story of Greed, Terror, and Heroism in Colonial Africa* by Adam Hochschild. *Nobodies: Modern American Slave Labor and the Dark Side of the New Global Economy* by John Bowe exposes the slave labor used today and how it is often tied to our food. Readers may also enjoy the fiction novel *The Discovery of Chocolate* by James Runcie about a young Spaniard who is part of the Conquistadors and is introduced to the magical chocolate drink of Montezuma. Readers may enjoy novels where chocolate is central such as Joanne Harris's *Chocolat* and its sequel. Roald Dahl's children's classic, *The Complete Adventures of Charlie and Mr. Wonka*, may be a whimsical adult read.

Ogle, Maureen

Ambitious Brew: The Story of American Beer. Orlando: Harcourt, 2006. 422pp. ISBN 9780151010127.

This well-researched account traces the history of beer brewing in America and the transformation of the American-style beer. Prior to the mid-nineteenth century, beer was not a popular drink in America. With the wave of German immigrants that came to America in the second half of the 19th century, they brought with them their love of beer and recreated the beer gardens that were popular back home. Soon, the taste for beer caught on with Americans. Breweries began opening in cities with large German immigrant populations, such as New York, St. Louis, and Milwaukee, making European-style beers. Ogle traces the histories of the brewers that rose to success, such as Phillip Best, Frederick Pabst, and Adophus Busch and how beer was transformed from the darker ale of its predecessors to the paler, lighter beers now popular in America today. Ogle includes vivid descriptions of the brewing process and inside stories of the families behind the leaders of the brewing industry.

> **Subjects:** American History, Beer, Brewing Industry
>
> **Now Try:** *Travels with Barley: A Journey Through Beer Culture in America* by Ken Wells is an entertaining tour of breweries and bars across America. *Dethroning the King: The Hostile Takeover of Anheuser-Busch, an American Icon*, by Julie MacIntosh, is a fascinating account of the takeover of one of the most well-known brands of American beer. Brian Yaeger visits a variety of breweries across America in *Red, White, and Brew*. *Pint Sized Ireland: In Search of the Perfect Guinness* by Evan McHugh is a tour of Ireland's famous brew. Tom Standage looks at the drinks that helped shape history, including beer, in *A History of the World in Six Glasses*. *America Walks into a Bar: A Spirited History of Taverns and Saloons, Speakeasies and Grog Shops* by Christine Sismondo is an entertaining history of an American cultural institution.

Pendergrast, Mark

Uncommon Grounds: The History of Coffee and How it Transformed Our World. New York: Basic Books, 1999. 520pp. ISBN 9780465036318.

In this detailed and wide-ranging history, Pendergrast traces the discovery of coffee and the history of its expansion throughout the world. He explores the various uses of coffee, first as a medicinal drink and later as a social drink and a patriotic drink, and its role in spawning revolutions and abetting slavery. The contemporary social and environmental impacts of coffee are also explored, from the exploitation of farmers, to economic inequalities, and deforestation. Pendergrast also details the effects on the world's economies, particularly Latin America, as well as the rise and fall of many regional brands and the creation of several coffee dynasties, that occurred when coffee became a major American industry.

Subjects: Coffee, Economics, Slavery, Social Issues, World History

Now Try: Other histories of coffee that may be of interest are Antony Wild's *Coffee: A Dark History*, and Stewart Lee Allen's *The Devil's Cup: A History of the World According to Coffee*. *God in a Cup: The Obsessive Quest for the Perfect Cup* by Michael Weissman explains how coffee is grown and produced and examines the socioeconomic impact of coffee. Dean Cycon investigates the coffee industry in *Javatrekker: Dispatches From the World of Fair Trade Coffee*. *Starbucked* by Taylor Clark traces the rise of the famous Starbucks chain. Howard Schultz, CEO of Starbucks, chronicles the steps the company took to restore its performance in *Onward: How Starbucks Fought for its Life Without Losing its Soul*. Readers may also enjoy the historical fiction novel *The Coffee Trader* by David Liss, about a Jewish trader attempting to introduce coffee to 17th-century Amsterdam.

Quinzio, Jeri

Of Sugar and Snow: A History of Ice Cream Making. Berkeley, CA: University of California Press, 2009. 279pp. ISBN 9780520248618.

Many myths surround the invention of ice cream. Emperor Nero, Marco Polo, and Catherine de Medici have all been rumored to have discovered ice cream. Quinzio dispels these myths and traces the origins of this popular dessert to the 16th-century Europeans whose experiments with mixing ice and salt led to the discovery of freezing. Although first applied to wine, the technique spread throughout Europe and England, and finally to America, where its popularity exploded. Quinzio explains how ice cream is made and how the invention of modern refrigeration made this dessert, which was once for the elite and upper classes, accessible to everyone.

Subjects: Ice Cream, Recipes, Science

Awards: IACP Award

Now Try: A number of books on the history and making of ice cream are currently available, including *Ice Cream U* by Lee Stout, which examines the success of Penn State's Creamery and how they became known as Ice Cream U. *Ice Cream: A Global History* by Laura Weiss, is part of the Reaktion Books Edible series and a quick read. *Ice Cream: The Delicious History* by Marilyn Powell is another detailed history. *The Perfect Scoop* by David Lebovitz is a colorful and tantalizing cookbook of ice cream recipes. Although somewhat scholarly, readers interested in how ice cream is made may want to try *The Science of Ice Cream* by C. Clarke, which explains the chemistry of producing ice cream and techniques used to assess it. Readers open to documentary viewing might also consider Rick Seback's program *An Ice Cream Show*.

Rain, Patricia

Vanilla: The Cultural History of the World's Most Popular Flavor and Fragrance. New York: J. P. Tarcher/Penguin, 2004. 371pp. ISBN 9781585423637.

Today, vanilla can be found in many everyday products, including our food, coffee, perfumes, lotions, and candles. This popular flavor and scent comes from the seed pods of a rare orchid. Rain, a vanilla broker, deftly traces the history of vanilla and its production to Mexico, the discovery of vanilla by the Europeans, and its dispersal to other countries. The demand for vanilla has affected food, medicine, politics, indigenous producers, perfume and confection industries, and spurred trade routes. Rain also addresses the effects vanilla cultivation has had on indigenous populations and local economies, as well as the issues raised by the production of synthetic vanilla. This insightful history is infused with folklore, trivia, and recipes.

> **Subjects:** Recipes, Spices, Vanilla, World History

> **Now Try:** Readers may want to consider checking out Rain's *Vanilla Cookbook*. Tim Ecott's *Vanilla* is another well researched history of vanilla. Readers may also be interested in Luigi Berliocchi's book *The Orchid in Lore and Legend*, a fascinating, comprehensive account of orchids. Other micro-histories that might appeal are Carol Off's *Bitter Chocolate* and Mark Pendergrast's *Uncommon Grounds*. Vanilla is interesting in many ways for its evocative scent; other books which cover olfactory subjects are Chandler Burr's *Perfect Scent: A Year inside the Perfume Industry in Paris and New York* and Amy Stewart's *Flower Confidential* (in which she describes how scent has been bred out of most modern flowers in favor of bloom longevity and hardiness).

Richardson, Tim

Sweets: A History of Candy. New York: Bloomsbury, 2002. 392pp. ISBN 9781582342290.

Humans have been attracted to sweet foods since prehistoric times. Richardson chronicles the history of sweets from the earliest sweets to the development of modern sweets. Sweets were initially used for medicinal purposes, but when its popularity grew, the demand for sugar led to slavery. Richardson also details some of the major figures in the candy business, including Hershey, Cadbury, Mars, and Lindt. He provides a scientific explanation of why we like sweets and recounts his own favorites and childhood candy memories, as well as comparing international preferences for sweets.

Subjects: Candy, Slavery, Sugar, World History

Now Try: Readers may also want to try Elizabeth Abbott's *Sugar: A Bittersweet History,* which illustrates how the desire for sugar changed the course of history. Deborah Cadbury traces the history of the major chocolate makers, including Hershey, Cadbury, and Mars in *Chocolate Wars.* Steve Almond visits candy makers and seeks out his favorite childhood candy in *Candyfreak: A Journey through the Chocolate Underbelly of America.* Hilary Liftin recalls the events of her life as experienced through candy in *Candy and Me.* Fiction readers may enjoy *True Confections* by Katherine Weber, a story of a woman in charge of running the family candy factory.

Rosenblum, Mort

Olives: The Life and Lore of a Noble Fruit. New York: North Point Press, 2006. 316pp. ISBN 9780865475038.

When Rosenblum bought a farm in Provence, he acquired a number of neglected olive trees. Intent on restoring the trees to health, he sets out to learn more about this revered fruit. His travels take him throughout Greece, Spain, Italy, Israel, and the United States. Rosenblum details the olive's history and how it shaped the course of nations since the time of ancient Greece. Throughout the Mediterranean he meets farmers who teach him about growing and caring for olive trees but also enlighten him as to the difficulties of farming. He is educated on the differences between olives and their oils and learns about the production of olive oil. The politics and environmental issues that affect the market are also explored.

Subjects: Investigative Stories, Olive Oil, Olives, Travel, World History

Now Try: Readers may also enjoy some of Rosenblum's other works, such *Chocolate: A Bittersweet Saga of Dark and Light* or his memoir of living and traveling on the Seine, *The Secret Life of the Seine.* Carol Drinkwater recounts her experiences buying a restoring an olive farm in Provence in *The Olive Farm.* Tom Mueller's *Extra Virginity: The Sublime and Scandalous World of Olive Oil* is an intriguing investigation into the fraudulent practices in the olive oil industry.

Satin, Morton

Death in the Pot: The Impact of Food Poisoning on History. Amherst: Prometheus Books, 2007. 258pp. ISBN 9781591025146.

Satin proposes that food-borne diseases and contamination are a phenomenon of nature, rather than a result of modern intensive agriculture and food processing. By considering the physical and archeological evidence as well as historical documentation, he illustrates that food-borne diseases have been a problem throughout history, as far back as the Stone Age. Lead poisoning was a common affliction among the Greeks and Romans. Poisoning from moldy grains was a frequent problem during the Middle Ages and was probably what caused the strange behaviors that led to the Salem Witch Trials. The court of Louis XIV suffered from parasitic diseases. Arsenic poisoning may have contributed to the madness of George III. Fascinating historical accounts, as well as the explanations of the biology of diseases will make this popular with readers who enjoy history as well as science.

Subjects: Agriculture, Food Poisoning, Medicine, Science, World History

Now Try: *Swindled: The Dark History of Food Fraud, From Poisoned Candy to Counterfeit Coffee* by Bee Wilson chronicles the history of corrupted foods that have been poisoning people since the 19th century. *Typhoid Mary: An Urban Historical* by Anthony Bourdain is a brief history of the woman charged with the 1904 outbreak of typhoid fever in Long Island. *Poisoned: The True Story of the Deadly E. Coli Outbreak That Changed the Way Americans Eat* by Jeff Benedict is a disturbing account of the 1993 outbreak of *Escherichia coli*. Ben Hewitt's *Making Supper Safe: One Man's Quest to Learn the Truth about Food Safety* also examines the current issue of food-borne illnesses. *The Blue Death: Disease, Disaster, and the Water We Drink* by Robert D. Morris chronicles historical and current epidemics transferred through water, as well as the history of public water filtration systems. Eric Schlosser's *Fast Food Nation* exposes instances of contamination in the fast-food industry. Tom Mueller's *Extra Virginity: The Sublime and Scandalous World of Olive Oil* is an intriguing investigation into the fraudulent practices in the olive oil industry.

Schivelbusch, Wolfgang

Tastes of Paradise: A Social History of Spices, Stimulants, and Intoxicants. New York: Pantheon, 1992. 236pp. ISBN 9780394579849.

Although short, this history provides a fascinating account of the discovery, popularity, and use of spices, stimulants, and intoxicants from the medieval period to the modern age. In medieval Europe people used copious amounts of spices such as salt, pepper, cinnamon, and nutmeg to preserve food and mask spoiled meats. Stimulants such as coffee, tea, and chocolate and intoxicants like alcohol and opium were often used to enhance pleasure and even numb the senses. This unique and accessible work examines how these items affected cultures' customs and behavior norms.

Subjects: Chocolate, Coffee, Opium, Spices, Spirits, Tea

Now Try: *Spice: The History of a Temptation* by Jack Turner traces the history of the allure of spices. *The Taste of Conquest* by Michael Krondl traces the history of the international spice trade and the rise and fall of the three most important spice centers in Europe: Venice, Amsterdam, and Lisbon. Readers may also enjoy micro-histories of spices and stimulants such as *The Secrets of Saffron: The Vagabond Life of the World's Most Seductive Spice* by Pat Willard, *Nathaniel's Nutmeg* by Giles Milton, *Vanilla* by Patricia Rain, *Opium* by Martin Booth, and *For All the Tea in China* by Sarah Rose. Marvin Harris examines the diversity of human food habits in *Good to Eat: Riddles of Food and Culture*.

Shephard, Sue

Pickled, Potted, and Canned: How the Art and Science of Food Preserving Changed the World. New York: Simon and Schuster, 2000. 366pp. ISBN 9780743216333.

Food preservation has been integral to human progress. Food preservation made it possible for nomadic people to settle and build agrarian communities. Continuously evolving preservation techniques have allowed people to travel further and further distances, both on land and in space, which has led to advancements in exploration and trade. Shephard describes the earliest methods of food preservation such as drying, salting, smoking, and fermenting. As scientists made strides in understanding the biological causes of food deterioration, new methods of food preservation were discovered such as heat processing, canning, refrigeration, freezing, and dehydrating, and the development of additives and preservatives. Shephard includes fascinating examples of preservation, including the discovery of an ancient Egyptian baby preserved in honey and the practice of preserving fish by burying it in sand.

Subjects: Food Preservation, Science, World History

Now Try: *Catching Fire: How Cooking Made Us Human* by Richard Wrangham explores how the evolution of cooking was essential to the evolution of humanity. Readers may also enjoy other histories of scientific discoveries that were essential to civilization such as *Eureka!: Scientific Breakthroughs That Changed the World* by Leslie Alan Horvitz or *The Evolution of Useful Things* by Henry Petroski. Readers interested in a how-to on food preservation should consider the classic *Putting Food By* by Ruth Hertzberg, Janet Greene, and Beatrice Vaughn. The blog Food In Jars (www.foodinjars.com) shares the ins and outs of canning and includes recipes.

Turner, Jack

Spice: The History of a Temptation. New York: Knopf, 2004. 352pp. ISBN 9780375407215.

Since the Roman ages, spices have been valued for their ability to enhance food, treat maladies, enhance sex, and aid in spiritual matters. This thorough account of the spice trade examines how the desire for spices fueled discovery and led to the reshaping of the world. Turner profiles the spice seekers, explorers such as Magellan, Columbus, and de Gama and chronicles the competition between European countries, particularly Spain and Portugal. Once a highly desired commodity, the appeal of spices has evolved over time, spices are now a common condiment and afterthought.

Subjects: Exploration, Spices, Trade

Now Try: Other good suggestions for histories about the spices include *The Taste of Conquest: The Rise and Fall of the Three Great Cities of Spice* by Michael Krondl, *Dangerous Tastes: The Story of Spices* by Andrew Dalby, *The Scents of Eden: A History of the Spice Trade* by Charles Corn, and *Nathaniel's Nutmeg: Or the True and Incredible Adventures of the Spice Trader Who Changed the Course of History* by Giles Milton. Readers may also enjoy micro-histories of other foods that changed the world, such as *Seeds of Change: Six Plants That Transformed Mankind* by Henry Hobhouse, Mark Kurlansky's *Salt* or *Cod*, or *Bitter Chocolate* by Carol Off.

Wilson, Bee

Swindled: The Dark History of Food Fraud, From Poisoned Candy to Counterfeit Coffee. Princeton: Princeton University Press, 2008. 384pp. ISBN 9780691138206.

In this entertaining history, Wilson tells of the many foods and drinks that have been cheapened, poisoned, diluted, substituted, mislabeled, and faked since the beginning of the 19th century. In Britain, lead was often used to dye sweets, arsenic was used to dye wine, coffee was frequently adulterated and many grocery staples were padded. Frederick Accum, a German chemist, exposed these adulterations in his treatise on the adulteration of food and culinary poisoning. In America, when society shifted from a predominantly agricultural society to an industrial society, new technologies led to more food tampering. Swill milk led to the deaths of many children in 1850s' New York City and the price fixing of Chicago's meat packing industry led to the Pure Food and Drug Act of 1906. Wilson also explores more current instances of food frauds, such as the frequent substitution of one food for another (basmati rice, saffron, truffles), organic fraud, and baby formula scandal in China.

> **Subjects:** Food Poisoning, Fraud

> **Now Try:** Readers may also want to consider *Death in the Pot: The Impact of Food Poisoning on History* by Morton Satin. The *Billionaire's Vinegar: The Mystery of the World's Most Expensive Bottle of Wine* by Benjamin Wallace recounts the quest to determine the authenticity of the most expensive bottle of wine ever sold. *Extra Virginity: The Sublime and Scandalous World of Olive Oil* by Tom Mueller exposes the common practice of adulterated olive oil. *Newton and the Counterfeiter: The Unknown Detective Career of the World's Greatest Scientist* by Thomas Levenson is an account of Sir Isaac Newton's career as Warden of the Royal Mint and his pursuit of a master counterfeiter.

Zuckerman, Larry

The Potato: How the Humble Spud Rescued the Western World. Boston: Faber & Faber, 1998. 304pp. ISBN 9780571199518.

Zuckerman presents a detailed yet accessible history of the impact of the potato on western civilization. The potato is a hardy, easy-to-grow vegetable that yields a large amount of food on little land and thin soil and has been grown in America as far back as 7,000 years. Spanish conquerors first discovered the potato as a crop of the Incas. However, the Spanish viewed the potato as a food for peasants and did not bring the potato back to Europe for several years. Once introduced in Europe it was widely unpopular for much of the 17th and 18th centuries. The Irish were the first to accept the potato as a field crop and by the 18th century the potato was a staple of the Irish diet. Zuckerman illustrates how the potato saved many populations, not just the Irish, from starvation and improved the daily lives of many people.

> **Subjects:** Potato, World History

> **Now Try:** Readers interested in the history of the Irish Potato Famine may want to consider *The Great Hunger: Ireland: 1845–1849* by Cecil Woodham-Smith or *The Famine*

Ships: The Irish Exodus to America by Edward Laxton. *Crunch: A History of the Great American Potato Chip* by Dirk Burhans is an entertaining history of how the potato became one of America's favorite snack foods. Readers should also consider *Seeds of Change: Six Plants that Transformed Mankind* by Henry Hobhouse. *The Story of Corn* by Betty Fussell is another micro-history of a plant that had an enormous impact on western civilization.

Consider Starting With . . .

These well-known and popular titles are likely to appeal to most readers interested in history.

Kamp, David. *The United States of Arugula: How We Became a Gourmet Nation.*

Kimball, Christopher. *Fannie's Last Supper: Re-Creating One Amazing Meal from Fannie Farmer's 1896 Cookbook.*

Kurlansky, Mark. *The Big Oyster: History on the Half Shell.*

Standage, Tom. *A History of the World in Six Glasses.*

Wallace, Benjamin. The *Billionaire's Vinegar: The Mystery of the World's Most Expensive Bottle of Wine.*

Ziegelman, Jane. *97 Orchard: An Edible History of Five Immigrant Families in One New York Tenement.*

References

Arnold, John H. 2000. *History: A Very Short Introduction.* New York: Oxford University Press.

Cognard-Black, Jennifer, and Goldthwaite, Melissa A. 2008. "Books That Cook: Teaching Food and Food Literature in the English Classroom." *College English* 70 (4): 421.

Cords, Sarah Statz. 2006. *The Real Story: A Guide to Nonfiction Reading Interests.* Westport, CT: Libraries Unlimited.

Gdula, Stephen. 2007. *The Warmest Room in the House: How the Kitchen Became the Heart of the Twentieth-Century American Home.* New York: Bloomsbury.

Kurlansky, Mark. 2002. *Choice Cuts: A Savory Selection of Food Writing From Around the World and Throughout History.* New York: Ballantine Books.

Lepore, Jill. 2002. "Historical Writing and the Revival of Narrative." Nieman Narrative Journalism Conference, Cambridge, Massachusetts, Spring 2001.

Messer, Peter C. 2006. "History and Biography." *Encyclopedia of the New American Nation* 2: 159–61.

Montagne, Renee, and Nancy Pearl. 2005. "Nancy Pearl Discusses Some Examples of Micro-Histories." *NPR Morning Edition*, March 23 (radio broadcast).

Wyatt, Neal. 2007. *The Readers' Advisory Guide to Nonfiction*. Chicago: American Library Association.

Chapter 6

Food Science

Definition of Food Science

In his chapter on popular science readers' advisory, Rick Roche defines science broadly as "knowledge gained through experience" (Roche 2010, 143). The first true scientific writings may be the astronomical reports from the fourth-century BC. Greek philosophers also sought to explain the natural world. Aristotle recorded his observations of the cosmological and natural world in *Physics*, which was considered "natural philosophy" (Cords 2006). Science writing became less philosophical and more focused on observation and experimentation in the 16th century. But it wasn't until the early 19th century that popular science writing came about. McGill University chemistry professor Joe Schwarcz credits Jane Haldimand Marcet as the inventor of popular science writing (Schwarcz 2009). Married to a physician, Marcet took an interest in chemistry lectures she attended with her husband, but often found them to be confusing. Her husband was adept at explaining the concepts to her and she became convinced that this conversational style of education was very effective. Jane created *Conversations on Chemistry* in 1806, which was written as a series of conversations between a teacher and her students. Jane's imaginative way of introducing these concepts was a huge success, making difficult scientific principles accessible to the public, especially women (Schwarz 2009). Today, science writing ranges from more technical descriptions written for scientists, to popular science writing that is easily accessible to general readers.

Although it is not as prolific as some of the other Food Literature genres, Food Science is becoming a popular topic in publishing. Despite its hefty list price of $625, Nathan Myhrvold's five-volume set *Modernist Cuisine*, about food prep and science, has sold over 45,000 copies and generated about $2 million (McLaughlin 2012). The Institute of Food Technologists defines food science as "the discipline in which the engineering, biological, and physical sciences are used to study the nature of foods, the causes of deterioration, the principles underlying food processing, and the improvement of foods for the consuming public" (Heldman 2006, 11). Food Science literature draws from biology, chemistry, physics, molecular gastronomy, engineering, and mathematics.

There are a number of technical Food Science books available, but the titles featured in this chapter fall in the popular science writing category, that make the science of food accessible to the general reader. Food Science books explain the whys and hows of cooking and can help us enjoy the culinary process almost as much as its results.

Food Science explains the whys and hows of cooking. These titles tend to be very detailed and descriptive, but can range in tone from serious and straightforward to informal, fun, and even humorous.

Appeal of Food Science

Science is a part of everyday life. Science is involved in our household products to the cars that we drive, and as *Library Journal* columnist and readers' advisory author Neal Wyatt mentions, when we wonder if half a cup is really the same as four ounces (Wyatt 2007). Food Science writing is appealing because it offers explanations for our everyday world and makes difficult topics easier to understand. The opportunity for learning is another appealing aspect of Food Science writing. Why does bread rise? How does a microwave work? How is chocolate made? People are curious about these things and enjoy titles that can explain difficult scientific concepts in an easy-to-understand, nonthreatening manner. Food Science titles are typically detailed, but they don't necessarily have to be serious (Wyatt 2007). Tone can vary from serious and straightforward to informal, fun, and even humorous.

The titles included in this section have a wide appeal. They are easy to understand and written for the general reader. While they will certainly be of interest to readers who enjoy cooking, they may also be of interest to readers who don't cook but simply enjoy knowledge of food. Readers who enjoy Food Science titles may also enjoy other popular science writing. There are also television series that focus on the science behind cooking, which readers may find enjoyable. Food Science titles are often quick reads, and some incorporate humor and a light, fun tone. These titles may also appeal to young adult readers.

Organization of the Chapter

Because there are fewer Food Science titles in Food Literature, this chapter is not broken down into subsections based on subject. Some of the titles in this chapter are lengthier and incorporate more detailed descriptions, and some are shorter and less formal in tone.

Brown, Alton

I'm Just Here for the Food: Food + Heat = Cooking. New York: Stewart, Tabori & Chang, 2002. 287pp. ISBN 9781584790839.

Alton Brown is the popular star of the Food Network show *Good Eats*. Brown is known for his scientific explanations of cooking methods; he refers to himself as more of a mechanic than a chef. His interest is not in creating new recipes, but understanding how food works and how to control the process of cooking. In this title, he aims to make sense of food and cooking by understanding the science behind it. Chapters are divided by cooking method, such as braising, frying, grilling, and searing, rather than by dish or meal. Brown includes many illustrations and sidebars of information, as well as a thorough index.

Subjects: Brown, Alton, Chemistry, Cooking Methods, Quick Reads, Recipes

Award: James Beard Award

Now Try: Brown's *I'm Just Here for More Food: Food x Mixing + Heat = Baking* addresses the science of baking. Brown also has a series of books based on his television show, *Good Eats* (*The Early Years*, *The Middle Years*, and *The Later Years*). Readers may also enjoy Brown's account of his travels around the country sampling road food, *Feasting on Asphalt*. Robert L. Wolke's *What Einstein Told His Cook* and Jeff Potter's *Cooking for Geeks* are other entertaining yet informative explanations of the science behind cooking. Howard Hillman is another popular food science writer. Try *The New Kitchen Science: A Guide to Know the Hows and Whys for Fun and Success in the Kitchen*. The Food Network series *Food Detectives* may also be appealing.

Corriher, Shirley O.

Cookwise: The Hows and Whys of Successful Cooking. New York: William Morrow, 1997. 524pp. ISBN 9780688102296.

In an easy-to-understand manner, Corriher explains the science of foods, such as the anatomy of an egg, how fruits and vegetables ripen, and the differences between types of flours. She also explains the effects of cooking on foods and the proper methods to insure successful outcomes. To lighten the tone, personal stories of Corriher's own cooking mishaps are also included as examples. Lengthy and detailed explanations will appeal to readers interested in the scientific side of cooking.

Subjects: Cooking Methods, Recipes

Now Try: Corriher's title *Bakewise: The Hows and Whys of Successful Baking* won a James Beard Award. Harold McGee's *On Food and Cooking: The Science and Lore of the Kitchen* is a similar title that explains the science behind cooking techniques. Pam Anderson's *How to Cook Without a Book* teaches readers how foods work together in an effort to help them cook more intuitively rather than relying on a recipe. *Cook's Illustrated* magazine or *The Cook's Illustrated Cookbook* may also be appealing for the rigorous testing and explanations of why some techniques work and others don't.

Hartel, Richard, and Hartel, AnnKate

Food Bites: The Science of the Food We Eat. New York: Copernicus Books, 2008. 190pp. ISBN 9780387758442.

Richard Hartel is a professor of food engineering and has written a column on all things related to food science for a Madison, Wisconsin newspaper. The contents of his column are collected in this short, but fact-filled book. Over the past one hundred years, food preparation has moved away from the home kitchen and into processing plants, and food scientists are responsible for the large-scale production of food. Hartel explains the basics of food science, such as freeze drying, preserving, irradiation, and food safety. He also explores how some of our favorite foods are produced, such as peanut butter, chocolate, orange juice, and my favorite: peeps.

Subjects: Chemistry, Essays, Food Production, Food Safety, Mathematics, Quick Reads

Now Try: Readers may enjoy titles that delve further into the topics Hartel discusses. Steve Ettlinger investigates the production of one of America's most famous snack cakes in *Twinkie, Deconstructed: My Journey to Discover How the Ingredients Found in Processed Foods Are Grown, Mined (Yes, Mined), and Manipulated into What America Eats.* Sue Shephard details the history of food preservation in *Pickled, Potted, and Canned: How the Art and Science of Food Preserving Changed the World.* Marion Nestle examines the food industry and food safety in *Safe Food: The Politics of Food Safety.* Readers may also enjoy the entertaining science writing of Len Fisher, such as *How to Dunk a Doughnut* or *Weighing the Soul.*

McGee, Harold

On Food and Cooking: The Science and Lore of the Kitchen. New York: Scribner, 2004. 884pp. ISBN 9780684800011.

Originally published in 1984, this classic tome has been revised and updated. Extensively detailed, yet written in a conversational style, McGee explains the scientific nature of foods: the chemical makeup and how cooking transforms a particular food. The physical nature of digestion and how foods interact with the body are also covered. He also explores where foods came from, when and why particular cooking habits took hold, and the diverse methods of preparation. Although it can be read from cover to cover, readers can also read the book in sections, focusing on a particular food.

Subject: Chemistry, History, Recipes

Awards: IACP Award

Now Try: McGee continues his exploration of food science in *The Curious Cook: More Kitchen Science and Lore* and *Keys to Good Cooking.* McGee draws on neuroscience and chemistry to discuss flavor. Readers interested in this concept may want to check out

Neurogastronomy: How the Brain Creates Flavor and Why It Matters by Gordon M. Shepherd. Although not as comprehensive, readers may enjoy Simon Quellen Field's *Culinary Reactions: The Everyday Chemistry of Cooking*. Field also investigates the science behind common household items in *Why There's Antifreeze in Your Toothpaste*. Readers may want to check out the French Culinary Institute's Tech 'N Stuff blog at www.cookingissues.com, with covers all the technical aspects of cooking.

Myhrvold, Nathan, Young, Chris, and Bilet, Maxime

Modernist Cuisine: The Art and Science of Cooking. Bellevue, WA: Cooking Lab, 2011. 2438pp. ISBN 9780982761007.

Myhrvold is a scientist and former Chief Technology Officer of Microsoft. Having also attended cooking school and worked in a restaurant, Myhrvold began experimenting with *sous vide* cooking, which led him to create a cooking lab. He and his team of chefs and scientists conducted scientific experiments to gain a better understanding of cooking. Their experiments resulted in this comprehensive 2,400-page, six-volume collection that covers the history and fundamentals of cooking, techniques and equipment, meat and vegetables, ingredients and preparations, as well as recipes. The set covers the science behind traditional food preparation techniques as well as molecular gastronomy and other new techniques, such as *sous vide* cooking. Vividly illustrated, cross-sectional photographs make this a visually appealing read.

> **Subjects:** Chemistry, Cooking Methods, Molecular Gastronomy, Recipes, *Sous Vide*

> **Now Try:** *The Kitchen as Laboratory* edited by Cesar Vega, Job Ubbink, and Erik van der Linden is a fascinating collection of essays by chefs and scientists exploring the science of food. Readers who are interested in some of the concepts featured here may want to consider Hervé This's *Molecular Gastronomy: Exploring the Science of Flavor* or Thomas Keller's *Under Pressure: Cooking Sous Vide*. Books by some of the masters of molecular gastronomy may also be appealing. Try *Modern Gastronomy: A to Z* by Ferran Adrià, *Alinea* by Grant Achatz, and *Noma: Time and Place in Nordic Cuisine* by René Redzepi.

Parsons, Russ

How to Read a French Fry: And Other Stories of Intriguing Kitchen Science. Boston: Houghton Mifflin, 2001. 334pp. ISBN 9780395967836.

In the early 1900s, it was common for a recipe to include the phrase "prepare in the usual manner." But over the past few generations, recipes have been including more and more instructions. Why? Because as people are cooking less, they are less familiar with why foods are prepared the way they are. Parsons attempts to explain the science behind important cooking techniques in order to give cooks a better understanding of cooking and more confidence in the kitchen. In easy-to-understand language and a conversational tone, the author explains why chopping an onion makes us cry, why different types and cuts of meat are cooked differently, and of course, how to read a French fry.

Subjects: Cooking Methods, Recipes

Now Try: Parson's title is a nonthreatening introduction into food science. Readers who want to delve deeper may want to consider Harold McGee's tome *On Food and Cooking* or Shirley O. Corriher's *Cookwise*. Other entertaining titles about food trivia and science are *Lobsters Scream When You Boil Them* by Bruce Weinstein and Marc Scarbrough, *What Einstein Told His Cook* by Robert L. Wolke, and *Froth: The Science of Beer* by Mark Denny. Other accessible explanations of science may also be appealing, such as *Why Things Break* by Mark Eberhart or *What Makes Flamingos Pink* by Bill McLain.

Potter, Jeff

Cooking for Geeks: Real Science, Great Hacks, and Good Food. Sebastopol, CA: O'Reilly, 2010. 412pp. ISBN 9780596805883.

The science of the kitchen is explored in this entertaining and accessible book. Potter explains what happens to food when it cooks, how recipes work, and encourages readers to experiment with cooking. The first section starts with the basics of the kitchen: utensils, ingredients, and the aspects of taste and flavor. The second section explores the important reactions in cooking and variables such as time, temperature, and air. The final section addresses the creative aspects of cooking: how leaveners and chemicals can be used to alter food, and explains some of the creative techniques being used by chefs, such as *sous vide* cooking and liquid nitrogen. Potter also includes interviews with well-known researchers, scientists, chefs, and food writers. The informal style and humor will appeal to those who are intimidated by the science.

Subjects: Chefs, Chemistry, Cooking Methods, Food Writers, *Sous Vide*, Scientists

Now Try: Readers who enjoy the informal and humorous tone may also enjoy Alton Brown's books, such as *I'm Just Here for the Food*. Hervé This illuminates the fundamentals of cooking in *Kitchen Mysteries: Revealing the Science of Cooking*. Howard Hillman's *The New Kitchen Science: A Guide to Know the Hows and Whys for Fun and Success in the Kitchen* may also be of interest. Ed Sobey explains the science behind the appliances in the kitchens in *The Way Kitchens Work*. Sobey's *The Way Toys Work: The Science Behind the Magic 8 Ball, Etch-a-Sketch, Boomerang and More* may also be of interest to readers who enjoy explanations of everyday items. Chad Orzel's *How to Teach Physics to Your Dog* approaches physics with similar humor and a light tone.

Ruhlman, Michael

Ratio: The Simple Codes behind the Craft of Everyday Cooking. New York: Scribner, 2009. 224pp. ISBN 9781416566113.

Ruhlman proposes that understanding proper ratios in cooking will allow you to cook without consulting a recipe. Fundamental ingredients such as butter, milk, eggs, and flour are described, and how they interact with each other. Understanding these relationships is the key to proper cooking technique. The book is divided into sections for dough, stocks, sausages, sauces, and custards, and identifies 33 ratios. Rulhman explains the properties of each ratio and the result of variations on those ratios.

Subjects: Cooking Methods, Recipes

Now Try: Readers may want to consider one of Ruhlman's other cookbooks, such as *The Elements of Cooking* or his memoirs, such as *The Making of a Chef*. Pam Anderson's *How to Cook Without a Book* also focuses on teaching cooks how to break away from recipes. Readers may also enjoy the blog Ideas in Food (www.ideasinfood.com). Written by Aki Kamozawa and H. Alexander Talbot, they share their ideas and experiments on using creativity in cooking. America's Test Kitchen takes the science of baking very seriously, rigorously testing different variations on recipes. Try *The Complete America's Test Kitchen TV Show Cookbook 2001–2012*.

Taber, George

To Cork or Not to Cork: Tradition, Romance, Science, and the Battle for the Wine Bottle. New York: Scribner, 2007. 278pp. ISBN 9780743299343.

How many times have you pulled a cork from a bottle of wine? How many times have you given any consideration to that cork? For some, the cork is the center of a passionate debate. But you don't have to be a wine lover to appreciate Taber's fascinating account of this topic. Taber traces the discovery of cork back to Roman times, and explains where it comes from, its chemistry, how it is harvested and manufactured. Although cork has been used for centuries, a chemical compound found in cork can sometimes cause cork taint which can ruin a bottle of wine. This has sparked a heated discussion of whether cork is the best material for sealing wine.

Subjects: Chemistry, Cork, History, Micro-Science, Wine

Awards: IACP Award

Now Try: Taber also wrote an account of an historic wine tasting in *Judgment of Paris: California vs. France and the Historic 1976 Paris Tasting That Revolutionized Wine*. Benjamin Wallace's *The Billionaire's Vinegar* is a fascinating account of a wine hoax. Tyler Colman explores the politics of wine in *Wine Politics: How Governments, Environmentalists, Mobsters and Critics Influence the Wines We Drink*. *The Botanist and the Vintner: How Wine Was Saved for the World* by Christopher Campbell explains the history and science of the phylloxera infestation that almost destroyed all of France's grapevines.

This, Hervé

Molecular Gastronomy: Exploring the Science of Flavor. New York: Columbia University Press, 2006. 377pp. ISBN 9780231133128.

Molecular gastronomy studies the physical and chemical processes that occur while cooking. This is a chemist and the creator of the first lab devoted to molecular gastronomy. This's short but fascinating book begins with secrets of the kitchen, explaining the chemical effects of cooking on foods. Why do soufflés rise? Why should you use a copper pan when making preserves? This moves on to discuss the physiology of flavor and the brain's perception of tastes. How does salt affect taste? How does chewing affect food? Although highly scientific, This's easy-to-understand style make this an accessible read for anyone interested in the science of food.

Subjects: Chemistry, Cooking Methods, Molecular Gastronomy

Now Try: This again turns to chemistry to understand the properties of foods and the transformations they are capable of undergoing in *Building a Meal*. Nathan Myhrvold shares the discoveries made in his molecular gastronomy lab in *Modernist Cuisine: The Art and Science of Cooking*. Ferran Adrià illustrates the use of molecular gastronomy in his restaurant in *A Day at El Bulli*. *The Fat Duck Cookbook* is written by Heston Blumenthal, another chef who incorporates molecular gastronomy in his cooking. Readers who enjoy blogs may want to check out Linda Miller Nicholson's blog Salty Seattle (www.saltyseattle.com), which features avant-garde food and molecular gastronomy. Want to try molecular gastronomy at home? Try *Molecular Cuisine: Twenty Techniques, Forty Recipes* by Anne Cazor, Christine Lienard, and Gui Alinat.

Wolke, Robert L.

What Einstein Told His Cook: Kitchen Science Explained. New York: W. W. Norton & Co., 2002. 350pp. ISBN 9780393011838.

With this enlightening yet entertaining book, Wolke helps readers understand the chemical and physical principles that explain the behaviors of our foods with clear, easy-to-understand explanations. He answers everyday questions that come up when cooking, debunks misconceptions, explains food labeling, and offers technical illustrations and tips. The humorous and conversational tone proves that the science of cooking can be fun.

Subjects: Chemistry, Cooking Methods, Food Labels, Humor

Now Try: Readers may also enjoy some of Wolke's other titles, such as *What Einstein Told His Cook 2*. Wolke has also written *What Einstein Didn't Know: Scientific Answers to Everyday Questions* and *What Einstein Told His Barber*. Other science titles that make science more accessible may also be appealing. Len Fisher introduces the basic principles of science using objects of everyday life in *How to Dunk a Doughnut: The Science of Everyday Life*. Mark Eberhart explains the basic principles of chemistry in *Why Things Break: Understanding the World by the Way It Comes Apart*. Alex Boese shares amusing scientific experiments in *Elephants on Acid: And Other Bizarre Experiments*.

Wrangham, Richard

Catching Fire: How Cooking Made Us Human. New York: Basic Books, 2009. 309pp. ISBN 9780465013623.

Wrangham asserts that the evolutionary success of humans is due to the discovery of fire and cooking. When humans learned to control fire, this led to the advent of cooked foods. The shift from raw to cooked food caused the digestive track to shrink, the brain grew, and eventually led to the creation of households, communities, and the sexual division of labor. Wrangham's provocative theory and fascinating evidence will appeal to fans of food science as well as history.

Subjects: Fire, History, Human Evolution, Micro-Science, Prehistoric Peoples

Now Try: Readers may want to consider *Near a Thousand Tables* by Felipe Fernandez-Armesto, who contends that the evolution of human culture resulted from advances in food. John S. Allen examines the relationship between eating and evolution in *The Omnivorous Mind: Our Evolving Relationship with Food*. Michael Cook's *A Brief History of the Human Race* and Nick Lane's *Life Ascending: The Ten Great Inventions of Evolution* may be of interest to readers who are interested in evolution. Jared Diamond's *Guns, Germs, and Steel* considers how the development of technologies and immunities in Western civilizations allowed them to succeed.

Consider Starting With . . .

Readers who are new to Food Science may want to consider starting with the following titles.

McGee, Harold. *On Food and Cooking: The Science and Lore of the Kitchen.*

This, Hervé. *Molecular Gastronomy: Exploring the Science of Flavor.*

Wolke, Robert L. *What Einstein Told His Cook: Kitchen Science Explained.*

References

Cords, Sarah Statz. 2006. *The Real Story: A Guide to Nonfiction Reading Interests.* Westport, CT: Libraries Unlimited.

Heldman, Dennis R. 2006. "IFT and the Food Science Profession." *Food Technology* (October): 11.

McLaughlin, Katy. 2012. "The $450 Cookbook is Going Strong." *Speakeasy* (blog). May 1. http://blogs.wsj.com/speakeasy/2012/05/01/the-450-cookbook-is-going-strong/

Schwarcz, Joe. 2009. "Jane Haldimand Marcet a popular science writer." *Canadian Chemical News* (July–August): 14.

Roche, Rick. 2010. "Everything Popular Science." In *Integrated Advisory Service: Breaking Through the Book Boundary to Better Serve Library Users,* ed. Jessica E. Moyer. Santa Barbara, CA: Libraries Unlimited, 143–181.

Part IV

Stylistic Genres

Chapter 7

Investigative Food Writing

Definition of Investigative Food Writing

In *The Inside Scoop: A Guide to Nonfiction Investigative Writing and Exposés*, Sarah Statz Cords explains investigative writing in simple terms: research was done and someone was talked to (Cords 2009). Investigative writing involves extensive research and often includes interviews or firsthand experience by the author. Stories are often dramatic and typically address a topic of public interest, such as crime, political corruption, or corporate wrongdoing.

Cords traces the beginnings of investigative writing to the early days of American journalism from the frontline reports of the Civil War battlefields. The first book of investigative writing was Ida Tarbell's *The History of the Standard Oil Company*, which was published in 1904 and exposed the operating procedures and methods of its chairman, John D. Rockefeller. Since then, several works of investigative writing have become classics, including Nellie Bly's *Ten Days in a Mad-House*, Studs Terkel's *Working*, Bob Woodward's *All the President's Men*, and Barbara Ehrenreich's *Nickel and Dimed: On (Not) Getting By in America* (Cords 2006).

Currently, one popular topic of investigative writing is the food industry. Many investigative works have examined the social and environmental impacts of the food industry, explained health issues caused by foods, and exposed animal welfare issues. The number of these publications continues to grow, but there have been a few notable classics over the past century.

Although a fictional account of the meat packing business, Upton Sinclair's 1906 novel *The Jungle*, was the first investigative work to shed light on the issues of the industrial food industry. Inspired by Chicago's stockyards, Sinclair spent seven weeks working incognito in the stockyards. He vividly describes the filth, disease, dangerous and inhumane conditions, and the daily grind in slaughterhouses. Although his original intent was to expose the exploitation of the American factory worker, the public focused on the food safety issues. This led to the passage of the Meat Inspection Act and the Pure Food and Drug Act of 1906, which later led to the establishment of the Food and Drug Administration (Bachelder 2006).

In 1962, Rachel Carson's book *Silent Spring* documented the detrimental effects of pesticides on the environment, which led to the ban of the pesticide DDT in 1972. Carson's landmark work is included in Modern Library's Best 20th Century Nonfiction. In 1964 Ruth Harrison shocked the world with her account of factory farming in her influential book *Animal Machines*. Factory farm conditions were not widely known at this time. In 1971, Frances Moore Lappé published *Diet for a Small Planet*, which was the first book to expose the enormous waste caused by the U.S. grain-fed meat industry. She argued that the current global food system is responsible for world hunger and advocated a vegetarian diet. Jim Mason's and Peter Singer's 1980 publication, *Animal Factories*, is another noteworthy investigation that lifted the veil on the exploitation of factory farmed animals.

More recently, several investigative writings and documentaries of current food issues have garnered much attention. Eric Schlosser's *Fast Food Nation*, published in 2001, exposed issues of obesity, fast-food chains, and the meat packing industry. Morgan Spurlock's documentary film *Super Size Me*, in which he consumed McDonald's food three times per day for a month, was nominated for Best Documentary at the 2004 Academy Awards. *Food, Inc.*, which first appeared as a documentary film and was later published in print form, addresses several of the issues of the food industry, was also nominated for Best Documentary at the 2010 Academy Awards. Michael Pollan's seminal 2006 publication *The Omnivore's Dilemma* spent over 100 weeks on the *New York Times* best-seller list and was named among the 10 best books of 2006 by the *New York Times*.

Appeal of Investigative Food Writing

Investigative Writing is popular because it presents compelling, dramatic stories that address topics of public interest. Often these are stories of crime, political corruption, or corporate wrongdoing. In the case of Investigative Food Writing, these stories are often about health issues, food safety, animal welfare, or environmental issues. Investigative Food Writing often exposes new information about a little-known subject. Readers discover surprising, often shocking information about food or the food industry. Investigative Food Writing also presents inside information on a subject. Authors conduct in-depth research and interviews in order to present detailed facts and evidence; and they frequently incorporate a dramatic writing style with a sensational tone to create captivating, engaging stories.

Readers who enjoy Investigative Food Writing may also enjoy other general Investigative Writing titles that present compelling stories. There are also a number of compelling, dramatic food documentaries that may also be appealing. Environmental writing, such as titles like Rachel Carson's *Silent Spring* and Jane Goodall's *In the Shadow of Man* may be of interest to readers who enjoy the environmental issues that are raised in many of the Investigative Food titles.

Organization of the Chapter

Investigative Food Writing is broken down into three subgenres. Titles considered **In-Depth Reporting** tend to be more detailed with less visible participation from the author. With **Immersion Journalism**, the author typically becomes personally involved in the investigation. **Food Exposés** tend to be more shocking; bringing an unknown subject to light.

In-Depth Reporting

In-Depth Reporting titles exhibit more detail with less visible participation from the author. The author takes as unbiased an approach as possible, and does not insert himself or herself into the story. These titles tend to be well researched. Authors often conduct multiple interviews and include factual data and extensive details.

> In-Depth Reporting are compelling stories about food issues. The author takes as unbiased an approach as possible, and does not insert himself or herself into the story. These titles tend to be well researched and include extensive details and data.

Abend, Lisa

The Sorcerer's Apprentices: A Season in the Kitchen at Ferran Adrià's El Bulli. New York: Free Press, 2011. 295pp. ISBN 9781439175552.

El Bulli was one of the most famous restaurants in the world. A five-time winner of Best Restaurant in the World and three Michelin stars, it was owned by Ferran Adrià. When Abend's friend referred to El Bulli as "just food," she decided to prove this wasn't the case. Adrià is the leader in molecular gastronomy and one of the most important chefs of our time, using ingredients and techniques in his restaurant never used before to create works of art. Each year, Adrià's kitchen created a new menu, incorporating new ingredients and new techniques. Few people realize that Adrià had up to 45 other chefs working with him in his kitchen. These stagiaires were experienced chefs who came to apprentice for Adrià, working long hours for no pay, just to have the experience of working with this famous chef. Abend spends a season observing Adrià's kitchen, providing readers a glimpse into this famous restaurant, the demanding pace, grueling hours, and the drive to succeed.

Subjects: Adrià, Ferran, Chefs, El Bulli, Molecular Gastronomy, Restaurants

Now Try: Colman Andrews's biography of the famous chef, *Ferran*, may be suggested. Adrià presents a look inside his restaurant in *A Day at El Bulli*. *The Family Meal* is Adrià's first cookbook for the home cook. William Echikson's *Burgundy Stars: A Year in the Life of a Great French Restaurant* and Leslie Brenner's *The Fourth Star: Dispatches from Inside Daniel Boulud's Celebrated New York Restaurant* are other inside accounts of starred restaurants. Readers interested in more details about molecular gastronomy should try Hervé This's *Molecular Gastronomy*.

Abramsky, Sasha

Breadline USA: The Hidden Scandal of American Hunger and How to Fix It. Sausalito, CA: PoliPoint Press, 2009. 209pp. ISBN 9780981709116.

One way of determining the success of a society is how well it can feed its people; and America has always been known for its abundance of food. In addition to an excess of food, America is also known for having a problem with obesity and weight-related health issues. Despite the abundance of food and rising instances of obesity, America has a hunger problem. Millions of Americans are food insecure. Abramsky looks at the global economic conditions and domestic policies that have led to this problem. Increased prices of natural resources, an outdated poverty threshold, welfare reforms, and the recent financial crisis have all contributed. The author interviews numerous people around the country who deal with hunger on a daily basis and visits food pantries. He also attempts to live under the same economic situations as hungry Americans, which provides an eye-opening perspective of what it's like to worry about food.

Subjects: Health Issues, Hunger, Poverty

Now Try: In *Stuffed and Starved: The Hidden Battle for the World Food System*, Raj Patel examines the global imbalance of food resources and worldwide hunger. Mark Winne also examines food insecurity and the ever-increasing food gap in *Closing the Food Gap: Resetting the Table in the Land of Plenty*. Tracie McMillan works undercover in the various jobs in the food industry to learn about American's eating habits in *The American Way of Eating: Undercover at Walmart, Applebee's, Farm Fields and the Dinner Table*.

Behr, Edward

The Artful Eater: A Gourmet Investigates the Ingredients of Great Food. Peacham, VT: Art of Eating, 2004. 293pp. ISBN 9780974784106.

A food writer and the publisher of the quarterly food magazine *The Art of Eating*, Behr compiles columns from his newsletter that focus on the quest for finding good food. Behr illustrates how basic ingredients can differ greatly and contribute to the taste; and explores such questions as, What makes food good? Examining individual ingredients such as eggs, vanilla, apples, coffee, and ham; he traces the origins and history of various ingredients and explores their differences. What is the difference between farmed and wild mussels? Can ham stand up to Italian prosciutto? Is there a difference between Mexican and Tahitian vanilla? Behr also laments how some foods have vanished or how some foods, such as salt, have faced scrutiny. His investigations are infused with artful descriptions of flavors.

Subjects: Essays, Gastronomy

Now Try: Readers who are intrigued by Behr's investigation may want to consider titles that explore terroir, or taste of place, such as *American Terroir* by Rowan Jacobsen, *Taste of Place* by Amy Trubek, or *Desert Terroir* by Gary Paul Nabhan. Readers may also want to consider Michael Ruhlman's *Ratio*, in which he explains how proper ratios between fundamental ingredients are the key to successful cooking. Other compilations of essays may also be of interest, such as Jeffrey Steingarten's *The Man Who Ate Everything* or Alan Richman's *Fork it Over*.

Bourette, Susan

Meat: A Love Story: Pasture to Plate, the Search for the Perfect Meal. New York: G. P. Putnam and Sons, 2008. 274pp. ISBN 9780399154867.

Meat is the new black. In Toronto, once chic vegetarian cafes are now being displaced by carnivore chic butchers and delis. Butchers used to be a blue-collar job; now yuppies are signing up for introductory courses in butchery. When Bourette went undercover in a meat processing plant for a journal article, her experience put her off meat. But her stints as a vegetarian have been short-lived. She likes eating meat and wonders if there isn't a better way to get meat than from the horrible processing plants like the one in which she worked. Bourette seeks out people who hunt, or raise and butcher animals; visiting cattle ranchers in Texas, moose hunters in Canada, whale hunters in northern Alaska, and a humane, sustainable farm in upstate New York.

Subjects: Butchery, Meat, Travel

Now Try: There are a number of titles that explore the idea of a more ethical way of eating meat, such as *The Butcher and the Vegetarian* by Tara Austen Weaver, *The Mindful Carnivore* by Tovar Cerulli, *Girl Hunter: Revolutionizing the Way We Eat One Hunt at a Time* by Georgia Pellegrini, *Righteous Porkchop: Finding a Life and Good Food Beyond Factory Farms* by Nicolette Hahn Niman, or Catherine Friend's *The Compassionate Carnivore: Or, How to Keep Animals Happy, Save Old MacDonald's Farm, Reduce Your Hoofprint, and Still Eat Meat*. Steve Rinella takes a respectful attitude towards the animals he hunts in *The Scavenger's Guide to Haute Cuisine*. Readers who are interested in the butchery aspect of Bourette's story may want to consider Julie Powell's *Cleaving*.

Brenner, Leslie

The Fourth Star: Dispatches from Inside Daniel Boulud's Celebrated New York Restaurant. New York: Clarkson Potter, 2002. 314pp. ISBN 9780609608081.

When a *New York Times* reviewer demoted Daniel Boulud's celebrated restaurant Daniel from four stars to three in 1999, Boulud was determined to regain the fourth star. This author spent a year behind the scenes at Daniel as its staff labored tirelessly to regain its star. Brenner illustrates not only the jobs of the chef and cooks, but also those in the front of the house, such as the reservationist and hostess. Stories of the hectic pace of the kitchen, the difficulties of accommodating demanding patrons, and the heightened tensions that come from having so much at stake come alive in this engaging account.

Subjects: Boulud, Daniel, Chefs, New York City, Restaurants, Work Relationships

Now Try: *Burgundy Stars: A Year in the Life of a Great French Restaurant* by William Echikson recounts Chef Bernard Loiseau's campaign to earn three Michelin stars for his French restaurant La Côte d'Or. Lisa Abend profiles the army of chefs at one of the most famous restaurants in *The Sorcerer's Apprentices: A Season in the Kitchen at Ferran Adrià's El Bulli.* Steven Shaw's *Turning the Table: Restaurants From the Inside Out* is an entertaining and quick read for those interested in an overview of the workings of an upscale restaurant, including front of the house management, the demands of the kitchen, issues with food sources, history of ratings, and the stress of opening a restaurant. *Service Included: Four Star Secrets of an Eavesdropping Waiter* by Phoebe Damrosch is an entertaining account of the demands of working in a four-star restaurant.

Caro, Mark

The Foie Gras Wars: How a 5,000-Year-Old Delicacy Inspired the World's Fiercest Food Fight. New York: Simon & Schuster, 2009. 357pp. ISBN 9781416556688.

When the famous Chicago chef Charlie Trotter announced that he was removing foie gras from his menu, the long-heated debate over this delicacy erupted. In this in-depth account, Caro documents both sides of the debate. Caro traces the history of foie gras back to the ancient Greeks and Egyptians and explains the process for making foie gras. Outlining the ethical and animal welfare issues, he examines the current treatment of animals in both France and America and visits farms and speaks with farmers who raise animals on both large and small scales. This unbiased investigation presents the views of chefs, politicians, and animal activists on both sides of the argument.

Subjects: Animal Welfare, Chefs, Ethics, Foie Gras, Trotter, Charlie

Now Try: Michael Ginor's *Foie Gras: A Passion* provides a thorough exploration of foie gras, including pictures and recipes. David Kamp's *The United States of Arugula* explores how we became a nation interested in gourmet foods like foie gras. Jonathan Safran Foer's *Eating Animals* exposes the cruelty involved in raising animals for meat. Eric Schlosser's *Fast Food Nation* exposes the ethical issues of eating fast-food. Catherine Friend's *The Compassionate Carnivore* provides the side of the debate for eating ethically raised animals. Readers may also be interested in a history of French cuisine, which is known for its foie gras. Try Susan Pinkard's *A Revolution in Taste: The Rise in French Cuisine.*

Costa, Temra

Farmer Jane: Women Changing the Way We Eat. Layton, Utah: Gibbs Smith, 2010. 224pp. ISBN 9781423605621.

> A revolution is taking place in this country that is changing how we eat and farm. People are starting to question where their food comes from, farmers' markets and community supported agriculture programs are gaining popularity, and there has been an increase in small farms. Costa argues that women are big players in this revolution but have been underrepresented in the public sphere. Seeking to rectify this, Costa profiles 26 women who have played major roles in the movement towards sustainable food and farming, from advocating social change to promoting local and seasonal foods to creating community gardens.

> **Subjects:** Agriculture, Food Movements, Local Foods, Quick Reads, Women's Nonfiction

> **Now Try:** Readers may be interested in the works of some of the women featured in this book such as *Farm City* by Novella Carpenter and *Diet for a Hot Planet* by Anna Lappé. Lisa Hamilton's *Deeply Rooted* profiles a number of unconventional farmers focused on sustainable farming. Katherine Gustafson's *Change Comes to Dinner: How Vertical Farmers, Urban Growers, and Other Innovators Are Revolutionizing How America Eats* also profiles people who are making changes in the way we eat. Ben Hewitt explores a small town that created its own sustainable local food system in *The Town That Food Saved*. Mark Winne's *Food Rebels, Guerilla Gardeners, and Smart-Cooking' Mamas: Fighting Back in an Age of Industrial Agriculture* is another investigative title that may appeal to these readers.

Critser, Greg

Fat Land: How Americans Became the Fattest People in the World. Boston: Houghton Mifflin Co., 2003. 232pp. ISBN 9780618164721.

> Although obesity rates are rising worldwide, the United States was one of the first countries to be recognized for obesity and it still ranks amongst the top countries for obesity. Critser examines the factors that evolved to produce this problem. He traces the rise of cheap food from the 1970s, when soaring food costs led to consumer demand for cheaper foods. This led to the development of high fructose corn syrup (HFCS), which has been blamed for obesity. The restaurants that encouraged people to eat more, which led to value meals and bigger serving sizes have also been blamed for obesity. The changes that occurred during the late 20th century in family, school, culture, and religion led to convenience foods, more eating out, acceptance of gluttony, and less physical activity, which have all played a role in the obesity crisis.

> **Subjects:** Food Industry, Health Issues, Obesity, Society

Now Try: Barry Popkin's *The World is Fat* is another fascinating investigation of the obesity crisis. David Kessler's *The End of Overeating: Taking Control of the Insatiable American Appetite explains* how the food industry uses the right combination of sugar, fat and salt to create food with hyperpalatability. Jeff O'Connell's *Sugar Nation* looks at America's deadly addiction to sugar. Hank Cardello's *Stuffed: An Insider's Look at Who's (Really) Making America Fat and How the Food Industry Can Fix It* also explores the obesity crisis in America. Critser presents another shocking investigation of the pharmaceutical industry in *Generation Rx: How Prescription Drugs Are Altering American Lives, Minds, and Bodies*. Morgan Spurlock's book, *Don't Eat This Book* and documentary, *Super Size Me*, investigates how the fast-food industry contributes to obesity in America.

Dornenburg, Andrew, and Page, Karen

Dining Out: Secrets from America's Leading Critics, Chefs, and Restaurateurs. New York: Wiley, 1998. 343pp. ISBN 9780471292777.

The authors provide an overview of restaurant history and the beginnings of restaurant reviews in America. A number of professionals are interviewed for a behind-the-scenes look at the restaurant business. Readers will find out what it takes to create a great dining experience, what it's like to be a restaurant critic, how critics get into the field, how reviews are written, and how critics remain anonymous. Famous critics such as Ruth Reichl and Gael Greene provide tips for diners on getting a good dining experience and talk about their favorite restaurants.

Subjects: American History, Dining, Restaurant Critics, Restaurants

Now Try: Readers who enjoy the inside scoop on restaurant critics may want to try the memoirs of food critics such as *Garlic and Sapphires: The Secret Life of a Critic in Disguise* by Ruth Reichl and *Eating My Words: An Appetite for Life* by Mimi Sheraton. *The Sorcerer's Apprentices: A Season in the Kitchen at Ferran Adrià's El Bulli* by Lisa Abend and *The Fourth Star: Dispatches from Inside Daniel Boulud's Celebrated New York Restaurant* by Leslie Brenner both provide a behind-the-scenes look at how two of the world's best restaurants are run. Titles from successful restaurant owners may also be appealing, such as *Lessons in Excellence* from Charlie Trotter by Paul Clarke and *Setting the Table: The Transforming Power of Hospitality in Business* by Danny Meyer. Page and Dornenberg also won a James Beard Award for their title *The Flavor Bible: The Essential Guide to Culinary Creativity, Based on the Wisdom of America's Most Imaginative Chefs*.

Echikson, William

Noble Rot: A Bordeaux Wine Revolution. New York: W. W. Norton & Company, 2004. 302pp. ISBN 9780393051629.

Bordeaux has always been synonymous with fine wine. However, in the past few decades, as Australia and California entered the wine-making business, and revolutionary garage wine makers began appearing, Bordeaux's supremacy has been challenged. Many family-run French vineyards, unable to compete with modern production and marketing methods, have begun to fail. Echikson investigates the new production techniques and the innovative winemakers who are challenging Bordeaux's wines. He also profiles the French winemakers who began fighting back against encroaching foreign corporations; and discusses the improvements that must be made in order to remain contenders.

Subjects: France, Wine, Wine Industry

Now Try: Benjamin Lewin also examines the revolution occurring in Bordeaux in *What Price Bordeaux?* Readers may also enjoy George Taber's *Judgment of Paris: California vs. France and the Historic 1976 Paris Tasting That Revolutionized Wine*, which describes the 1976 wine tasting that declared a California wine superior to a French wine and launched the California wine industry. Mike examines the current state of the wine industry and its future in *Wine Wars: The Curse of the Blue Nun, the Miracle of Two Buck Chuck, and the Revenge of the Terroirists*. Lawrence Osbourne details the steps of wine production from the vineyards to winemaking to marketing in *The Accidental Connoisseur: An Irreverent Journey Through the Wine World*. Mike Weiss chronicles a successful Sonoma winery in *A Very Good Year: The Journey of a California Wine from Vine to Table*. Christopher Campbell's historical account of the phylloxera infestation that almost destroyed French vineyards may also be appealing: *The Botanist and the Vintner: How Wine Was Saved for the World*.

Fishkoff, Sue

Kosher Nation: Why More and More of America's Food Answers to a Higher Authority. New York: Schocken Books, 2010. 364pp. ISBN 97808052 42652.

The kosher industry in the United States is growing, despite the small number of observant Jews. Eighty-five percent of kosher consumers are not Jewish. Fishkoff provides a fascinating look at the kosher industry and its history. She explains kashrut, the Jewish dietary laws and how kosher food is produced. The reader is introduced to rabbis who oversee kosher food production, restaurants, and catering services, as well as rabbis who assist families in koshering their kitchens. Fishkoff also examines why so many people besides observant Jews choose kosher products. Readers unfamiliar with kashrut laws and kosher rules will find a thorough investigation and compelling presentation of a complex topic.

Subjects: Dietary Laws, Kosher, Kosher Food Industry, Judaism, Religion

Now Try: Jonathan Safran Foer's documentary *If This is Kosher . . .* exposes the animal abuse at the world's largest kosher slaughterhouse. *Brave New Judaism: When Science and Scripture Collide* by Miryam Wahrman considers contemporary ethical issues and Jewish law, asking whether GMOs can be kosher. *97 Orchard: An Edible History of Five Immigrant Families in One New York Tenement* by Jane Ziegelman traces the impact of immigrant food habits on American cuisine, particularly Jewish foods. Laura Alpern details the history of the biggest producer of Matzo in *Manischewitz: The Matzo Family, The Making of an American Icon*. Fishkoff investigates Lubavitcher Judaism, a sect of Orthodox Jewry most people are unaware of, and the goal of its outreach program to make all Jews more observant in *The Rebbe's Army: Inside the World of Chabad-Lubavitch*. Judith Shulevitz explores the history of the Sabbath in *The Sabbath World: Glimpses of a Different Order of Time*.

Friedman, Andrew

Knives At Dawn: America's Quest for Culinary Glory at the Legendary Bocuse d'Or Competition. New York: Free Press, 2009. 304pp. ISBN 9781439153079.

The Bocuse d'Or is the most prestigious cooking competition in the world. Twenty-four countries compete for gold, silver, and bronze medals, with each country represented by a team of two: a chef and an assistant and five hours to produce a meat platter and a fish platter. Elaborate, intricate details, precision, and timing are essential. Friedman follows Chef Timothy Hollingsworth of the French Laundry, and his assistant, Adina Guest, as they spend three months in intensive training preparing for this legendary competition. This is a pulse-pounding account of the U.S. team's preparation for, and participation in, this competition.

> **Subjects**: Bocuse d'Or, Chefs, Cooking Competitions, Florida, France

> **Now Try**: Readers may enjoy the essay collection edited by Friedman, *Don't Try This At Home: Culinary Catastrophes From the World's Greatest Chefs*. In *The Soul of a Chef*, Michael Ruhlman describes the rigorous cooking that is required to pass the Certified Master Chef exam, and also details the career of Chef Thomas Keller, Hollingsworth's mentor. The documentary, *The Kings of Pastry*, follows the competition for the Meilleurs Ouvriers de France, the ultimate pastry competition. One could argue that cooking at this level is just as rigorous as an athletic competition, so this book would be a good read not only for those interested in food, but also those that are interested in sports competitions. David Halberstam's *The Amateurs* also chronicles the preparation, practices, and training to prepare for competition, the stories of the competitors, and the account of the actual competition.

Fromartz, Samuel

Organic, Inc.: Natural Foods and How They Grew. Orlando: Harcourt, 2006. ISBN 9780151011308. 294pp.

Organic foods have an image of being pure, wholesome, natural, healthy, environmentally friendly foods that have been produced by small, local farmers. But are they? The organic food industry has become a multibillion dollar industry and the biggest organic producers are owned by major food corporations. Fromartz traces the evolution of the organic food movement from the pioneers in the early 20th century to the industrialized, commercialized business that it is today. Organic food came about in the early 20th century as a reaction to the new agricultural methods that were employed to raise output. As studies of the pesticides found in conventionally grown foods began appearing in the 1980s and 1990s, national organic food regulations were passed. Fromartz explains what the term organic really means and what the regulations require. The author visits both small farms and large-scale operations and compares conventional methods with organic methods. He explores whether organic methods offer a viable alternative to conventional practices and whether the smaller organic farmers will be able to compete with the big organic farms.

Subjects: Farming, Organic Food Industry

Now Try: Maria Rodale argues for the viability of the organic food industry in *Organic Manifesto*. Pamela Ronald makes a case for a combination of organic farming and genetic engineering in *Tomorrow's Table: Organic Farming, Genetics, and the Future of Food*. Cindy Burke explains the basics of organic foods in *To Buy or Not to Buy Organic*. Scott Chaskey chronicles a year working on an organic farm in *This Common Ground*. William Alexander discovers the difficulties of organic farming firsthand in *The $64 Tomato*. Readers may also enjoy Michael Shaffer's examination of the pet industry in *One Nation Under Dog: Adventures in the New World of Prozac-Popping Puppies, Dog-Park Politics, and Organic Pet Food*.

Gollner, Adam Leith

The Fruit Hunters: A Story of Nature, Adventure, Commerce, and Obsession. Scribner, 2008. 279pp. ISBN 9780743296946.

There are hundreds of varieties of fruits in the world, of which we only eat a few. Throughout history fruit has fueled wars and the discovery of new worlds. Gollner explores our love affair with fruit, its history, and the science of fruit reproduction. Traveling throughout the world, Gollner samples exotic fruits never seen in the United States and meets other fruit-obsessed characters. Fruit tourism has become a popular trend and has raised the issue of fruitlegging. Gollner investigates some of the other current issues, such as engineering fruits and genetically modified fruits, marketing fruits as health treatments, mass production and transportation, environmental degradation, and loss of flavor.

Subjects: Food Industry, Fruit, Genetically Modified Organisms, Travel

Now Try: Readers may also enjoy Dan Koeppel's investigation of *Banana: The Fate of the Fruit That Changed the World*. Plants were another motivation for exploration throughout history. Readers may want to check out Mary Gribbin's *Flower Hunters*, Andrea Wulf's *The Brother Gardeners: A Generation of Gentlemen Naturalists and the Birth of an Obsession*, Susan Orlean's *The Orchid Thief*, and Mark Honigsbaum's *The Fever Trail*. Readers interested in how foods are changing due to human intervention might also consider Thomas Pawlick's *The End of Food*.

Greenberg, Paul

Four Fish: The Future of the Last Wild Food. New York: Penguin Press, 2010. 284pp. ISBN 9781594202568.

Pollution, habitat destruction, and overfishing have caused a big decline in wild fish populations, but aquaculture is the fastest growing food system in the world. Greenberg looks at the four fish that dominate the modern seafood market: salmon, sea bass, cod, and tuna. The current state of each species is examined and how each relates to the future of the ocean. Greenberg argues that sustainably farmed fish will be a necessary part of the future of aquaculture. Traveling the world from Cape Cod to Vietnam, Alaska, and Norway, he investigates wild fishing practices and mega-farms. He visits a farm using genetic techniques and learns how polychlorinated biphenyls and mercury are found in fish. The author's solutions for improving aquaculture and steps that must be taken to preserve the dwindling populations are proposed.

> **Subjects:** Aquaculture, Environmental Issues, Fish, Fishing Practices, Genetically Modified Organisms, Health Issues
>
> **Awards:** James Beard Award
>
> **Now Try:** Mark Kurlansky's *Cod: A Biography of the Fish that Changed the World, King of Fish: The Thousand-Year Run of Salmon* by David R. Montgomery and Richard Ellis's *Tuna: A Love Story* provide an even more in-depth look at two of the species examined in this book. Molyneaux's *Swimming in Circles: Aquaculture and the End of Wild Oceans* investigates the argument that fish farming is a viable solution to the ocean's dwindling fish populations. Fiction readers may enjoy *The Fisherman's Son* by Mike Koepf about a boy whose father is a fisherman, struggling to survive against the problems of the commercial fishing industry.

Grescoe, Taras

Bottomfeeder: How to Eat Ethically in a World of Vanishing Seafood. New York: Bloomsbury USA, 2008. 336pp. ISBN 9781596912250.

Grescoe explains the need for caution when consuming fish. Overfishing and destructive fishing methods have harmed the ocean's fish supplies. Farmed fish can have a very negative impact on the environment as well. In addition, some species have high levels of mercury, antibiotics, or other contaminants. Grescoe provides surprising information about the seafood industry and fishing practices and very clearly outlines the issues. A clear breakdown of the species that are acceptable to eat is provided at the end.

> **Subjects:** Animal Welfare, Environmental Conservation, Fishing Practices, Seafood
>
> **Awards:** IACP Award
>
> **Now Try:** There are a number of books that illustrate the issues of overfishing, such as *The End of the Line: How Overfishing is Changing the World and What We Eat* by Charles Clover and *The Empty Ocean* by Richard Ellis. *The Secret Life of Lobsters: How Fishermen and Scientists are Unraveling the Mysteries of Our Favorite Crustacean* by Trevor Corsan

provides a more intimate look at one aspect of the fishing industry. *The Compassionate Carnivore: Or, How to Keep Animals Happy, Save Old MacDonald's Farm, Reduce Your Hoofprint, and Still Eat Meat* looks at the ethics of the meat industry and provides suggestions for more ethical options. Readers may also enjoy Grescoe's other title, an investigation of unusual foods, *The Devil's Picnic: Around the World in Pursuit of Forbidden Fruit*.

Hewitt, Ben

The Town that Food Saved: How One Community Found Vitality in Local Food. Emmaus: Rodale, 2009. 234pp. ISBN 9781605296869.

Arguing that industrial agriculture is failing, Hewitt champions the need for the localization of food production and investigates the small town of Hardwick, Vermont, which is attempting to create a local food system. Encouraging small, local food-based businesses, Hardwick has managed to infuse its community with much-needed jobs and money. Hewitt explores some of these businesses and the conditions for their success. He also examines some of the issues raised by these local businesses, such as how many of the locals can't afford to buy these local food products, which are then shipped out to bigger cities.

Subjects: Business, Community Life, Farming, Food Systems, Industrial Agriculture, Local Food, Small Communities

Now Try: Wendell Berry advocates for sustainable agriculture and local food systems in *Bringing it to the Table: On Farming and Food*. Darrin Nordahl also advocates for local food systems in *Public Produce: The New Urban Agriculture*. In *Deeply Rooted: Unconventional Farmers in the Age of Agribusiness*, Lisa M. Hamilton profiles small farmers and ranchers who are committed to agriculture, not industry. Temra Costa profiles women who have advocated for local and sustainable farming in *Farmer Jane: Women Changing the Way We Eat*. Hewitt's latest title, *Making Supper Safe: One Man's Quest to Learn the Truth about Food Safety*, investigates instances of contaminated foods and the vulnerability of the U.S. food industry.

Jacobsen, Rowan

American Terroir: Savoring the Flavors of Our Woods, Waters, and Fields. New York: Bloomsbury USA, 2010. 272pp. ISBN 9781596916487.

The term terroir, or taste of place, is a French term used to describe the way local conditions of the climate and soil affect the flavors of wine. With the current trend toward local food, Jacobsen explores how terroir can affect the flavors of foods, and produce exceptional and products with its own unique taste. Jacobsen travels throughout North America to visit producers and examine the factors that make their foods unique. From Vermont maple syrup to Panamanian coffee beans, Alaskan salmon, apples, honey, oysters, wild mushrooms, wine, cheese, and chocolate, Jacobsen covers some of America's iconic foods. Although a quick read, readers will find this to be a compelling and informative investigation.

> **Subjects:** Local Food, Terroir, Travel

> **Now Try:** Amy B. Trubek presents another investigation of terroir: *The Taste of Place: A Cultural Journey into Terroir*. Gary Paul Nabhan explores the terroir of the American Southwest in *Desert Terroir*. Brian Sommers explains terroir in relation to wine in *The Geography of Wine: How Landscapes, Cultures, Terroir, and the Weather Make a Good Drop*. Jacobsen explores the differences between the various types of oysters in *A Geography of Oysters: The Connoisseur's Guide to Oyster Eating in North America*. Other titles that focus on regional cuisines and specialties may also be appealing, such as Calvin Trillin's *Feeding a Yen* or Mort Rosenblum's *A Goose in Toulouse: And Other Culinary Adventures in France*.

Lambrecht, Bill

Dinner at the New Gene Café: How Genetic Engineering Is Changing What We Eat, How We Live, and the Global Politics of Food. New York: St. Martin's Press, 2001. 383pp. ISBN 9780312265755.

The use of genetically modified foods, or GMOs, is a very controversial topic. In this comprehensive account, Lambrecht explains the history of the debate and the science and politics surrounding GMOs. Lambrecht provides testimony from all sides of the debate, interviewing farmers, scientists, activists, government officials, and industry leaders. The clear explanations and balanced review of this topical subject make this a good choice for all readers, especially those who are unfamiliar with the subject.

> **Subjects:** Agriculture, Business, Food Industry, Genetically Modified Organisms

> **Now Try:** Alan McHughen's *Pandora's Picnic Basket: The Potentials and Hazards of Genetically Modified Foods* is another fair and balanced examination of the risks and benefits of GMOs. Jeffrey M. Smith's *Seeds of Deception: Exposing Industry and Government Lies About the Safety of the Genetically Engineered Foods You're Eating* is clearly a biased account of GMOs, however it does explore the dark side of GMOs, including stolen evidence, omitted data, bribes, threats, and grotesque results. Pamela C. Ronald makes an argument for the coexistence of GMOs and organic in *Tomorrow's Table: Organic Farming, Genetics, and the Future of Food*. Marion Nestle examines the safety of the food industry in *Safe Food: Bacteria, Biotechnology, and Bioterrorism*. *The Hundred-Year Lie: How Food and Medicine Are Destroying Your Health* by Randall Fitzgerald looks at the consequences of the synthetic chemicals used in the food and pharmaceutical industries.

Rosenblum, Mort

A Goose in Toulouse: And Other Culinary Adventures in France. New York: Hyperion, 2000. 285pp. ISBN 9780786864652.

Rosenblum looks at the importance of food in France and the culinary specialties that have defined it as a leader in gourmet cuisine. Each chapter focuses on a specialty, such as Roquefort cheese, champagne, goat cheese, truffles, calvados, foie gras, and of course, wine. Rosenblum details the production of these foods and introduces some of the people who make them. He also reflects on the infamous Michelin Guide. Globalization and how it is changing the way the French eat and the current state of French food is also explored. Vivid descriptions of meals and personal interviews with producers create a strong sense of France's food culture.

Subjects: France, French Cuisine, Globalization, Local Food, Travel, Wine

Now Try: Rosenblum has other titles that may be of interest. *Olives: The Life and Lore of a Noble Fruit* investigates the history of the olive and the olive industry. *Chocolate: Bittersweet Saga of Dark and Light* covers the history of chocolate. Michael Steinberger also explores the current state of French cuisine in *Au Revoir to All That*. Other titles about France and food may also be appealing, such as *The Sweet Life in Paris: Delicious Adventures in the World's Most Glorious and Perplexing City* by David Lebovitz, *Lunch in Paris: A Love Story, with Recipes* by Elizabeth Bard, *French Lessons: Adventures with Knife, Fork, and Corkscrew* by Peter Mayle, or M.F.K Fisher's *Long Ago in France: The Years in Dijon*. For a broader history of France, try Graham Robb's *The Discovery of France: A Historical Geography*.

Sax, David

Save the Deli: In Search of Perfect Pastrami, Crusty Rye, and the Heart of the Jewish Delicatessen. Boston: Houghton Mifflin Harcourt, 2009. 319pp. ISBN 9780151013845.

Jewish delicatessens, which first appeared in New York City in the 19th century and have been a cornerstone of Jewish food, are slowly disappearing. Many traditional delicatessen products are also disappearing from menus. Sax, an avid lover of delicatessens, travels the country to investigate the reasons for the decline, and to determine if the deli can be saved. Beginning his investigation in New York City, Sax chronicles the introduction of delis when masses of Jewish immigrants came to the United States and its dispersal throughout the United States as Jews left New York City for other cities such as Detroit, Chicago, and San Francisco. He finds that assimilation, homogenization, and the desire for healthier foods have turned many people away from delicatessens. Perhaps the most entertaining is his description of how delicatessen foods are made and his highlights of outstanding delis across the country.

Subjects: Delicatessens, Travel

Awards: James Beard Award

Now Try: Milton Parker, owner of the Carnegie deli, traces the history of his deli from 1937 as well as the history of deli food in America in *How to Feed Friends and Influence People: The Carnegie Deli . . . A Giant Sandwich, a Little Deli, a Huge Success*. Ben Ryder Howe recounts his experience owning a deli in Brooklyn in *My Korean Deli: How I Risked My Career and Mortgaged My*

Future for a Convenience Store. Adam Richman explores the history of some of the most iconic American foods from around the country in *America the Edible: A Hungry History, from Sea to Dining Sea*. Readers may also enjoy the documentary and companion cookbook, *Sandwiches That You Will Like*, which features regional favorites from around the country.

Shell, Ellen Ruppel

Cheap: The High Cost of Discount Culture. New York: Penguin Press, 2009. 296pp. ISBN 9781594202155.

Shell chronicles America's never-ending demand for cheaper goods. Taking us back to the beginnings of discounted goods in the 1800s, she examines the effects our insistence for cheaper prices has had on our economy, as well as the world's economy. Although the overall focus of the book is on all goods, Shell does devote a portion of the book to food. Shell outlines how advancements in technology and government subsidies have allowed us access to extremely cheap food. She explains that the price of food in American supermarkets does not reflect the true cost, which is our health, the environment, and the social welfare of other countries.

> **Subjects**: American History, Consumer Behavior, Economics, Food Industry

> **Now Try**: Although more academic, Michael Carolan's *The Real Cost of Cheap Food* expands on the issues raised in Shell's book. Eric Schlosser details how the demand for cheaper food led to the unacceptable practices of the fast-food industry in *Fast Food Nation: The Dark Side of the All-American Meal*. In *Cheap We Trust: The Story of a Misunderstood American Virtue* by Lauren Weber examines America's appreciation for thriftiness. Titles that detail the author's attempt to consume less may also be appealing. Try Judith Levine's *Not Buying It: My Year Without Shopping* and Sara Bongiorni's *A Year Without 'Made in China': One Family's True Life Adventure in the Global Economy*.

Vileisis, Ann

Kitchen Literacy: How We Lost Knowledge of Where Food Comes from and Why We Need to Get It Back. Washington: Island Press/Shearwater Books, 2008. 332pp. ISBN 9781597261449.

Vileisis contends that most Americans have lost touch with their food. They have no idea where there food comes from or how it is produced and we have distanced ourselves from food and nature. Recent stories in the news about pathogens found in factory farmed meat and pesticides contaminating the environment have led many to wonder about the origins of the food found in supermarkets. Vileisis looks to history to understand the present state. She traces our relationship with food back to the 18th century, when most women raised their own foods or got it from someone they knew. Vileisis draws on diaries of women and cookbooks to illustrate how people ate during that time. In the 19th century, industrialization and urbanization transplanted many rural residents to cities where they were distanced from their food sources. Initial disgust over meat packing plants and canned foods was won over by the low costs of mass produced foods. Social and economic changes, as well as World War II led to more convenience foods. Vileisis provides a detailed and well-researched outline of the current state of food, which is further enhanced by her use of primary sources.

Subjects: Food Industry, History, Society

Now Try: Readers may also appreciate Wendell Berry's *The Unsettling of America: Culture and Agriculture*. Berry argues that agribusiness has estranged Americans from the land, and therefore, the food we eat. Marion Nestle explores current issues of food safety in *Safe Food: The Politics of Food Safety, Updated and Expanded*. Michael Pollan investigates the sources of our major food chains in *The Omnivore's Dilemma: A Natural History of Four Meals*. Eric Schlosser exposes the origins of fast-food and its impact on our health in *Fast Food Nation: The Dark Side of the All-American Meal*. Geoff Andrews chronicles the history and politics of the Slow Food movement in *The Slow Food Story*. Readers may also be interested in Vileisis's investigation of America's disappearing wetlands, *Discovering the Unknown Landscape: A History Of America's Wetlands*.

Winne, Mark

Food Rebels, Guerrilla Gardeners, and Smart-Cookin' Mamas: Fighting Back in an Age of Industrial Agriculture. Boston: Beacon Press, 2011. 200pp. ISBN 9780807047330.

Author and longtime executive director of a community food system organization in Connecticut, Winne opens his book about new methods of raising and eating food with an alarmist hypothetical chapter on America's food system in 2020—a system ruled by a few powerful corporate interests. He follows that introduction with chapters on current American eating habits, agricultural production, and governmental regulation (or lack thereof) of food; in later chapters he provides character profiles of individuals living their beliefs in community agriculture and organization. It's a short book, but a meaty one that demands a thoughtful response from its readers.

Subjects: Agriculture, Community Life, Food Movements, Government, Nonprofits

Now Try: Winne is also the author of the food book *Closing the Food Gap*. Other titles about how consumers can take more personal charge of their food choices and sourcing might be suggested to these readers, such as Frances Moore Lappé's *Diet for a Small Planet* or Mark Pollan's *Food Rules*. Also of interest might be books about community food (and other) movements, such as Ben Hewitt's *The Town that Food Saved*, Katherine Gustafson's *Change Comes to Dinner: How Vertical Farmers, Urban Growers, and Other Innovators Are*

Revolutionizing How America Eats, or Lisa Hamilton's *Deeply Rooted: Unconventional Farmers in the Age of Agribusiness. The Slow Food Story* by Geoff Andrews chronicles the history and politics of the Slow Food movement, which embraces a return to fresh, seasonal, local products.

Immersion Journalism

With Immersion Journalism, the author is typically personally involved in the investigation. The author still conducts research and interviews, but often also inserts himself or herself into the story. The author may have a personal interest in the story, such as Steve Almond's fixation with candy. The author may attempt a particular task or journey in order to have a better understanding of the topic in which he or she is researching, such as Holly Bishop's attempt at beekeeping. While the authors may have a personal interest in the topic at hand, the focus of the book is more on the story and less on the author's personal life, as it can be in the Personal Endeavor memoirs. The authors also tend to have a definitive end to their investigation, whereas the authors of Personal Endeavor memoirs attempt to make lifelong changes. Immersion Journalism titles have a more intimate feeling to them, and the writing tends to be more conversational. Because the stories are more personal, readers who enjoy Immersion Journalism may also enjoy titles from the Memoir chapter such as the Working Life Memoirs or Personal Endeavor memoirs.

> In Immersion Journalism titles, the author inserts himself or herself into the story in order to obtain a better understanding of the topic. These titles tend to have a more intimate, conversational tone.

Almond, Steve

Candyfreak: A Journey Through the Chocolate Underbelly of America. Chapel Hill, NC: Algonquin Books, 2004. 266pp. ISBN 9781565124219.

Almond is a self-described candyfreak. He is obsessed with candy. He admits that he keeps three to seven pounds of candy in his house at all times and has a stash of the discontinued Kit Kat Darks hidden in an undisclosed location. He waxes poetic about the candies he has eaten throughout his life. Wondering what became of some of his favorite childhood candies, Almond embarks on a mission to learn about the candy-making business. Finding it difficult to tour the factories of some of the big name brands because of the secrecy, Almond focuses on the smaller, regional candy makers, learning that they struggle to survive in an industry ruled by the big guys. Traveling throughout the country, Almond visits candy manufacturers and meets other candyfreaks, collectors, historians, and entrepreneurs. This is a humorous, quick read.

Subjects: Candy, Humor, Quick Reads, Travel

Now Try: Another candy fanatic, Tim Richardson explores the history of candy and the variety of sweets in the market today in *Sweets: A History of Candy*. Kate Hopkins also travelled through the United States and Europe investigating the history of candy in *Sweet Tooth: The Bittersweet History of Candy*. In *Candy and Me: A Girl's Tale of Life, Love, and Sugar,* Hilary Liftin remembers the candies she associates with different periods of her life. Fiction readers may enjoy the novel *True Confections* by Katharine Weber, about a woman running a candy factory. Readers may enjoy other titles about an author's investigation into a particular topic, such as Jason Wilson's *Boozehound: On the Trail of the Rare, the Obscure, and the Overrated in Spirits*, Ken Wells's *Travels With Barley*, or Sarah Vowell's *Assassination Vacation*. Fans of Almond's humorous writing style will want to check out one of his other titles, including *Death by Pad Thai*, *Not That You Asked*, and *Rock and Roll Will Save Your Life* as well as his novels *My Life in Heavy Metal* and *Which Brings Me to You*.

Baur, Gene

Farm Sanctuary: Changing Hearts and Minds about Animals and Food.
New York: Simon & Schuster, 2008. 286pp. ISBN 9780743291583.

After rescuing an ill sheep that had been left to die at a stockyard, Gene Baur founded Farm Sanctuary in 1986. Since then, Farm Sanctuary has rescued thousands of farm animals from the ill treatment of factory farms, stockyards, and slaughterhouses. Baur provides a vivid and often disturbing picture of how factory animals are treated, and profiles many of the individual animals that have been rescued, providing insight into animal psychology and dispelling myths about animal feelings. The history of industrial farming, the roots of factory farms, and the current state of farming today are also considered. Baur also recounts Farm Sanctuary's struggles to bring about changes in farming practices and animal cruelty laws, including battles with the enormous agribusiness lobby, the USDA, and Congress.

Subjects: Animals, Animal Welfare, Factory Farms, Food Industry

Now Try: Readers who enjoyed Baur's descriptions of the rescued animals and their individual personalities and behaviors may enjoy Jeffrey Moussaieff Masson's *The Pig Who Sang to the Moon: The Emotional World of Farm Animals* or Jonathan Balcombe's *Pleasurable Kingdom: Animals and the Nature of Feeling Good*. Temple Grandin has played a big role in changing conditions at slaughterhouses to create more humane conditions. Reader may want to consider one of her books, such as *Animals in Translation: Using the Mysteries of Autism to Decode Animal Behavior*. Readers who are interested in more stories about individuals who are fighting factory farms may enjoy David Kirby's *Animal Factory: The Looming Threat of Industrial Pig, Dairy, and Poultry Farms to Humans and the Environment*. A slightly different type of story is told in Peter Lovenheim's *Portrait of a Burger as a Young Calf*; out of a desire to better understand where his food comes from, Lovenheim adopts a calf destined to become one of his food sources.

Bishop, Holly

Robbing the Bees—A Biography of Honey—the Sweet Liquid Gold that Seduced the World. New York: Free Press, 2005. 324pp. ISBN 9780743250214.

Since ancient times, humans have revered and lusted for honey. This fascinating title explains the science of bees, hive society, and honey production. The evolution of honey and beeswax harvesting, and the evolving uses of honey throughout history are covered. Bishop visits a respected Florida beekeeper, who is known for producing Tupelo honey, an uncommon and highly regarded type of honey. In order to gain a better firsthand experience with beekeeping and honey production, Bishop acquires her own hive, which provides the story with a bit of humor. Despite the scientific and historical information, Bishop's lively and familiar prose style keep this account from becoming too dense.

Subjects: Beekeeping, Bees, Honey, Recipes

Now Try: Beekeeping has become a popular topic recently among urban farmers and there are a number of books on this topic. Readers may want to try *Letters From the Hive: An Intimate History of Bees, Honey, and Humankind* by Stephen Buchmann, C. Marina Marchese's account of becoming a beekeeper in *Honeybee: Lessons from an Accidental Beekeeper,* or Hannah Nordhaus's *The Beekeeper's Lament: How One Man and Half a Billion Honey Bees Help Feed America. Sweetness and Light: The Mysterious History of the Honeybee* by Hattie Ellis provides a more in-depth and detailed historical account of the natural history of bees and their role in society since the Stone Age. Readers interested in the mysterious colony collapse disorder should try Rowan Jacobsen's *Fruitless Fall: The Collapse of the Honey Bee and the Coming Agricultural Crisis. The Queen Must Die: And Other Affairs of Bees and Men* by William Longgood explains bee physiology and social structure. The documentary *The Vanishing of the Bees* may also be of interest. Readers who like the in-depth look at a particular insect or animal may want to consider Sharman Apt Russell's *An Obsession with Butterflies: Our Long Love Affair with a Singular Insect,* Robert Sullivan's *Rats: Observations on the History and Habitat of the City's Most Unwanted Inhabitants,* and Richard Schweid's *The Cockroach Papers: A Compendium of History and Lore.*

Bone, Eugenia

Mycophilia: Revelations from the Weird World of Mushrooms. New York: Rodale, 2011. 348pp. ISBN 9781605294070.

Mycophilia comes from the Greek word mycophilos, meaning fungus loving. After finding a cache of porcini mushrooms while hiking in Colorado, Bone became intrigued with mushrooms. Since then, she began mushroom hunting and studying mushrooms. She joins the New York Mycological Society, attends lectures, and participates in group hunts in search of morels. Broadening her range, she finds small but dedicated groups of quirky mushroom lovers all over the country who educate her on the vast variety of mushrooms, the biology of mushrooms, and the differences between poisonous and edible mushrooms. Bone also explores the use of mushrooms throughout history and the possibility for their use in cleaning up pollutants and wastes, in vaccine production, and in biodiesel fuel.

Subjects: Mushrooms, Science, Travel

Now Try: In *Chanterelle Dreams, Amanita Nightmares: The Love, Lore, and Mystique of Mushrooms,* Greg A. Marley introduces readers to the history and uses of mushrooms and provides a guide for those interested in foraging. Paul Stamets explores the ways mushrooms can be used in *Mycelium Running: How Mushrooms Can Help Save the World.* Readers may enjoy cookbooks that feature wild foods, such as Hank Shaw's *Hunt, Gather, Cook: Finding the Forgotten Feast* or Connie Green's *The Wild Table: Seasonal Foraged Food and Recipes.*

Buford, Bill

Heat: An Amateur's Adventures as Kitchen Slave, Line Cook, Pasta-maker, and Apprentice to a Dante-quoting Butcher in Tuscany. New York: Alfred A. Knopf, 2006. 318pp. ISBN 9781400041206.

Buford is a journalist and amateur home cook. After meeting famous chef Mario Batali and striking up a friendship, he is offered the opportunity to apprentice in Mario's famous kitchen, Babbo. Although a fairly good home cook, Buford has never worked in a professional kitchen. He is immediately thrown into the fray and introduced to the fast pace, difficult tasks, quest for perfection, and hierarchy of the kitchen staff. In between his tales, Buford provides a history of Batali's career and rise to success, as well as Batali's true personality of enjoying drinking and sex versus the wholesome version the public is shown. Buford also travels to England to interview Marco Pierre White, the famous chef who once employed Mario, and to Italy to study technique from Mario's teachers.

Subjects: Batali, Mario, Chefs, Restaurants, White, Marco Pierre

Awards: *New York Times* Notable Book

Now Try: Michael Ruhlman, a journalist, entered the CIA to document the training of professional chefs in *The Making of a Chef: Mastering Heat at the Culinary Institute of America.* Katherine Darling also recounts her experiences in culinary school in *Under the Table.* Readers who enjoyed Buford's fast pace, behind-the-scenes style may enjoy Marco Pierre White's memoir, *The Devil in the Kitchen: Sex, Pain, Madness, and the Making of a Great Chef,* Anthony Bourdain's *Kitchen Confidential: Adventures in the Culinary Underbelly,* or Jason Sheehan's *Cooking Dirty: A Story of Life, Sex, Love and Death in the Kitchen.* Readers may also enjoy other immersion journalism titles such as *Working in the Shadows: A Year of Doing the Jobs (Most) Americans Won't Do* by Gabriel Thompson, *Nickel and Dimed: On (Not) Getting By in America* by Barbara Ehrenreich, *or Newjack: A Year as a Prison Guard in New York's Most Infamous Maximum Security Jail* by Ted Conover. These readers might also enjoy the television series *MasterChef,* in which (primarily) amateur home chefs compete to win the approval of several celebrity chef judges.

Corson, Trevor

The Zen of Fish: The Story of Sushi, from Samurai to Supermarket. New York: HarperCollins Publishers, 2007. 372pp. ISBN 9780060883508.

Corson observes classes at the California Sushi Academy to learn about the art of making sushi. Not only did he learn about how sushi is made, but he also covers all you ever wanted to know about sushi. The history of how sushi came about in Japan, the extensive training a sushi chef receives in Japan, how sushi became popular in the United States and how it has been adapted for Americans are all explored. Corson learns the process of making sushi, variations of sushi, information on the various fish that is used, how components such as soy sauce, rice, nori, and rice vinegar are made, and the etiquette of eating sushi. Observing the students in the California Sushi Academy, Corson focuses on one female student's experiences and the challenges she faces as a woman working in a male-dominated field.

Subjects: Chefs, Culinary School, Japan, Sushi

Now Try: Sasha Issenberg's *Sushi Economy: Globalization and the Making of a Modern Delicacy* is another thorough exploration into the world of sushi. Ken Kawasumi's *The Encyclopedia of Sushi Rolls* illustrates the basic techniques of sushi preparation as well as special techniques to create visually stunning sushi. Readers may also want to consider Victoria Abbott Riccardi's *Untangling My Chopsticks: A Culinary Sojourn in Kyoto*, the author's account of learning kaiseki, the ritualized cuisine that accompanies the formal Japanese tea ceremony. Readers who enjoy Trevor's style may also enjoy his investigation into the decline of lobster populations off the coast of Maine in *The Secret Life of Lobsters: How Fishermen and Scientists Are Unraveling the Mysteries of Our Favorite Crustacean*.

Cycon, Dean

Javatrekker: Dispatches from the World of Fair Trade Coffee. White River Junction: Chelsea Green Pub., 2007. 239pp. ISBN 9781933392707.

Although one of the most popular beverages in America, few coffee drinkers are aware of the socio-political issues created by coffee production. Nor do they understand the complexity of the coffee trade, or even know where their coffee comes from and who produces it. Cycon visits a number of countries, including Columbia, Ethiopia, Kenya, Peru, and Nicaragua to investigate the immense, complex coffee trade and meet the struggling coffee farmers. Exploring the major problems caused by the coffee trade, Cycon discovers negative effects on immigration, women's rights, pollution, poverty, and indigenous rights. His investigation of the social issues with the combination of the personal stories of the coffee farmers and life in coffee villages provides a unique, entertaining view point that will appeal to readers who enjoy exposes as well as travel.

Subjects: Coffee, Coffee Industry, Environmental Issues, Social Issues, Travel

Now Try: Readers interested in the history of coffee and its current issues may want to try *Uncommon Grounds: The History of Coffee and How It Transformed Our World* by Mark

Pendergrast, *The Devil's Cup: A History of the World According to Coffee* by Stewart Lee Allen or *The Coffee Book: Anatomy of an Industry from Crop to the Last Drop* by Nina Luttinger and Gregory Dicum. *The Coke Machine: The Dirty Truth Behind the World's Favorite Soft Drink* by Michael Blanding investigates the issues caused by the production of another popular American beverage. Fred Pearce investigates the origins of other popular goods in *Confessions of an Eco-Sinner: Tracking Down the Sources of My Stuff*. John Bowe's *Nobodies: Modern American Slave Labor and the Dark Side of the New Global Economy* and Gabriel Thompson's *Working in the Shadows: A Year of Doing the Jobs [Most] Americans Won't Do* both investigate modern slavery and food production.

Fagone, Jason

Horsemen of the Esophagus: Competitive Eating and the Big Fat American Dream. New York: Crown Publishers, 2006. 303pp. ISBN 9780307237385.

Fagone gives readers a backstage pass into the world of competitive eating. Traveling around the country to 27 contests, readers are introduced to a subculture that few are familiar with. Some of the well-known characters on the competitive eating circuit are profiled, including Dave "Coondog" O'Karma, Bill "El Wingador" Simmons, and Sonya "the Black Widow" Thomas. Fagone learns the tricks and techniques of competitive eating and gets a firsthand look at how serious these competitions are. He also travels to Japan to meet Takeru Kobayashi, who holds several world records in eating and won the Nathan's Annual Hot Dog Eating Contest for five years in a row. Shocking and often humorous, with interesting characters and play-by-plays of the competitions, readers will easily get swept up into this fascinating story.

> **Subjects:** Eating Competitions, Travel
>
> **Now Try:** In *Eat This Book: A Year of Gorging and Glory on the Competitive Eating Circuit*, Ryan Nerz chronicles his experience as an announcer for the International Federation of Competitive Eating. Readers will recognize many of the characters seen in Fagone's book, but will enjoy the insider perspective. Readers who enjoy the inside look at little known competitions may also enjoy Stefan Fatsis's *Word Freak: Heartbreak, Triumph, Genius, and Obsession in the World of Competitive Scrabble Players* or Ken Jennings's *Brainiac: Adventures in the Curious, Competitive, Compulsive World of Trivia Buffs*.

Friend, Catherine

The Compassionate Carnivore: Or, How to Keep Animals Happy, Save Old MacDonald's Farm, Reduce Your Hoofprint, and Still Eat Meat. Da Capo Press, 2008. 291pp. ISBN 9781600940071.

Like many others, Friend believes that factory farmed meat is cruel to animals, harmful to the environment, and bad for our health. While some feel that vegetarianism is the only way to fight factory farming, Friend readily admits that she enjoys eating meat and has no plans to quit. She believes that by educating ourselves, we can make more humane choices in the meat we eat. Interspersing stories of her own farming experiences, she explains the different methods of raising and slaughtering animals. The differences in the labeling terms are also explained (organic, free-range, vegetarian-fed, finished, etc.) and the author provides suggestions for finding humanely raised meat. Friend's non-judgmental tone and less hard-line approach make this a more accessible guide for the average carnivore.

Subjects: Animal Welfare, Farming Practices, Meat

Now Try: Readers interested in the experience of living on a farm and raising animals may want to try Friend's memoirs *Hit By a Farm: How I Learned to Stop Worrying and Love the Barn* and *Sheepish*, or Barbara Kingsolver's memoir of her year spent growing her own food and raising poultry, *Animal, Vegetable, Miracle: A Year of Food Life*. Readers interested in the animal welfare aspect may enjoy *Farm Sanctuary: Changing Hearts and Minds about Animals and Food* by Gene Bauer. Although Bauer advocates veganism, he also provides suggestions for meat eaters who want to make more ethical choices. Tovar Cerulli's *The Mindful Carnivore* contemplates the debate over a meat or vegetarian diet.

Garbee, Jenn

Secret Suppers: Rogue Chefs and Underground Restaurants in Warehouses, Townhouses, Open Fields, and Everywhere in Between. Seattle: Sasquatch Books, 2008. 248pp. ISBN 9781570615467.

Underground restaurants are the latest craze with foodies. A kind of combination supper club, dinner party, and restaurant, underground restaurants are held in a variety of locations without permits or licenses and are typically kept on the down low, as they exist on the fringe of legality. Chefs who are looking to experiment and don't want to be hindered by their restaurant's menu have begun holding these secret dinners for diners looking for a new eating experience. Garbee investigates several of these popular events, profiling the chefs as well as some of the diners, and providing details of the menus. The dinners are diverse in size and geography, ranging all over the country, and can be as many as 100 guests or as few as 12. The chefs may be professional chefs wanting to experiment with new dishes or hobby chefs. Either way, diners never know what to expect, except that they will experience something new and different.

Subjects: Restaurants, Underground Dining

Now Try: Kerstin Rodgers, owner of the famous London Underground Restaurant, combines her experiences, recipes, menus, and advice in *Supper Club: Recipes and Notes from the Underground Restaurant*. Cathy Erway chronicles her experiences with new food adventures, including underground restaurants, in *The Art of Eating In: How I Learned to Stop Spending and Love the Stove*. Another popular culinary craze gaining popularity is the food truck. Heather Shouse explores trucks across the country in *Food Trucks: Dispatches and Recipes from the Best Kitchens on Wheels*. Sandor Ellix Katz profiles several different underground food movements in *The Revolution Will Not Be*

Microwaved: Inside America's Underground Food Movements. New York magazine also frequently contains articles about the latest food crazes. Mark Boyle's *The Moneyless Man* might also be considered for his creative attempts at living for free.

Lee, Jennifer 8

The Fortune Cookie Chronicles: Adventures in the World of Chinese Food. New York: Twelve, 2008. 307pp. ISBN 9780446580076.

In 2005, 110 people won the lottery playing numbers they received in fortune cookies. This prompted Lee to examine the history of the fortune cookie, as well as the history and popularity of Chinese food in America. Lee travels the country visiting Chinese restaurants, including those that gave out the cookies with the winning numbers. She examines the difference between true Chinese food and American Chinese food, as well as the immigration of Chinese to America, the development of American Chinese dishes such as Chop Suey, the invention of fortune cookies and the fortune writers, and the beginning of food delivery. Lee finishes her investigation by visiting Chinese restaurants throughout the world to determine the best Chinese restaurant.

Subjects: American History, Chinese Cuisine, Chinese Culture, Immigrants, Travel

Now Try: Readers will also enjoy Andrew Coe's thorough exploration of Chinese food in *America in Chop Suey: A Cultural History of Chinese Food in the United States*. Bonnie Tsui's *American Chinatown: A People's History of Five Neighborhoods* is a vibrant tour of the five (San Francisco, Los Angeles, New York, Las Vegas, and Honolulu) Chinatown communities in America. Cecelia Chiang, founder of San Francisco's Mandarin restaurant, recalls her early life in China, immigration to America, and the influence of Chinese cuisine in America in *The Seventh Daughter: My Culinary Journey from Beijing to San Francisco*. Trevor Corson details how sushi became popular in the United States and has been adapted for American palates in *The Zen of Fish: The Story of Sushi, from Samurai to Supermarket*. Twelve, the publisher of Lee's book, publishes only 12 titles a year. Readers may want to consider some of their other sociological titles, such as Eric Weiner's *The Geography of Bliss*, Bryan Christy's *The Lizard King*, and Sheena Iyengar's *How We Choose*.

Lovenheim, Peter

Portrait of a Burger as a Young Calf: The Story of One Man, Two Cows, and The Feeding of a Nation. New York: Harmony Books, 2002. 272pp. ISBN 9780609605912.

Fewer than 2 percent of Americans are engaged in farming, and as a result, many know very little about where their food comes from.

Lovenheim decides that he wants to follow the cycle of a cow from conception to slaughter to better understand the process our food goes through to get onto our plate. Partnering with a dairy farm, he is given access to the farm to watch the insemination of the cows, and the birth of calves. He buys three calves and has them moved to a farm where they will be raised for beef. Throughout their lives he makes frequent trips to the farms to observe farming practiced. He witnesses how ill cows are treated, how natural animal inclinations are ignored or prohibited, and the use of chemicals and growth hormones. But he also learns how hard the life of a farmer can be: long hours, hard labor, injuries, and little money. Lovenheim attempts to be nonjudgmental and unbiased, but there are instances where the ethics of his project trouble him and his decision whether to slaughter his calves weighs heavy on his mind. He delivers an engrossing, up-close look at the daily work of a meat farm and attempts to address both sides of the ethical dilemmas.

Subjects: Animal Welfare, Farmers, Farming Practices, Meat

Now Try: Michael Pollan investigates how meat gets from farm to plate in *The Omnivore's Dilemma*. Readers may also enjoy Steve Ettlinger's detailed investigation of the twinkie in *Twinkie, Deconstructed: My Journey to Discover How the Ingredients Found in Processed Foods Are Grown, Mined (Yes, Mined), and Manipulated into What America Eats*. Other inside looks at farmer's lives are Keith Stewart's *It's a Long Road to a Tomato*, Mike Madison's memoir *Blithe Tomato: An Insider's Wry Look at Farmers' Market Society*, Michael Ableman's *On Good Land*, and Jane Brox's *Here and Nowhere Else: Late Seasons of a Farm and Its Family*. Lovenheim also wrote *In the Neighborhood: The Search for Community on an American Street, One Sleepover at a Time*.

McMillan, Tracie

American Way of Eating: Undercover at Walmart, Applebee's, Farm Fields and the Dinner Table. New York: Scribner, 2012. 319pp. ISBN 9781439171967.

With the growing obesity crisis in the United States, Americans are constantly hearing that we should eat healthy, fresh foods, and eliminate processed foods from our diet. But eating fresh, healthy foods is often more expensive than fast-food or processed food, and therefore out of reach for many Americans. McMillan goes undercover in a number of food-related jobs to see where the average American's food comes from. She begins with farm labor in California, working alongside migrant workers in the fields under grueling conditions. Her second foray takes her to Walmart, where she works as a produce clerk, illuminating many of the store's behind-the-scenes practices. Finally, she takes a kitchen job at the largest chain restaurant, Applebee's, where much of the food is prepared off-site. Aside from providing shocking details of working conditions and standard practices within these companies, she also recounts the difficulties she faced trying to eat well on her meager wages.

Subjects: Farming, Food Habits, Food Industry, Health Issues, Immigrants, Labor, Nutrition, Poverty, Restaurants

Now Try: Gabriel Thompson also recounts his experiences working under-cover in food-related jobs in *Working in the Shadows*. Steve Striffler takes a job in a poultry processing plant to better understand the current issues of the poultry industry in *Chicken: The Dangerous Transformation of America's Favorite Food*. Barbara Ehrenreich's *Nickel and Dimed* recounts her experiences trying to get by while working in minimum-wage level jobs. David Shipler investi-gates the lives of the working poor in America in *The Working Poor: Invisible in America*. *Fast Food Nation* by Eric Schlosser is an eye-opening account of the fast-food industry.

Nabhan, Gary Paul

Desert Terroir: Exploring the Unique Flavors and Sundry Places of the Borderlands. Austin: University of Texas Press, 2012. 144pp. ISBN 9780292725898.

Terroir is a term used to describe how characteristics of the land affect the flavors of the foods produced from it. Nabhan attempts to discover what creates the unique terroir of the desert borderlands of Mexico and the United States. In his travels throughout the borderlands, he is introduced to local foods such as wild oregano, prickly pear cactus, mesquite torti-llas, and a Mexican breed of cattle. Attempting to subsist on only local foods from this area, he quickly learns how difficult it is to raise food in this region. Nabhan explains how the desert ecology, such as the soil and water (or lack thereof), affects the tastes of these foods. He also explores how cultural history can affect terroir, tracing the history of the Spanish and Arab immigrants to the region. A quick read, this will appeal to read-ers interested in this unique perspective on terroir.

Subjects: American Southwest, History, Terroir, Travel

Now Try: Rowan Jacobsen travels throughout America seeking terroir in *American Terroir*. Amy B. Trubek presents another investigation of terroir: *The Taste of Place: A Cultural Journey into Terroir*. Brian Sommers explains terroir in relation to wine in *The Geography of Wine: How Landscapes, Cultures, Terroir, and the Weather Make a Good Drop*. Mort Rosenblum's *A Goose in Toulouse: And Other Culinary Adventures in France* focuses on the regional cuisines and specialties of France. Readers may also enjoy some of the Extreme Cuisine titles that fea-ture exotic local foods, such as *Eat My Globe* by Simon Majumdar. Nabhan has a number of other titles that may be appealing. Try *Coming Home to Eat: The Pleasures and Politics of Local Food, Chasing Chiles: Hot Spots Along the Pepper Trail,* or *Renewing America's Food Traditions: Saving and Savoring the Continent's Most Endangered Foods*.

Pearce, Fred

Confessions of an Eco-Sinner: Tracking Down the Sources of My Stuff. Beacon Press, 2008. 276pp. ISBN 9780807085882.

Although Pearce's mission to track down the sources of his stuff encompasses clothes, metals, and plastics, one section is devoted to food. Pearce travels around the world to see where coffee beans, cocoa, and green beans come from. He also tracks down the source of most of our wild fish and prawns, as well as palm oil and bananas. From Africa to India, Pearce provides an inside look at where our food comes from and the people who produce it.

Subjects: Environment Issues, Food Production, Travel

Now Try: Readers who enjoy learning where products come from may also enjoy *Where Underpants Come From* by Joe Bennett or *Fugitive Denim: A Moving Story of People and Pants in the Borderless World of Global Trade* by Rachel Louise Snyder. Mike Berners-Lee looks at the carbon footprint of our stuff in *How Bad Are Bananas?: The Carbon Footprint of Everything*. One of Pearce's most compelling chapters is the chapter on the endangerment of the banana. Readers interested in more detail can try *Banana: The Fate of the Fruit That Changed the World* by Dan Koeppel. Dean Cycon investigates where our coffee comes from and the people who produce it in *Javatrekker: Dispatches From the World of Fair Trade Coffee*. Steve Ettlinger traces the ingredients of the popular American snack food in *Twinkie, Deconstructed: My Journey to Discover How the Ingredients Found in Processed Foods Are Grown, Mined (Yes, Mined), and Manipulated into What America Eats*. Elizabeth Royte investigates the bottled water industry in *Bottlemania: How Water Went on Sale and Why We Bought It*. Titles that examine the environmental costs of our stuff and what happens to it when we are finished with it, may want to consider Elizabeth Royte's *Garbage Land: On the Secret Trail of Trash* or Annie Leonard's *The Story of Stuff: The Impact of Overconsumption on the Planet, Our Communities, and Our Health-And How We Can Make It Better*.

Pollan, Michael

The Omnivore's Dilemma: A Natural History of Four Meals. New York: Penguin Press, 2006. 450pp. ISBN 9781594200823.

Pollan examines the major food chains in the United States: the conventional industrial food industry, the organic food industry (both on a large and small scale), and the hunter-gatherer method. Using a particular meal to illustrate his message, he traces a McDonald's meal to Iowa corn farms, an organic meal to a small Virginia farm, and attempts to procure his own food by hunting wild boar and gathering mushrooms. Pollan paints a portrait of the American way of eating and its consequences on our health and the health of the planet.

Subjects: Environmental Issues, Farms, Food Industry, Foraging, Health Issues, Hunting, Organic Food Industry

Awards: James Beard Award, *New York Times* Notable Book

Now Try: Pollan's *In Defense of Food: An Eater's Manifesto* also won a James Beard Award and is a good option for readers who want a pared down version of *The Omnivore's Dilemma*. Readers who like Pollan's style may want to check out *The Botany of Desire: A Plant's-Eye View of the World*. During his investigation, Pollan spends time with sustainable farmer Joel Salatin of Polyface Farms. Readers may want to check out some of Salatin's books, such as *Folks, This Ain't Normal: A Farmer's Advice for*

Happier Hens, Healthier People, and a Better World or *Everything I Want To Do Is Illegal: War Stories From the Local Food Front*. In Peter Lovenheim's *Portrait of a Burger as a Young Calf: The Story of One Man, Two Cows, and the Feeding of a Nation*, the author purchases two calves to observe the process of getting meat on our table. Langdon Cook explores foraging in *Fat of the Land*. Georgia Pellegrini hunts for her own food in *Girl Hunter*. Erich Schlosser's *Fast Food Nation* is an eye-opening account of the fast-food industry. Paul Greenberg's *Four Fish: The Future of the Last Wild Food* is an examination of the state of the fishing industry. Wendell Berry also examines the agricultural industry and the exploitation of the land in *The Unsettling of America: Culture and Agriculture*.

Rehak, Melanie

Eating for Beginners: An Education in the Pleasures of Food from Chefs, Farmers, and One Picky Kid. Boston: Houghton Mifflin Harcourt, 2010. 275pp. ISBN 9780151014378.

Battling a picky toddler and confused by all the information that is thrown at us regarding how to eat, Rehak decides to investigate what is most important when it comes to food. What should we eat? Is organic more important, or local? Rehak takes a job working in the kitchen of a neighborhood restaurant that is committed to supporting local farmers. Working for some of the producers of the restaurant's food, she also helps make cheese on a dairy farm, lends a hand on an organic vegetable farm, and goes to sea to fish for monkfish. Along the way she begins to understand the compromises that must sometimes be made and decides what is important to her and her family. This is a touching and lighthearted story of a woman who wants to do the right thing for her child and struggles with daily battles with a toddler. Although Rehak does spend time working in a restaurant kitchen, readers will get no chaotic, fast-paced, foul language-infused tale like many other kitchen memoirs. The restaurant Rehak works for seems oddly calm and peaceful.

> **Subjects:** Children, Farms, Food Industry, Restaurants

> **Now Try:** Readers who enjoyed the charming and humorous struggles of feeding a picky toddler may also enjoy Matthew Amster-Burton's struggle to raise an adventurous eater in *Hungry Monkey: A Food-Loving Father's Quest to Raise an Adventurous Eater*. Emily Franklin chronicles her attempts to introduce her children to new foods and instill in them a love of food and cooking in *Too Many Cooks: Kitchen Adventures with 1 Mom, 4 Kids, and 102 Recipes*. Jennifer Reese's narrative cookbook *Make the Bread, Buy the Butter* also seeks to help readers make sense of which foods to make from scratch and which ones to buy. Readers who enjoyed Rehak's charming story and lighthearted tone may also enjoy Novella Carpenter's *Farm City: The Education of an Urban Farmer*. Rehak also wrote *Girl Sleuth: Nancy Drew and the Women Who Created Her*, which traces the creation and history of the famous character, Nancy Drew.

Ruhlman, Michael

The Making of a Chef: Mastering Heat at the Culinary Institute of America. New York: Henry Holt and Co., 1997. 305pp. ISBN 9780805046748.

Ruhlman, a journalist, entered the Culinary Institute of America (CIA) to document the training of professional chefs. He joined the classes, learned the basics of cooking, and also experienced the pressures of restaurant work by working and serving in the CIA's restaurants. His immersion introduced him to the intense, high pressure, fast-paced life of a chef and the career's demand for absolute perfection. Aside from his own experiences, Ruhlman introduces the readers to his classmates and teachers, whom he respects. This insider's view provides an engrossing account of what it is like to attend cooking school.

> **Subjects**: Chefs, Culinary Institute of America, Culinary School, Personal Endeavor

> **Now Try**: Ruhlman continued his investigation, following with *The Soul of a Chef*, where he describes the exam one must take to become a Certified Master Chef. In *The Reach of a Chef*, he looks at the world of professional cooking since the rise of the celebrity chef, and how things have changed at the CIA since his attendance. Readers may also enjoy other accounts of culinary school such as Katherine Darling's account of culinary school in *Under the Table: Saucy Tales from Culinary School*, Kathleen Flinn's *The Sharper Your Knife the Less You Cry: Love, Laughter, and Tears at the World's Most Famous Cooking School*, or *Beaten, Seared, and Sauced: On Becoming a Chef at the Culinary Institute of America* by Jonathan Dixon. Readers who enjoyed Ruhlman's writing style may also enjoy his other title *House: A Memoir* of his experience trying to restore a neglected old house.

Schatzker, Mark

Steak: One Man's Search for the World's Tastiest Piece of Beef. New York: Viking, 2010. 290pp. ISBN 9780670021819.

Steak is the king of meat. Mark Schatzker fondly remembers the taste of a perfect steak he ate years ago, and wonders why so much steak today is simply mediocre. Why is it so hard to get a good steak? In search of the answer, Schatzker travels around the world investigating various methods of cattle production. In Texas he compares the difference between corn-fed and grass-fed cattle. He compares different cattle breeds in Scotland, France, and Italy. And in Japan he considers the famed kobe and Wagyu beef. Schatzker investigates what makes a steak taste good, the science behind good meat. He also explores modern cattle production versus more traditional methods.

> **Subjects:** Agriculture, Animal Welfare, Meat, Science, Travel

> **Now Try:** Readers who are interested in a more detailed history of the beef industry in America should try Betty Fussell's *Raising Steaks: The Life and Times of American Beef* or Jeremy Rifkin's *Beyond Beef: The Rise and Fall of the Cattle Culture*. In *The Shameless Carnivore: A Manifesto for Meat Lovers*, Scott Gold chronicles his attempt to consume 31 different meats in 31 days. Readers may also want to check out *The River Cottage Meat Book* by Hugh Fearnley-Whittings, which was a James Beard Cookbook of the Year. Readers

who enjoyed Schatzker's search for the perfect steak may also appreciate Kate Hopkins's search for the perfect whiskey in *99 Drams of Whiskey: The Accidental Hedonist's Quest for the Perfect Shot and the History of the Drink*.

Singer, Peter

The Way We Eat: Why Our Food Choices Matter. Emmaus: Rodale, 2006. 328pp. ISBN 9781579548896.

Singer asks the provoking question: what is the true cost of the food we eat? Singer explores the impact that food has on people, animals, and the environment. He follows three families to trace the origins of their food and examine the issues associated with each. The families represent three common diets: the standard American diet high in low-cost meat, dairy, and refined carbs; the conscientious omnivores who choose humane and free-range products; and the vegan diet. Singer is a member of the animal liberation movement, so this is clearly a biased account, however, his use of the individual families makes for a personalized and interesting account.

Subjects: Animal Welfare, Environmental Issues, Ethics, Food Industry, Health Issues, Nutrition

Now Try: In *The Omnivore's Dilemma: A Natural History of Four Meals* Michael Pollan also explores common American diets and their costs on society and health. Jonathan Safran Foer explores the ethical issues of eating meat in *Eating Animals*. Anna Lappé investigates the environmental costs of the meat industry in *Diet for a Hot Planet: The Climate Crisis at the End of Your Fork and What You Can Do About It*. Raj Patel details how the current world food system has created obesity in some parts of the world while there is starvation in others in *Stuffed and Starved: The Hidden Battle for the World Food System*. Singer, a philosopher and animal rights activist, has written a number of other books. Readers may want to start with his groundbreaking 1975 title, *Animal Liberation*. He has also written *Animal Factories* and *In Defense of Animals*. He has written on other subjects as well, including *The Life You Can Save: Acting Now to End World Poverty* and *One World: The Ethics of Globalization*.

Spurlock, Morgan

Don't Eat This Book: Fast Food and the Supersizing of America. New York: G. P. Putnam's Sons, 2005. 306pp. ISBN 9780399152603.

In 2003, Spurlock spent a 30-day period eating only fast-food from McDonald's to see how it would affect his health and weight. His experiment was documented in the Academy Award nominated documentary *Super Size Me*. In this entertaining book, Spurlock expounds on his experiment and the fast-food industry's relationship to the obesity epidemic in this country. The rise of the fast-food industry and the economic conditions that created demand for cheaper food and larger portions are chronicled. He also examines the industry's marketing efforts, especially towards children and the government lobbies that protect their interests. Spurlock's conversational tone and personal experiences make this an engaging and quick read.

> **Subjects:** Diet, Fast-Food, Food Industry, Health Issues, Humor, Junk Food, McDonald's, Obesity

> **Now Try:** Eric Schlosser's *Fast Food Nation: The Dark Side of the All-American Meal* is another shocking expose of the fast-food industry. Other titles that explore how the food industry has played a role in the rise of obesity and diet-related illnesses may also be of interest. Try *Food Fight: The Inside Story of The Food Industry, America's Obesity Crisis,* and *What We Can Do About It* by Kelly Brownell, *Appetite for Profit: How the Food Industry Undermines Our Health and How to Fight Back* by Michele Simon, or Greg Critser's *Fat Land: How Americans Became the Fattest People in the World.* Readers may be interested in watching Spurlock's documentary, *Super Size Me.* Readers who enjoy Spurlock's humorous, conversational style may also enjoy his other title, *Where in the World is Osama Bin Laden?* in which he investigates terrorism and religious fundamentalism. Spurlock's documentary series *30 Days* may also be appealing. In this series, Spurlock spent 30 days living with a different culture or different lifestyle or working a specific job. Some of his experiences include working as a coal miner, living with illegal immigrants, a Muslim family, a Christian family, and spending 30 days in prison.

Steinberger, Michael

Au Revoir to All That: Food, Wine, and the End of France. New York: Bloomsbury, 2009. 243pp. ISBN 9781596913530.

France was once the capital of great cuisine. Lately, however, the most influential chefs and best restaurants in the world are no longer found in France. France has seen a decline in sales of its wines and cheeses, as well as the disappearance of many bistros. Steinberger finds that he has experienced increasingly disappointing meals while in France, and so decides to journey through France to determine the cause of the decline in French cuisine. In this amusing and engaging investigation, Steinberger talks with famous chefs, winemakers, bakers, and other food artisans. He interviews the head of McDonald's Europe to discuss the rise in popularity of McDonald's. Steinberger also discovers new, innovative chefs and artisans who are working to put France back at the top of great cuisine. This insightful journey presents an interesting perspective on France's changing culture and its cuisine.

> **Subjects:** France, French Cuisine, French Culture, McDonald's, Travel, Wine

> **Now Try:** *Corkscrewed: Adventures in the New French Wine Country* by Robert Camuto investigates the new generation of French winemakers. *A Goose in Toulouse: And Other Culinary Adventures in France* by Mort Rosenblum covers the culinary specialties that France is famous for and the changes in France's culinary culture. Peter Mayle's *French Lessons: Adventures with Knife, Fork, and Corkscrew* is a humorous culinary tour of France. David Sax explores the disappearing state of the delicatessen in America in

Save the Deli: In Search of Perfect Pastrami, Crusty Rye, and the Heart of the Jewish Delicatessen.

Striffler, Steve

Chicken: The Dangerous Transformation of America's Favorite Food. New Haven: Yale University Press, 2005. 195pp. ISBN 9780300095296.

Striffler draws on his own experiences working in a poultry processing plant to explore the issues surrounding the current poultry industry. The history of chicken consumption in American and the development of the modern poultry industry after World War II is presented in vivid detail. The poultry industry's growing dependence on immigrant labor has caused an influx of immigrants in areas with poultry factories and has altered the ethnic makeup of Middle America. In addition, chickens have been physically changed by the poultry industry to provide a cheap source of protein and have earned an unwarranted healthy image. Striffler's personal experiences provide a vivid and detailed account of the inner workings of a poultry plant and its animal and human rights abuses.

Subjects: Animal Welfare, Food Industry, Immigrants, Labor, Poultry, Quick Reads, Working Conditions

Now Try: Readers who enjoyed the inside view of working in the poultry industry may also enjoy Gabriel Thompson's account of working in various food industries in *Working in the Shadows: A Year of Doing the Jobs [Most] Americans Won't Do.* David Kirby's *Animal Factory: The Looming Threat of Industrial Pig, Dairy, and Poultry Farms to Humans and the Environment* exposes the negative effects of the factory farming industry. Richard Longworth explores the Rust Belt, factory farming jobs, and how immigration is affecting the region in *Caught in the Middle: America's Heartland in the Age of Globalism.* Readers also may find Upton Sinclair's classic novel *The Jungle* appealing, which exposed the ethical and health issues created by the Chicago stockyards.

Sutherland, Amy

Cookoff: Recipe Fever in America. New York: Viking, 2003. 333pp. ISBN 9780670032518.

Sutherland spends a year following the competitive cooking circuit. While the Pillsbury Bake-Off is the most coveted award, there are hundreds of other competitions throughout the country. Traveling across the country, Sutherland investigates both large and small competitions, including the National Chicken and Nation Beef Cook-Offs, National Cornbread, and Great Garlic and meets veteran participants as well as amateurs. Sutherland also examines the rules of competition, the fierce competitiveness of the contestants, and squabbles that often break out. Interesting characters and the unique competitions make this an engrossing read.

Subjects: Cooking Competitions, Recipes, Travel, Year in the Life

Now Try: Sutherland also spent a year following the students of Moorpark College's Exotic Animal Training and Management Program, which she chronicles in *Kicked, Bitten, and Scratched: Life and Lessons at the World's Premier School for Exotic Animal Trainers*. She recounts the rigorous demands of the programs and the competitiveness of the participants. William Brohaugh's *The Grill of Victory: Hot Competition on the Barbecue Circuit* also provides a behind-the-scenes glimpse of competitive cooking and the contestants. Readers may also enjoy Jane and Michael Stern's *Two for the Road* or Calvin Trillin's *Feeding a Yen*, where the authors travel across the country sampling local foods and meeting interesting characters.

Thompson, Gabriel

Working in the Shadows: A Year of Doing the Jobs [Most] Americans Won't Do. New York: Nation Books, 2010. 298pp. ISBN 9781568584089.

In response to the claim that immigrants are taking American jobs, Thompson attempts some of the jobs that are known for employing large numbers of immigrants, which are all linked to food. First in Yuma, Arizona, Thompson takes a job cutting lettuce in the fields. In Alabama, he works in a chicken processing plant, and in New York City, he works at a restaurant delivering food. Although Thompson is primarily interested in what it is like to do these jobs, and why they are mostly filled by immigrants; his account also provides interesting details of jobs in the food industry.

Subjects: Animal Processing Plants, Farming, Immigrants, Labor, Restaurants, Working Conditions

Now Try: Tracie McMillan worked in various jobs in the food industry to understand how Americans eat in *The American Way of Eating: Undercover at Walmart, Applebee's, Farm Fields and the Dinner Table*. Barbara Ehrenreich's *Nickel and Dimed: On (Not) Getting By in America* is another example of immersion journalism where she takes on jobs most Americans won't do. Barry Estabrook's *Tomatoland* looks at the tomato industry and the life of its workers. Pete Jordan travels the country washing dishes in *Dishwasher: One Man's Quest to Wash Dishes in All Fifty States*. John Bowe exposes modern slave labor in *Nobodies: Modern American Slave Labor and the Dark Side of the New Global Economy*. Gary Rivlin investigates the poverty businesses that get rich by taking advantage of the working poor in *Broke, USA: From Pawnshops to Poverty, Inc: How the Working Poor Became Big Business*. Thompson has also written about the lives of immigrants in *There's No Jose Here: Following the Hidden Lives of Mexican Immigrants*. Readers may want to consider T. C. Boyle's *The Tortilla Curtain*, which portrays the difficult lives of illegal immigrants.

Wilson, Jason

Boozehound: On the Trail of the Rare, the Obscure, and the Overrated in Spirits. Berkeley: Ten Speed Press, 2010. 232pp. ISBN 9781580082884.

The spirits columnist for the *Washington Post*, Wilson purports that cocktails are traditional American foodways. Before Prohibition, bartending was a craft that was appreciated. But Prohibition broke the cultural chain of bartending knowledge and caused many spirits to go out of style. Wilson believes that many spirits that disappeared during Prohibition are being rediscovered by many Americans and attempts to raise awareness and appreciation for lesser-known spirits. Wilson provides the history of many classic cocktails, such as the martini, and how and why recipes have changed over the years. He travels throughout the world sampling various spirits, explaining how they are made, and their history. Along with his fascinating account of both classic and rare spirits, he includes recipes and humorous drinking stories, and rails against popular drinking trends, such as the flavored vodkas.

Subjects: American History, Cocktails, Journalism, Prohibition, Spirits, Travel

Now Try: David Wondrich's *Imbibe!* chronicles the life of Jerry Thomas, father of the American bar and the history of classic American drinks. William Grimes offers a history of American cocktails in *Straight Up or On the Rocks*. Readers interested in other histories and explorations of spirits may want to try Max Watman's *Chasing the White Dog: An Amateur Outlaw's Adventures in Moonshine* or Kat Hopkins's *99 Drams of Whiskey: The Accidental Hedonist's Quest for the Perfect Shot and the History of the Drink*. Readers may also enjoy Kingsley Amis's *Everyday Drinking*, a collection of humorous essays on drinking. Peter Krass chronicles the history of one of America's most legendary moonshiners in *Blood and Whiskey: The Life and Times of Jack Daniel*.

Food Exposés

Food Exposés are compelling to readers because they tend to be more sensational and shocking. These titles often focus on a subject about which the public knows little. Eric Schlosser's *Fast Food Nation* is one of the most well-known titles of Food Exposés; bringing to light the negative aspects of the fast-food industry. The author is usually biased or has an agenda, and attempts to persuade the reader. Authors of Exposés do conduct research and interviews and present facts; however, they do not always present both sides of the story. These titles are dramatic, shocking, and often more conversational than In-Depth Food Reporting.

> Food Exposés bring to light food issues about which the public knows little. The author is usually biased and may often only cover one side of the issue. These titles are dramatic and shocking, contain factual data, and are more conversational in tone.

Bittman, Mark

Food Matters: A Guide to Conscious Eating With More Than 75 Recipes. New York: Simon & Schuster, 2008. 336pp. ISBN 9781416575641.

The main message Bittman attempts to make is that Americans eat too much meat and refined carbohydrates, which has a negative impact on our health and weight. Bittman explains how the industrialization of food production has led to overconsumption. He proposes that Americans reduce the amount of meat they currently eat, eliminate junk food, eat fewer refined carbohydrates, and eat more vegetables, fruits, and grains. Although there are many other titles that touch on this topic, this book is a good introduction to the issues. The simple recipes that are included also add interest.

> **Subjects:** Food Industry, Health Issues, Nutrition, Recipes
>
> **Now Try:** Bittman has created a lengthier cookbook to accompany this title, *The Food Matters Cookbook: 500 Revolutionary Recipes for Better Living*. Readers may also be interested in his classic cookbooks, *How to Cook Everything* and *How to Cook Everything Vegetarian*. Readers interested in delving deeper in this subject may want to look at Michael Pollan's *In Defense of Food: An Eater's Manifesto*. Marion Nestle also addresses responsible food choices in *What to Eat*. Nina Planck makes a case for eating real foods and condemns processed foods in *Real Food: What to Eat and Why*. Fans of Bittman might also want to watch DVDs of his travel series *Spain: On the Road Again*, also featuring Mario Batali.

Blanding, Michael

The Coke Machine: The Dirty Truth behind the World's Favorite Soft Drink. New York: Avery, 2010. 375pp. ISBN 9781583334065.

Coca-Cola is one of the most profitable companies in the world and one of the most widely recognized products. In this shocking and gripping exposé, Blanding details the history of the company and examines the accusations about Coca-Cola's global impact. Coca-Cola is accused of decimating water supplies in villages in India and Mexico, busting up unions in Turkey and Guatemala, creating obesity in America, murdering union organizers in Columbia, and ignoring international health, labor, and environmental standards. For a company that has long projected an image of wholesomeness and harmony, this is a fascinating exposé.

> **Subjects:** Business, Coca-Cola Company, Health Issues, Labor, Soft Drink Industry
>
> **Now Try:** Other histories of Coca-Cola may also be appealing, such as *For God, Country, and Coca-Cola: The Definitive History of the Great American Soft Drink and the Company That Makes It* by Mark Pendergrast or Constance Hays's *The Real Thing: Truth and Power at the Coca-Cola Company*. Mark Thomas travelled the world investigating the marketing practices, environmental and labor issues, and production of Coca-Cola in *Belching Out the Devil: Global Adventures with Coca-Cola*. John Barlow's novel *Intoxicated* is a humorous spoof of the soft drink industry. In Max Barry's humorous novel *Syrup*, a young marketing graduate pitches an idea for a new cola to Coca-Cola. Readers may

also find other investigations of the beverage industry appealing, such as Elizabeth Royte's *Bottlemania: How Water Went on Sale and Why We Bought It*, Dean Cycon's *Javatrekker: Dispatches From the World of Fair Trade Coffee*, and Taylor Clark's *Starbucked: A Double Tall Tale of Caffeine, Commerce, and Culture*.

Charles, Daniel

Lords of the Harvest: Biotech, Big Money and the Future of Food. Cambridge: Perseus, 2001. 348pp. ISBN 9780738202914.

Genetic engineering of crops is a highly controversial topic but it is also a big business that is changing the face of modern agriculture. Proponents of these designer crops claim great benefits, including hardier and more productive crops and healthier foods, but opponents question the true effects on health and the dangers to the environment. In this detailed and unbiased investigation, Charles traces the history of genetic engineering in plants, focusing on key players such as Monsanto, the American chemical giant. He also details the controversy between biotechnology and consumer advocacy, and illuminates how genetically modified organisms (GMOs)have become a highly political, profit-driven business.

Subjects: Agriculture, Business, Food Industry, Genetically Modified Organisms

Now Try: *Dinner at the New Gene Café: How Genetic Engineering is Changing What We Eat, How We Live, and the Global Politics of Food* by Bill Lambrecht and *Eating in the Dark: America's Experiment with Genetically Engineered Food* by Kathleen Hart are also thorough investigations of GMOs. Peter Pringle's *Food, Inc.: Mendel to Monsanto—the Promises and Perils of the Biotech Harvest* examines the revolution of GMOs and how it will affect the world food supply. Marie-Monique Robin lists Monsanto as one of the world's greatest polluters in *The World According to Monsanto: Pollution, Corruption, and the Control of the World's Food Supply*. There is a documentary by the same title as well. Titles that promote the necessity for sustainable rather than corporate agriculture may also be appealing. Try Wes Jackson's *Consulting the Genius of the Place: An Ecological Approach to a New Agriculture* or Wendell Berry's *Bringing It to the Table: On Farming and Food*.

Deville, Nancy

Death by Supermarket: The Fattening, Dumbing Down, and Poisoning of America. Fort Lee, NJ: Barricade Books, 2007. 339pp. ISBN 9781569803325.

Deville argues that the typical American diet of processed foods is the major cause of the obesity epidemic and is also responsible for a number of degenerative diseases. The industrialization of food production changed the way Americans eat; giving us unlimited access to fast-food, frozen dinners, and processed sweets. The introduction of trans fats,

HFCS, monosodium glutamate (MSG), and aspartame has led to a country addicted to unhealthy fat and sugar. Deville explains MSG, HFCS, and aspartame—what they are, how they are made, and how they affect our bodies. The government agencies that should be protecting Americans from harmful factory foods have been bought by industry lobbyists. She illustrates how the Food and Drug Administration's (FDA) approval of MSG and aspartame were influenced by drug companies and huge corporations like Monsanto. Although Deville provides a wealth of information, the chapters are short, making this a quick read.

Subjects: Diet, Food Industry, Health Issues, Monsanto, Processed Foods, Quick Reads, Science

Now Try: Deville also touches on the food industry's push to get Americans to accept soy as a healthy alternative. She references Kaayla Daniel's book, *The Whole Soy Story*. Titles about America's addiction to sugar and the safety of sugar substitutes may be suggested. Try *Sugar Nation* by Jeff O'Connell or *Sweet Deception* by Joseph Mercola and the documentary by the same title. Other titles about the food industry and its effects on America's health may be of interest, such as *Stuffed* by Hank Cardello, *Fat Politics* by J. Eric Oliver, and *The World is Fat* by Barry Popkin. *Twinkie, Deconstructed: My Journey to Discover How the Ingredients Found in Processed Foods Are Grown, Mined (Yes, Mined), and Manipulated into What America Eats* by Steve Ettlinger is an in-depth investigation of the ingredients found in America's most famous processed food.

Estabrook, Barry

Tomatoland: How Modern Industrial Agriculture Destroyed Our Most Alluring Fruit. Kansas City: Andrews McMeel Publishing, 2011. 220pp. ISBN 9781449401092. The tomato is the second most popular vegetable in this country (behind lettuce) and the tomato industry is a $5 billion business. The tomatoes we find in the grocery store are always a bright, shiny red and perfectly shaped. But they don't actually taste very good. Tomatoes are bred for hardiness, picked while still green and firm, and artificially gassed with ethylene until they turn red. Estabrook asks why modern industrial agriculture can't seem to deliver a decent tasting tomato. He begins his investigation in Peru, the birthplace of the tomato and moves to Florida, which accounts for one-third of the fresh tomatoes grown in this country. What he finds is an environment not ideally suited to grow tomatoes, a crop that requires hundreds of pesticides, and workers that suffer from ailments due to exposure to these chemicals and are kept in a state of near slavery. Visiting laboratories, large commercial farms, and small-scale farmers, Estabrook presents insight into commercial farming and a thought-provoking argument as to what tomatoes should and can taste like.

Subjects: Industrial Agriculture, Health Issues, Tomatoes, Working Conditions

Now Try: Arthur Allen's *Ripe: The Search for the Perfect Tomato* may also be of interest. Thomas Pawlick investigates the changes that have occurred to our fruits and vegetables as a result of industrialized agriculture in *The End of Food: How the Food Industry is*

Destroying Our Food Supply—And What We Can Do About It. Gabrielle Thompson investigates working conditions in other food industry jobs in *Working in the Shadows*. Dan Koeppel investigates the current state of the banana in *Banana: The Fate of the Fruit That Changed the World*. A wide variety of other food Micro-histories, found in the History chapter of this volume, might also appeal to these readers.

Ettlinger, Steve

Twinkie, Deconstructed: My Journey to Discover How the Ingredients Found in Processed Foods Are Grown, Mined (Yes, Mined), and Manipulated Into What America Eats. New York: Hudson Street Press, 2007. 304pp. ISBN 9781594630187.

Twinkies contain many of the most common ingredients found in processed foods, such as high fructose corn syrup and Polysorbate 60. Although most of us have seen these terms before, most of us have no idea what they are or where they come from. Ettlinger sets out to demystify the ingredients of this popular snack. Each chapter focuses on a specific ingredient, how it is made and where it comes from. Although it is heavy on the details, this work is a fascinating account of these commonly used ingredients and how they became part of our diets.

> **Subjects:** Food Additives, Food Industry, Food Production, Processed Foods

> **Now Try:** Readers interested in learning more about the ingredients in processed foods may enjoy *What Are You Really Eating: How to Become Label Savy* by Amanda Ursell, *Eating Between the Lines* by Kimberly Lord Stewart, or *Sweet Deception: Why Splenda, NutraSweet, and the FDA May Be Hazardous to Your Health* by Joseph Mercola. Readers that enjoy the details of how the ingredients are produced may enjoy many of the titles about food science such as *Food Bites: The Science of the Foods We Eat* by Richard W. Hartel. Thomas Thwaites undertook a similarly eye-opening task in his science memoir *The Toaster Project: Or a Heroic Attempt to Build a Simple Electric Appliance from Scratch*.

Foer, Jonathan Safran

Eating Animals. New York: Little, Brown and Co., 2010. 341pp. ISBN 9780316069908.

Known best for his novels, author Foer delves into investigative journalism in this work, describing where our meat comes from, how it is produced, how the animals are treated, and the economical, social, and environmental effects of eating meat. Interspersed with the factual information, Foer also includes family stories and anecdotes, as well as philosophical explorations of the ethics of eating meat.

> **Subjects**: Agriculture, Animals, Animal Welfare, Factory Farms, Meat, Vegetarianism

Now Try: *Why We Love Dogs, Eat Pigs, and Wear Cows: An Introduction to Carnism* by Melanie Joy explores why humans love some animals but are willing to eat others, and describes the inhumane treatment of slaughter animals. Jeffrey Moussaieff Masson presents his arguments for eliminating meat from our diets in *The Face On Your Plate: The Truth About Food*. Nicole Hahn Niman, wife of one of the nation's most famous sustainable ranchers, details the issues of industrialized meat farming and advocates for humane and sustainable farming in *Righteous Porkchop: Finding a Life and Good Food Beyond Factory Farms*. David Kirby exposes the practices of factory farms in *Animal Factory: The Looming Threat of Industrial Pig, Dairy, and Poultry Farms to Humans and the Environment*. Readers may also be interested in Foer's documentary exposing the inhumane practices found at the largest kosher slaughterhouse, *If This is Kosher*. . . . Foer has also written two popular fiction novels, *Everything is Illuminated* and *Extremely Loud and Incredibly Close*.

Fussell, Betty

Raising Steaks: The Life and Times of American Beef. Orlando: Harcourt, 2008. 402pp. ISBN 9780151012022.

Fussell traces the history of the beef industry in America from the 17th century to today. Visiting ranches and feedlots across the country, she meets the ranchers and cowboys who raise the cattle for our beef. She visits a slaughterhouse and interviews Temple Grandin, who has played a big role in the creation of more humane slaughtering methods. The buffalo, beef's current competitor, is also considered. Fussell voices the concerns over the immensity of today's beef industry and examines the collision of individualism of the ranchers with corporate technology in order to turn cattle into meat for America.

Subjects: Beef, Farmers, Food Industry, Grandin, Temple, Meat

Now Try: *Beef: The Untold Story of How Milk, Meat, and Muscle Shaped the World* by Andrew Rimas and *Beyond Beef* by Jeremy Rifkin both explore the history of the beef industry and the issues faced by the current industry. In Mark Schatzker's interesting investigation, *Steak: One Man's Search for the World's Tastiest Piece of Beef*, he attempts to find out why it is so difficult to find a truly great steak today. M. R. Montgomery traces the evolution of domesticated cattle in *A Cow's Life: The Surprising History of Cattle, and How the Black Angus Came to Be Home on the Range*. In Scott Gold's *Shameless Carnivore: A Manifesto for Meat Lovers*, the author attempts to consume 31 meats in 31 days. Readers may also be interested in *The Butcher's Guide to Well-Raised Meat: How to Buy, Cut, and Cook Great Beef, Lamb, Pork, Poultry, and More* by Joshua and Jessica Applestone of Fleisher's butcher shop (featured in Julie Powell's memoir, Cleaving). Fussell has also written *The Story of Corn*.

Katz, Sandor Ellix

The Revolution Will Not Be Microwaved: Inside America's Underground Food Movements. Vermont: Chelsea Green Publishing, 2006. 378pp. ISBN 9781933392110.

Real foods, as opposed to processed food products, are becoming increasingly illegal. Laws dictating food standards, driven by industrialized agriculture, have made foods like raw milk, illegal. Katz profiles some of the local underground food movements that are refusing to bend to these laws, such as local bread makers, raw milk and raw meat enthusiasts, guerilla gardeners, seed savers, foragers, and freegans. Katz includes numerous resources for the reader, including books, films, organizations, and websites.

Subjects: Activism, Food Habits, Food Movements, Food Supply, Foraging, Industrial Agriculture, Local Food, Meat, Raw Food, Slow Food

Now Try: Readers may want to consider one of the other titles referenced in Katz's book, such as *Tangled Routes: Women, Work, and Globalization on the Tomato Trail* by Deborah Barndt. Gary Paul Nabhan advocates local food in *Coming Home To Eat: The Pleasures and Politics of Local Food*. Readers may enjoy *Everything I Want to Do is Illegal* by Joel Salatin, a well-known food rebel. Euell Gibbons was a leader in food foraging. Try his book *Stalking the Wild Asparagus*. Readers may want to consider books about people who are part of the underground food movements such as Mark Winne's *Food Rebels, Guerrilla Gardeners, and Smart-Cookin' Mamas: Fighting Back in an Age of Industrial Agriculture*, Temra Costa's *Farmer Jane: Women Changing The Way We Eat* and Jennifer Cockrall-King's *Food and the City: Urban Agriculture and the New Food Revolution*.

Kirby, David

Animal Factory: The Looming Threat of Industrial Pig, Dairy and Poultry Farms to Humans and the Environment. New York: St. Martin's Press, 2010. 492pp. ISBN 9780312380588.

In this thoroughly researched account, Kirby examines the ill effects of Concentrated Animal Feeding Operations (CAFOs), more commonly known as factory farms. Kirby explains how CAFOs operate and illustrates the enormous amount of animal waste that is produced. He documents how CAFOs have been responsible for health crises such as swine and bird flues, recalls on grocery products due to *E. coli* contaminations, and negative impacts to the surrounding land, air, and water. Personalizing the message, three individuals who fought back against CAFOs are profiled: a North Carolina fisherman whose river was being destroyed by a local hog farm; an Illinois woman fighting a local dairy farm, and a Washington woman fighting a nearby cattle farm that was fouling the air and water. This book will be of interest not only to readers concerned with environmental impact of CAFOs, but also to those who enjoy stories of people who fight big businesses.

Subjects: Environmental Issues, Factory Farms, Health Issues, Meat

Now Try: Anna Lappé explores the environmental impact of CAFOs in *Diet for a Hot Planet: The Climate Crisis at the End of Your Fork and What You Can Do about It*. Michael Pollan investigates the industrial food chain in *The Omnivore's Dilemma: A Natural History of Four Meals*. Readers who enjoy stories of people fighting back against the destructive practices of large corporations may enjoy Gillian Klucas's story of the residents of Leadville, Colorado who fought back against the destructive mining companies in *Leadville: The Struggle To Revive An American Town* or *A Civil Action* by Jonathan Harr. Kirby has also written *Evidence of Harm: Mercury in Vaccines and the Autism Epidemic.*

Knecht, G. Bruce

Hooked: Pirates, Poaching, and the Perfect Fish. Emmaus: Rodale, 2006. 278pp. ISBN 9781594861109.

When the Patagonian Toothfish was discovered and renamed "Chilean Sea Bass," it quickly became the latest culinary craze and was fished almost to the point of extinction. Although efforts have been made to protect the fish, the lucrative demand for the fish has prompted piracy and illegal fishing. In this fast-paced, absorbing account, Knecht details the commercial history of the toothfish, while interweaving the story of a dangerous chase in the South Indian Ocean to catch a pirate vessel that is illegally hunting toothfish.

Subject: Fishing, Piracy

Now Try: Sebastian Junger's *The Perfect Storm: A True Story of Men Against the Sea* offers another gripping high seas account of the dangerous job of fishing for Swordfish. Kieran Mulvaney's *The Whaling Season* and Peter Heller's *The Whale Warriors* both offer passionate accounts of the attempts to end commercial whaling. Other titles that look at the poaching of wildlife may also be appealing, such as Craig Welch's *Shell Games: Rogues, Smugglers, and the Hunt for Nature's Bounty* and Richard Ellis's *Tiger Bone & Rhino Horn: The Destruction of Wildlife for Traditional Chinese Medicine*. Mark Kurlansky provides a history of cod and how it has been fished almost to the point of extinction in *Cod: A Biography of the Fish That Changed the World*. Paul Greenberg examines the current state and future of the four main commercial fish: cod, tuna, salmon, and sea bass in *Four Fish: The Future of the Last Wild Food*.

Lappé, Anna

Diet for a Hot Planet: The Climate Crisis at the End of Your Fork and What You Can Do About It. New York: Bloomsbury, 2010. 313pp. ISBN 9781596916593.

While many other writers have focused on how horrible factory farming is for the animals as well as for people and how it has created a system of cheap food and an obese population with health issues, Lappé takes a different look at the effect of the food industry. Filled with statistics, studies, and details, she posits that industrialized food, especially factory farming, has a direct link to global warming and the climate. She visits various farmers all over the world who are using environmentally friendly farming techniques. Although heavy on the statistics, it offers a fresh take on the negative effects of industrialized food.

Subjects: Agriculture, Environmental Issues, Factory Farms, Farming, Food Industry, Global Warming

Now Try: Anna's mother, Frances Moore Lappé, wrote the revolutionary book, *Diet for a Small Planet*, in 1971, which challenged the meat industry and proposed that a vegetarian diet could not only be healthy, but could also ease world hunger. Christopher D. Cook's *Diet for a Dead Planet: Big Business and the Coming Food Crisis* also accuses factory farms of damaging the environment. Other environmental titles may also be appealing, such as Rachel Carson's classic title, *Silent Spring*, Tim Flannery's *The Weather Makers: How Man is Changing the Climate and What it Means for Life on Earth*, and Bill McKibben's *Eaarth: A Survivor's Guide*. Lappé has also written a cookbook, *Grub: Ideas for an Urban Organic Kitchen*.

Layman, Howard

Mad Cowboy: Plain Truth from the Cattle Rancher Who Won't Eat Meat. New York: Scribner, 1998. 223pp. ISBN 9780684845166.

In 1996, Howard Layman appeared on the Oprah Winfrey show on a program about Mad Cow disease. Having been a cattle rancher, he shared insights into the cattle industry and his belief that America was not safe from Mad Cow disease. Both Lyman and Winfrey were sued by a group of Texas cattlemen for food disparagement. Layman recounts the issues surrounding the lawsuit, as well as the reasons he chose to leave the cattle industry after 20 years and become a vegetarian. He laments the decline of the family farm, the environmental and health problems caused by current industry practices, and the difficulties he faced trying to return his farm to organic practices. While the writing is less polished than others in this genre, Layman's unique viewpoint and frank, and often humorous, writing style will appeal to readers.

> **Subjects:** Food Industry, Food Safety, Health Issues, Industrialized Agriculture, Meat, Winfrey, Oprah

> **Now Try:** Layman follows up this title with *No More Bull: The Mad Cowboy Targets America's Worst Enemy: Our Diet*. Readers interested in learning more about Mad Cow disease may want to consider *How the Cows Turned Mad: Unlocking the Mysteries of Mad Cow Disease* by Maxime Schwartz, *Mad Cow U.S.A.* by Sheldon Rampton and John Stauber, and *Brain Trust: The Hidden Connection Between Mad Cow and Misdiagnosed Alzheimer's Disease* by Colm Kelleher. Histories of the beef industry may also be good suggestions. Try Jeremy Rifkin's *Beyond Beef: The Rise and Fall of the Cattle Culture* or M. R. Montgomery's *A Cow's Life: The Surprising History of Cattle, and How the Black Angus Came to Be Home on the Range*. Upton Sinclair's classic novel *The Jungle* was the first to expose the ills of the meat packing industry.

McWilliams, James E.

Just Food: Where Locavores Get it Wrong and How We Can Truly Eat Responsibly. New York: Little, Brown and Company, 2009. 258pp. ISBN 9780316033749.

A locavore is the term used to describe a person who eats foods that have been grown or produced locally, or within a certain radius. This has become a popular movement, prompting a rise in local farmers' markets and many newly released cookbooks promote using locally grown foods. McWilliams argues, however, that the locavore approach has limitations and is not a viable answer to sustainable food production on a global level. Believing that food miles are insignificant in the grand scheme of food production, McWilliams argues that consumers should look at the overall cost of producing food, such as energy use and sustainability. He also challenges conventional views of organic foods and genetically modified foods. While McWilliams did anger a number of foodies with this book, he does state that he is not against the locavore movement, but believes that proponents should look at the bigger picture. McWilliams tackles this controversial topic with an abundance of factual evidence and scientific data, without coming off as judgmental or high-handed.

Subjects: Food Industry, Genetically Modified Organisms, Local Food, Locavore

Now Try: In *The Town that Food Saved: How One Community Found Vitality in Local Food*, Ben Hewitt examines some of the issues raised by creating a local food system, such as how many of the locals can't afford to buy these local food products, which are then shipped out to bigger cities. Wendell Berry also advocates for sustainable agriculture in *Bringing it to the Table: On Farming and Food*. Michael Pollan examines the major food chains in America, including sustainable agriculture and local foraging in *The Omnivore's Dilemma: A Natural History of Four Meals*. Readers may find personal memoirs of an individual's attempt to eat locally, such as Barbara Kingsolver's *Animal, Vegetable, Miracle: A Year of Food Life*, Spring Warren's *The Quarter-Acre Farm: How I Kept the Patio, Lost the Lawn, and Fed My Family for a Year*, Gary Paul Nabhan's *Coming Home to Eat: The Pleasures and Politics of Local Foods*, and *Plenty: Eating Locally on the 100-Mile Diet* by Alisa Smith and J. B. Mackinnon.

Menzel, Peter, and Faith D'Aluisio

Hungry Planet: What the World Eats. Napa, CA: Material World, 2005. 287pp. ISBN 9781580086813.

The authors of this photo journal visited 30 families in 24 countries in order to explore the differences in the way people eat. Each family was photographed with a display of all the foods they eat in an entire week. This book is a compilation of these photographs, as well as brief descriptions of each family's daily life. The photographs clearly reflect that although the world produces enough food for everyone, its distribution is anything but equal. The photos also reveal the striking differences in the consumption of processed foods between countries.

Subjects: Food Habits, Photo Essays, Travel

Awards: James Beard Award

Now Try: Menzel has also depicted the differences in diets around the world in *What I Eat: Around the World in 80 Diets*. Readers who enjoyed the striking diversity of the photographs may also enjoy Menzel's other photo essay with Sandra Eisert, *Material World: A Global Family Portrait*. Erik Millstone's *The Atlas of Food: Who Eats What, Where,* *and Why* will appeal to readers interested in the distribution of the world's food. *The Foodlover's Atlas of the World* by Martha Rose Schulman will appeal to readers who enjoy reading about international culinary traditions.

Mueller, Tom

Extra Virginity: The Sublime and Scandalous World of Olive Oil. New York: W. W. Norton & Co., 2012. 238pp. ISBN 9780393070217.

The use of oil is an ancient tradition, going back to Christ, Mohammed, and the Egyptian pharaohs. Today, olive oil is a popular cooking oil, touted for its health benefits, and there are hundreds of olive oils on supermarket shelves. But as with any valued commodity, fraud is an ever-present threat. Inspectors have been checking for fraudulent practices in olive growers and millers as far back as 24 BC. Most of the olive oils that grace the supermarket shelves today are adulterated in some way; not fit for eating, according to many olive growers. The laws dictating what can be labeled as extra virgin olive oil are never enforced, leading to a widespread practice of selling inferior, tainted oils, or oil that has been cut with cheaper oils. Mueller begins his investigation by traveling to Italy to meet olive growers and learns how it is produced and what makes the oil extra virgin. He also participates in a taste test to recognize the differences among the varieties of olive oils and consults with scientists to understand the properties of olive oil. His investigation continues as he travels to Spain, North Africa, the West Bank, Crete, California, Chile, and South Africa, meeting producers, studying the history of olive oil cultivation and its use in sacred rituals, investigating the health benefits, and examining the effects of globalization on small producers. Mueller's engaging investigation and vivid writing will appeal to fans of investigative writing, travel writing, history, and business.

Subjects: Business, Fraud, History, Italy, Olives, Olive Oil, Travel

Now Try: Mort Rosenblum bought a neglected olive farm in Provence in *Olives*. Carol Drinkwater shares her experience buying an olive farm in Provence in *The Olive Farm: A Memoir of Life, Love, and Olive Oil in the South of France*. In *Extra Virgin: A Young Woman Discovers the Italian Riviera, Where Every Month Is Enchanted*, Annie Hawes and her sister move to the Italian coast to escape the dreariness of England and find themselves in a town of olive growers. Other stories of food fraud may be of interest, such as Benjamin Wallace's *The Billionaire's Vinegar*.

Nestle, Marion

Food Politics: How the Food Industry Influences Nutrition and Health. Berkeley: University of California Press, 2002. 457pp. ISBN 9780520224650.

Nestle, a professor of nutrition and food studies, exposes the great lengths the food industry goes to influence what we eat. Concerned with protecting its economic interests, the food industry makes financial contributions and lobbies Congress and government agencies for favorable laws, discourages government regulation, and influences the USDA's dietary guidelines. Health experts are often hired to support the nutritional claims made by the food industry and discredit nutritional recommendations that might threaten sales. The food industry also spends a lot of money marketing their products, especially to children. Although Nestle includes an abundance of facts, she deftly explains difficult concepts and presents an informative and shocking expose.

Subjects: Food Industry, Food Policy, Health Issues, Nutrition, Politics

Awards: James Beard Award

Now Try: Readers will also want to check out Nestle's expose of the pet food industry in *Pet Food Politics: The Chihuahua in the Coal Mine*, as well as *Food Safety: The Politics of Food Safety*. Michele Simon investigates the food industry's role in shaping nutrition policies in America in *Appetite for Profit: How the Food Industry Undermines Our Health and How to Fight Back*. David Kessler explains how food corporations have conditioned people to overeat in *The End of Overeating: Controlling the Insatiable American Appetite*.

Parsons, Russ

How to Pick a Peach: The Search for Flavor From Farm to Table. Boston: Houghton Mifflin, 2007. 412pp. ISBN 9780618463480.

Parsons champions the case for eating locally and seasonally. Today, fruits and vegetables are grown on a mass scale and shipped all over the world, all year long. But produce that is trucked or flown in from far away locations lose their freshness. Parsons explains how the food industry has designed fruits and vegetables that are disease-free, slow to spoil, sturdier, and better suited for shipping. Although this allows us to have any fruit or vegetable year round, the quality and taste of the produce is sacrificed. Parsons advocates for eating produce only when it is in season and from sources as local as possible. He outlines when fruits and vegetables are in season, how to choose the ripest one, and the simplest way of preparing it.

Subjects: Food Industry, Genetically Modified Organisms, Industrial Agriculture, Plant Breeding, Produce

Now Try: Thomas Pawlick's experience with a tasteless tomato in his local grocery chain prompted him to investigate the decline of quality and taste in produce that is shipped long distances in *The End of Food: How the Food Industry is Destroying Our Food Supply—and What We Can Do About It*. In *Ripe: The Search for the Perfect Tomato*, Arthur Allen traces the journey of the typical tomato from field to table and explains why many are lacking flavor. Barry Eastabrook investigates the tasteless supermarket tomato in *Tomatoland: How Modern Industrial Agriculture Destroyed Our Most Alluring Fruit*.

Pawlick, Thomas

The End of Food: How the Food Industry is Destroying Our Food Supply—and What We Can Do About It. Fort Lee: Barricade Books, 2006. 256pp. ISBN 9781569803028.

When Pawlick purchased a tomato from his local chain grocery store, he got a hard, tasteless, unripe vegetable and wondered what had happened to the fresh, flavorful vegetables he remembered as a child. After conducting some research, he found that in order to maximize profit, the industrial food system created produce that will withstand pests, transport, and lengthy shelf life. As a result, not only has there been a decline in flavor, but the nutritional, vitamin, and mineral contents in produce have declined and contaminants are increasing. Pawlick also examines the impact the industrial food system has had on the environment, as well as its role in the decline of small family farms. The easy-to-read writing style and well-researched investigation make this an appealing read.

> **Subjects:** Environmental Issues, Farming, Food Industry, Genetically Modified Organisms, Industrial Agriculture, Tomatoes
>
> **Now Try:** Paul Roberts's *The End of Food* also examines the negative effects that large scale food production has on food. Barry Estabrook's *Tomatoland* is another investigation of the tomato industry. Russ Parsons investigates the decline of mass produced fruits and vegetables in *How to Pick a Peach: The Search for Flavor From Farm to Table*. Jill Richardson advocates for sustainable agriculture in *Recipe for America: Why Our Food System is Broken and What We Can Do to Fix It*. Pawlick has also written *The War in the Country: How the Fight to Save Rural Life Will Shape Our Future* about the battle between Big Ag and small, local farms.

Pence, Gregory

Designer Food: Mutant Harvest or Bread Basket for the World? Lanham: Rowman & Littlefield Publishers, Inc., 2002. 233pp. ISBN 9780742508392.

The use of GMOs remains a controversial topic. Gregory Pence is a proponent for the use of GMOs and believes that opponents have deceived the public with inaccurate information. In this scholarly examination, Pence debunks many of the myths surrounding both organic foods and GMOs as well as many of the fears of GMOs. He traces the history and politics of GMOs and explores other issues such as ethics and safety.

> **Subjects:** Food Industry, Food Safety, Genetically Modified Organisms, Globalization, Organic Foods, Scholarly
>
> **Now Try:** Kathleen Hart also explores the controversy of genetically modified foods (GMFs) in *Eating in the Dark: America's Experiment with Genetically Engineered Food*. Nina Fedoroff and Nancy Marie Brown also advocate for the use of GMFs. In their accessible book *Mendel in the Kitchen: A Scientist's*

View of Genetically Modified Foods, they explain genetics and genetic engineering and the low risk of consuming modified foods. *Tomorrow's Table: Organic Farming, Genetics, and the Future of Food* by Pamela C. Ronald and Raoul W. Adamchak makes a case for the use of GMFs in organic farming. Peter Pringle addresses the controversies of GMFs in *Food, Inc.: Mendel to Monsanto: The Promises and Perils of the Biotech Harvest*.

Schlosser, Eric

Fast Food Nation: The Dark Side of the All-American Meal. Boston: Houghton Mifflin Company, 2001. 356pp. ISBN 9780395977897.

In this benchmark title, Schlosser exposes the destructiveness of the fast-food industry. Schlosser argues that fast-food has widened the chasm between the rich and the poor, fueled obesity, and caused the homogenization of our landscape. He traces the changes in society that led to the infiltration of fast-food and its impact on American lives. He also explains how the industry exploits youths and minorities and illustrates the effects of mass production on quality and safety. Schlosser's description of how the food is made and why it tastes so good is a shocking revelation.

Subjects: Business, Fast-food Industry, Food Industry, Health Issues

Awards: ALA Notable Book

Now Try: Schlosser's follow-up, *Chew On This* provides much of the same information found in *Fast Food Nation*, however the personal stories of people whose lives have been affected by fast-food are quite illuminating. Morgan Spurlock's personal experiment of consuming fast-food in *Don't Eat This Book: Fast Food and the Supersizing of America* will also appeal to fans of Schlosser's easy-to-read style. In *The American Way of Eating: Undercover at Walmart, Applebee's, Farm Fields and the Dinner Table*, Tracie McMillan shares her experiences working at various jobs in the food industry. *The Meat You Eat: How Corporate Farming Has Endangered America's Food Supply* by Ken Midkiff details the deplorable conditions of factory farms and slaughterhouses. Schlosser has also written *Reefer Madness: Sex, Drugs, and Cheap Labor in the American Black Market*, an expose of the illegal drug market.

Schonwald, Josh

The Taste of Tomorrow: Dispatches From the Future of Food. New York: Harper Collins, 2012. 294pp. ISBN 9780061804212.

What will the typical meal look like in the year 2035? Schonwald travels the world meeting with scientists, farmers, food engineers, and chefs in an attempt to answer this question. His quest begins with salad greens, as he looks for the next big salad ingredient. The future of meat will include the next salmon, rabbit, emu, and even meat that is grown in labs. The author concludes that our future foods will have to be more environmentally friendly, which leads him to consider the benefits of GMOs. A former opponent, the author's investigation leads him to change his mind, as he discovers that GMOs can provide healthier and more environmentally friendly foods.

> **Subjects:** Aquaculture, Environmental Issues, Farming, Food Science, GMOs, Meat

> **Now Try:** Readers may want to try some of the titles mentioned in Schonwald's book, such as *Tomorrow's Table* by Pamela Roland, *The Botany of Desire* by Michael Pollan, *Seeds of Deception* by Jeffrey Smith, and *Food Fray* by Lisa Weasel. Like Schonwald, James McWilliams challenges the conventional views of GMOs in *Just Food: Where Locavores Get it Wrong and How We Can Truly Eat Responsibly.* Gregory Pence also makes a case for GMOs in *Designer Food: Mutant Harvest or Bread Basket for the World?* Readers may be interested in other titles that project life in the future, such as *Physics of the Future: How Science Will Shape Human Destiny and Our Daily Lives by the Year 2100* by Michio Kaku or George Friedman's *The Next 100 Years.*

Smith, Jeffrey M.

Seeds of Deception: Exposing Industry and Government Lies About the Safety of the Genetically Engineered Foods You're Eating. Fairfield: Yes! Books, 2003. 289pp. ISBN 9780972966580.

> Smith tackles the controversial topic of GMOs, presenting the opposing case. The dark side of GMOs is exposed, including stolen and suppressed evidence, omitted data, bribes, threats, and grotesque results. Smith illuminates the industry manipulation and political collusion that occurs. Although this is clearly a biased account of GMOs, Smith presents a captivating and disturbing picture of this controversial subject.

> **Subject:** Food Industry, Genetically Modified Organisms, Politics

> **Now Try:** There are several other books that address this controversial issue. Try Peter Pringle's *Food, Inc.: Mendel to Monsanto—The Promises and Perils of the Biotech Harvest*, Bill Lambrecht's *Dinner at the New Gene Café: How Genetic Engineering is Changing What We Eat, How We Live, and the Global Politics of Food*, Marie-Monique Robin's *The World According to Monsanto: Pollution, Corruption, and the Control of the World's Food Supply*, and Lisa Weasel's *Food Fray: Inside the Controversy Over Genetically Modified Food.* Readers looking for a basic introduction to genetic science may want to check out *The Wonder of Genetics: The Creepy, the Curious, and the Commonplace* by Richard V. Kowles.

Stuart, Tristram

Waste: Uncovering the Global Food Scandal. New York: W. W. Norton & Co., 2009. 451pp. ISBN 9780393068368.

> Stuart argues that hunger exists in the world because so much food is wasted. He examines the enormous levels of food waste created by affluent countries, such as the United States and Western Europe, from the farmers, to the grocery stores and consumers. The factors that cause

food to be wasted in countries where poverty and hunger is rampant, such as Pakistan, are considered. Stuart suggests solutions for the reader, such as reducing the amount of food one buys, not sticking to the strict and overly cautious expiration dates, and composting. One of Stuart's personal solutions was to become a freegan which is someone who essentially dumpster dives for food. His adventures in reclaiming discarded foods are not only entertaining but also eye-opening.

Subjects: Climate, Food Industry, Poverty, Waste

Awards: IACP Award

Now Try: Jonathan Bloom also explores the issue of waste in *American Wasteland: How America Throws Away Nearly Half of Its Food (and What We Can Do About It)*. In *Garbage Land: On the Secret Trail of Trash*, Elizabeth Royte spends the year analyzing her own trash and visiting landfills and recycling centers to trace the lasting effect of our waste. Royte's examination of the bottled water industry and its effects on the environment may also be appealing: *Bottlemania: How Water Went on Sale and Why We Bought It*. *The Story of Stuff: How Our Obsession With Stuff is Trashing the Planet, Our Communities, and Our Health* by Annie Leonard tracks the journeys of everyday items once we are through with them. Stuart has also written a history of vegetarianism, *The Bloodless Revolution: A Cultural History of Vegetarianism: From 1600 to Modern Times*.

Wallace, Benjamin

The Billionaire's Vinegar: The Mystery of the World's Most Expensive Bottle of Wine. New York: Crown Publishers, 2008. 319pp. ISBN 9780307338778.

In 1985, a new record was set for the most expensive bottle of wine ever sold at auction. A 1787 Chateau Lafite that was said to have been owned by Thomas Jefferson was bought for $156,000. From the very beginning, the authenticity of the bottle was questioned. Its owner was a secretive German wine collector, who balked at providing the details of its discovery. Although Christie's examined the bottle and determined it to be authentic, speculation continued. Wallace traces the controversy surrounding the famous bottle, as well as the investigation into its authenticity. This will appeal to fans interested in the history of wine in America, as well as fans of true crime stories of forgeries.

Subjects: Christie's Auction House, Forgeries, History, Jefferson, Thomas, True Crime, Wine, Wine Collecting

Now Try: "Wine Scams" in *The Best Food Writing 2009* is a fascinating essay about creating fake wine. *Swindled: The Dark History of Food Fraud, from Poisoned Candy to Counterfeit Coffee* by Bee Wilson is a history adulterated foods in the 19th century. *Extra Virginity: The Sublime and Scandalous World of Olive Oil* by Tom Mueller is another exposé of corrupted food. Readers interested in the historical details of Thomas Jefferson may want to consider *The Founding Foodies: How Washington, Jefferson, and Franklin Revolutionized American Cuisine* by Dave DeWitt. Other titles about fakes and forgeries may also be appealing, such as *Fakes & Forgeries: The True Crime Stories of History's Greatest Deceptions: The Criminals, the Scams, and the Victims* by Brian Innes, *Provenance: How a*

Con Man and a Forger Rewrote the History of Modern Art by Laney Salisbury and Aly Sujo, *Catch Me If You Can* by Frank Abagnale, or *Flawless: Inside the Largest Diamond Heist in History* by Scott Andrew Selby and Greg Campbell.

Waltner-Toews, David

Food, Sex and Salmonella: Why Our Food is Making Us Sick. Berkeley: Greystone Books, 2008. 248pp. ISBN 9781553652717.

Every year over one billion people get sick due to infections transmitted through food and water. Waltner-Toews argues that our insatiable appetites for exotic and out-of-season foods places demands on our food supplies that creates a host of natural and man-made toxins. In this shocking expose the author examines food-borne illnesses caused by bacteria, viruses, and parasites, as well as the chemicals that have entered the food supply and the effects they can have on our health and the environment. He explains how common food-borne illnesses such as salmonella, *E. coli*, and botulism get into food.

Subjects: Food Industry, Food Safety, Food-borne Illnesses, Health Issues

Now Try: Ben Hewitt's *Making Supper Safe: One Man's Quest to Learn the Truth about Food Safety* also examines the issue of food-borne illnesses. Readers will also find shocking evidence in Marion Nestle's *Safe Food: The Politics of Food Safety*. Robert Morris's *The Blue Death: The Intriguing Past and Present Danger of the Water You Drink* traces the history of cholera and examines the current safety issues with our water supply systems. *Poisoned: The True Story of the Deadly E. Coli Outbreak That Changed the Way Americans Eat* by Jeff Benedict describes a deadly outbreak of *E. coli* in 1993. *Death in the Pot: The Impact of Food Poisoning on History* by Morton Satin is a fascinating account of food poisonings throughout history.

Weber, Karl, ed.

Food Inc.: A Participant Guide: How Industrial Food is Making Us Sicker, Fatter, and Poorer-And What You Can Do About It. New York: PublicAffairs, 2009. 321pp. ISBN 9781586486945.

Based on the documentary film of the same name, this collection of short essays exposes the dirty secrets of the food industry. Written by food writers, farmers, and various relevant watchdog organizations, each essay focuses on an individual issue such as organic foods, health and humane issues of factory farms, GMFs, pesticides, global warming, worker exploitation, and world hunger. This is a good selection for the reader who is not looking for in-depth information, but just a broad overview of all the issues.

Subjects: Animal Welfare, Environmental Issues, Food Industry, Genetically Modified Organisms, Health Issues, Laborers, Organic Foods

Now Try: Readers may also want to view the companion documentary, *Food, Inc.* Because this collection covers a wide variety of topics, there are several other titles that may appeal to readers: *Animal Factory: The Looming Threat of Industrial Pig, Dairy, and Poultry Farms to Humans and the Environment* by David Kirby; *Working in the Shadows: A Year of Doing the Jobs (Most) Americans Won't Do* by Gabriel Thompson; and *Diet for a Hot Planet: The Climate Crisis at the End of Your Fork and What You Can Do About It* by Anna Lappé.

Winne, Mark

Closing the Food Gap: Resetting the Table in the Land of Plenty. Boston: Beacon Press, 2008. 199pp. ISBN 9780807047309.

Despite the abundance of food in America, food insecurity is common and there is an ever-widening gap in the food system. Most impoverished families don't have enough money to buy a sufficient supply of nutritious foods. Less affluent areas tend to have too few choices of healthy, affordable food and are oversaturated with unhealthy food options. These food deserts tend to have higher obesity rates. Winne traces the history of the widening food gap since the 1960s and the development of food affluence and gastronomical expectations. Food activists are making attempts at narrowing the gap, including creating community gardens, inner-city farmers' markets, food banks, and youth-run urban farms. Winne's account of his personal experiences working toward closing the food gap add a personal, informal touch to the writing.

Subjects: Community Gardens, Farmers Markets, Food Deserts, Hunger, Poverty

Now Try: Other titles that examine poverty and hunger in America are Sasha Abramsky's *Breadline USA: The Hidden Scandal of American Hunger* and *All You Can Eat: How Hungry Is America* by Joel Berg. Raj Patel examines the situations that have created a global imbalance in food that has created an epidemic of obesity while some starve in *Stuffed and Starved: The Hidden Battle for the World Food System.* Readers may also be interested in Winne's other title *Food Rebels, Guerrilla Gardeners, and Smart-Cookin' Mamas: Fighting Back in an Age of Industrial Agriculture.*

Consider Starting With . . .

These titles are considered benchmarks of Investigative Food Writing and are a good place to start for those new to the genre.

Almond, Steve. *Candyfreak: A Journey Through the Chocolate Underbelly of America.*

Lappé Frances Moore. *Diet for a Small Planet.*

Pollan, Michael. *The Omnivore's Dilemma: A History of Four Meals.*

Schlosser, Eric. *Fast Food Nation: The Dark Side of the All-American Meal.*

Weber, Karl. *Food Inc.: A Participant Guide: How Industrial Food is Making Us Sicker, Fatter, and Poorer—And What You Can Do About It.*

References

Bachelder, Chris. 2006. "The Jungle at 100: Why the Reputation of Upton Sinclair's Good Book Has Gone Bad." *Mother Jones* (January/February), 71.

Cords, Sarah Statz. 2006. *The Real Story: A Guide to Nonfiction Reading Interests*. Westport: Libraries Unlimited.

Cords, Sarah Statz. 2009. *The Inside Scoop: A Guide to Nonfiction Investigative Writing and Exposes*. Westport: Libraries Unlimited.

1

2

3

4

5

6

7

8

9

Chapter 8

Narrative Cookbooks

Definition of Narrative Cookbooks

A cookbook is essentially an instruction manual for the preparation of food (Haber 2003). Often it contains a collection of recipes, with instructions on cooking techniques, and information on ingredients. The earliest collection of recipes found dates back to the first century. Cookbooks have always been popular sellers. Favorite Recipes Press states that the cookbook market has sustained a 5 percent growth rate annually since 1984 (www.favoriterecipespress.com 2010). Even in the recent difficult economic times, when sales of adult nonfiction have been down, cookbook sales were up 4 percent in the first part of 2009 (Keeler 2009).

Why do cookbooks remain so popular despite the vast number of cooking websites available on the Internet? One food book editor said, "You can Google chicken and asparagus and get a thousand recipes. But in a cookbook, the author tells you why he likes the recipe and how it works" (Daley 2010). Many cookbooks have traditionally been straightforward collections of recipes and instructions. But Favorite Recipes Press states that cookbooks have become more than just a collection of recipes. Many cookbooks now include vivid photography, interesting sidebar information, and stories that engage the reader (www.favoriterecipespress.com 2010). And many cookbooks are leaving the kitchen and finding their way to the coffee table. Neal Wyatt refers to this type of cookbook as a Narrative Cookbook, describing them as part memoir, part food history, part essay, and part cookbook (Wyatt 2007). The main focus of the Narrative Cookbook is the recipes, but there will be the added element of a lengthier narrative and a stronger feel for the author's voice.

With the wide use of the Internet and the thousands of recipes that are available online, one wonders whether the desire for cookbooks may fade. Holly Hughes, editor of the *Best Food Writing* series, says that recipe websites are missing something: gorgeous photographs, colorful writing, meticulously tested recipes, and a write-up that gives some history and context to the recipe (Hughes 2010).

Narrative Cookbooks are a collection of recipes that also include a lengthier narrative. These titles have a strong feel for the author's voice, engaging stories, and are visually appealing.

Appeal of Narrative Cookbooks

Many readers will want to try the recipes in narrative cookbooks, but narrative cookbooks can also function like armchair travel books. Readers who may not be interested in attempting recipes may still enjoy reading about the author's experiences cooking. Because the author's voice is prevalent throughout, readers for whom character is an appeal factor may enjoy narrative cookbooks. Story is also another major element of narrative cookbooks. The story is not as detailed or in-depth as food literature in other genres, but the theme of the story runs throughout the collection of recipes. The type of story can vary greatly, however. Some authors may tell a personal story, such as a romance or meeting their spouse. Some may tell the history of a region. And some may just be a collection of the author's experiences with food or cooking. Narrative Cookbooks are also visually appealing, including vivid photography.

Because Narrative Cookbooks have such a wide appeal, there are a number of other titles that may appeal to readers who enjoy Narrative Cookbooks. Those who enjoy the brief passages in these titles may also enjoy Food Essays. Readers who enjoy the sense of place captured in some Narrative Cookbooks may also enjoy Food Travel Lit. Food Memoirs may be appealing to readers who enjoy the personal stories found in Narrative Cookbooks.

Ahern, Shauna James, and Ahern, Daniel

Gluten-Free Girl and the Chef. Hoboken: John Wiley, 2010. 288pp. ISBN 9780470419717.

When Shauna James Ahern was diagnosed with celiac disease, she began blogging about living with the disease and learning to find foods she could enjoy. She also met and married a chef. Together they began experimenting with cooking and finding delicious foods that were safe for Shauna to eat. This vivid narrative cookbook intersperses the story of their romance and marriage with a wide variety of gluten-free recipes created by Daniel Ahern. Readers will enjoy the bright photographs, tempting recipes, and endearing love story.

Subjects: Celiac Disease, Marriage, Recipes, Relationships

Now Try: Ahern continues her blog at glutenfreegirl.com. Her memoir *Gluten-Free Girl: How I Found the Food That Loves Me Back . . . And How You Can Too* recounts how she discovered her disease, explains Celiac disease, and how she learned to live with it. Erin McKenna, owner of the famous New York bakery BabyCakes, a gluten-free bakery, creates favorite recipes that are gluten-free in *BabyCakes Covers the Classics: Gluten-Free*

Vegan Recipes from Donuts to Snickerdoodles. Karen Morgan, owner of the famous Blackbird Bakery and author of the blog The Art of Gluten Free Baking, presents *Blackbird Bakery Gluten-Free: 75 Recipes for Irresistible Gluten-Free Desserts and Pastries*.

Alford, Jeffrey, and Duguid, Naomi

Beyond the Great Wall: Recipes and Travels in the Other China. New York: Artisan, 2008. 376pp. ISBN 9781579653019.

Three-fifths of China is made up of people who historically are not ethnically Chinese. Within China lie what were distinct countries and regions, including Tibet, Inner Mongolia, Yunnan, and Guizhou. As a result, there are a number of Tibetan, Mongol, Tuvan, and Kirghiz peoples whose food and culture are often overlooked when people consider China. As a result of the economic changes currently occurring in China, the cultural survival of the foods and culture of these societies have been impacted. The authors explore the foods of these regions, as well as the land, history, and its peoples. Vivid photographs of the land and the people are stunning, as are the simple recipes.

Awards: IACP Award, James Beard Award

Subjects: China, Multicultural Issues, Recipes, Travel

Now Try: *Hot Sour Salty Sweet: A Culinary Journey Through Southeast Asia* and *Mangoes & Curry Leaves: Culinary Travels Through the Great Subcontinent* are other narrative cookbooks by Alford and Duguid. Readers may enjoy other cookbooks featuring Chinese cooking such as Fuchsia Dunlop's *Land of Plenty: A Treasury of Authentic Sichuan Cooking* or *Revolutionary Chinese Cookbook: Recipes from Hunan Province*, or *Mastering the Art of Chinese Cooking* by Eileen Yin-Fei Lo. Jen Lin-Liu travels and cooks her way through China in *Serve the People: A Stir-Fried Journey Through China*. Peter Hessler's books about travel and China may also be of interest. Try *Oracle Bones: A Journey Through Time in China* or *River Town: Two Years on the Yangtze*.

Colwin, Laurie

Home Cooking: A Writer in the Kitchen. New York: Vintage Books, 1988. 193pp. ISBN 9780307474414.

Colwin, a novelist, weaves together her thoughts and memories of food and cooking with simple, comforting recipes. Colwin recalls cooking in her small apartment, ponders eating dinner alone, contemplates how to cook for fussy eaters, and describes English food she experienced on a trip abroad. Lighthearted and humorous, the joy Colwin takes from food is evident in this quick, touching read.

Subjects: Quick Reads, Recipes

Now Try: Colwin followed this title with *More Home Cooking: A Writer Returns to the Kitchen*. Colwin also wrote several fiction novels including *Happy All* *the Time* and *The Lone Pilgrim. Roast Chicken and Other Stories* by Simon Hopkinson is another charming Narrative Cookbook with simple recipes. Michael Lee West's *Consuming Passions: A Food-Obsessed Life* is a charming collection of Southern home cooking, stories, and advice. *In the Kitchen with A Good Appetite: 150 Recipes and Stories About the Food You Love* by Melissa Clark has a similar conversational style and lighthearted tone.

Dabney, Joseph E.

Smokehouse Ham, Spoon Bread and Scuppernog Wine: The Folklore and Art of Southern Appalachian Cooking. Nashville: Cumberland House, 1998. 493pp. ISBN 9781888952933.

This engaging narrative cookbook combines Appalachian recipes with a fascinating history of the area and the people. Dabney describes the life of Appalachia's first settlers, the folklore and superstitions, and the importance of food and how it was prepared. Traditional Appalachian foods are described, such as cornbread, biscuits, wild boar, opossum, raccoon, moonshine, and sassafrass tea. Dabney's history of this region, vibrant language, photographs, firsthand accounts, and authentic recipes will appeal to readers who enjoy history and cultural explorations.

Subjects: Appalachia, History, Recipes

Now Try: Dabney turns his attention to the Southern Lowcountry in *The Food, Folklore, and Art of Lowcountry Cooking: A Celebration of the Foods, History, and Romance Handed Down from England, Africa, the Caribbean, France, Germany, and Scotland.* In the late 1960s, Eliot Wigginton created the magazine *Foxfire* in an effort to record the traditional culture of the Southern Appalachians. Those magazines have been compiled into a series that covers everything from hog dressing to midwifery. Start with the first in the series, *The Foxfire Book: Hog Dressing, Log Cabin Building, Mountain Crafts and Foods, Planting by the Signs, Snake Lore, Hunting Tales, Faith Healing, Moonshining.* Joan E. Aller's *Cider Beans, Wild Greens, and Dandelion Jelly: Recipes from Southern Appalachia* is another wonderful narrative cookbook that combines traditional Appalachian recipes with a history of the region and people and beautiful photographs.

Drummond, Ree

The Pioneer Woman Cooks: Recipes from an Accidental Country Girl. New York: William Morrow, 2009. 247pp. ISBN 9780061658198.

Drummond had left her life in Oklahoma for the big city. But passing through her old hometown she met and unexpectedly fell in love with a cowboy. Leaving her city life behind, she married the cowboy and moved to his ranch. In this narrative cookbook, Drummond describes her life on the ranch, her husband and her children, and how she learned to cook hearty meals for hungry cowboys. Drummond combines easy recipes, simple instructions, colorful photographs (which display almost a step-by-step illustrated guide to her recipes), and a cheerful tone.

Subjects: Family, Marriage, Ranching, Relationships, Recipes

Now Try: Drummond's new memoir, *The Pioneer Woman: Black Heels to Tractor Wheels*, details the story of her romance and her move from the city to the farm. Drummond also maintains her blog, The Pioneer Woman Cooks at thepioneerwoman.com. Kristin Kimball left her city life to move to a farm when she fell in love with a farmer. Readers may enjoy her memoir, *The Dirty Life: A Memoir of Farming, Food, and Love*. Readers may also enjoy Barbara Kingsolver's account of the year she and her family spent growing their own food in *Animal, Vegetable, Miracle: A Year of Food Life*.

Foose, Martha Hall

Screen Doors and Sweet Tea: Recipes and Tales from a Southern Cook. New York: Clarkson Potter/Publishers, 2008. 248pp. ISBN 9780307351401.

Foose brings the South to life with stories about life in the South and the people, places, and events that inspired her collection of recipes. Winner of the 2009 James Beard Award for American Cooking, this book will appeal not only to cooks, but also to readers who appreciate a strong sense of place and charming stories.

Subjects: American South, Recipes

Awards: James Beard Award

Now Try: Foose follows up with another narrative cookbook, *A Southerly Course: Recipes and Stories from Close to Home*. John T. Edge chronicles the restaurants, food, and people of the South in *Southern Belly*. James Villas was a well-known food writer who grew up in the South. Try his cookbook, *The Glory of Southern Cooking*. Edna Lewis was an African American chef, best known for her books on traditional Southern cuisine. Try her cookbook, *The Taste of Country Cooking*. Paula Deen's *Southern Cooking Bible* is a cookbook by another famous Southern cook. *Bon Appetit, Y'all: Recipes and Stories from Three Generations of Southern Cooking* by Virginia Willis is another cookbook filled with Southern charm. Readers may also enjoy the writings of Southern humorist Celia Rivenbark. Try *Bless Your Heart, Tramp: And Other Southern Endearments*.

Hesser, Amanda

The Cook and the Gardener: A Year of Recipes and Writings for the French Countryside. New York: W.W. Norton, 1999. 632pp. ISBN 9780393046687.

Hesser, a food writer for the *New York Times*, spent a year cooking at a chateau in France. The garden, which provides a bounty of food that Hesser uses in her cooking, is cared for by a crusty, surly, old Frenchman. Hesser provides a month-by-month account of her time in France, highlighting the garden's produce and the recipes she created, along with stories of her attempt at befriending the gardener. Beautifully descriptive, this narrative cookbook will appeal to readers who enjoy a strong sense of place.

Subjects: France, Gardening, Recipes, Relationships

Awards: IACP Award

Now Try: Hesser also wrote a memoir of falling in love, *Cooking for Mr. Latte: A Food Lover's Courtship, with Recipes.* Richard Goodman recounts keeping a vegetable garden in a small French village in *French Dirt: The Story of a Garden in the South of France.* Georgeanne Brennan describes life and food in Provence in *A Pig in Provence: Good Food and Simple Pleasures in the South of France.* Didi Emmons chronicles a year in a garden in *Wild Flavors: One Chef's Transformative Year Cooking from Eva's Farm.* Novelist Joanne Harris (known for her best-selling novel, *Chocolat*) shares her collection of family recipes that have been passed down in *My French Kitchen: A Book of 120 Treasured Recipes.*

Nathan, Joan

Quiches, Kugels, and Couscous: My Search for Jewish Cooking in France. New York: Alfred A. Knopf, 2010. 387pp. ISBN 9780307267597.

Nathan combines a well-researched history of the Jews in France and an entertaining journey through the kitchens and markets of France, to create a rich narrative cookbook illustrating the Jewish influence on French cuisine, as well as the French influence on Jewish cuisine. Visiting Paris, Alsace, and the Loire Valley, Nathan collects a wide array of dishes, which she provides the history and details the influence of local culture. Many of the dishes she finds bear the influence of Alsatian, Provecal, Moroccan, Algerian, and Eastern European cuisines. Along the way, she meets colorful locals and incorporates their stories into her narrative.

Subjects: Food Habits, France, French Cuisine, History, Jewish Cuisine, Recipes, Travel

Now Try: Nathan won James Beard Awards and IACP Awards for her cookbooks *Jewish Cooking in America* and *New American Cooking. Aromas of Aleppo* by Poopa Dweck is a vivid narrative cookbook that includes a social and culinary history of Syrian Jews. *The Bialy Eaters* by Mimi Sheraton traces the history of this Jewish bread. *97 Orchard: An Edible History of Five Immigrant Families in One New York Tenement* by Jane Ziegelman is a compelling history of the influence of immigrant cultures, including Jewish, on American cuisine.

Nguyen, Pauline, and Nguyen, Luke

Secrets of the Red Lantern: Stories and Recipes from the Heart. Kansas City: Andrews McMeel Publishing, 2008. 344pp. ISBN 9780740777431.

The authors of this vivid narrative cookbook escaped Vietnam shortly after the Vietnam War and spent a year in a Thai refugee camp. After that, they moved to Australia, where they opened a Vietnamese restaurant, the Red Lantern. Their parents were trained chefs and restaurant life was home to them. The Red Lantern served as a link to their home and helped assuage their homesickness. The family's history and immigration are recounted along with the success of the Red Lantern restaurant. Traditional Vietnamese recipes and explanations of Vietnamese food are included, along with family photos and striking photos of food.

Subjects: Family Relationships, Immigrants, Recipes, Vietnam War, Vietnamese Cuisine

Now Try: Luke Nguyen has also written *My Vietnam: Stories and Recipes*. Kim Fay's *Communion: A Culinary Journey Through Vietnam* is a wonderful narrative cookbook of her travels in Vietnam. *The Seventh Daughter: My Culinary Journey from Beijing to San Francisco* by Cecilia Chiang is another narrative cookbook about an immigrant who opened a restaurant in her new country.

Roden, Claudia

Arabesque: A Taste of Morocco, Turkey, and Lebanon. New York: Knopf, 2006. 341pp. ISBN 9780307264985.

Morocco, Turkey, and Lebanon are part of the Mediterranean culinary culture that has been influenced by the Islamic world, Moorish Spain, and the Ottoman Empire. The flavorful, unique cuisines of these countries are immensely popular; however, the traditional cooking methods are inconvenient for modern cooks. Roden introduces readers to the history of these cuisines, the regional dishes, and the various traditions surrounding meals and eating. The classic recipes are updated for the modern cook.

Subjects: Lebanon, Morocco, Recipes, Travel, Turkey

Now Try: Roden has also written *The Food of Spain*. Greg Malouf presents a vivid narrative cookbook in *Turquoise: A Chef's Travels in Turkey*. Readers may want to consider Expatriate titles such as Suzanna Clarke's *A House in Fez: Building a Life in the Ancient Heart of Morocco* or Tahir Shah's *The Caliph's House: A Year in Casablanca*.

Shopsin, Kenny, and Carreno, Carolynn

Eat Me: The Food and Philosophy of Kenny Shopsin. New York : Alfred A. Knopf, 2008. 260pp. ISBN 9780307264930.

Kenny Shopsin is the owner of Shopsin's restaurant in New York City, which has become a neighborhood institution. But Shopsin runs his restaurant a little differently than most others. There are rules you must follow when you eat here, and if you don't, you'll be asked to leave. You might also be asked to leave if Shopsin thinks you won't fit in with his customers. Shopsin explains his philosophy in this entertaining narrative cookbook. He recounts how he began his business, first as a neighborhood grocer, then as a restaurant, and shares stories of his children growing up in the store and then coming to work for him. His customers and the relationships he has forged over the years are a source of pride for him. Shopsin is not a trained chef, but enjoys cooking and creating his own unique recipes. An unconventional character, Shopsin's antics make for a humorous, entertaining read.

Subjects: Community Life, Family Relationships, Humor, New York City, Recipes, Restaurants

Now Try: Another cookbook from an unconventional restaurant is *Mission Street Food: Recipes and Ideas from an Improbable Restaurant* by Anthony Myint and Karen Leibowitz. *Everyone Comes to Elaine's* by A. E. Hotchner profiles another New York institution. Other unique family businesses are described in Ben Ryder Howe's *My Korean Deli: Risking It All for a Convenience Store* and Frances and Ginger Park's *Chocolate Chocolate: The True Story of Two Sisters, Tons of Treats, and the Little Shop that Could.*

Slater, Nigel

The Kitchen Diaries: A Year in the Kitchen with Nigel Slater. New York: Gotham Books, 2006. 392pp. ISBN 9781592402342.

For one year, Slater keeps a daily record of the dishes he creates for himself and his friends and family. Slater reflects on the seasonal aspect of food and details the foods that are in season at the time. Observations on the weather, as well as his daily life, lends to the feel of a true diary.

Subjects: Recipes, Seasonal Foods

Now Try: Slater has written a number of cookbooks as well as his memoir, *Toast: The Story of a Boy's Hunger*. His latest, *Tender: A Cook and His Vegetable Patch*, is a guide to growing and cooking vegetables. Chef David Tanis's cookbook *Heart of the Artichoke and Other Kitchen Journeys* has a similar conversational style and simple recipes. Readers may also enjoy Simon Hopkinson's *Roast Chicken and Other Stories*. Skye Gyngell reflects on the seasons in *A Year In My Kitchen*.

Thorne, John

Outlaw Cook. New York: Farrar Straus Giroux, 1992. 378pp. ISBN 9780374228385.

Thorne, the author of the well-known newsletter "Simple Cooking" combines articles from his newsletter, recipes, and narrative commentary. Thorne recalls the fresh, simple foods eaten during the summers of his childhood while on vacation, and how he learned the pleasure of food when he began cooking for himself as an adult. Espousing simple foods, he encourages cooks to experiment heavily, turning to recipes only as a guideline. Thorne's recipes are simple and traditional, and explore regional dishes, as well as the historical background of recipes.

Subjects: Memoir, Recipes

Now Try: Thorne has a number of other titles. In *Serious Pig: An American Cook in Search of His Roots* Thorne tracks down the origins of some of his favorite regional recipes. Also consider *Pot on the Fire: Further Exploits of a Renegade Cook* or *Mouth Wide Open: A Cook and His Appetite*. Readers may also enjoy Jason Epstein's short memoir, *Eating*, which also recounts early meals and discovering the pleasures of food. Elizabeth David's *An Omlette and a Glass of Wine* is a charming collection of recipes and contemplations of food.

Tilson, Jake

A Tale of 12 Kitchens: Family Cooking in Four Countries. New York: Artisan, 2006. 256pp. ISBN 9781579653200.

This vibrant narrative cookbook and scrapbook tells the story of the Tilson family's love for food and cooking. Tilson lovingly recalls his childhood home in the English countryside where the kitchen was the heart of the family and the garden provided fresh produce. He vividly describes summers in Italy, foraging for herbs and visiting markets, as well as other family travels where the sampling of local foods was the highlight. As an adult, Tilson continued his search for new and exciting foods in Paris and New York City. This unique cookbook includes recipes from all over the globe, as well as mementos, family photographs, and even labels from beloved food packages.

> **Subjects:** Family Relationships, Recipes, Travel

> **Now Try:** *The World is a Kitchen: Cooking Your Way Through Culture*, edited by Michele Anna Jordan and Susan Brady, illustrates cultures and cuisines around the world and includes a number of recipes. Readers may also enjoy titles about travel and food such as *Around the World in 80 Dinners: The Ultimate Culinary Adventure* by Bill Jamison and Cheryl Alters Jamison or *Two for the Road: Our Love Affair With American Food* by Jane and Michael Stern.

Wolf, Bonny

Talking with My Mouth Full: Crab Cakes, Bundt Cakes, and other Kitchen Stories. New York: St. Martin's Press, 2006. 255pp. ISBN 9780312353575.

Wolf, a commentator on National Public Radio, combines personal stories with her thoughts on food and cooking, as well as recipes and instruction. She reflects on regional foods, comfort foods, and food traditions, including toast, kugel, popovers, crab cakes, Jell-O, and even fair food. Basic recipes with simple how-to advice are included. The brief, lighthearted stories combined with simple, traditional recipes will appeal to readers who enjoy a light tone.

> **Subjects:** Food Traditions, Local Food, Recipes

> **Now Try:** Readers may also enjoy *All Cakes Considered* from NPR producer Melissa Gray. Other narrative cookbooks with a similar conversational style and lighthearted tone are *In the Kitchen with A Good Appetite: 150 Recipes and Stories About the Food You Love* by Melissa Clark and Laurie Colwin's *Home Cooking: A Writer in the Kitchen*. Readers may also enjoy Elizabeth David's reflections in An *Omlette and a Glass of Wine*.

Consider Starting With . . .

Fans of narrative cookbooks, as well as readers new to the genre, are likely to enjoy these popular narrative cookbooks.

Colwin, Laurie. *Home Cooking: A Writer in the Kitchen.*

Hesser, Amanda. *The Cook and the Gardener: A Year of Recipes and Writings for the French Countryside.*

Slater, Nigel. *The Kitchen Diaries: A Year in the Kitchen With Nigel Slater.*

References

Daley, Bill. 2010. "Cookbooks Are Still Something to Savor." (June 17). Available at www.philly.com (accessed June 29, 2010).

Favorite Recipes Press. 2010. Available at www.favoriterecipespress.com (accessed September 29).

Haber, Barbara. 2003. "Cookbooks." In *Encyclopedia of Food and Culture*, 452–56. New York: Charles Scribner's Sons.

Keeler, Janet K. 2009. "Bestselling Ingredients." *The St. Petersburg Times* (May 13): 1E.

Wyatt, Neal. 2007. *The Readers' Advisory Guide to Nonfiction*. Chicago: American Library Association.

Chapter 9

Food Essays

Definition of Food Essays

The word essay derives from the French essayer, meaning to try or to attempt (Merriam-Webster 2011). In the 16th century, the Frenchman Michel de Montaigne played a large role in the development of the essay as a literary genre. Before Montaigne, scholars used the term to describe formal philosophical works. Montaigne was the first to apply the term *essai* to short, informal writings in the style of everyday speech. He wanted to emphasize that his writing was an attempt to express his thoughts and experiences. Montaigne's essays were published in two volumes in 1580, titled *Essais*. Francis Bacon was the first to use the term essay in English to describe his works. He published his essays in 1597, 1612, and 1625. Ben Johnson first used the word essayist in English in 1609 (Grendler 2004).

An essay is a short piece of writing often written from the author's personal point of view. The essay has served as a vehicle for literary, social, and political criticism. Essays have also consisted of the author's observations on daily life and personal reflections. Aldous Huxley said that the essay was a device for saying almost everything about almost anything.

Food is a popular topic for essays. These essays are often published in food and travel magazines, as well as newspapers. Topics range from food and travel to current issues in food. Often essays from a particular publication or by a particular author are compiled into books. In this book, the annotations of Food Essays that focus on a particular subject are placed in that chapter. The Food Essays included in this chapter are compilations of various subjects. Readers who enjoy Food Essays may enjoy full-length works on a particular subject.

Food Essays are collections of short pieces of writing and are compilations of various topics from food and travel to food issues. These titles range from humorous to more serious, historical, or contemporary.

Appeal of Food Essays

Essays are appealing because they are quick reads. Readers may want something they can pick up and put down without having to be involved in a lengthy work. Readers' advisor Catherine Sheldrick Ross's research found that many nonfiction readers enjoy the aspect of "dipping in" to short pieces (Ross 2004). Readers who enjoy a variety of topics may also enjoy Food Essays, which can contain essays on particular restaurants, travels, cooking, and food issues. Readers who are new to Food Literature may want to begin with a collection of Food Essays. This allows them to explore different topics without committing to an entire book, and may lead them to other titles. Essays can be humorous or more serious, historical or contemporary, or a combination.

Bauer, Douglas

Death By Pad Thai: And Other Unforgettable Meals. New York: Three Rivers Press, 2006. 239pp. ISBN 9780307337849.

Bauer presents a collection of essays by well-known writers who describe their most memorable meal. Steve Almond describes his creation of a magnificent lobster pad thai, while Andre Dubus III longs for his birthday dinner with his family after his parents' divorce. For Amy Bloom, Richard Russo, Peter Mayle, Ann Packer, Diana Abu-Jaber, Aimee Bender, and Jane and Michael Stern, food is the center of these nostalgic, sometimes humorous, sometimes heart wrenching, tales.

Subjects: Humor, Recipes, Relationships, Restaurants, Writers

Now Try: *Food and Booze: A Tin House Literary Feast* edited by Michelle Wildgen includes a number of essays and recipes from food writers and novelists, including Steve Almond. Readers may also want to try some of the titles written by the authors featured here. Andre Dubus reflects on his difficult childhood in *Townie: A Memoir.* Aimee Bender's novel *The Particular Sadness of Lemon Cake* portrays a young girl who can taste the emotions of others in the foods they create. Diana Abu-Jaber's novel *Crescent* weaves the story of a love affair between a chef and a professor.

Berry, Wendell

Bringing It to the Table: On Farming and Food. Berkeley, CA: Counterpoint, 2009. 234pp. ISBN 9781582435435.

Wendell Berry is a famous American writer, cultural critic, activist, and farmer. A forefather of the Slow Food Movement, Berry was one of the first to point out the dangers of industrialized agriculture and the separation of food production from food preparation and consumption. This collection includes essays written by Berry between 1971 and 2006 on farming, farmers, and food. Berry presents his philosophy on the ideal farming practices that connect to the nature of the place. He considers the differences between small and large farms, advocating for farmers who are in touch with their land and animals and practice responsible husbandry. He also addresses the issue of organic food versus food that is locally grown and prepared at home. Although some essays were written years ago, Berry's eloquent writing is fresh and still relevant today.

Subjects: Agriculture, Farmers, Farming, Organic Foods

Now Try: Readers who enjoy Berry's thought-provoking essays may want to try Berry's classic work, *The Unsettling of America: Culture and Agriculture*, as well as his novels, most of which feature rural settings, including *Jayber Crow* and *That Distant Land: The Collected Stories*. Michael Pollan frequently cites Berry in his writings, so readers may also consider *The Omnivore's Dilemma*. Readers may also want to consider *Consulting the Genius of the Place: An Ecological Approach to a New Agriculture* by Wes Jackson, who is closely associated with Berry.

David, Elizabeth

An Omlette and a Glass of Wine. New York: Viking, 1985. 318pp. ISBN 9780670807697.

Elizabeth David is a well-known British cookbook author and food writer. This is a collection of articles written for a variety of publications and varies in format, including book reviews, travel pieces, restaurant reviews, recipes, and thoughts on food and cooking. David recalls life with rationing after World War II, her thoughts on tinned foods, and describes many of the various food samples she has received. She also recalls her travels, foods she has tried, and cooks she has met. The brief essays make this a quick read and the variety of topics provide interest.

Subjects: Recipes, Restaurants, Travel, World War II

Now Try: David has a number of cookbooks that may appeal to readers. Try *French Provincial Cooking* or *Italian Food*. *Writing at the Kitchen Table* by Artemis Cooper is the authorized biography of David. Readers who enjoy her writing style may also enjoy M.F.K. Fisher's writing. Start with *The Art of Eating*. Readers may also enjoy the food writing of Roy Andries de Groot in *The Auberge of the Flowering Hearth*.

Davidson, Alan, and Saberi, Helen

The Wilder Shores of Gastronomy: Twenty Years of the Best Food Writing From the Journal Petits Propos Culinaires. Berkeley, CA: Ten Speed Press, 2002. 497pp. ISBN 9781580084178.

In 1979, food writers Elizabeth David, Richard Olney, and Alan and Jane Davidson created *Petits Propos Culinaires*, an English language magazine of the history of food and cookery. This anthology highlights some of the best pieces from this magazine. Aside from the founders, there are essays from other notable food writers such as Harold McGee, Jane Grigson, and Claudia Roden. A wide range of topics is covered and will be of particular interest to fans of history and biography, as well as readers who enjoy fascinating details of exotic foods.

Subjects: Biography, Gastronomy, History

Now Try: Readers interested in reading additional pieces by writers featured in this collection may want to try Alan Davidson's collection of essays, *A Kipper With My Tea*, *Reflexions* by Richard Olney, or Elizabeth David's *An Omlette and a Glass of Wine*. Readers who enjoy essays by a variety of food writers may want to try *Endless Feasts: 60 Years of Writing from Gourmet Magazine*.

Donohue, John

Man With a Pan: Culinary Adventures of Fathers Who Cook for Their Families. Chapel Hill, NC: Algonquin Books, 2011. 326pp. ISBN 9781565129856.

Traditionally, cooking for the family has been considered women's work, but thanks to changes in society and gender roles, more men are heading into the kitchen. Donohue compiles essays from chefs, food writers, and average American men who all are responsible for cooking for their families, whether out of necessity or simply because they enjoy it. From Mario Batali, whose son enjoys foie gras and duck testicles to Peter Kaminsky, whose daughter doesn't like to eat anything, these quick essays are touching and humorous.

Subjects: Batali, Mario, Bittman, Mark, Blogs, Family Relationships, Fathers, Harrison, Jim, Humor, Kurlansky, Mark, Parenting, Quick Reads, Recipes, Ruhlman, Michael, Writers

Now Try: Readers may also enjoy other touching and amusing stories of fathers who cook for their children, such as *Hungry Monkey* by Matthew Amster-Burton and *Cooking for Gracie* by Keith Dixon. In *How to Cook Like a Man*, Daniel Duane recalls his efforts to learn to cook when he became a father using Alice Waters as his guide. *Home Game: An Accidental Guide to Fatherhood* by Michael Lewis is another lighthearted and humorous account of fatherhood, as is Austin Murphy's *How Tough Could It Be? The Trials and Errors of a Sportswriter Turned Stay-at-Home Dad*. Readers may want to consider titles by some of the food writers featured in this collection. *The Raw and the Cooked: Adventures of a Roving Gourmand* by Jim Harrison is another collection of Food Essays. *The Making of a Chef* by Michael Ruhlman or *Food Matters* by Mark Bittman are other possibilities. Donohue maintains his blog at www.stayatstovedad.com.

Dunea, Melanie

My Last Supper: 50 Great Chefs and Their Final Meals. New York: Bloomsbury USA, 2007. 216pp. ISBN 9781596912878.

If you could plan your last meal, what would you have? This is a common game among chefs and Dunea asks some of the most well-known and celebrated chefs. Jacques Pépin, Mario Batali, Gordon Ramsay, Thomas Keller, and

Ferran Adrià are just a few of the chefs who imagine their perfect last supper. But with chefs, it's not only a matter of what would be served for the last meal, they also imagine where they would eat, who would join them, what wine would be served, and what music would be playing. Some chefs describe elaborate meals of exotic foods and some describe simple meals at home with their families. This quick read provides interesting insight into chefs' favorite foods and descriptive details.

Subjects: Chefs, Family Relationships, Meals

Now Try: *My Last Supper: The Next Course* features 50 more chefs describing their ideal last meal. Andrew Caldwell describes the last meals of some of the most famous and infamous figures in history in *Their Last Suppers: Legends of History and Their Final Meals. Chef's Story* by Dorothy Hamilton features chefs talking about what got them into the business. For fun, try *1001 Foods You Must Taste Before You Die* edited by Frances Case and *1001 Wines You Must Taste Before You Die* edited by Neil Beckett. Anthony Bourdain's collection *Medium Raw*, contains an essay that details a decadent meal that is the stuff of legend among chefs and foodies.

Ferrari-Adler, Jenni

Alone in the Kitchen with an Eggplant. New York: Riverhead Books, 2007. 272pp. ISBN 9781594489471.

Laurie Colwin's essay "Alone in the Kitchen With an Eggplant," which describes her experiments cooking eggplant while living alone in her tiny New York apartment, was the inspiration of this collection of essays about eating alone. Some writers, such as Holly Hughes, see eating alone as a rare luxury. Amanda Hesser describes her favorite luxurious recipe when eating alone: truffled egg toast. Some writers, such as Haruki Murakami and Nora Ephron, find solace and comfort in foods when they eat alone. Still others, such as Marcella Hazan and Laura Calder, feel that food and eating are better when shared with someone you love. Humorous, touching, and endearing, these diverse essays will appeal to readers who enjoy light, quick reads.

Subjects: Almond, Steve, Colwin, Laurie, Fisher, M.F.K., Hazan, Marcella, Hesser, Amanda, Hughes, Holly, Humor, Quick Reads, Recipes, Relationships, Writers

Now Try: Deborah Madison's *What We Eat When We Eat Alone* is an enjoyable exploration of the pros and cons of eating alone and looks at what, and how, people eat when no one is watching. Judith Jones encourages eating alone in *The Pleasures of Cooking for One*. Readers may want to consider titles by the authors featured in this collection. Try Laurie Colwin's *Home Cooking*, Amanda Hesser's *Cooking for Mr. Latte*, Nora Ephron's novel *Heartburn*, and Marcella Hazan's *Amarcord: Marcella Remembers*.

George, Donald W.

A Moveable Feast: Life-Changing Food Adventures Around the World. London: Lonely Planet, 2010. 296pp. ISBN 9781742202297.

George says that travel and food are inseparably intertwined. When we travel, food becomes a pathway into the place we are visiting. Food allows the traveler a deeper connection to the culture he or she is visiting. In this vein, George collects 38 essays from chefs, food critics, and travel writers. The essays cover the world from the heartland of America to Mongolia and a wide variety of foods, from barbecue to bats. The authors explore not only the culinary delights (or oddities) of a location, but also attempt to gain a better understanding of the local culture as well.

> **Subject:** Bourdain, Anthony, Chefs, Extreme Cuisine, Gates, Stefan, Kurlansky, Mark, Lebovitz, David, Local Culture, Restaurant Critics, Travel, Writers, Zimmern, Andrew
>
> **Now Try:** Readers who appreciate the idea of food as a pathway to understanding a culture may want to consider Anthony Bourdain's *A Cook's Tour* and Andrew Zimmern's *The Bizarre Truth*. J. Maarten Troost's *Lost on Planet China* is an entertaining and insightful look at China's culture, including food. Readers may also be interested in Ernest Hemingway's memoir of the same title, *A Moveable Feast*, which recounts his years living in Paris.

Harrison, Jim

The Raw and the Cooked: Adventures of a Roving Gourmand. New York: Grove Press, 2001. 271pp. ISBN 9780802116987.

Harrison is a well-known novelist and a passionate food writer. His literary essays extolling the pleasures of food are collected here. Harrison's desire for genuine food and a relationship to the natural world are evident in his essays about hunting and fishing trips, as well as the meals he creates from wild game. Harrison laments the lack of snack food in Los Angeles and chalks about bouts of gout and indigestion as a necessary trade-off for life's greatest pleasures. Harrison recalls the luscious meals he has created and meals he has eaten in famous restaurants. Harrison's passion for food comes across in every essay and will appeal to readers who enjoy highly literary works with descriptive prose.

> **Subjects:** Fishing, Hunting, Travel
>
> **Now Try:** Consider some of Harrison's novels, including *True North* and *The English Major*, as well as his poetry, such as *In Search of Small Gods*. Readers who enjoy his literary writing style may also enjoy M.F.K. Fisher's works, such as *The Art of Eating*. Readers who enjoy his reflections on nature and hunting may want to consider Steven Rinella's *The Scavenger's Guide to Haute Cuisine. Hunt, Gather, Cook: Finding the Forgotten Feast* by Hank Shaw may be appealing to readers interested in hunting and foraging.

Hesser, Amanda

Eat, Memory: Great Writers at the Table: A Collection of Essays From the New York Times. New York: W. W. Norton & Company, 2009. 204pp. ISBN 9780393067637.

> Hesser, an editor and food writer, compiles 26 essays from the *New York Times Magazine* from novelists, cooks, food writers, and journalists who recall how foods have influenced their lives. Gary Shteyngart, Ann Patchett, Tom Perrotta, and Gabrielle Hamilton are just a few of the writers who reflect on the foods that spark memories of people and places.

> **Subjects:** Apple, R. W., Jr., Child, Julia, Hamilton, Gabrielle, Writers

> **Now Try**: Amanda Hesser has written her own memoir, *Cooking for Mr. Latte*. Readers may also enjoy the yearly edition of *The Best Food Writing*, edited by Holly Hughes. Titles by the authors featured in this collection may also be appealing. Try *Gabrielle Hamilton's Blood, Bones and Butter: The Inadvertent Education of a Reluctant Chef, Far Flung and Well Fed* by R. W. Apple, *Sag Harbor* by Colson Whitehead, or *The Leftovers* by Tom Perotta.

Hughes, Holly, ed.

The Best Food Writing 2010. Cambridge, MA: Da Capo, 2010. 352pp. ISBN 9780738213811.

> This compilation of essays from chefs, food writers, and amateur foodies is brought tougher from a variety of sources, including memoirs, popular food magazines, general interest magazines, and blogs. In her introduction, editor Holly Hughes laments the closing of *Gourmet* magazine, but believes that despite this, food writing is not a dying subject. Food writing is alive and well; much of the best writing is being published online on a number of serious food websites. The essays featured here run the gamut of topics, from pieces on both sides of the locavore trend, ethical meat eating, the dethroning of El Bulli, and the relevancy of Zagat's. Some essays examine a specific food trend, such as avocados, kimchi, underground charcuterie, and Kyoto's tofu. Also included are sections from food titles that are annotated elsewhere in this book, including Novella Carpenter, Jason Sheehan, and William Alexander.

> **Subjects:** Alexander, William, Carpenter, Novella, El Bulli, Food Issues, Restaurants, Sheehan, Jason, Travel, Zagat's

> **Now Try:** This is the 10th year of this series, so readers may want to go back and look at previous years. Readers may enjoy reading the full-length titles of the essays featured here, such as William Alexander's *52 Loaves*, Novella Carpenter's *Farm City*, or Jason Sheehan's *Cooking Dirty*. *The Best American Travel Writing* series may also be appealing to readers who enjoy the essays that feature travel.

Kurlansky, Mark

Choice Cuts: A Savory Selection of Food Writing from Around the World and Throughout History. New York: Ballantine Books, 2002. 473pp. ISBN 9780345457103.

Kurlansky presents an anthology of food writing throughout history, including pieces from notable foodies such as Brillat-Savarin, Escoffier, A. J. Liebling, M.F.K. Fisher, James Beard, Elizabeth David, Clementine Paddleford, and Mrs. Beeton. Kurlansky also includes pieces from writers such as Ernest Hemingway, John Steinbeck, Charles Dickens, and even philosophers such as Plato and Pliny the Edler. Some essays present specific knowledge of food while others illuminate broader subjects, and some just express the author's love of food or recall memorable meals. Readers will find both historical and modern pieces and a variety of writing styles.

Subjects: Chefs, History, Writers

Now Try: Readers may also want to consider Molly O'Neill's *American Food Writing: An Anthology with Classic Recipes*, which contains over 250 years of American food writing. Other titles by or about the writers featured in this collection may also be appealing, such as Escoffier's *Memoirs of My Life*, Elizabeth David's biography *Writing at the Table*, and *Hometown Appetites: The Story of Clementine Paddleford, the Forgotten Food Writer Who Chronicled How America Ate* by Kelly Alexander and Cynthia Harris.

McInerney, Jay

Hedonist in the Cellar: Adventures in Wine. New York: A. A. Knopf, 2006. 243pp. ISBN 9781400044825.

McInerney, a novelist and wine columnist for *House & Garden* magazine, compiles five years of his essays on his exploration of wine. McInerney covers the science and technique of winemaking, and explores the geography, history, and culture of a wine's origin. Recognizing that there is a wider world of wine than just France, he investigates lesser known wines from South America, South Africa, New York, and New Zealand. He also seeks out smaller winemakers as well as the larger producers. McInerney admits that when it comes to wine, he is an amateur. His essays are infused with wit, unpretentious prose, and a genuine sense of discovery that make his writing accessible to all readers.

Subjects: France, History, Humor, New York, New Zealand, Wine, Winemaking, South America, South Africa

Now Try: Readers wanting more of McInerney's writing may want to try his other collections of wine essays such as *The Juice: Vinous Veritas* and *Bacchus and Me* or one of his fiction novels, such as *Bright Lights, Big City*, or *The Good Life*. Kermit Lynch tours France in search of the great French wines in *Adventures on the Wine Route*. Other attempts to demystify the world of wine may also be of interest. Try *Red, White and Drunk All Over* by Natalie MacLean or *The Accidental Connoisseur* by Lawrence Osborne. Readers interested in other novelists who have written food books should consider Jonathan Safran Foer's *Eating Animals* or Jim Harrison's *The Raw and the Cooked*.

O'Neill, Molly

American Food Writing: An Anthology with Classic Recipes. New York: Library of America, 2007. 753pp. ISBN 9781598530056.

This anthology compiles over 250 years of American culinary history with recipes, letters, diary entries, menus, and essays. Writers, chefs, critics, and foodies describe their delight in food, restaurants, and discoveries of new foods while traveling. Thomas Jefferson's recipe for ice cream begins the collection. A Southerner describes a Virginian barbeque, illustrating the role of the slaves in preparing food. A description of the eating houses that began popping up in New York City in the mid-19th century. Nathaniel Hawthorne describes the joys of gathering his own food. Thoreau describes the delight of watermelon. David Sedaris describes dining out in New York City. Many historical and contemporary icons are included: M.F.K. Fisher, Michael Pollan, Calvin Trillan, Laurie Colwin, Brillat-Savarin, Harriet Beecher Stowe, Clementine Paddleford, and Betty Fussell.

Subjects: Chefs, Recipes, Restaurant Critics, Restaurants, Travel, Writers

Now Try: O'Neill has also written a memoir, *Mostly True: A Memoir of Family, Food, and Baseball*, as well as a cookbook featuring traditional American recipes, *One Big Table: 600 Recipes From the Nation's Best Home Cooks, Farmers, Fishermen, Pit-Masters, and Chefs*. Readers may also enjoy Mark Kurlansky's anthology of food writing throughout history, *Choice Cuts: A Savory Selection of Food Writing From Around the World and Throughout History*. Also consider some of the writers featured in this collection: Michael Pollan's *The Omnivore's Dilemma*, Calvin Trillin's *Feeding a Yen*, Laurie Colwin's *Home Cooking*, and Betty Fussell's *Raising Steaks*.

Reed, Dale Volberg, and Reed, John Shelton

Cornbread Nation 4: The Best of Southern Food Writing. Athens, GA: University of Georgia Press, 2008. 308pp. ISBN 9780820330891.

This series from the Southern Foodway's Alliance features pieces published in a variety of magazines, newspapers, and books that celebrate the people, traditions, and tastes of the American South. Edna Lewis, R. W. Apple, Jr., Rick Bragg, and Pat Conroy include their musings on southern life and food. Typical southern foods such as roux, Tabasco, crawfish, red beans and rice, bread puddings, and shrimp po'boys are all featured, as is an ode to the southern institution, the Waffle House. The down home spirit of the south shines through in these essays and the traditional recipes will entice both southerners and Yankees.

Subjects: American South, Apple, R. W., Jr., Food Traditions, Lewis, Edna, Recipes

Now Try: *Cornbread Nation* consists of six volumes. Readers who enjoy the essays that capture the feel of life and food in the south may want to consider the other volumes in this series. *Screen Doors and Sweet Tea* by Martha Hall Foose is a narrative cookbook that also captures the charming Southern setting. Jospeh Dabney's *The Food, Folklore, and Art of Lowcountry Cooking: A Celebration of the Foods, History, and Romance Handed Down from England, Africa, the Caribbean, France, Germany, and Scotland* includes history, culture, and recipes of the South. Sara Roahen describes moving to New Orleans in *Gumbo Tales: Finding My Place at the New Orleans Table*. Readers may also enjoy titles by some of the authors featured in this collection, such as *Far Flung and Well Fed* by R. W. Apple. Edna Lewis's cookbook, *The Taste of Country Cooking*, Rick Bragg's memoir *All Over But the Shoutin'*, and Pat Conroy's novel *South of Broad*.

Reichl, Ruth

Endless Feasts: Sixty Years of Writing From Gourmet. New York: Modern Library, 2002. 401pp. ISBN 9780679642503.

Founded in 1941, *Gourmet* magazine was the first U.S. magazine devoted to food, and was the leading magazine on food and travel until its discontinuation in 2009. Reichl, *Gourmet's* last editor compiles some of the best pieces to appear in the magazine over the past 60 years. The magazine was known to feature some of the best food writers of the time. Included are pieces from James Beard, M.F.K. Fisher, Madhur Jaffrey and Laurie Colwin, Elizabeth David, and Paul Theroux. Pieces from novelists such as Annie Proux, Pat Conroy, and Ray Bradbury are also featured. The collection includes pieces on a wide range of topics, including travel and the changes in eating habits.

Subjects: Food Writers, *Gourmet*, Recipes, Travel, Writers

Now Try: Readers may be interested in other collections from *Gourmet*, such as *Remembrance of Things Paris: Sixty Years of Writing From Gourmet* and *History in a Glass: Sixty Years of Wine Writing From Gourmet*. Readers may also want to consider a title by Ruth Reichl, the last editor-in-chief of *Gourmet*. Start with *Tender at the Bone*. *Secret Ingredients* by David Remnick is collection of food essays from the *New Yorker*.

Remnick, David, ed.

Secret Ingredients: The New Yorker Book of Food and Drink. New York: Random House, 2007. 582pp. ISBN 9781400065479.

David Remnick has compiled some of the best food writing from the *New Yorker* magazine, since its inception. Pieces date back to the 1930s and include many famous food writers, such as A. J. Liebling, Calvin Trillin, M.F.K. Fisher, and Anthony Bourdain. Pieces illustrate the changes in restaurants and dining out, experiences trying local delicacies, and memories of specific foods. Short works of fiction are also included.

Subjects: Fiction, Fishing, Foraging, Humor, Local Delicacies, *New Yorker*, Quick Reads, Restaurants

Now Try: Remnick has compiled other essays on other topics that may be appealing. Check out *Disquiet Please!: More Humor Writing From the New Yorker*, *The Only Game in Town: Sports Writing From the New Yorker*, and *Fierce Pajamas: An Anthology of Humor*

Writing From the New Yorker. Readers may also want to consider titles by the authors featured in this collection. Try *Between Meals: An Appetite for Paris* by A. J. Leibling, *Blue Trout And Black Truffles: The Perigrinations of an Epicure* by Joseph Wechsberg, *How to Cook a Wolf* by M.F.K. Fisher, *The Raw and the Cooked* by Jim Harrison, and *Oracle Bones: A Journey Through Time in China* by Peter Hessler.

Richman, Alan

Fork It Over: The Intrepid Adventures of a Professional Eater. New York: HarperCollins, 2004. 324pp. ISBN 9780060586294.

A food critic for *GQ* magazine, this collection is a compilation of Richman's magazine columns over the past decade. In these entertaining essays, Richman infuses a humorous tone throughout his essays. In one essay Richman distinguishes between a joint and a dive. He offers humorous tips for eating in an empty restaurant. Richman reveals how he may be the only soldier to gain weight while serving in Vietnam. Richman also recalls the occasion he dined with Sharon Stone and his visit to Louis Farrakhan's Nation of Islam restaurant.

Subjects: *GQ*, Humor, Restaurants, Travel

Now Try: Readers who enjoy Richman's humorous style, quick pace, and entertaining stories may also enjoy Jeffrey Steingarten's *It Must Have Been Something I Ate* or *The Man Who Ate Everything*, R. W. Apple's *Far Flung and Well Fed*, or Calvin Trillin's *Alice, Let's Eat.*

Steingarten, Jeffrey

The Man Who Ate Everything: And Other Gastronomic Feats, Disputes and Pleasurable Pursuits. New York: Knopf, 1997. 514pp. ISBN 9780679430889.

A food critic for *Vogue* magazine, this collection includes essays that have appeared in *Vogue*, as well as other magazines. Steingarten, a passionate foodie, goes to great lengths to test new recipes, such as *la pain au levain naturel*, piecrust, or French fries cooked in horse fat. He travels far and wide to taste delicacies such as Wagyu beef, truffles, and choucroute. Weight gain is a common issue for foodies, and Steingarten reluctantly tries a popular French diet, visits a weight loss clinic, and samples various low-fat products. Readers will enjoy Steingarten's humorous essays, varied topics, great descriptions, short chapters, and recipes.

Subjects: Humor, Recipes, Travel, *Vogue*, Weight Loss

Now Try: Steingarten's *It Must Have Been Something I Ate* combines more humorous, entertaining essays on a variety of topics. Readers who enjoy Steingarten's humorous style may also enjoy Alan Richman's *Fork It Over: The Intrepid Adventures of a Professional Eater.* William Alexander is another passionate foodie who goes to great lengths when it comes to cooking. Try his memoir *52 Loaves: One Man's Relentless Pursuit of Truth, Meaning, and a Perfect Crust.*

Stefan Gates is also willing to try anything in the name of food. Try his collection of essays, *Gastronaut: Adventures in Food for the Romantic, the Foolhardy, and the Brave.*

Witherspoon, Kimberly, and Friedman, Andrew

Don't Try This At Home: Culinary Catastrophes From the World's Greatest Chefs. New York: Bloomsbury, 2005. 308pp. ISBN 9781596910706.

Even the best chefs have had their moments. This collection compiles the stories of 40 celebrated chefs and their worst culinary disasters. Anthony Bourdain recalls the worst New Year's Eve meltdown. Mario Batali describes how he took revenge on a chef. Ferran Adrià found his lobsters spoiled right before a private dinner party for 3,200 guests. Gabrielle Hamilton hired a blind line cook. Daniel Boulud and Tom Colicchio describe the difficulties of taking food on the road. Drunk chefs, demanding patrons, and screaming bosses are all here. The essays are humorous, frank, cringe-inducing, behind-the-scenes stories of restaurant life.

> **Subjects:** Adrià, Ferran, Batali, Mario, Blumenthal, Heston, Boulud, Daniel, Bourdain, Anthony, Chefs, Hamilton, Gabrielle, Henderson, Fergus, Luongo, Pino, Oliver, Jamie, Restaurants
>
> **Now Try:** Witherspoon also compiled a collection of essays from famous cooks, *How I Learned to Cook: Culinary Educations From the World's Greatest Chefs*. Other titles that provide a behind-the-scenes look at restaurants may also be appealing, such as Anthony Bourdain's *Kitchen Confidential: Adventures in the Culinary Underbelly*, Bill Buford's *Heat: An Amateur's Adventures as Kitchen Slave, Line Cook, Pasta-Maker, and Apprentice to a Dante-Quoting Butcher in Tuscany*, Jason Sheehan's *Cooking Dirty: A Story of Life, Sex, Love, and Death in the Kitchen*, and *Service Included: Four-Star Secrets of an Eavesdropping Waiter* by Phoebe Damrosch.

Consider Starting With . . .

Readers new to Food Essays may want to consider starting with these benchmark titles.

David, Elizabeth. *An Omelette and a Glass of Wine.*

Hughes, Holly. *Best Food Writing.*

Remnick, David, editor. *Secret Ingredients: The New Yorker Book of Food and Drink.*

Steingarten, Jeffrey. *The Man Who Ate Everything: And Other Gastronomic Feats, Disputes and Pleasurable Pursuits.*

References

Grendler, Paul F. 2004. "Montaigne, Michel de 1533–1592 French Essay Writer." In *Renaissance: An Encylcopedia for Students*, 89–90. New York: Charles Scribner's Sons.

Merriam-Webster. 2011. http://www.merriam-webster.com/dictionary/essay (accessed September 4).

Ross, Catherine Sheldrick. 2004. "Reading Nonfiction for Pleasure: What Motivates Readers?" In *Nonfiction Readers' Advisory*, ed. Robert Burgin, 105–120. Westport, CT: Libraries Unlimited.

Wikipedia. 2011. http://en.wikipedia.org/wiki/Essays (accessed September 4, 2011).

1

2

3

4

5

6

7

8

9

Appendix A

Cooks and Their Books

The titles listed below are some of the most well-known cookbooks or from the most well-known cooks and chefs. This is not meant to be a comprehensive list of cookbooks, but to provide a list of cookbooks and cooks that will be familiar to most people. These are some of the must know titles.

America's Test Kitchen. *The New Best Recipe.*
America's Test Kitchen is a public television cooking show dedicated to the careful testing of recipes in order to create foolproof recipes. America's Test Kitchen publishes the monthly magazine, *Cook's Illustrated*, as well as numerous cookbooks. Their cookbooks are known for lengthy descriptions and explanations of the various methods that were tested and how they came up with the final recipe.

Anderson, Pam. *How to Cook Without a Book: Recipes and Techniques Every Cook Should Know by Heart.*
Anderson is a well-known food writer and cookbook author. She has five cookbooks; *How to Cook Without a Book* was a James Beard Award nominee.

Batali, Mario. *Simple Italian Food: Recipes From My Two Villages.*
Batali is an American chef, cookbook author, and television personality, known for specializing in Italian cuisine. Batali has opened several restaurants, including Babbo in New York City. Batali was the star of the Food Network's *Molto Mario* and *Iron Chef America* and the PBS series *Spain . . . On the Road Again* with Gwyneth Paltrow.

Bayless, Rick. *Mexican Everyday.*
Bayless is an American chef known for his specialization in Mexican cuisine. He owns three Mexican restaurants, including Frontera Grill in Chicago; and hosts the PBS series *Mexico . . . One Plate at a Time.* He has published other Mexican cookbooks as well.

Beard, James. *American Cookery.*
Beard was an American chef and food writer. He is considered the father of American cuisine. He published over 20 cookbooks. The James Beard Foundation was

established in 1986 after Beard's death. The James Beard Foundation Awards are given annually to honor the best chefs, restaurants, cookbook authors, and other food professionals in the United States.

Beeton, Isabella. *Mrs. Beeton's Book of Household Management*.
This book was originally published in 1861 in London. It has an iconic status in Britain and is still available today. The book was intended as a guide for the middle classes for running a house, and includes recipes and tips on cooking, how to deal with servants' pay, and children's health.

Bittman, Mark. *How to Cook Everything*.
Bittman is an American food writer and cookbook author. He has written for numerous publications, including the *New York Times*. This cooking reference is known for its easy-to-understand instructions and illustrations. Bittman has also published *How to Cook Everything Vegetarian*.

Blumenthal, Heston. *The Fat Duck Cookbook*.
Blumenthal is an English chef and owner of the award-winning restaurant, The Fat Duck.

Child, Julia. *Mastering the Art of French Cooking*.
This classic cookbook, published in 1961, is credited with bringing French cuisine to the American home cook. Child went on to publish numerous cookbooks and star in her own television series.

Claiborne, Craig. *The New York Times Cookbook* (1990).
Claiborne was the former food editor for the *New York Times*. The *New York Times* began publishing a cookbook of its best recipes in 1961. As editor, Claiborne compiled an edition in 1990 and *The New York Times Cookbook* in 1995. Claiborne has also published a number of\ cookbooks of his own recipes as well.

David, Elizabeth. *Italian Food*.
David was a British food writer who specialized in French and Italian cuisines. She is credited with introducing the British with French and Italian cooking. David has published several cookbooks, including *French Country Cooking* and *French Provincial Cooking*.

De Laurentis, Giada. *Everyday Italian*.
De Laurentis is an Italian American chef and television personality. She is known for her television series on the Food Network: *Giada at Home*, *Everyday Italian*, and *Giada's Weekend Getaways*. De Laurentis has published several cookbooks.

Fairchild, Barbara. *The Bon Appétit Cookbook*.
Fairchild is the editor-in-chief of *Bon Appétit* magazine. This cookbook features over 1,000 recipes from the magazine's history. Fairchild has published two other cookbooks for *Bon Appétit*.

Farmer, Fannie. *The Boston Cooking School Cook Book*.
Fannie Farmer attended the Boston Cooking School in the late 1880s. In 1896 she published *The Boston Cooking School Cook Book*, which became the bestselling cookbook of the era. The book is now in its 13th edition.

Fearnley-Whittingstall, Hugh. *The River Cottage Meat Book.*
Fearnley-Whittingstall is a British chef, food writer, and television personality. He is best known for his British television series River Cottage, in which he lives in a rural English cottage and attempts to eat locally. Fearnley-Whittingstall has written a number of River Cottage cookbooks; the *River Cottage Meat Book* is a James Beard Award winner.

Flay, Bobby. *Bobby Flay's Boy Meets Grill.*
Flay is an American chef, cookbook author, restaurateur, and television personality. He owns several restaurants across the United States. Flay has starred in several Food Network shows, including *Boys Meets Grill* and *Throwdown! With Bobby Flay*. Flay is also an Iron Chef and frequently appears on *Iron Chef America*.

Garten, Ina. *The Barefoot Contessa Cookbook.*
Garten is an American cook, cookbook author, and television personality, best known as the Barefoot Contessa from her Food Network television series. Garten published her first cookbook, *The Barefoot Contessa Cookbook* in 1999. Since then, she has published several other cookbooks. Interesting note: Garten was once a White House nuclear policy analyst.

Greenspan, Dorie. *Around My French Table: More Than 300 Recipes From My Home to Yours.*
Greenspan has published several cookbooks, which have won James Beard awards and IACP awards. She also writes for *Bon Appétit* magazine and frequently appears on NPR.

Hazan, Marcella. *The Essentials of Classic Italian Cooking.*
Hazan is an Italian American cookbook author and is credited with bringing Italian cooking to the average American cook.

Hesser, Amanda. *The Essential New York Times Cookbook.*
Hesser is a food writer and editor for the *New York Times*. In 2010, she compiled the new edition of the *New York Times* cookbook. Hesser is also the cofounder of food52.com and author of *The Food52 Cookbook, Cooking for Mr. Latte*, and *The Cook and the Gardener*.

Jaffrey, Madhur. *At Home with Madhur Jaffrey: Simple, Delectable Dishes from India, Pakistan, Bangladesh, and Sri Lanka.*
Jaffrey is an Indian actress and cookbook author, often credited with introducing Indian cooking to the Western world.

Katzen, Mollie. *The Moosewood Cookbook.*
Katzen is one of the bestselling cookbook authors of all time and has been inducted into the James Beard Hall of Fame. She is known for promoting gourmet vegetarian food. The *Moosewood Cookbook* was originally published in 1978, is one of the top 10 best-selling cookbooks of all time and one of the most popular vegetarian cookbooks. The book has since been revised and updated. Katzen has also written several other cookbooks, including *The Enchanted Broccoli Forest, Still Life With Menu*, and *Vegetable Heaven*.

Keller, Thomas. *The French Laundry Cookbook.*
Thomas Keller is the creator and owner of the award-winning French Laundry restaurant in Napa Valley, California. He is also the owner of Per Se in New York City. Both restaurants have been awarded three Michelin stars.

Lagasse, Emeril *From Emeril's Kitchens: Favorite Recipes from Emeril's Restaurants.*
Lagasse is a well-known chef, television celebrity, restaurateur, and cookbook author. He is best known for his Food Network series, *Emeril Live* and *The Essence of Emeril*. He is also known for his catch phrases "Bam!" and "kick it up a notch."

Lawson, Nigella. *How to Eat.*
Lawson is a British cookbook author. She published *How to Eat* in 1998, which became a best seller. Her second book, *How to Be a Domestic Goddess*, was published in 2000 and was awarded British Book Award Author of the Year. Since then she has published several other books, including *Nigella Bites*, *Nigella Express*, and *Forever Summer*.

Lewis, Edna. *The Taste of Country Cooking.*
Edna Lewis was an African American chef best known for traditional southern cuisine.

Madison, Deborah. *Vegetarian Cooking for Everyone.*
Madison is a popular cookbook author and food writer. She has several cookbooks featuring vegetarian and local, seasonal cooking.

Oliver, Jamie. *The Naked Chef.*
Oliver is an English chef, restaurateur, and television personality. He is known as the Naked Chef and for his campaign to improve diets and remove processed foods from schools. Oliver has starred in *The Naked Chef*, *Jamie's Kitchen*, *Jamie's School Dinners*, and *Jamie Oliver's Food Revolution*. Oliver has published several cookbooks.

Phaidon Press. *The Silver Spoon.*
Originally published in Italy in 1950, this cookbook is considered the Italian Joy of Cooking. It contains over 2,000 traditional Italian recipes from all regions of Italy. It was translated into English in 2005.

Puck, Wolfgang. *Modern French Cooking for the American Kitchen.*
Puck is a celebrity chef and restaurateur. He owns several restaurants, most notably Spago and has appeared on *Iron Chef America*.

Ramsay, Gordon. *A Chef for All Seasons.*
Ramsay is a Scottish chef, restaurateur, and television personality. Ramsay is best known for his fiery temper on his reality televisions shows *Kitchen Nightmares*, *Hell's Kitchen*, *MasterChef*, and *The F-Word*. Ramsay has published several cookbooks.

Ray, Rachael. *30 Minute Meals.*
Ray is a celebrity cook and television personality. Ray is known for her Food Network television series *30 Minute Meals* and *$40 a Day*, as well as her day time talk

show *Rachael Ray*. Ray is known for teaching simple recipes that take less than 30 minutes and her bubbly personality. She has published several other cookbooks, as well as a monthly magazine, *Every Day With Rachael Ray*.

Reichl, Ruth, ed. *The Gourmet Cookbook: More Than 1,000 Recipes.*
Gourmet magazine was founded in 1941 and was published until 2009. Reichl, the final editor-in-chief of *Gourmet*, compiled recipes from *Gourmet*'s history. She also compiled *Gourmet Today: More Than 1,000 All-New Recipes for the Contemporary Ki\tchen*.

Rombauer, Irma, and Marion Rombauer Becker. *The Joy of Cooking.*
This classic American cookbook was originally published in 1936 and has been in print ever since. A 75th anniversary edition was published in 2006.

Rosso, Julee, and Sheila Lukins. *The Silver Palate Cookbook.*
This classic American cookbook was originally published in 1982. The 25th anniversary edition was published in 2007.

Stewart, Martha. *Martha Stewart's Cooking School: Lessons and Recipes for the Home Cook.*
Stewart is a well-known television personality, author, magazine publisher, and businesswoman. She is the publisher of *Martha Stewart Living* magazine, host of the television show *Martha*, and creator of numerous cookbooks and books on crafts, gardening, and housekeeping.

Waters, Alice. *The Chez Panisse Menu Cookbook.*
Waters is the owner of the famous Chez Panisse restaurant located in Berkeley, California. She is considered one of the most influential figures in food and a leader in the organic food movement. Waters has a number of other popular cookbooks.

Wells, Patricia. *The Provence Cookbook.*
Wells is a journalist, cookbook author, and owner of a cooking school in France. She specializes in French cuisine.

Appendix B

Other Formats

Books are not the only format that may be appealing to foodies. There are a number of food magazines that include not only recipes and cooking information, but also interesting articles about cuisine and culinary trends. The Internet is a vast source of entertainment and information; there are probably thousands of blogs devoted to food. Readers may also enjoy documentaries or television series that are focused on food and cooking.

Food Journals or Magazines

These are some of the most well-known food magazines, journals, and newsletters.

The Art of Eating
This magazine is written exclusively by food writer Edward Behr. It first appeared as a food letter in 1986, and is now published four times a year. *The Art of Eating* focuses on the best food and wine—how it is produced and where to find it. There is no advertising. The magazine contains in-depth articles, recipes, wine reviews, restaurant reviews, book reviews, addresses for exceptional open-air markets, individual growers and craftsmen, bakers, cheese makers, wineries, olive-oil mills, charcutiers, and chocolatiers.

Bon Appétit
Bon Appétit was started in 1956. It is a monthly magazine that focuses on food and entertainment.

Cooking Light
Cooking Light is a monthly magazine that was founded in 1987. The magazine is dedicated to healthy living. It includes healthy recipes and covers food trends, fitness, and health news.

Cook's Illustrated
Cook's Illustrated is published by America's Test Kitchen and was founded in 1980. The magazine is published every two months and includes recipes, equip-

ment reviews, taste tests, and tips on cooking techniques. The magazine includes step-by-step illustrations on cooking methods and rigorously tested recipes.

Diner Journal

Diner Journal is a quarterly publication that includes original art, essays, and recipes.

Eating Well

Eating Well magazine is published monthly and focuses on helping readers make healthy eating a way of life. The magazine includes recipes, cooking tips, information on food and health trends, and promotes organic, nonprocessed foods.

Edible Communities

Edible Communities is an organization that publishes a group of magazines that is dedicated to local foods and culinary news. As of 2010, there are 62 Edible magazines, including *Edible San Francisco*, *Edible Boston*, and *Edible Chicago*. Each magazine has news tailored to that specific local food scene. It emphasizes organic and sustainable foods.

Every Day With Rachael Ray

This magazine features Food Network celebrity cook, Rachael Ray. The magazine includes Ray's signature 30 Minute Meal recipes, as well as cooking tips, entertaining ideas, and travel ideas.

Fine Cooking

Fine Cooking is devoted to teaching the art of cooking. It includes step-by-step illustrations and photographs and detailed instructions.

Food and Wine

Food and Wine features fine cuisine, recipes, restaurant reviews, wine pairing, articles, and travel suggestions.

Food Network Magazine

This magazine is published by the Food Network and features recipes from Food Network stars, as well as cooking tips and trends.

Gastronomica

Gastronomica is a quarterly magazine published by the University of California. It covers a wide range of food topics and includes vivid photography. Articles are well researched and thorough.

Living Without

This magazine is for people with food allergies and sensitivities. It includes gluten-free and dairy-free recipes, the latest medical information, and product reviews.

Meatpaper

Meatpaper is a quarterly magazine that began publication in 2006. *Meatpaper* is dedicated to all things meat. It does not focus primarily on recipes, but instead on the politics and ethics of food. It is known for its original art, including illustrations, paintings, and photographs.

Saveur

Saveur is a gourmet food and wine magazine that explores world cuisines and includes recipes, news about the latest culinary trends, and tips on cooking techniques. This magazine contains beautifully vivid photographs.

Simple Cooking

John Thorne began this simple newsletter in 1983. It is published five times per year and sent electronically. Issues include brief articles and recipes.

Urban Farm

Urban farming is growing in popularity. This magazine is published every two months and includes articles on growing food, caring for livestock, and green living.

Vegetarian Times

Vegetarian Times is a monthly magazine devoted to vegetarians who are focused on a healthy lifestyle. The magazine includes recipes and cooking techniques, health information, and tips for eco-friendly lifestyles and green products.

Blogs

There is no shortage of food blogs currently in existence. The wonderful thing about the Internet is that everyone has the opportunity to write about their passions. The bad thing about the Internet is that everyone writes about their passions, and this includes food. This is by no means a comprehensive list of food blogs, but instead a list of some of the most well-known blogs. Some have been nominated or received awards and some are simply outstanding food blogs. Because of the plethora of food blogs in existence, in order to stand out, a food blog must be unique and visually stunning. Most of these food blogs contain stunning photography.

80 Breakfasts—80breakfasts.blogspot.com

Written by a blogger in the Philippines who loves breakfast.

5 Second Rule—5secondrule.typepad.com

This Silicon Valley blogger muses about food issues and shares recipes and photographs of food.

101 Cookbooks—101cookbooks.com

Written by Heidi Swanson, this blog focuses on natural, whole foods and ingredients and vegetarian recipes. Swanson has published three cookbooks, including *Super Natural Cooking*, which was a James Beard Foundation Award nominee.

Accidental Hedonist—accidentalhedonist.com

Written by Kate Hopkins, author of *99 Drams of Whiskey*, this blog covers all things related to spirits.

Amateur Gourmet—www.amateurgourmet.com

While in law school Adam Roberts began blogging about cooking. His blog caught the attention of publishers, and in 2007 he published *The Amateur Gourmet:*

How to Shop, Chop, and Table-Hop Like a Pro (Almost). He is now a full-time food writer and will publish his first cookbook in Fall of 2012.

Anthony Bourdain—blog.travelchannel.com/anthony-bourdain/
Bourdain is a best-seller author and star of the Travel Channel's popular show *No Reservations*. Bourdain blogs about his travels and thoughts on food and culture.

Bake or Break—www.bakeorbreak.com
This blogger writes about her adventures in baking. The recipes and photographs will make your mouth water.

Bakerella—www.bakerella.com
Angie Dudley created the Bakerella blog to write about her adventures in baking. When her cake pops became a hit, she published the book *Cake Pops*. Her blog features photos and recipes for cake pops, but other sweet treats as well, such as cakes, cookies, and pie.

Beyond the Plate—www.beyondtheplate.net
Danielle Tsi is a foodie and a photographer. Her aim is to talk about the stories behind the food by focusing on local producers. She posts recipes, beautiful photographs, and stories of farmers, fishermen, and food artisans.

Bitter Sweet—www.bittersweetblog.wordpress.com
Hannah Kaminsky is a food photographer and a vegan. She is the author of the cookbooks *Vegan Desserts* and *My Sweet Vegan*. Her blog includes the photographs and recipes of her creations.

Blue Kitchen—www.blue-kitchen.com
Terry Boyd, a food blogger from Chitown shares homemade, easy-to-prepare recipes.

The Boy Who Bakes—theboywhobakes.co.uk
Edd Kimber was the winner of the BBC's Great British Bake Off in 2010, is the author of the cookbook, *The Boy Who Bakes*, and teaches macaroon classes in London. His blog includes delicious recipes with a hint of British charm.

Brown Eyed Baker—www.browneyedbaker.com
This Pennsylvanian blogger shares her tantalizing creations. Most are sweets, but there are a few savory recipes as well.

CakeSpy—www.cakespy.com
Created by Jessie Oleson, CakeSpy is a "Dessert Detective Agency." They write about bakeries, conduct baking experiments, and feature delicious baked goods.

Cakewrecks—www.cakewrecks.com
Cakewrecks's motto is "When professional cakes go horribly, hilariously wrong." This blog contains photographs of humorous misspellings and misshapen cakes. Its enormous popularity led to the publication of two books.

Cannelle et Vanille—www.cannellevanille.com
Aran Goyoaga is a Basque ex-pat who has been living in the United States since 1998. A freelance food writer and photographer, she includes vibrant photographs and recipes. Her first cookbook will be published in Fall of 2012.

Chez Pim—www.chezpim.com
Pim Techamuanvivit is a food writer living in San Francisco. Pim shares her adventures in the kitchen, as well as her foodie adventures all over the world.

Chocolate and Zucchini—www.chocolateandzucchini.com
Chocolate and Zucchini is written by Parisian Clotilde Dusoulier, who lives in Monmartre, Paris. She shares her passion for all things related to food.

Chow—www.chow.com
While not a blog, this popular food site incorporates recipes, news, discussion, and advice on food and cooking.

Confessions of a Cookbook Queen—www.confessionsofacookbookqueen.com
Arkansas blogger Kristan says "If I could, I would paint my life pink, sprinkle it with glitter, and give everyone a cupcake" and this is the theme of her blog: a sparkly pink blog with a fun, casual writing style and creative, mouthwatering desserts.

Cooking in Pajamas—cookinginpajamas.onsugar.com
Although this blog is not the most visually appealing, Gwenn Weiss shares some amazing recipes, tips for cooking, and information on food trends.

Cooking Issues—www.cookingissues.com
The French Culinary Institute (FCI) "Tech'N Stuff" blog, headed by the FCI's leaders, covers the technical aspects of cooking. Some posts cover topics as simple as salting meat before searing, and some go into science-y topics like cooking *sous vide* for fans of food science.

Cooking With Amy—cookingwithamy.blogspot.com
Amy Sherman is a San Francisco-based food writer and cookbook author. Her blog contains original recipes, reviews, commentary, news, and culinary travel information.

Cream Puffs in Venice—www.creampuffsinvenice.ca
Ivonne lives in Toronto and comes from a large Italian family. She shares her amazing photographs.

Culinate—www.culinate.com
This multifaceted website features articles, cooking tips, interviews, recipes, podcasts, food news, and blog posts.

Curd Nerds—curdnerds.com
Devoted to all things cheese, this blog covers the science of cheesemaking, features cheesemakers, and books about cheese.

David Lebovitz (Saveur's Best Culinary Travel Blog 2011)—www.davidlebovitz. com

> Lebovitz is a Chez Panisse alum, pastry chef, and cookbook author. In his blog, he shares his recipes and stories of encounters with food.

Deep End Dining—www.deependdining.com

> This blog is dedicated to seeking out uncommon foods and exotic cuisines. Although not the most visually appealing blog, fans of extreme cuisine will eat this up.

Delicious: Days—www.deliciousdays.com

> Nicole Stich shares her love of food and photography. Recipes paired with impressive photographs as well as food news can be found here. Stich also published a cookbook, *delicious days*.

Dessert First—dessertfirstgirl.com

> Anita is a San Francisco native with a love for all things sweet. Also a freelance photographer, Anita includes gorgeous photographs of her sweet treats.

Donal Skehan—www.donalskehan.com

> Donal is an Irish cook, food writer, and photographer. He has published two cookbooks: *Good Mood Food* and *Kitchen Hero*.

Dorie Greenspan—www.doriegreenspan.com

> Greenspan has published 10 cookbooks and won six James Beard Foundation and IACP awards. Her blog includes recipes, products she loves, and guides to restaurants and food shops in Paris.

A Dork and His Pork—www.adorkandhispork.com

> This Cincinnati blogger writes about his love of all things pork.

Drink Dogma (Saveur's Best Cocktail Blog 2011)—www.drinkdogma.com

> This blog is written by the owners of a Huston bar, Anvil Bar & Refuge. They share opinions on cocktails and stories from the world of bartending.

Eat Live Run—www.eatliverun.com

> A graduate of Le Cordon Bleu, pastry chef and baker, Jenna Weber shares her favorite recipes here. Her first book, *White Jacket Required*, a memoir of her time in culinary school, will be released in Fall of 2012.

Eat the Love—www.eatthelove.com

> Irvin Lin lives in San Francisco and shares his love of baking on his blog. Lin combines recipes for indulgent desserts with his humorous, friendly tone.

Eating Asia—eatingasia.typepad.com

> Robyn Eckhardt is a freelance food and travel writer. David Hagerman is a photographer. Based in Malaysia, but also covering other areas of Asia, the two chronicle their experiences with traditional Asian foods with stunning photographs.

Eats Well With Others—www.joanne-eatswellwithothers.com

> Joanne began blogging during her senior year at MIT while recovering from anorexia. When she entered medical school, she discovered a love of cooking.

She shares her love of food and healthy recipes filled with fruits and vegetables, along with the occasional sweet treat.

eGullet—www.egullet.org

This website, produced by the Society for Culinary Arts & Letters, is dedicated to the advancement of the culinary arts. The online forums are available to all to read, however, membership in the Society is required for participation. Society membership also gives access to the literary journal, the *Daily Gullet*.

Evan's Kitchen Ramblings—bossacafez.blogspot.com

Great writing isn't what makes this a standout blog. The vibrant, colorful, dream-like photographs are incredible. Evangeline blogs mainly about her dessert creations, but also has some savory creations as well. This is dessert couture at its finest.

Ezra Pound Cake—www.ezrapoundcake.com

Rebecca Crump is a food writer and a baker. She blogs about recipes she has tried, as well as her own creations. She includes main courses, appetizers, sides, meatless recipes, and desserts.

Food52—www.food52.com

Amanda Hesser and Merrill Stubbs began the Food52 website to give people around the world a chance to share their own recipes and discuss food. From this site, they decided to create a crowd-sourced cookbook. They created recipe contests and chose the best recipes. The website also contains articles and food news. Hesser and Stubbs published *The Food52 Cookbook* in October 2011.

Food Blogga—foodblogga.blogspot.com

Susan Russo is a food writer and a cookbook author. She published *The Encyclopedia of Sandwiches* and *Recipes Every Man Should Know*. Her blog contains recipes, photographs of her creations, cookbook recommendations, and bits about foods and food trends.

Food in Jars—www.foodinjars.com

Marisa McClellan grew up in Oregon, canning the local blueberries, blackberries, and apples. She blogs about the ins and outs of canning and shares recipes for canning. Her cookbook is scheduled for publication in Spring of 2012.

Food Porn Daily—www.foodporndaily.com

Food Porn Daily is a daily photograph of enticing, delicious foods, created by Amanda Simpson. Recipes are not usually included with the photograph, which may be frustrating to readers, but Simpson has published *Food Porn Daily: The Cookbook*.

Gluten-Free Girl and the Chef—glutenfreegirlcom

Shauna James Ahern was diagnosed with celiac disease in 2005. After removing gluten from her diet, her health improved and she began blogging about food and the changes in her diet. Later she met and fell in love with a chef, who began changing his recipes to create dishes she could eat. Shauna blogs about their life together and the gluten-free recipes they create. She has published *Gluten-Free Girl* and *Gluten-Free Girl and the Chef*.

How Sweet It Is—www.howsweeteats.com

Jessica shares a variety of recipes for healthy meals, comfort foods, and indulgent desserts. The "crumbs" section of her blog contains her posts on other aspects of her daily life.

Hunter Angler Gardner Cook—honest-food.net

Hank Shaw hunts, fishes, gardens, and forages for his food. His philosophy is eating honest food; nothing that is packaged in plastic and nothing that comes from a factory farm. His blog contains recipes using wild game, fish, and foraged foods. A former political journalist, he is now a food writer. Shaw published *Hunt, Gather, Cook: Finding the Forgotten Feast* in May 2011.

I Made That!—lookimadethat.com

This blogger's goal is to make all her meals from scratch. She posts recipes along with her photos of the process.

Ideas in Food—ideasinfood.com

Aki Kamozawa and H. Alexander Talbot published *Ideas in Food: Great Recipes and Why They Work*, a handbook that teaches cooks how to unleash their creativity and intensify flavors. On their blog they continue to share their ideas and experiments.

It's Not You, It's Brie—itsnotyouitsbrie.com

Cheese aficionado Kirstin Jackson shares luscious descriptions and photographs of cheeses, and recommends her favorite cheese-related reads.

Joe Pastry—www.joepastry.com

Joe has been working in the food industry since he was 16. His passion is baking and he shares his creations, as well as baking tutorials. He also blogs about current food issues and the food industry.

Joy the Baker (Saveur's Best Baking and Dessert Blog of 2011)—www.joythebaker.com

Joy adds humor to her accounts of creating delicious baked goods and includes stunning photography.

Just Bento—justbento.com

Written by Makiko Itoh, Just Bento is dedicated to healthy, simple bento box lunches. Some of her recipes are traditional Japanese, but others are not. She includes recipes and any and all things related to the bento box.

Just Hungry—www.justhungry.com

Makiko Itoh also writes Just Bento, a blog dedicated to Japanese food and cooking.

Kiss My Spatula—kissmyspatula.com

Literary musings on food, unique recipes, and stunning, professional-quality photography make this blog appealing to fans of Frances Mayes's writing and food porn.

The Kitchn—www.thekitchn.com
> Part of the popular Apartment Therapy website, whose mission is "helping people make their homes more beautiful, organized and healthy by connecting them to a wealth of resources, ideas and community online," this site includes recipes, food news, information on food products, and interviews with cooks, food writers, and farmers.

La Tartine Gourmande—www.latartinegourmande.com
> Beatrice Peltre is a French expatriate living in Boston. She is a food stylist, photographer, and writer. She shares recipes and stories of her life. Her blog is notable for the vibrantly colorful photographs. The cookbook is scheduled for publication in February 2012.

Leite's Culinaria—www.leitesculinaria.com
> Leite's Culinaria is dedicated to educating and entertaining cooks and readers of all levels who are interested in the diverse world of food. This website offers articles, interviews, essays, and slide shows on food and popular culture and history. Recipes, culinary resources, and cooking tips are also provided.

Lettuce Eat Kale—lettuceeatkale.com
> Sarah Henry is a freelance food writer living in Berkeley, California. She shares stories about established and emerging food artisans, covers issues such as school food and food security, and reports on cultural food trends, like the thriving DIY movement.

Lick My Spoon—lickmyspoon.com
> Stephanie is a freelance food writer in San Francisco. She shares recipes, restaurant reviews, information on food and wine events, and stories of her food discoveries she makes on her travels.

Lottie and Doof—www.lottieanddoof.com
> This Chicago-based food blogger shares his recipes for baking and thoughts on food politics.

Love and Olive Oil—www.loveandoliveoil.com
> Lindsay Landis and her husband Taylor share their love of food and cooking. Recipes are mostly sweet, but there are some savories as well along with gorgeous photography. Landis's first cookbook *The Cookie Dough Lover's Cookbook* is due out in June 2012.

Mark Bittman—markbittman.com
> Food writer and cookbook author, Mark Bittman is well known for his cookbook series *How to Cook Everything* and his book *Food Matters*. His blog includes recipes as well as news and his thoughts on the state of the food industry.

Melissa Clark—melissaclark.typepad.com (blog)
> Melissa Clark is a food writer and cookbook author. She writes for the *New York Times* and many other popular publications. She has written and collaborated on over 30 cookbooks.

Michael Ruhlman—ruhlman.com
> Ruhlman has published several titles on cooking, including *The Making of a Chef*, *The Elements of Cooking*, and *Ratio: The Simple Codes Behind the Craft of Everyday Cooking*. On his blog, Ruhlman shares recipes, interviews with famous cooks and food writers, and news about food issues.

Ms. Marmitelover's Underground Restaurant—marmitelover.blogspot.com
> Kerstin Rodgers is a cook and a photographer. She launched one of the UK's first supperclubs, The Underground Restaurant in 2009. The blog contains recipes, menus, and photographs.

Nom! Nom! Nom!—nomnomnomblog.com
> Kris Holechek is a vegan baker living in Minnesota. She blogs about vegan cooking and baking and believes that everyone can have delicious treats despite dietary restrictions. She has published three cookbooks, including *Have Your Cake and Vegan Too*.

Not Eating Out in New York—www.noteatingoutinny.com
> Cathy Erway is the author of *The Art of Eating In: How I Learned to Stop Spending and Love the Stove*. Erway is a proponent of cooking at home rather than eating out. She blogs about meals she has prepared and features other home cooks and local markets and food events.

Not Quite Nigella—www.notquitenigella.com
> Lorraine Elliot is a food enthusiast who shares recipes as well as stories and photographs of her adventures in eating. Her memoir, *Not Quite Nigella*, will be out in 2012.

Not Without Salt—notwithoutsalt.com
> This former pastry chef blogs about her life raising and feeding her three children. Her recipes range from sweet to savory.

Orangette—orangette.blogspot.com
> Molly Wizenberg lives in Seattle and is a food writer. Her blog includes her musings on food, recipes, and gorgeous photographs of food and of her travels.

Peas and Thank You—peasandthankyou.com
> Sarah Matheny decided to eliminate meat from her diet to ensure a healthy diet for her children. She blogs about her life with her family and creating vegetarian meals her children will enjoy. Her cookbook, *Peas and Thank You*, was published in 2011.

Pinch My Salt—pinchmysalt.com
> This Californian blogger started this blog while living in Sicily in order to share the tastes of Italy. Although back in the United States, she continues to share her love of food and cooking.

The Pioneer Woman Cooks—thepioneerwoman.com
> Ree Drummond was a city girl until she met and married a cattle rancher and moved to the country. Her blog contains not only recipes, but also her photos and updates of life on the ranch.

Poor Girl Gourmet—poorgirlgourmet.blogspot.com

Amy McCoy is the Poor Girl Gourmet. Her mission is to eat the best food while spending as little as possible. On her blog she shares her recipes and writes about food, farmers, markets, artisans, and her travels. Her cookbook is *Poor Girl Gourmet: Eat in Style on a Bare-Bones Budget.*

Rambling Spoon—ramblingspoon.com

Karen Coates is a journalist who writes about food, the environment, and social issues around the world. Her blog consists of recipes and details of her experiences growing food, stories of her travels, and experiences with exotic foods, and foods from other cultures.

Rasa Malaysia—rasamalaysia.com

Bee Yinn Low is the author of *Easy Chinese Recipes*. Her blog features easy Asian recipes from Chinese, Japanese, Thai, Malaysian, Singaporean, and Indian.

Salty Seattle—saltyseattle.com

Linda Miller Nicholson lives in Seattle and has a reputation for avant-garde food and molecular gastronomy. Humorous and a bit snarky, she shares her unique and creative recipes on her blog.

Sassy Radish—www.sassyradish.com

Sassy Radish is written by Olga Massov, a writer and a recipe tester/developer. Her goal is to help home cooks make good, simple food. She believes that good food doesn't have to be complicated or fancy. She shares recipes for easy-to-prepare meals and tips on cooking techniques, as well as stories from her childhood in Russia and her life in the United States.

Serious Eats—www.seriouseats.com

Serious Eats is all about celebrating and sharing food through blogs and online community. The site includes the latest food news and commentary, recipes from cookbook writers and chefs, advice on eating out all over the world, and food photography.

Seven Spoons—www.sevenspoons.net

Tara blogs from Ontario, Canada. Her blog is a collection of recipes and stories about family and food.

Simply Recipes—simplyrecipes.com

Elise Bauer lives in California and shares her family recipes and new recipes she has created. She provides step-by-step instructions and photographs of her recipes.

Smitten Kitchen (Saveur's Best Cooking Blog 2011)—www.smittenkitchen.com

Smitten Kitchen features "fearless cooking from a tiny kitchen in New York City." Recipes feature comfort foods that are accessible and easy to prepare with beautiful photography.

Souvlaki for the Soul—souvlakiforthesoul.com

This Australian blogger shares recipes, travel stories, and wonderful photography.

Sprinkle Bakes—www.sprinklebakes.com

> Heather Baird combines her artistic talents and love of baking to present unique and beautiful desserts. The blog features a vibrant design and gorgeous photographs. Her first cookbook, inspired by the blog, *SprinkleBakes*, will be released in spring of 2012.

The Sprouted Kitchen—sproutedkitchen.com

> This blog features recipes that use local, healthy ingredients such as whole grains, unsaturated fats, and natural alternatives to sugar and includes stunning photographs.

Steamy Kitchen—steamykitchen.com

> Jaden Hair is a television chef, food writer, and photographer. Her blog features, fresh, fast, and easy recipes, as well as crafts and her favorite food finds. Hair published *The Steamy Kitchen* cookbook in 2009.

Sunday Suppers—sunday-suppers.com

> Photographer Karen Mordechai created Sunday Suppers, a combination cooking class and group dinner. Led by chefs, participants use fresh, local, organic ingredients to create seasonal meals. Inspired by the events, this blog shares recipes and restaurant reviews, as well as beautifully styled photographs.

Tartelette—tarteletteblog.com

> Helene Dujardin is a French expat living in South Carolina. A former pastry chef, her blog is devoted to food and photography. She has written the book *Plate to Pixel: Digital Food Photography and Styling*.

Tea and Cookies—teaandcookiesblog.com

> Tara Austen Weaver, author of *The Butcher and the Vegetarian*, blogs about food, cooking, travel, books, gardening, farmers, and artisanal food producers.

Traveler's Lunchbox—www.travelerslunchbox.com

> Melissa Kronenthal blogs about her travels abroad, recipes, cookbooks, and life.

Vanilla Garlic—vanillagarlic.com

> Garrett McCord is a food writer and a pastry chef. He loves cheese, desserts, espresso, and spirits. He blogs about the connection between food and life.

Vinography (Saveur's Best Wine Blog 2011)—www.vinography.com

> This blog is a respected source for wine writing, wine reviews, restaurant reviews, editorials, book reviews, wine news, and wine event coverage.

The Wednesday Chef—www.thewednesdaychef.com

> Luisa Weiss is a writer and home cook living in Berlin, Germany. She shares stories of her life in Berlin and recipes she tries.

What Katie Ate (Saveur's Best Photography Blog 2011)—whatkatieate.blogspot.com

> Katie Quinn Davies is a food photographer from Sydney, Australia. Her blog features gorgeous, professional-quality photographs of meals she prepares.

Wild Yeast—www.wildyeastblog.com

>This blogger lives in Northern California and blogs about her hobby, baking bread.

Yum Sugar—www.yumsugar.com

>Although not really a blog, this website is a division of SugarInc.com, and features recipes, how-tos, food news, and food products.

Zester Daily—www.zesterdaily.com

>This website is committed to providing excellent reporting and writing on all aspects of food.

Documentaries

Readers who enjoy the titles in the Investigative Writing chapter may be interested in one of these documentaries.

Animals: Friend or Food

>Jason Young tries out farm life, to see if raising and killing his own meat will change him and his attitude toward meat.

Bad Seed

>This documentary exposes the prevalence of GMOs in the world's food supply.

Bananas!

>This is a documentary of a landmark legal case in which Nicaraguan banana plantation workers fought against the Dole Food Corporation for its use of banned pesticides.

Blue Gold

>Based on the book by the same name by Maude Barlow and Tony Clarke, this documentary examines the environmental and political implications of the planet's dwindling water supply, the problems created by the commoditization of water, and speculates that future wars will be fought over water.

Colony

>Bees play a vital role in pollinating the world's fruits and vegetables. But colony collapse disorder is devastating bee populations. This documentary examines the impacts of colony collapse disorder and the beekeepers who are facing this crisis.

The End of the Line

>The increasing demand for seafood for consumption has taken a toll on the world's oceans and threatens the survival of many species.

Food, Inc.

>This documentary examines the nation's food industry and how it is controlled by a few giant corporations. Also explored are the treatment of factory-farmed animals, the difficulties facing small farmers competing against corporate giants,

the health issues raised by industrial agriculture, and small farmers who are practicing more sustainable methods of farming.

Food Fight

Michael Pollan and Alice Waters look at Industrialized Agriculture and the local, organic food movement.

Food Stamped

This documentary explores whether it is possible to eat healthy on a food stamp budget.

Forks Over Knives

This documentary proposes a plant-based diet as the solution to common health issues, such as diabetes, high blood pressure, and stroke.

Fresh

This documentary features farmers and businesspeople who are challenging industrial food system and working toward better alternatives.

The Future of Food

The controversial issue of the genetic engineering of food crops is examined along with the anti-GMO movement.

The Harvest

Agricultural child labor in America is examined. This documentary profiles three children who work in tomato fields and apple orchards up to 12 hours a day in order to help support their families.

The Garden

A 14-acre lot in South Central Los Angeles was turned into the largest community garden in the United States.

If This is Kosher . . .

Author Jonathan Safran Foer investigates the inhumane practices at a Kosher slaughterhouse.

Ingredients

Farmers and chefs who are working to build a sustainable and local food system with nutritional and delicious foods are featured.

Killer At Large

The rising epidemic of American obesity and its related social and political problems are examined.

King Corn

Two best friends move to the Midwest after attending college on the East coast, to learn where their food comes from. Raising their own crop of corn, they become familiar with genetically modified seeds and fertilizers and attempt to follow the trail of their corn through the food system.

Locavore: Local Diet—Healthy Planet

This documentary advocates a return to a local diet and features pioneers of the locavore movement.

Meat the Truth
> The link between livestock farming and global warming is investigated.

McLibel
> McDonald's has used the UK libel laws to suppress criticism from organizations such as the BBC and *The Guardian*. When two ordinary Brits stood up to McDonald's, their court case exposed the dark side of this famous fast food restaurant.

Modern Meat
> PBS's *Frontline* series investigates the meat industry; interviews industry insiders and federal regulators, presents facts about food-borne illnesses and explores the industry's influence in Washington.

Patent for a Pig
> Monsanto, the huge American biotechnology company, has applied for a patent for a pig in 160 countries. Aside from the issues surrounding the use of genetically modified animals, farmers are concerned that if the patent is approved, Monsanto will have to be paid for every pig in the world that carries the patented genetic marker.

Poison on the Platter
> This documentary examines how everyone's lives will be adversely affected by the use of GMOs.

The Real Dirt of Farmer John
> John Peterson is a third-generation farmer. This documentary chronicles the difficulties he has faced against America's shift towards industrialized agriculture.

Super Size Me
> For 30 days Morgan Spurlock consumes only food from McDonald's menu. He investigates the fast-food industry and the growing obesity crisis in America, and covers the effects the diet has on his own health. Spurlock also published a book by the same title.

Sweet Misery
> This documentary considers the safety of aspartame and the FDA's questionable process of approving the sweetener.

Tapped
> The role of the bottled water industry and its effects on pollution and climate change is examined.

Two Angry Moms
> Upset with the national child obesity crisis and the inferior lunches being served in their children's schools, two women investigated what parents need to do to get better foods into schools.

Waste = Food
> The waste produced by humans is rapidly filling landfills and depleting natural resources. A group of scientists have invented a concept of designing all products in such a way that at the end of its lifecycle, the materials become a new resource.

The World According to Monsanto
    This is an in-depth look at the most powerful company in the agricultural industry.

The Vanishing of the Bees
    This documentary examines the mysterious disappearance of honeybees due to Colony Collapse Disorder and the crisis it presents for the fruit and vegetable industries.

Films

This is a brief list of some popular feature films in which food is featured heavily.

301/302
    A chef tries to entice her anorexic neighbor with her fabulous meals.

Babette's Feast
    In 19th-century Denmark, two sisters hold a dinner to commemorate the 100th birthday of their father. Their French housekeeper and cook prepare a feast.

Big Night
    Two brothers attempt to save their failing Italian restaurant on one special night.

A Chef in Love
    A French chef falls in love with a princess when travelling in Georgia in the 1920s.

Chocolat
    A woman opens a chocolate shop in a conservative French village during Lent.

Delicatessen
    In a post-apocalyptic society where food is rare, the owner of a delicatessen occasionally acquires meat from questionable sources.

Eat Drink Man Woman
    A chef lives with his three adult daughters in Taipei, where their family lives revolves around the ritual of the Sunday dinner.

Fast Food Nation
    When cow feces are found in a fast-food chain's best-selling burger, the company's marketing director discovers the truth about the production of its food.

Julie and Julia
    The life of Julia Child is told interspersed with the life of blogger Julie Powell, who attempted to cook all of the recipes in Child's *Mastering the Art of French Cooking*.

Like Water for Chocolate
    When Tita is forced to make the wedding cake for the man whom she loves, the guests can taste her sadness.

Love's Kitchen
> A successful chef and restaurateur is distraught over the death of his wife. When he decides to turn a country pub into a gourmet restaurant, he meets an American food critic and finds love again.

Mostly Martha
> A successful, obsessive German chef finds herself the guardian of her niece after her sister dies. When an Italian chef is hired to assist in her kitchen, she feels threatened by his presence.

No Reservations
> The American version of *Mostly Martha*.

Ratatouille
> In this animated film, a rat named Remy discovers a love of food and cooking and helps a young chef achieve success.

Soul Food
> When the family matriarch is hospitalized, the traditional Sunday family dinners end and tensions among the children rise.

Tampopo
> A truck driver helps a family turn around their fledgling noodle shop.

Tortilla Soup
> A Mexican American chef lives with his three adult daughters in Los Angeles and serves them lavish dinners.

Waitress
> An unhappily married waitress is saving her money, hoping to leave her husband. She also hopes to win a pie-baking contest and practices by baking her pies at the restaurant, which are a huge success.

Woman on Top
> When a Brazilian chef's husband cheats on her, she leaves him, moves to San Francisco and begins hosting a TV show.

Television Series

With two channels devoted entirely to food, and a number of other networks that air food shows, this is by no means a comprehensive list of televisions shows. This list attempts to include some of the more popular series that are currently on television. There are also a number of popular series that are no longer airing, but many are available on DVD.

Ace of Cakes
> This Food Network show features Duff Goldman of Charm City Cakes in Baltimore. He creates elaborate and unique cake designs.

Bizarre Foods
> Andrew Zimmern travels the world seeking bizarre foods in this Travel Channel series.

Cake Boss
> Buddy Valastro runs this family-owned bakery in New Jersey in this TLC series.

Chopped
> The Food Network presents this cooking competition pitting four up-and-coming chefs against each other.

DC Cupcakes
> This TLC series features two sisters who run a Georgetown cupcake shop.

Hell's Kitchen
> Fox presents this reality television cooking competition, hosted by Gordon Ramsay, in which teams compete in various competitions.

Iron Chef America
> The Food Network presents this showdown between two world-class chefs and their quest to prepare an entire meal made from a secret ingredient.

Kitchen Nightmares
> Fox presents this reality series in which Gordon Ramsay attempts to help restaurant owners save their fledgling businesses.

The Layover
> For the Travel Channel, Anthony Bourdain travels to major cities throughout the world, taking viewers to the must-try restaurants if they are only in town for a few hours.

Man vs. Food
> Adam Richman travels the country attempting to eat some of the biggest food challenges on this Travel Channel series.

MasterChef
> This Fox cooking competition is open to amateur cooks and is co-hosted by chefs Gordon Ramsay and Graham Elliot and restaurateur Joe Bastianich.

Top Chef
> A Bravo reality cooking competition in which contestants are given culinary challenges and judged by food professionals.

Appendix C

Food in Fiction

Following are fiction titles that feature food as a main part of the story's focus. These titles may be appealing to readers who enjoy nonfiction Food Lit. The titles are broken down by genre: literary, women's fiction, romance, chick lit, mystery, historical fiction, and Christian fiction.

Literary

Abu-Jaber, Diana. *Crescent.*
Thirty-nine-year-old Sirine is a chef in a Lebanese restaurant where she provides a taste of home to Arabs in Los Angeles and discovers love in an unexpected romance.

Ali, Monica. *In the Kitchen.*
The executive chef of a London hotel dreams of owning his own restaurant, but his complicated personal life, his crazy kitchen crew, and the murder of the night porter in his restaurant causes him to crack.

Averill, Thomas Fox. *Secrets of the Tsil Café.*
A young man comes of age in a family for whom food is their livelihood, but is divided between his mother's Italian cooking and catering business and his father's Southwestern style restaurant.

Barbery, uriel. *Gourmet Rhapsody.*
While lying on his death bed, a food critic searches his memories, trying to recall a forgotten perfect flavor he experienced in his youth.

Bates, Judy Fong. *Midnight at the Dragon Café.*
A Chinese family immigrates to Ontario in the 1950s and opens their own restaurant, struggling with isolation and dangerous secrets.

Bender, Aimee. *The Particular Sadness of Lemon Cake.*
Upon turning nine, Rose discovers that she can taste the emotions of people in the foods they prepare.

Brite, Poppy Z. *Liquor.*

Two New Orleans cooks come up with an idea to create an upscale restaurant where all the dishes are laced with liquor. With no money to fund their venture, the two rely on a wealthy celebrity chef, who has his own motives for backing the business.

Esquivel, Laura. *Like Water for Chocolate.*

Tita, the youngest of three daughters, is expected to remain single and care for her mother. When she falls in love with her sister's fiancé, she uses her cooking to convey her love for him.

Fox, Andrew. *The Good Humor Man: or, Calorie 3501.*

This satirical story depicts a future in which the American government enforces strict dietary laws and Good Humor Men are tasked with ferreting out high calorie contraband.

Harris, Joanne. *Chocolat.*

When Vianne Rocher opens a chocolate shop in a small conservative French village, the villagers are torn between their Lenten abstinences and the exquisite, luscious confections.

Kalpakian, Laura. *American Cookery.*

Eden Douglas develops a love of food from a young age and is determined to break away from her strict Mormon upbringing. Eden's recipes mark important events and represent the influential people in her life.

Kurlansky, Mark. *Edible Stories.*

This collection of short stories follows the lives of various Seattle residents for whom food plays an important role.

Lanchester, John. *The Debt to Pleasure.*

A gastronomic Englishman reminisces about memorable meals and his love for French food and wine while harboring a sinister secret.

Mayle, Peter. *A Good Year.*

When an Englishman inherits a vineyard in Provence, he finds the house and vineyards in disrepair, another claim on the estate, and a possible scandal involving the caretaker.

Mones, Nicole. *The Last Chinese Chef.*

A food writer who is grieving over the death of her husband travels to China to profile an up-and-coming young American-born Jewish Chinese chef.

Morais, Richard. *The Hundred-Foot Journey.*

After tragedy strikes an Indian family from Bombay, they relocate to small French village, where they introduce Indian cuisine to the town with their restaurant, sparking a war with the local French chef.

Neilson, Melany. *The Persia Café.*

Fannie Leary and her aunt run the Persia Café in a small Mississippi town during the 1960s. When Fannie discovers the body of a murdered young African American man, she is forever changed.

O'Nan, Stewart. *Last Night at the Lobster.*

The manager of a failing Red Lobster in a run-down strip mall has to keep his staff together for one last shift.

Parkin, Gaile. *Baking Cakes in Kigali.*

Talented baker Angel Tungaraza serves up delicious confections while serving as confidant and advisor to her customers in war-torn Rwanda.

Prior, Lily. *La Cucina.*

Rosa's cooking was legendary in her small Italian village. Suffering a broken heart, she retreated to her kitchen until a visiting English chef awakens her passion.

Prunty Morag. *Recipes for a Perfect Marriage.*

Shortly after her hasty marriage, Tressa realizes she has made a mistake. Seeking solace and advice, she turns to the diaries of her late grandmother, who chronicled her struggles with marriage along with her traditional, comforting recipes.

Rayner, Jay. *Eating Crow.*

A venomous restaurant critic begins apologizing to everyone he has wronged after his apology to the widow of a chef who committed suicide after his bad review earns him celebrity status, and he realizes he has a penchant for apologies.

Singh, Jaspreet. *Chef.*

Kip reminisces about his time as a cook for a general in a military camp in Kashmir as he is returning to cook for the general's daughter's wedding.

Smith, Mark Haskell. *Delicious.*

A young Hawaiian chef's family catering business is threatened by a competing business with Mafia connections.

Spiller, Nancy. *Entertaining Disasters.*

When a Los Angeles food writer begins planning a dinner party, the expectations for the perfect party send her into a panic.

Truong, Monique. *The Book of Salt.*

A personal cook traveling with Gertrude Stein and Alice B. Toklas considers whether he will accompany the couple to America, while reminiscing about his childhood in Vietnam.

Vapnyar, Lara. *Broccoli and Other Tales of Food and Love.*

This collection of short stories explores the lives of immigrants living in Brooklyn who find solace in the foods of their homeland.

Waggoner, Susan. *Better than Chocolate.*
Food writer Annie Wilkins and her husband Tom, a research scientist, leave their university jobs so that Tom can take a job with a cooperation developing chocolate that is fat, calorie, and carb-free. When he succeeds and the product is a hit, their lives are forever changed.

Women's Fiction or Romance or Chick Lit

Allen, Sarah Addison. *Garden Spells.*
All of the Waverly women have mysterious gifts. Claire's gift of creating dishes that affect the eater in curious ways has led to her successful catering business.

Andrews, Mary Kay. *Deep Dish.*
Sparks fly when Gina, a southern chef, competes against Tate, for a highly prized spot on the Cooking Channel.

Asher, Bridget. *The Provence Cure for the Brokenhearted.*
Grieving for her deceased husband, Heidi returns to her family's cottage in Provence, pouring herself into repairing the cottage.

Ballis, Stacey. *Good Enough to Eat.*
When Melanie loses 145 pounds and her husband leaves her for a heavy woman, she throws her heartache into her new restaurant that features healthy fare.

Bauermeister, Erica. *The School of Essential Ingredients.*
Lillian teaches a cooking class in her restaurant every Monday night. Each student comes with his or her own drama, and as they learn to cook, they also learn about the power of food to heal and comfort.

Binchy, Maeve. *Quentins.*
A filmmaker wants to make a documentary about Dublin's legendary Quentins restaurant.

Capella, Anthony. *The Food of Love.*
In this Cyrano-like story, Tomasso, a waiter, attempts to woo Laura, young American woman traveling in Italy, by claiming he is a chef. Tomasso turns to his friend Bruno, an actual chef, to help him prepare mouthwatering meals to win Laura's heart.

Chiaverini, Jennifer. *The Quilter's Kitchen.*
Part of Chiaverini's Elm Creek Quilts series, the newest member of Elm Creek's quilting circle is a chef who puts her talents to use when she begins compiling a cookbook for the group.

Criswell, Millie. *The Trouble with Mary.*
When Mary confronts the local food critic who gave her Italian restaurant a bad review, sparks fly between the two.

Fforde, Katie. *Second Thyme Around.*
Perdita, a producer of organic greens, finds herself thrust back together with her ex-husband, who comes back to town as new chef at the local inn. When the two are cast as cohosts on a local cooking show, they struggle to prevent their growing attraction.

Flagg, Fannie. *Fried Green Tomatoes at the Whistle Stop Café.*
An elderly woman tells the story of Idgie and Ruth, who run a railroad café in the 1930s, which is known for its good barbeque.

Gee, Darien. *Friendship Bread.*
A woman who is grieving for the loss of her son finds a starter batch of Amish friendship bread on her porch one morning. As she begins baking the bread and sharing the starter with others, she begins to heal.

Hendricks, Judith Ryan. *Bread Alone.*
When her husband leaves her for another woman, Wynter leaves Los Angeles for Seattle, where she takes a job in a bakery, finding solace in bread making.

Hilderbrand, Elin. *The Blue Bistro.*
Adrienne lands a job as the hostess of an upscale restaurant on Nantucket Island, which is scheduled to be sold at the end of summer.

Hinton, J. Lynne. *Friendship Cake.*
When a women's church group decides to create a cookbook, they share their joys and sorrows as well as their recipes, creating lasting friendships.

Israel, Andrea. *The Recipe Club: A Tale of Food and Friendship.*
Two lifelong friends, Val and Lilly, share their hopes, dreams, secrets, and favorite recipes over the years through letters.

Jacobs, Kate. *Comfort Food.*
As TV celebrity chef Augusta Simpson approaches her 50th birthday, her show's falling ratings prompt her producers to bring in a new cohost: a younger beauty queen.

Jacobs, Melissa. *Love, Life and Linguini.*
Successful Philadelphia restaurant consultant leaves her cheating boyfriend and returns home to help save her family's fledgling restaurant.

James, Kay-Marie. *Cooking for Harry: A Low-Carbohydrate Novel.*
After 25 years of marriage and overeating, Harry decides to go on a diet. His new lifestyle leaves his wife, Francie, feeling left out.

Kafka, Kimberly. *Miranda's Vines.*
Successful chef Miranda leaves her promising career in San Francisco behind to return to Oregon to take over her family's endangered vineyard and care for her injured friend.

Killham, Nina. *How to Cook a Tart.*
Jasmine March is a cookbook author whose love for rich, fattening dishes has left her unpopular in today's diet-obsessed culture. Struggling with an anorexic

daughter trying to lose her virginity and a husband whose midlife crisis includes a mistress, Jasmine, has more than she can handle when she discovers her husband's mistress murdered on her kitchen floor.

King, Mia. *Table Manners.*
Deidre McIntosh is a successful cooking show host with her own line of sweets and a great relationship with one of Seattle's most eligible bachelors. But the reappearance of her boyfriend's ex-fiancé makes Deidre insecure about their relationship.

Kirchner, Bharti. *Pastries: A Novel of Desserts and Discoveries.*
Sunya, a pastry chef, is struggling with relationship troubles, her mother's obnoxious boyfriend, and a big chain bakery that threatens her own small shop. Hoping to recover from her slump, Sunya heads to a baking school in Japan to rediscover the joy of baking.

Lopez, Josefina. *Hungry Woman in Paris.*
After losing a loved one and ending a relationship, a confused and depressed young woman flees to Paris and enrolls in cooking school.

Lynch, Sarah-Kate. *Blessed Are the Cheesemakers.*
When a young woman's marriage ends in divorce, she returns to her estranged grandfather's dairy farm in Ireland and begins to pick up the pieces of her life while finding joy in cheese making.

Lynch, Sarah-Kate. *By Bread Alone.*
Esme consoles herself after a family tragedy by baking bread and reminiscing about the summer she spent in France, learning to bake bread and falling in love.

Lynch, Sarah-Kate. *Dolci di Love.*
When Lily Turner discovers her husband has a secret second family in Tuscany, she travels to Italy to track him down and is taken in by two elderly widows who own a bakery.

Lynch, Sarah-Kate. *House of Daughters.*
Three half-sisters inherit their father's fledgling champagne vineyard and set about bringing it back to life while they mend their fragile relationship.

Mallery, Susan. *Delicious.*
When Cal Buchanan's family restaurant is in danger of failing, he brings in the best chef he can find: his ex-wife. As the two are forced to work closely, sparks fly.

Martin, Deirdre. *Just a Taste.*
When Vivi opens a French bistro across the street from Anthony's Italian restaurant, the competition between the two quickly turn into a heated romance.

McCouch, Hannah. *Girl Cook.*
A young female chef tries to make her way in the competitive Manhattan restaurant scene while looking for love. *Library Journal* called it Anthony Bourdain meets Bridget Jones.

Mehran, Marsha. *Pomegranate Soup.*
Three sisters flee Iran for a small village in Ireland, where they open their own café, winning over the townspeople with their exotic fare.

Nathan, Melissa. *The Waitress.*
Waiting tables until she can figure out what to do with her life, Katie's life becomes even more complicated when her love interest buys the restaurant where she works.

Nelson, Jenny. *Georgia's Kitchen.*
Georgia Gray, a talented chef, has it all: a great job, great friends, and a great fiancé. When Georgia receives a bad review, she calls off her engagement and escapes to Italy, where she finds solace in the beautiful countryside, luscious food, and fine wines.

Norris, Frances. *Blue Plate Special.*
Julia is a food stylist for a gourmet magazine but is unhappy with her job and is dealing with the recent deaths of her parents. With the help of a therapist and her friends, she begins to recognize her depression and starts to create a new life for herself.

O'Neal, Barbara. *The Lost Recipe for Happiness.*
Santa Fe chef Elena Alvarez has just been fired from her job. When she is offered a job opening a new restaurant in Aspen, she finds fresh start.

Owens, Sharon. *The Tea House on Mulberry Street.*
An old tea house in Belfast is like home to a handful of locals, all contemplating making changes in their lives.

Palmer, Liza. *Seeing Me Naked.*
Elisabeth is a pastry chef at a hot Los Angeles restaurant. Elisabeth faces pressure from her demanding head chef, her disapproving father, and is unfulfilled with her relationship with her childhood sweetheart, until a new job offer and a new guy turn things around for her.

Parkhurst, Brooke. *Belle in the Big Apple.*
Belle leaves her home in Mobile, Alabama for New York City, where she takes a job as a journalist for a corrupt conservative news channel. Belle eventually leaves her job to pursue her passion for Southern cooking.

Pezzelli, Peter. *Francesca's Kitchen.*
A widow whose children are all grown up decides to take a job as a nanny, and uses her culinary skills to comfort her adopted family.

Prior, Lily. *La Cucina.*
While working as a librarian in Palermo, Italy, Rosa meets a mysterious English chef and the two quickly begin a passionate affair while sharing their love of food.

Senate, Melissa. *The Love Goddess' Cooking School.*
When Holly inherits her Grandmother's Italian cooking school, she returns home determined to carry on her grandmother's cooking.

Wingate, Lisa. *Texas Cooking.*
> A Washington, DC reporter is sent to Texas to write about small town life and Texas cooking and ends up falling in love with the simple life as well as a local bad boy.

Mystery or Crime

Aames, Avery. *The Long Quiche Goodbye.*
> A murder interrupts the grand opening of Charlotte Bessette's new cheese shop. This is the first in the Cheese Shop series of three mysteries.

Beck, Jessica. *Glazed Murder.*
> When a dead body is dumped on the doorstop of her donut shop, Suzanne Hart attempts to find the killer. The first in the Donut Shop series of eight mysteries.

Bishop, Claudia. *A Taste for Murder.*
> Sarah Quilliam manages a local inn with her sister Meg, who is the chef. When a murder occurs at the inn, the sisters attempt to solve the mystery. The first in the Hemlock Falls series of 17.

Bliss, Miranda. *Cooking up Murder.*
> Two best friends take a cooking class together and become involved in a murder when a body is found in the parking lot after class. The first in the Cooking Class series of five.

Bourdain, Anthony. *Bone in the Throat.*
> Tommy Pagano takes a job as a chef in his uncle's Italian restaurant in Little Italy, but finds himself embroiled with mafia hit men and FBI stings. Bourdain has also written two other crime novels, *Gone Bamboo* and *The Bobby Gold Stories.*

Campion, Alexander. *Grave Gourmet.*
> A young Parisian police detective is assigned to the case of a murdered executive whose body is found in the freezer of Paris's best restaurant. The first in the Capucine Culinary series of three.

Carl, JoAnna. *The Chocolate Cat Caper.*
> Lee McKinney takes a job working for her aunt's luxury chocolate business and becomes involved in a murder when a client eats poisoned chocolate. The first in the Chocoholic series of 11.

Cavender, Chris. *A Slice of Murder.*
> Pizzeria owner Eleanor Swift stumbles on a murder victim when making a delivery. The first in the Pizza Lovers series of four.

Childs, Laura. *Eggs in Purgatory.*
> When three best friends open a café, their first customer is murdered. The first in the Cackleberry Club series of three. Childs also has another mystery series featuring a tea shop, *Death by Darjeeling.*

Conant-Park, Jessica, and Conant, Susan. *Steamed.*

The first of five in the Gourmet Girl mystery series introduces Chloe Carter, a foodie who has been unsuccessful at love. When Chloe goes on a blind date with a fellow foodie who is killed, Chloe ends up investigating the murder.

Coyle, Cleo. *On What Grounds.*

Clare is the manager of the village coffee shop. When the assistant manager's murder is chalked up to robbery, Clare decides to investigate on her own. The first of 11 in the Coffeehouse Mystery series.

Crawford, Isis. *A Catered Murder.*

When two sisters cater their high-school reunion, they become involved in a murder investigation when one of the guests drops dead at the dinner. The first of six in the Mysteries with Recipes series.

Davidson, Diane Mott. *Catering to Nobody.*

Caterer Goldy Bear is hired to cater a wake, but when one of the guests is poisoned, Goldy becomes a prime suspect. The first of 16 in the Goldy Bear series.

Farmer, Jerrilyn. *Sympathy for the Devil.*

The first in a series introduces Madeline Bean, a caterer to Hollywood's celebrities. When Madeline caters a Halloween party for a notorious producer and a guest is killed, she finds herself embroiled in a mystery. The first of five in the Madeline Bean Catering series.

Fluke, Joanne. *Chocolate Chip Cookie Murder.*

Bakery owner Hannah Swenson finds the deliveryman murdered behind her bakery and assists the sheriff in the investigation. The first of 15 Hannah Swensen mysteries.

Gannascoli, Joseph. *A Meal to Die For.*

Brooklyn chef and mobster Benny "the Food Fence" Lacoco prepares an elaborate meal for fellow wise guys, while trying to guess which one of them is the rumored rat.

Goodhind, J. G. *A Taste to Die For.*

When the victorious chef of the Bath International Taste Extravaganza is murdered, Honey Driver, hotel owner, finds herself trying to clear her chef's name. The first of seven in the Honey Driver series.

Greenwood, Kerry. *Earthly Delights.*

Corinna Chapman, owner of Earthly Delights bakery, teams up with her offbeat neighbors to investigate a series of death threats. The first of six in the Corinna Chapman series.

Hyzy, Julie. *State of the Onion.*

This cozy mystery is the first in a series featuring White House assistant chef Olivia Paras. Here she competes for the top chef position and takes on the role of amateur sleuth after she catches a mysterious intruder at the White House. The first of five in the White House Chef series.

Johnson, Claire. *Beat Until Stiff.*
A pastry chef at a popular San Francisco restaurant finds herself involved in a murder investigation when she finds a coworker's dead body stuffed in a laundry bag. There are two titles in the Mary Ryan series.

King, Peter. *The Gourmet Detective.*
An ex-chef known as the Gourmet Detective works as a consultant on restaurant menus and tracks down hard to find ingredients. In this first novel of eight in the series, the Gourmet Detective is hired by a restaurant owner to find out who is trying to sabotage his restaurant. When a journalist is poisoned, the Gourmet Detective is asked to help Scotland Yard's Food Squad solve the case.

Laurence, Janet. *Death and the Epicure.*
English cook and caterer Darina Lisle is hired to write a cookbook for a gourmet food company. When a company employee is murdered, Darina gets involved in the investigation. There are six titles in the Darina Lisle series.

Myers, Tamar. *Too Many Cooks Spoil the Broth.*
Magdalena Yoder is a Mennonite innkeeper. Aside from trying to accommodate the guests many different dietary restrictions, Magdalena is further put out when two of her guests wind up dead. There are 18 titles in the Pennsylvania Dutch mystery series.

Page, Katherine Hall. *Body in the Big Apple.*
Caterer Faith Fairchild gets caught up in a mystery when a former high school classmate tells her she is being blackmailed. The first of 20 titles in the Faith Fairchild series.

Pence, Joanne. *Something's Cooking.*
Food columnist Angie Amalfi must help solve the murder of a frequent contributor to her column while trying to stay out of danger. The first of 14 Angie Amalfi mysteries.

Pickard, Nancy. *The Cooking School Murders.*
In the first of six in the Eugenia Potter series, Ms. Potter organizes a cooking class with a noted gourmand. However, when a murder involves the members of the class, Ms. Potter attempts to solve the crime.

Richman, Phyllis. *The Butter Did It.*
When Washington, DC's finest French chef is murdered, restaurant critic Chas Wheatley assists a gastronomic detective in the investigation. The first of three Chas Wheatley mysteries.

Watson, Wendy Lyn. *I Scream, You Scream.*
Ice cream shop owner Tally Jones investigates the murder of her ex-husband's new girlfriend. The first of three in the Mystery a la Mode series.

Wells, Melinda. *Killer Mousse.*

When Della Carmichael's cooking show ends in murder, she must prove her innocence. The first of four in the Della Cooks series.

History

Boyle, T. C. *The Road to Wellville.*

In 1907, a couple visits John Harvey Kellogg's health spa in Michigan in search of better health.

Ceely, Jonatha. *Mina.*

In 1848, a young Irish girl disguises herself as a boy to work on an English estate. As she works in the estate's kitchen, she develops a friendship with the chef.

Gleeson, Janet. *The Thief Taker.*

Agnes Meadowes is a cook to an English family of silversmiths in 18th-century London. When an apprentice is killed, a maid goes missing, and an expensive silver commission stolen, the family charge Agnes with unraveling the mysteries. The below stairs portrayal and descriptions of the 18th-century cook's life will appeal to fans of history.

Jones, Idwal. *High Bonnet: A Novel of Epicurean Adventures.*

Originally published in 1945, this story follows a young Frenchman as he works his way from candy maker up to apprentice chef to chef de cuisine in upscale French restaurants during the 1930s.

Newmark, Elle. *The Book of Unholy Mischief.*

In Renaissance Venice, an orphan boy is taken in as a chef's apprentice in the palace of the doge. While working in the kitchens he learns that the doge is searching for ancient book of alchemy.

Schell, Adam. *Tomato Rhapsody.*

In a 16th-century Tuscan village, a Jewish tomato farmer falls in love with the Catholic daughter of an olive tycoon.

Temple, Lou Jane. *The Spice Box.*

Bridget Heaney arrives in New York City during the Civil War, fleeing the potato famine in Ireland. She finds a job as a cook for a wealthy Jewish merchant, but when his son is murdered, Bridget helps the family to find the killer. Temple wrote a second Spice Box historical mystery, *Death du Jour.*

Widmer, Eleanor. *Up from Orchard Street.*

Three generations of a Russian Jewish immigrant family live on Orchard Street on the lower east side of New York City, with a matriarch who is known for cooking and operates a restaurant out of their tenement apartment.

Christian Fiction

Clark, Mindy Starns. *Under the Cajun Moon.*
A dying chef decides to publish his secret recipes while his daughter is caught up in a murder when she returns to take care of family business.

Hauck, Rachel. *Dining With Joy.*
Joy, a cooking show host harbors a big secret: she can't actually cook. When the producers bring in a chef to cohost, Joy hopes he can save her.

Wright, Vinita. *Velma Still Cooks in Leeway.*
Velma Brendle is the aging widower who owns Leeway's only café, where the dramas of the townspeople are played out.

Appendix D

Food Writing Awards

James Beard Foundation Book Awards

James Beard is considered by many to be the father of American cuisine. After his death in 1985, The James Beard Foundation was established to foster interest in the culinary arts. The James Beard Foundation Awards were established in 1990 to recognize the best talent in the food and beverage industry. The awards cover all aspects of the industry, including chefs, restaurateurs, food journalists, cookbook authors, and more. The James Beard Foundation Awards are awarded annually and have come to be thought of as the Oscars of the food world. Below is a list of the James Beard Foundation Book Awards from 2000 to 2011.

2011

Cookbook of the Year: *Oaxaca al Gusto: An Infinite Gastronomy* by Diana Kennedy

American Cooking: *Pig: King of the Southern Table* by James Villas

Baking and Dessert: *Good to the Grain: Baking with Whole-Grain Flours* by Kim Boyce

Beverage: *Secrets of the Sommeliers: How to Think Like the World's Top Wine Professionals* by Jordan Mackay and Rajat Parr

Cooking from a Professional Point of View: *Noma: Time and Place in Nordic Cuisine* by Rene Redzepi

General Cooking: *The Essential New York Times Cookbook: Classic Recipes for a New Century* by Amanda Hesser

Healthy Focus: *The Simple Art of EatingWell: 400 Easy Recipes, Tips and Techniques for Delicious, Healthy Meals* by Jessie Price

International: *Stir-Frying to the Sky's Edge: The Ultimate Guide to Mastery, with Authentic Recipes and Stories* by Grace Young

Photography: *Noma: Time and Place in Nordic Cuisine* by Rene Redzepi

Reference and Scholarship: *Salted: A Manifesto on the World's Most Essential Mineral* by Mark Bitterman

Single Subject: *Meat: A Kitchen Education* by James Peterson

Writing and Literature: *Four Fish: The Future of the Last Wild Food* by Paul Greenberg

2010

Cookbook of the Year: *The Country Cooking of Ireland* by Colman Andrews

Cookbook Hall of Fame: *A Book of Middle Eastern Food* by Claudia Roden

American Cooking: *Real Cajun* by Donald Link with Paula Disbrowe

Baking and Dessert: *Baking* by James Peterson

Beverage: *Been Doon So Long: A Randall Grahm Vinthology* by Randall Grahm

Cooking from a Professional Point of View: *The Fundamental Techniques of Classic Pastry Arts* by The French Culinary Institute with Judith Choate

General Cooking: *Ad Hoc at Home* by Thomas Keller with Dave Cruz

Healthy Focus: *Love Soup: 160 All-New Vegetarian Recipes from the Author of the Vegetarian Epicure* by Anna Thomas

International: *The Country Cooking of Ireland* by Colman Andrews

Reference and Scholarship: *Encyclopedia of Pasta* by Oretta Zanini de Vita

Single Subject: *Pasta Sfoglia* by Ron Suhanosky and Colleen

Writing and Literature: *Save the Deli* by David Sax

Photography: *Seven Fires: Grilling the Argentine Way* by Santiago Solo Monllor

2009

Cookbook of the Year: *Fat: An Appreciation of a Misunderstood Ingredient, with Recipes* by Jennifer McLagan

Cookbook Hall of Fame: Jane Grigson for her entire body of work, including: *The Art of Charcuterie, Good Things, Jane Grigson's Vegetable Book, The Mushroom Feast,* and *English Food*

American Cooking: *Screen Doors and Sweet Tea: Recipes and Tales from a Southern Cook* by Martha Hall Foose

Baking and Dessert: *Bakewise: The Hows and Whys of Successful Baking* by Shirley O. Corriher

Beverage: *WineWise: Your Complete Guide to Understanding, Selecting, and Enjoying Wine* by Steven Kolpan, Brian H. Smith, and Michael A. Weiss

Cooking from a Professional Point of View: *Alinea* by Grant Achatz

General Cooking: *How to Cook Everything (Completely Revised Tenth Anniversary Edition)* by Mark Bittman

Healthy Focus: *The Food You Crave: Luscious Recipes for a Healthy Life* by Ellie Krieger

International: *Beyond the Great Wall: Recipes and Travels in the Other China* by Jeffrey Alford, and Naomi Duguid

Reference and Scholarship: *The Flavor Bible: The Essential Guide to Culinary Creativity, Based on the Wisdom of America's Most Imaginative Chefs* by Karen Page, and Andrew Dornenburg

Single Subject: *Fat: An Appreciation of a Misunderstood Ingredient, with Recipes* by Jennifer McLagan

Writing and Literature: *In Defense of Food* by Michael Pollan

Photography: *The Big Fat Duck Cookbook* by Dominic Davies

2008

Cookbook of the Year: *The River Cottage Meat Book* by Hugh Fearnley-Whittingstall

Cookbook Hall of Fame: *Couscous and Other Good Food from Morocco* by Paula Wolfert

Asian Cooking: *My Bombay Kitchen: Traditional and Modern Parsi Home Cooking* by Niloufer Ichaporia King

Baking and Dessert: *Peter Reinhart's Whole Grain Breads: New Techniques, Extraordinary Flavor* by Peter Reinhart

Cooking from a Professional Point of View: *The Fundamental Techniques of Classic Cuisine* by The French Culinary Institute with Judith Choate

Entertaining: *Dish Entertains* by Trish Magwood

Americana: *A Love Affair with Southern Cooking* by Jean Anderson

General Cooking: *Cooking* by James Peterson

Healthy Focus: *The EatingWell Diet* by Jean Harvey-Berino with Joyce Hendley

International: *The Country Cooking of France* by Anne Willan

Reference: *A Geography of Oysters: The Connoisseur's Guide to Oyster Eating in North* by Rowan Jacobsen

Single Subject: *The River Cottage Meat Book* by Hugh Fearnley-Whittingstall

Wine and Spirits: *Imbibe!: From Absinthe Cocktail to Whiskey Smash, a Salute in Stories and Drinks to "Professor" Jerry Thomas, Pioneer of the American Bar* by David Wondrich

Writing on Food: *Animal, Vegetable, Miracle: A Year of Food Life* by Barbara Kingsolver

Photography: *The Country Cooking of France* by France Ruffenach

2007

Cookbook of the Year: *The Lee Bros. Southern Cookbook* by Matt Lee, and Ted Lee

Cookbook Hall of Fame: *Moosewood Cookbook* by Mollie Katzen

Asian Cooking: *Cradle of Flavor* by James Oseland

Baking and Dessert: *Baking: From My Home to Yours* by Dorie Greenspan

Cooking from a Professional Point of View: *Alain Ducasse's Desserts and Pastries* by Alain Ducasse, and Frederic Robert

Entertaining: *The Big Book of Outdoor Cooking and Entertaining* by Cheryl Alters Jamison, and Bill Jamison

Food of the Americas: *The Lee Bros. Southern Cookbook* by Matt Lee, and Ted Lee

General Cooking: *Tasty: Get Great Food on the Table Everyday* by Roy Finamore

Healthy Focus: *Whole Grains Every Day, Every Way* by Lorna Sass

International: *The Soul of a New Cuisine* by Marcus Samuelsson

Reference: *What to Eat* by Marion Nestle

Single Subject: *The Essence of Chocolate* by John Scharffenberger, and Robert Steinberg

Wine and Spirits: *Romancing the Vine* by Alan Tardi

Writing on Food: *The Omnivore's Dilemma* by Michael Pollan

Photography: *Michael Mina* by Michael Mina

2006

Cookbook of the Year *Hungry Planet: What the World Eats* by Peter Menzel, and Faith D'Aluisio

Cookbook Hall of Fame: *An Invitation to Indian Cooking* by Madhur Jaffrey

Baking and Desserts: *Dough: Simple Contemporary Bread* by Richard Bertinet

Cooking from a Professional Point of View: *Sunday Suppers at Lucques* by Suzanne Goin

Entertaining and Special Occasions: *Simple Soirées: Seasonal Menus for Sensational Dinner Parties* by Peggy Knickerbocker

Food of the Americas: *The New American Cooking* by Joan Nathan

General Cooking: *The Cook's Book* by Jill Norman

Healthy Focus: *Spices of Life: Simple and Delicious Recipes for Great Health* by Nina Simonds

International: *Molto Italiano* by Mario Batali

Reference: *Cheese: A Connoisseur's Guide to the World's Best* by Max McCalman, and David Gibbons

Single Subject: *Bones: Recipes, History & Lore Author* by Jennifer McLagan

Wine and Spirits: *Whiskey* by Michael Jackson

Writings on Food: *Hungry Planet: What the World Eats* by Peter Menzel, and Faith D'Aluisio

Photography: *Nobu Now* by Eiichi Takahashi

2005

Cookbook of the Year: *Rick Stein's Complete Seafood* by Rick Stein

Cookbook Hall of Fame: *The Great Scandinavian Baking Book* by Beatrice Ojakangas

General Cooking: *Weir Cooking in the City: More than 125 Recipes and Inspiring Ideas for Relaxed Entertaining* by Joanne Weir

Baking and Desserts: *A Blessing of Bread: The Many Rich Traditions of Jewish Bread Baking Around the World* by Maggie Glezer

Cooking from a Professional Point of View: *John Ash: Cooking One on One: Private Lessons in Simple, Contemporary Food, From a Master Teacher* by John Ash

Entertaining and Special Occasions: *Serena, Food & Stories: Feeding Friends Every Hour of the Day* by Serena Bass

Food of the Americas: *Food of the Americas: Native Recipes and Traditions* by Fernando Divina

Healthy Focus: *The New Mayo Clinic Cookbook: Eating Well for Better Health* by Cheryl Forberg

International: *The Provence Cookbook* by Patricia Wells

Photography: *Bouchon* by Thomas Keller

Reference: *On Food and Cooking: The Science and Lore of the Kitchen* by Harold McGee

Single Subject: *All About Braising: The Art of Uncomplicated Cooking* by Molly Stevens

Vegetarian: *Olive Trees and Honey: A Treasury of Vegetarian Recipes from Jewish Communities Around the World* by Gil Marks

Wine and Spirits: *Scotch Whiskey: A Liquid History* by Charles MacLean

Writing on Food: *Last Chance to Eat: The Fate of Taste in a Fast Food World* by Gina Mallet

2004

Cookbook of the Year: *The King Arthur Flour Baker's Companion* by King Arthur Flour

Cookbook Hall of Fame: *The Modern Art of Chinese Cooking* by Barbara Tropp

Baking: *The Secrets of Baking: Simple Techniques for Sophisticated Desserts* by Sherry Yard

Cooking from a Professional Point of View: *Flavor* by Rocco DiSpirito

Food of the Americas: *It's All American Food* by David Rosengarten

General Cooking: *The Quick Recipe* by The Editors of Cook's Illustrated Magazine

Healthy Focus and Vegetarian: *Taste Pure and Simple* by Michel Nischan

International: *From Curries to Kebabs* by Madhur Jaffrey

Single Subject: *The All American Cheese and Wine Book* by Laura Werlin

Tools and Techniques: *BBQ USA* by Steven Raichlen

Wine and Spirits: *Wines of South America* by Monty Waldins

Writing and Reference: *A Thousand Years Over a Hot Stove* by Laura Schenone

Photography: *Shunju: New Japanese Cuisine* by Masano Kawana

2003

Cookbook of the Year: *The Zuni Cafe Cookbook* by Judy Rodgers

Cookbook Hall of Fame: Edna Lewis for her entire body of work, including: *The Edna Lewis Cookbook, The Taste of Country Cooking, In Pursuit of Flavor,* and *The Gift of Southern Cooking*

Americana: *Foods of the Southwest Indian Nations* by Lois Ellen Frank

Baking: *Baking in America* by Greg Patent

General Cooking: *Local Flavors* by Deborah Madison

Cooking from a Professional Point of View: *The Zuni Cafe Cookbook* by Judy Rodgers

International: *Thai Food* by David Thompson

Literary: *Food Politics: How the Food Industry Influences Nutrition and Health* by Marion Nestle

Mediterranean: *Glorious French Food* by James Peterson

Photography: *The Anatomy of a Dish* by Diane Forley with Catherine Young; photographer Victor Schrager

Reference: *I'm Just Here for the Food* by Alton Brown

Single Subject: *The Flavors of Olive Oil* by Deborah Krasner

Tools and Techniques: *Process This!* by Jean Anderson

Vegetarian or Healthy Focus: *Passionate Vegetarian* by Crescent Dragonwagon

Wines and Spirits: *Michael Broadbent's Vintage Wine* by Michael Broadbent

2002

Cookbook of the Year: *The Bread Baker's Apprentice* by Peter Reinhart

Cookbook Hall of Fame: *North Atlantic Seafood* by Alan Davidson

Americana: *Mustards Grill Napa Valley Cookbook* by Cindy Pawlcyn with Brigid Callinan

Baking and Desserts: *The Bread Baker's Apprentice* by Peter Reinhart

Entertaining and Special Occasions: *Jacques Pépin Celebrates* by Jacques Pépin

General: *Back to the Table* by Art Smith

Healthy Focus: *A New Way to Cook* by Sally Schneider

International: *Madhur Jaffrey's Step-by-Step Cooking* by Madhur Jaffrey

Italian: *Sicilian Home Cooking* by Wanda, and Giovanna Tornabene with Michele Evans

Single Subject: *¡Ceviche!* by Guillermo Pernot with Aliza Green

Reference: *Larousse Gastronomique* by Librarie Larousse

Wine and Spirits: *Wine* edited by Andre Dominé

Writing on Food: *The Last Days of Haute Cuisine* by Patric Kuh

Photography: *Charlie Trotter's Meat and Game* by Charlie Trotter; photographer Tim Turner

2001

Cookbook of the Year: *Hot Sour Salty Sweet: A Culinary Journey Through Southeast Asia* by Jeffrey Alford, and Naomi Duguid

Cookbook Hall of Fame: *A Book of Mediterranean Food* by Elizabeth David

Americana: *Tom Douglas' Seattle Kitchen* by Tom Douglas

Baking and Desserts: *Artisan Baking Across America* by Maggie Glezer

Entertaining and Special Occasions: *Savor the Moment* by the Junior League of Boca Raton, Florida

General: *Think Like a Chef* by Tom Colicchio

Healthy Focus: *Healthy Jewish Cooking* by Steven Raichlen

International: *Mexico: One Plate at a Time* by Rick Bayless with JeanMarie Brownson, and Deann Groen Bayless

Single Subject: *The Good Egg* by Marie Simmons

Vegetarian: *The Modern Vegetarian Kitchen* by Peter Berley

Wine and Spirits: *American Vintage: The Rise of American Wine* by Paul Lukacs

Writing and Reference: *Pot on the Fire: Further Exploits of a Renegade Cook* by John Thorne with Matt Lewis Thorne

Photography: *Hot Sour Salty Sweet: A Culinary Journey Through Southeast Asia* by Jeffrey Alford, and Naomi Duguid; photographers Jeffrey Alford, Naomi Duguid, and Richard Jung

2000

Cookbook of the Year: *A Mediterranean Feast* by Clifford A. Wright

Cookbook Hall of Fame: *The Classic Italian Cookbook* by Marcella Hazan

Americana: *American Home Cooking* by Cheryl Alters Jamison, and Bill Jamison

Baking and Desserts: *The Bread Bible* by Beth Hensperger

Chefs and Restaurants: *The Kitchen Sessions with Charlie Trotter* by Charlie Trotter

Entertaining and Special Occasions: *Entertaining 1-2-3* by Rozanne Gold

General: *Julia and Jacques Cooking at Home* by Julia Child, and Jacques Pépin

Healthy Focus: *A Spoonful of Ginger* by Nina Simonds

International: *Madhur Jaffrey's World Vegetarian* by Madhur Jaffrey

Reference: *The Oxford Companion to Food* by Alan Davidson

Single Subject: *The Cook's Illustrated Complete Book of Poultry* by the editors of Cook's Illustrated magazine

Wine and Spirits: *Terroir* by James E. Wilson

Writing on Food: *A Mediterranean Feast* by Clifford A. Wright

Photography: *New Food Fast* by Donna Hay; photographer Petrina Tinslay

IACP Awards

Each year, the International Association of Culinary Professionals (IACP) recognizes outstanding accomplishments in cookbook writing, food journalism, professional excellence, and food photography. The IACP Cookbook Awards promote quality, creativity, and awareness of culinary literature with awards in 17 categories.

2011

Cookbook of the Year: *Around My French Table* by Dorie Greenspan

American: *The Lee Bros. Simple Fresh Southern* by Matt Lee, and Ted Lee

Baking: *Chewy Gooey Crispy Crunchy Melt-in-Your-Mouth Cookies* by Alice Medrich

Chefs and Restaurants: *Flying Pans: Two Chefs, One World* by Bernard Guillas, and Ron Oliver

Children, Youth and Family: *Sara Moulton's Everyday Family Dinners* by Sara Moulton

Compilations: *The Essential New York Times Cookbook* by Amanda Hesser

Culinary History: *Culinary Ephemera: An Illustrated History* by William Woys Weaver

First Book (The Julia Child Award): *Fried Chicken & Champagne: A Romp Through the Kitchen at Pomegranate Bistro* by Lisa Dupar

Food Matters: *American Wasteland* by Jonathan Bloom

Food Photography and Styling: *Noma: Time and Place in Nordic Cuisine* by René Redzepi

Food and Beverage Reference/Technical: *Food Styling: The Art of Preparing Food for the Camera* by Delores Custer

General: *Around My French Table: More Than 300 Recipes From My Home To Yours* by Dorie Greenspan

Health and Special Diet: *Essentials of Nutrition for Chefs* by Catharine Powers, and Mary Abbott Hess

International: *The Country Cooking of Ireland* by Coleman Andrews

Literary Food Writing: *As Always, Julia: The Letters of Julia Child & Avis DeVoto* by Joan Reardon

Professional Kitchens: *Wedding Cake Art and Design: A Professional Approach* by Toba Garrett

Single Subject: *Meat: A Kitchen Education* by James Peterson

Wine, Beer or Spirits: *Asian Palate* by Jeannie Cho Lee

Design Award: *Noma: Time and Place in Nordic Cuisine* by René Redzepi

Jane Grigson Award: *Chanterelle Dreams, Amanita Nightmares: The Love, Lore, and Mystique of Mushrooms* by Greg Marley

Jane Grigson Award: *What I Eat: Around the World in 80 Diets* by Peter Menzel, and Faith D'Aluisio

Judge's Choice Award: *Cooking with Italian Grandmothers: Recipes and Stories from Tuscany to Sicily* by Jessica Theroux

People's Choice Award: *Flying Pans: Two Chefs, One World* by Bernard Guillas, and Ron Oliver

2010

Cookbook of the Year: *Rose's Heavenly Cakes* by Rose Levy Beranbaum

American: *My New Orleans: The Cookbook* by John Besh

Baking: *Rose's Heavenly Cakes* by Rose Levy Beranbaum

Chefs and Restaurants: *Ad Hoc at Home* by Thomas Keller, and Dave Cruz

Children, Youth and Family: *William Sonoma Family Meals* by Maria Helm Sinsky

Compilations: *Gourmet Today* by Ruth Reichl

Culinary History: *Of Sugar and Snow: A History of Ice Cream Making* by Jeri Quinzio

First Book (The Julia Child Award): *The New Portuguese Table* by David Leite

Food Photography and Styling: *Williams-Sonoma Cooking for Friends* by Alison Attenborough, and Jamie Kimm

Food and Beverage Reference/Technical: *The Fundamental Techniques of Classic Pastry Arts* by The French Culinary Institute

General: *Stephanie Alexander's Kitchen Garden Companion* by Stephanie Alexander

Health and Special Diet: *The Cancer-Fighting Kitchen: Nourishing, Big-Flavor Recipes for Cancer Treatment and Recovery* by Rebecca Katz, and Mat Edelson

International: *Mastering the Art of Chinese Cooking* by Eileen Yin-Fei Lo

Literary Food Writing: *Waste* by Tristram Stuart

Professional Kitchens: *Baking and Pastry: Mastering the Art and Craft* by The Culinary Institute of America

Single Subject: *Go Fish* by Al Brown

Wine, Beer or Spirits: *World Whiskey* by Charles Maclean

Design Awards: *Thai Street Food* by David Thompson

People's Choice: *The Cancer-Fighting Kitchen: Nourishing, Big-Flavor Recipes for Cancer Treatment and Recovery* by Rebecca Katz, and Mat Edelson

2009

Book of the Year: *A16: Food & Wine* by Nate Appleman, and Shelley Lindgren with Kate Leahy

American: *Arthur Schwartz's Jewish Home Cooking: Yiddish Recipes Revised* by Arthur Schwartz

Baking: *The Art and Soul of Baking* by Sur La Table, and Cindy Mushet

Chefs & Restaurants: *Chanterelle: The Stories and Recipes of a Restaurant Classic* by David Waltuck, and Andrew Friedman

Compilations: *The Bon Appétit Fast Easy Fresh Cookbook* by Barbara Fairchild

First Book (The Julia Child Award): *A16: Food & Wine* by Nate Appleman, and Shelley Lindgren with Kate Leahy

Food Photography and Styling: *Chanterelle* by David Waltuck, and Andrew Friedman

Food Reference and Technical: *The Science of Good Food* by David Joachim, and Andrew Schloss with Philip Handel, Ph.D.

General: *Do It For Less! Weddings: How to Create Your Dream Wedding Without Breaking the Bank* by Denise Vivaldo

Health and Special Diet: *The Food You Crave* by Ellie Krieger

International: *Beyond the Great Wall* by Jeffrey Alford, and Naomi Duguid

Literary Food Writing: *Bottomfeeder* by Taras Grescoe

Single Subject: *Fat: An Appreciation of a Misunderstood Ingredient* by Jennifer McLagan

Wine, Beer and Spirits: *Ciderland* by James Crowden

Jane Grigson Award: *Shark's Fin and Sichuan Pepper: A Sweet-Sour Memoir of Eating in China* by Fuschia Dunlop

Design Award: *The Big Fat Duck Cookbook* by Heston Blumenthal

2008

Cookbook of the Year: *Fish Forever: The Definitive Guide to Understanding, Selecting and Preparing Healthy, Delicious and Environmentally Sustainable Seafood* by Paul Johnson

American: *The Pastry Queen Christmas: Big-Hearted Holiday Entertaining, Texas Style* by Rebecca Rather, and Alison Oresman

Bread, Other Baking and Sweets: *Local Breads: Sourdough and Whole-Grain Recipes from Europe's Best Artisan Bakers* by Daniel Leader, and Lauren Chattman

Chefs and Restaurants: *Morimoto: The New Art of Japanese Cooking* by Masaharu Morimoto

Compilations: *Chocolates and Confections: Formula, Theory, and Techniques for the Artisan Confectioner* by The Culinary Institute of America, and Peter P. Greweling

First Book (The Julia Child Award): *Morimoto: The New Art of Japanese Cooking* by Masaharu Morimoto

Food Photography and Styling: *Good Spirits: Recipes, Revelations, Refreshments, and Romance, Shaken and Served with a Twist* by Melissa Punch

Food Reference/Technical: *Food: The History of Taste* by Paul Freedman

General: Cook with Jamie: *My Guide to Making You A Better Cook* by Jamie Oliver

Health and Special Diet: *How to Cook Everything Vegetarian: Simple Meatless Recipes for Great Food* by Mark Bittman

International: *Turquoise* by Greg Malouf, and Lucy Malouf

Literary Food Writing Category: *Julia Child* by Laura Shapiro

Single Subject: *Fish Forever: The Definitive Guide to Understanding, Selecting, and Preparing Healthy, Delicious, and Environmentally Sustainable Seafood* by Paul Johnson

Wine, Beer or Spirits: *The World Atlas of Wine* by Hugh Johnson, and Jancis Robinson

Jane Grigson Award: *Beans: A History* by Ken Albala and *To Cork or Not to Cork: Tradition, Romance, Science and the Battle for the Wine Bottle* by George M. Taber

Design Award: *Egg* by Publisher: Flammarion

2007

Cookbook of the Year: *What to Drink with What You Eat: The Definitive Guide to Pairing Food with Wine, Beer, Spirits, Coffee, Tea—Even water—Based on Expert Advice from America's* by Andrew Dornenburg, and Karen Page

American: *The Lee Bros. Southern Cookbook: Stories and Recipes for Southerners and Would-be Southerners* by Matt Lee, and Ted Lee

Bread, Other Baking and Sweets: *Bread Matters: The State of Modern Bread and a Definitive Guide to Baking Your Own* by Andrew Whitley

Chefs and Restaurants: *Allegra McEvedy's Colour Cookbook* by Allegra McEvedy

Compilations: *All-New Complete Cooking Light Cookbook* by Cooking Light magazine

First Book (The Julia Child Award): *The Lee Bros. Southern Cookbook: Stories and Recipes for Southerners and Would-be Southerners* by Matt Lee, and Ted Lee

Food Photography and Styling: *Simple Chinese Cooking* by Earl Carter

Food Reference/Technical: *Modern Garde Manger by Robert Garlough and Angus Campbell and The Spice and Herb Bible, Second Edition* by Ian Hemphill

General: *The Improvisational Cook* by Sally Schneider

Health and Special Diet: *Lunch Lessons: Changing the Way We Feed Our Children* by Ann Cooper, and Lisa M. Holmes

International: *Cradle of Flavor: Home Cooking from the Spice Islands of Indonesia, Malaysia, and Singapore* by James Oseland

Literary Food Writing: *My Life in France* by Julia Child, and Alex Prud'homme

Single Subject: *A Passion for Ice Cream: 95 recipes for Fabulous Desserts* by Emily Luchetti

Wine, Beer or Spirits: *What to Drink with What You Eat: The Definitive Guide to Pairing Food with Wine, Beer, Spirits, Coffee, Tea—Even Water—Based on Expert Advice from America's Best Sommeliers* by Andrew Dornenburg, and Karen Page

The Design Award: *Au Pied De Cochon: The Album* by Martin Picard, and Jean-Francois Boily

The Jane Grigson Award: *Memories of Philippine Kitchens: Stories and Recipes from Far and Near* by Amy Besa, and Romy Dorotan

2006

Cookbook of the Year: *Dough: Simple Contemporary Breads* by Richard Bertinet

American: *The New American Cooking* by Joan Nathan

Bread, Other Baking, and Sweets: *Chocolate Chocolate* by Lisa Yockelson

Chefs and Restaurants: *Easy Entertaining* by Darina Allen

Compilations: *Cooking at De Gustibus at Macy's: Celebrating Twenty-five Years of Innovation* by Arlene Feltman Sailhac

First Book (The Julia Child Award): *Dough: Simple Contemporary Breads* by Richard Bertinet

Food Photography and Styling: *Chocolate Obsession: Confections and Treats to Create and Savor* by Maren Caruso

Food Reference/Technical: *The Food Substitutions Bible* by David Joachim

General: Recipes: *A Collection for the Modern Cook* by Susan Spungen

Health and Special Diet: *Spices of Life* by Nina Simonds

International: *Mangoes and Curry Leaves* by Jeffrey Alford and Naomi Duguid

Literary Food Writing: *Chocolate: A Bittersweet Saga of Dark and Light* by Mort Rosenblum

Single Subject: *Vegetable Love* by Barbara Kafka

Wine, Beer or Spirits: *A History of Wine in America* by Thomas Pinney

The Design Award: *Fonda San Miguel: Thirty Years of Food and Art* by Shearer Publishing

The Jane Grigson Award: *Matzoh Ball Gumbo: Culinary Tales of the Jewish South* by Marcie Cohen Ferris and *Washoku: Recipes from the Japanese Home Kitchen* by Elizabeth Andoh

2005

Cookbook of the Year: *Arthur Schwartz's New York City Food: An Opinionated History and More Than 100 Legendary Recipes* by Arthur Schwartz

American: *Arthur Schwartz's New York City Food: An Opinionated History and More Than 100 Legendary Recipes* by Arthur Schwartz

Bread, Other Baking and Sweets: *A Blessing of Bread: The Many Rich Traditions of Jewish Bread Making Around the World* by Maggie Glezer

Chefs and Restaurants: *Bouchon* by Thomas Keller

Compilations: *Cooking New American: How to Cook the Food You Love to Eat, 200 Recipes from Fine Cooking Magazine* by The Editors of Fine Cooking Magazine

First Book (The Julia Child Award): *Bread: A Baker's Book of Techniques and Recipes* by Jeffrey Hamelman

Food Photography and Styling: *Bouchon* by Deborah Jones

Food Reference/Technical: *On Food and Cooking: The Science and Lore of the Kitchen* by Harold McGee

General: *Williams-Sonoma Entertaining* by George Dolese

Health and Special Diet: *Getting Thin and Loving Food!: 200 Easy Recipes to Take You Where You Want to Be* by Kathleen Daelemans

International: *The Breath of a Wok: Unlocking the Spirit of Chinese Wok Cooking Through Recipes and Lore* by Grace Young, and Alan Richardson

Literary Food Writing: *Poet of the Appetites: The Lives and Lores of M.F.K. Fisher* by Joan Reardon

Single Subject: *All About Braising: The Art of Uncomplicated Cooking* by Molly Stevens

Wine, Beer or Spirits: *Everyday Dining with Wine* by Andrea Immer

The Design Award: *The Japanese Kitchen* by Kyle Cathie, Ltd.

The Jane Grigson Award: *The Breath of a Wok: Unlocking the Spirit of Chinese Wok Cooking Through Recipes and Lore* by Grace Young, and Alan Richardson

2004

Cookbook of the Year: *BitterSweet: Recipes And Tales From A Life In Chocolate* by Alice Medrich

American: *Gulf Coast Kitchens: Bright Flavors from Key West to the Yucatan* by Constance Snow

Bread, Other Baking and Sweets: *Great Cookies: Secrets To Sensational Sweets* by Carole Walter

Chefs and Restaurants: *Bistro Cooking at Home* by Gordon Hamersley with Joanne McAllister Smart

Compilations: *Cooking at Home with the Culinary Institute of America* by The Culinary Institute of America

First Book (The Julia Child Award): *I Am Almost Always Hungry: Seasonal Menus and Memorable Recipes* by Lora Zarubin

Food Reference and Technical: *The Advanced Professional Pastry Chef* by Bo Friberg

General: *Bonnie Stern's Essentials of Home Cooking* by Bonnie Stern

Health and Special Diet: *Entertaining For A Veggie Planet: 250 Down-To-Earth Recipes* by Didi Emmons

International: *The Slow Mediterranean Kitchen: Recipes for the Passionate Cook* by Paula Wolfert

Literary Food Writing: *Cooking for Mr. Latte: A Food Lover's Courtship, With Recipes* by Amanda Hesser

Single Subject: *BitterSweet: Recipes And Tales From A Life In Chocolate* by Alice Medrich

Wine, Beer or Spirits: *The Brewmaster's Table: Discovering the Pleasures of Real Beer with Real Food* by Garrett Oliver

The Design Award: *The Balthazar Cookbook* by Clarkson Potter

The Jane Grigson Award: *Cooking by Hand* by Paul Bertolli

2003

Cookbook of the Year: *Vegetables From Amaranth to Zucchini: The Essential Reference* by Elizabeth Schneider

American: *American Classics* by The Editors of Cook's Illustrated

Bread, Other Baking and Sweets: *Baking by Flavor* by Lisa Yockelson

Chefs and Restaurants: *Zuni Café Cookbook* by Judy Rodgers

First Book (The Julia Child Award): *The Craft of the Cocktail* by Dale DeGroff

Food Reference/Technical: *Vegetables From Amaranth to Zucchini: The Essential Reference* by Elizabeth Schneider

General: *Michael Chiarello's Casual Cooking* by Michael Chiarello, and Janet Fletchers

Health and Special Diet: *Betty Crocker's Living with Cancer* by Betty Crocker Editors

International: *1,000 Indian Recipes* by Neelam Batra

Literary Food Writing: *Near a Thousand Tables: The History of Food* by Felipe Fernández-Armesto

Single Subject: *Italian Classics* by the Editors of Cook's Illustrated

Wine, Beer or Spirits: *Vino Italiano: The Regional Wines of Italy* by Joseph Bastianich, and David Lynchs

2002

Cookbook of the Year: *The Bread Baker's Apprentice: Mastering the Art of Extraordinary Bread* by Peter Reinhart

American: *The America's Test Kitchen Cookbook: The Recipes, Equipment Ratings, and Science Experiments from the Hit Public Television Show* by The Editors of Cook's Illustrated

Bread, Other Baking and Sweets: *The Bread Baker's Apprentice: Mastering the Art of Extraordinary Bread* by Peter Reinhart

Chef & Restaurants: *Lidia's Italian-American Kitchen* by Lidia Matticchio Bastianich

First Book (The Julia Child Award): *Recipes From Home* by Barbara Shinn, and David Page

Food Reference/Technical: *Professional Baking* by Wayne Gisslen

General: *A New Way to Cook* by Sally Schneider

Health and Special Diet: *Healthy 1-2-3: The Ultimate Three-Ingredient Cookbook* by Rozanne Gold

International: *Savoring India: Recipes and Reflections on Indian Cooking* by Julie Sahni

Literary Food Writing: *On Rue Tatin* by Susan Herrmann Loomis

Single Subject: *How to Grill* by Steven Raichlen

Wine, Beer, or Spirits: *Bordeaux: People, Power, and Politics* by Stephen Brook

The Jane Grigson Award: *The Glorious Foods of Greece* by Diane Kochilas and *Bordeaux: People, Power, and Politics* by Stephen Brook

The Design Award: *Van Gough's Table at the Auberge Ravoux* by Artisan

2001

Cookbook of the Year: *In the Sweet Kitchen: The Definitive Guide to the Baker's Pantry* by Regan Daley

American: *The New American Cheese: Profiles of America's Great Cheesemakers and Recipes for Cooking with Cheese* by Laura Werlin

Bread, Other Baking and Sweets: *In the Sweet Kitchen: The Definitive Guide to the Baker's Pantry* by Regan Daley

Chef and Restaurant: *The Herbfarm Cookbook* by Jerry Traunfeld

First Book (The Julia Child Award): *Cracking the Coconut* by Su-Mei Yu

Food Reference/Technical: *The Oxford Companion to the Wines of North America* by Bruce Cass, and Jancis Robinson

General: *The Minimalist Cooks at Home: Recipes That Give You More Flavor from Fewer Ingredients in Less Time* by Mark Bittman

Health and Special Diet: *Fresh & Healthy: The All new Victor Chang Cardiac Research Institute Cookbook, Good Medicine, 100 Fabulous New Low-Fat Recipes* by Sally James

International: *Savoring Southeast Asia: Recipes & Reflections on Southeast Asian Cooking* by Joyce Jue

Literary Food: *The Soul of a Chef: The Journey Toward Perfection* by Michael Ruhlman

Single Subject: *The Modern Vegetarian Kitchen* by Peter Berley

Wine, Beer, or Spirits: *American Vintage: The Rise of American Wine* by Paul Lukacs

The Jane Grigson Award: *The Pepper Trail* by Jean Andrews

The Design Award: *Hot Sour Salty Sweet* by Artisan

2000

Cookbook of the Year: *The French Laundry Cookbook* by Thomas Keller

American: *American Home Cooking* by Cheryl Alters Jamison, and Bill Jamison

Bread, Other Baking and Sweets: *Simply Sensational Desserts* by Francois Payard

Chef and Restaurant: *Chez Panisse Cafe Cookbook* by Alice Waters

First Book (The Julia Child Award): *The French Laundry Cookbook* by Thomas Keller

Food Reference and Technical: *The Oxford Companion to Food* by Alan Davidson

General: *Julia & Jacques Cooking at Home* by Julia Child, and Jacques Pépin

Health and Special Diet: *A Spoonful of Ginger* by Nina Simonds

International: *The Wisdom of the Chinese Kitchen* by Grace Young

Literary Food: *The Cook and the Gardener: A Year of Recipes and Writings from the French Countryside* by Amanda Hesser

Single Subject: *Martha Stewart's Hors d'oeuvers Handbook* by Martha Stewart, and Susan Spungen

Wine, Beer, or Spirits: *Italian Wines 1998* by Daniele Cernilli, and Carlo Petrini

Author/Title Index

The page numbers where main entries appear are boldface.

Subject Index

About the Author

MELISSA BRACKNEY STOEGER is a Readers' Services Librarian at the Deerfield Public Library in Deerfield, Illinois. She has a Master of Library and Information Science from Dominican University. She is also a book reviewer for *Library Journal*.